BLACK DIRECTORS IN HOLLYWOOD

MELVIN DONALSON

 UNIVERSITY OF TEXAS PRESS, AUSTIN

First edition, 2003

Requests for permission to reproduce material from
this work should be sent to Permissions, University
of Texas Press, Box 7819, Austin, TX 78713-7819.

♾ The paper used in this book meets the minimum
requirements of ANSI/NISO Z39.48-1992 (R1997)
(Permanence of Paper).

Library of Congress Cataloging-in-Publication Data

Donalson, Melvin Burke, 1952–
Black directors in Hollywood / Melvin Donalson.
        p.   cm.
ISBN 0-292-70178-0 (cloth : alk. paper) —
ISBN 0-292-70179-9 (pbk. : alk. paper)
1. African Americans in motion pictures.   2. African
American motion picture producers and directors—
United States—Biography.   I. Title.
PN1995.9.N4D66   2003
791.43'0233'092273—dc21   2003006770

With love to my wife, Beverly, who appreciates the aesthetics of cinema, but who understands the powerful messages in the medium

CONTENTS

I began researching this book in the spring of 1997, but from summer 1998 to winter 1999 I set aside the project to write, coproduce, and direct a short film, entitled *A Room without Doors*. Given my desire to be a filmmaker, it was an opportunity that I could not walk away from, and with the extensive help and support of professionals in front of and behind the camera, I was able to complete my first film. The film went on to be screened at nine film festivals during the following year, and it was selected for inclusion in Showtime Network's Black Filmmakers Showcase in February 1999.

Among the many valuable lessons learned while making the film, I was forced to deal with the realities of filmmaking that often go unnoticed or without assessment by most film critics and scholars. My hope is that in shaping this book, I have been able to bring some of that experience to bear on my evaluations of the directing process, thus avoiding a mocking or arrogant posture.

As a professor who teaches film studies and popular culture, I know too well how scholars rush to find a haven in theory and academic jargon that sometimes become ends in themselves rather the means to illuminating a film. My concern was to avoid that entrapment with this book because I wanted to reach that same wide audience that the directors themselves have been seeking to reach. Therefore, I have not adopted a critical framework or a central thesis by which to analyze the directors, nor have I utilized an academic lexicon to render the text.

In the introduction to his book *Am I Black Enough for You: Popular Culture from the 'Hood and Beyond* (1997), scholar Todd Boyd writes about the emergence of black cultural critics, such as Cornel West, bell hooks, Henry Louis Gates Jr. and Michael Eric Dyson, who have revealed complex areas of African American culture to audiences that are both academic and popular; these intellectuals have worked to move away from an elitist, disconnected scholarship toward an accessible connection with black culture and a mainstream audience. Although I am not placing myself by any means within that circle of distinctive black intellectuals, I am embracing the spirit of their scholarship that acknowledges that all black cultural expressions warrant serious study, and deserve a wide audience. Consequently, *Black Directors in Hollywood* is designed to serve as a useful tool in undergraduate film, popular culture, and/or ethnic studies classes. At the same time, it has a practical appeal to any reader who inquires about the aspects and dimensions of ethnic directors in the Hollywood system. In researching the book, discrepancies about the release dates of films, the box-office grosses, the names of characters, and the spelling of actors' names occurred. My editors and I sought to find agreement among several sources in order to confirm details and facts. It remains possible, therefore, that some of the data in *Black Directors in Hollywood* may contradict information in other film books.

Finally, between the end of my research in 1999 and the numerous stages in the process of writing, editing, and completing the final published book in 2003, a number of new black directors and films have appeared. The absence of those filmmakers and works has been unavoidable given the scope of this book and the meticulous demands of publication. Even as I bemoan the fact that those black filmmakers and works are not included in my book, their contributions are an added cause for celebration.

Melvin Donalson
2003

ACKNOWLEDGMENTS

I need to extend my deepest appreciation and gratitude to numerous people who have, sometimes unknowingly, provided me with support and motivation throughout the six years of completing this book. First, I deeply thank two scholars whose professional and personal endeavors have continually inspired me on this project: Marcus Bruce and Wilfred Samuels. It is my great honor to be called their friend.

Next, I owe a debt to my colleagues at Pasadena City College who, over the years, shared many productive and thoughtful discussions: Harry Smallenburg, Mark McQueen, Phyllis Mael, Joseph Sierra, Amy Ulmer, Jane Hallinger, Roger Marheine, Loknath Persaud, Lola Praono-Gomez, Phil Pastras, Dan Meier, Judith Branzburg, Karen Holgerson, Diana Savas, and Yves Maglo. Likewise, at California State University–Los Angeles, two colleagues, in particular, contributed their helpful perspectives: Steven Jones and Alfred Bendixen.

Off campus, I continued to annoy my friends with this project, but always received patient and valuable feedback from them all: Kate Remo, Dave Kee, Reggie McDowell, Bill Paden, Laura Paden, Mary Peterson, Ron Peterson, Richard Doran, Elaine Doran, Jill Bruce, James Tobey, and John Jenkins. Just as encouraging to me has been the helpful and informative exchanges with a number of talented filmmakers and actors along the way: Jacqueline George, David Massey, Rodney Hooks, Dick Anthony Williams, Michael Beach, and Lloyd Roseman.

During my research I relied on the knowledgeable assistance from librarians and staff members at a number of sites: the Motion Picture Academy's Margaret Herrick Library; the Louis B. Mayer Library at the American Film Institute; the John F. Kennedy Library at California State University–Los Angeles; the UCLA Research Library; and the Tomas Rivera Library at the University of California–Riverside.

In locating and gathering stills, I received enthusiastic support from Mary Corliss and Terry Geesken at the Museum of Modern Art; Rodney Gray at Bill Duke Media; Jarene Fleming at Tim Reid Productions, Inc.; Joe Khoury at Del, Shaw, Moonves, Tanaka, and Finkelstein; Jenny Reith Beasley at the Indiana University Black Film Center/Archive; Book City Collectibles; and Pete Bateman and staff at the Larry Edmunds Bookstore in Hollywood, and Book Castle in Burbank, CA.

Additionally, I was fortunate to receive an NEH Research Award, which became an invaluable support in helping me complete this text. Any views, findings, conclusions, or recommendations expressed in this book do not necessarily reflect those of the National Endowment for the Humanities.

At the University of Texas Press, I still marvel at the endurance and patience of my editor, Jim Burr, as well as the steadfast consultation from the Press's assistant managing editor, Leslie Tingle. Moreover, for the final form of this book, I am indebted to the experience and contributions of two key people—Bob Fullilove, copyeditor, and Lynne F. Chapman, manuscript editor.

Finally, in the years of developing this project, I have been sustained by the love and care of my family: Beverly, Derek, Wilbert, Dorothy, Brian, Paulette Theresa McAuliffe, and the late Kevin McAuliffe.

BLACK DIRECTORS IN HOLLYWOOD

Of the many creative people who collaborate on a motion picture, the director is regarded as the pivotal individual who governs the aggregate elements for completing the final film. In contemporary American cinema, the director serves as both the guiding force behind a film's effective content and box-office success. Films, consequently, have been called a director's medium.

Since the mid-1960s in Hollywood, more than seventy black directors have attained this key position of director. Although this number appears high in the span of the last four decades, in actuality the number indicts commercial cinema when considering that Hollywood's first feature film was released in 1915.

To better understand both the director's responsibilities and the elusive nature of this position for black filmmakers, six significant questions must be examined.

Why is the director such a desired position in today's cinema?

A glance at any recent book about filmmaking or magazine article about Hollywood reveals the numerous established television and movie performers who have moved from in front of the camera to become directors — Clint Eastwood, Barbra Streisand, Robert Redford, Mel Gibson, Penny Marshall, Kevin Spacey, and Denzel Washington, just to name a few. Part of the reason behind the quest to direct stems from the power and leadership role inherent in the position. The director is in charge, and his/her decisions dictate the final film that the audience will view. Another part of the answer rests within the status and recognition received from both critics and the public. The immense audiences that movies have gained as the result of multiplex cinemas, network television, videocassettes, cable channels, DVDs, and film websites have given the medium its primary importance in American pop culture. For many critics and audiences, certain directors, such as Woody Allen, Spike Lee, Martin Scorsese, Steven Spielberg, and Quentin Tarantino, have become popular celebrities and icons. Consequently, many performers and aspiring filmmakers have been lured to grasp for that cinematic brass ring.

But the director's position wasn't always held in such high esteem. In the early silent era, the director had more of a supervisory than creative role, tending to all the many areas that needed to be coordinated to complete a film. In some ways, the director was burdened with being an effective manager who moved from one assigned project to another. With the development of synchronized sound films and the studio system in the 1920s, the producer was often viewed as a creative force as much as a business expert, and producers such as Irving Thalberg, Louis B. Mayer, Darryl F. Zanuck, and David O. Selznick dominated studios and shaped the final forms that films would take.

However, the appreciation of the crucial role of a director in making a film appeared in the late 1950s, when the critical philosophies of French film critics became popular. These critics, like François Truffaut, Claude Chabrol, Eric Roemer, and Jean-Luc Godard, were film enthusiasts who wrote their perspectives in a movie journal called *Cahiers du Cinema*. As critics, they were enamored of feature films by American directors such as Alfred Hitchcock, John Ford, and Howard Hawks. To the French critics these American directors revealed stylistic, visual elements within filmmaking that made them the film's author, or "auteur," the source and guiding hand for the movie's final form.

When these same French critics became directors, they were referred to as a "French New Wave" of filmmakers who alluded to American movies, American movie stars, and American directors in their own films. The bottom line was that the French New Wave critic-filmmakers evaluated American feature films as "serious" works of "art," not just commercial products churned out by the Hollywood factory.

By the 1960s, American film critics, particularly Andrew Sarris, helped to bring the "auteur" approach to American readers. And with the growth of college and university classes in film history, film criticism and semiology, and film production, the "auteur" theory became a popular critical approach that influenced the study and the making of American movies.

What does a director do on a given film?

The response to that question varies as much as the process of film production itself. In general, a director would be closely involved with the three major phases of completing a film: *preproduction, production,* and *postproduction.* In the *preproduction* phase, the director could be active in working on the final script; choosing the actors and primary technical personnel; rehearsing the actors; sharing ideas with the production designer, costume personnel, and makeup artists; and even finalizing decisions about locations. Then, when the *production* phase begins—that is to say the actual shooting of the film—the director does several things: he/she communicates closely with actors as they perform; orchestrates the mise-en-scène— the movements of people and things in front of the camera; and works in detail with the cinematographer and production designer for the angles and appearance of everything seen upon the screen. In *postproduction,* the director still remains busy: with the editor, the director works on the film's pacing, scene connections, and visual effects; with the sound personnel, the director works on the film's aural qualities; and with the music composer, the director makes suggestions about the film's score. Undoubtedly, the director's responsibilities are enormous, and some directors take command in all of these areas, while others rely on the expertise of their collaborators.

How can a director's work be evaluated?

Combining the ideas of the French New Wave critics, American critics, and film scholars, a director's work can be assessed for certain discernible aspects within a single film, or more ideally, within the body of his/her film works. Regardless, when working under the premise that a film is the personal artistic expression of the director, the following areas can be critiqued: (1) the visual techniques, such as camera angles, frame composition, altered reality, textures, and colors; (2) any recognizable storytelling elements, such as characterization, theme, and symbols emphasized in a film or recurring in successive films; (3) the pacing, editing, and rhythm(s) employed in telling the story; and (4) the utilization of both diegetic and nondiegetic music. In general, what becomes significant is the manner in which the director assembles these four areas in completing a coherent film that communicates to and affects the audience on various levels.

Why has the participation of black directors in Hollywood been so limited in the past, and how has it changed?

Simply stated, the Hollywood director has traditionally been a white male, and though American narrative films date back to 1903, it wasn't until the late 1960s that Hollywood allowed a black director to command a major film project. Two complex factors have contributed to this bleak history: (1) the history of the stereotypical screen images of blacks, and (2) the lack of a power base by blacks in the business of filmmaking.

The screen depiction of African Americans and their culture during the "golden years" of Hollywood—from 1915 to 1948—was dominated by recurring stereotypes. The three most popular stereotypes—the servant (slave); the mulatto; and the entertainer—were easily identified in decades of movies. The servant—as seen in plantation films such as *The Littlest Rebel* (1935) or *Gone with the Wind* (1939) or in urban films such as *You Can't Take It with You* (1938) or *Mildred Pierce* (1945)—was both black male and female who enjoyed drudgery and patriarchy. The mulatto—in films such as *Imitation of Life* (1934/1959) and *Show Boat* (1936/1951)—was usually a fair-complexioned black female whose character, often portrayed by a white actress, was confused and psychologically lost due to her racial marginality. The entertainer—in numerous films such as *Sun Valley Serenade* (1941) and *Ziegfeld Follies* (1946)—was a black male or female who sang, danced, played instruments, and clowned as the comic relief or as a specialty performance within a movie. Hollywood avoided the diverse roles of blacks in society, opting instead for narrow images that maligned both black women and men. The consistency of those depictions has been overwhelming in its power to validate myths, encouraging viewers of all races to dismiss the value of black experiences.

In 1949 Hollywood discovered that there was a business value in movies with serious social and ethnic themes. In particular, the racial concerns stemming from the genocide of World War II prompted a different direction in film content. As early as 1947 two movies—*Gentleman's Agreement*, the winner of the Academy Award for Best Picture, and *Crossfire*—focused on the treatment of Jews within American society. Two years later, four films appeared that continued to look at the problem of race in America, primarily the "Negro Problem": *Pinky, Lost Boundaries, Home of the Brave*, and *Intruder in the Dust.* Those four films did *not* have black producers and directors and, in some cases, used white performers to portray fair-complexioned black characters. But, importantly, those four films departed from earlier stereotypes and promised an improved set of black images for the future.

As depictions modified in their dimensions during the civil rights era, the status of blacks behind the camera did not alter. The tradition of an exclusive studio system remained, and likewise, the early years of television as a competing entertainment form did little to deviate from black stereotypes or to promote black participation behind the camera. But with a strong emphasis on integration, movies such as *No Way Out* (1950), *Edge of the City* (1957), and *A Raisin in the Sun* (1961), all starring Sidney Poitier, began to modify presentations of black people. In some films, black characters were given middle-class aspirations and personalities that mirrored respectability.

The overall history of narrow screen images of blacks resulted directly from the lack of decision-making power behind the camera. In both the creative and business aspects of filmmaking, blacks have traditionally had a minimal involvement as studio executives. In the motion picture business, which thrives on closed social networks, family affiliations, and venture capital, Hollywood powerbrokers have easily excluded blacks from the inner circles of creative development, financial planning, production, and distribution. Consequently, to those Hollywood powerbrokers, blacks were not capable or worthy of assuming the responsibilities and power given to a film director.

Despite the pejorative representation on screen and exclusion from power on the set, by the late 1960s, as the country underwent changes because of political, social, and racial issues, Hollywood films were inextricably caught within the dynamics of the time. The visible celebrations of black culture and the intense black political awareness found a reflection in American movies. The struggles, hostilities, and triumphs of black Americans in the inner-city environment became suitable story elements for Hollywood's action-oriented dramas. At the same time, black-oriented comedies that were laced with black vernacular, styles, and manners served as an exotic territory for laughter in Hollywood productions.

By the 1970s, it was apparent to studios that the stories, sensibilities, and perspectives of black filmmakers could impart a realism and believability that would translate into box-office dollars. Slowly, Hollywood began to seek out black writers and directors—very slowly. The movement toward using black directors in the 1970s was hardly an explosive one; instead, it was less than a trickling of opportunity, allowing only a few black directors to gain recognition. But soon, a few black directors became five, and the numbers increased further as access into studio productions, though still difficult, did occur on occasion. Even by the year 2000, statistics told the story: out of a total membership of 11,825 in the Directors Guild of America, only an estimated 350 members were black directors.[1]

What is the difference between a Hollywood film and an independent film?

The distinction between the Hollywood and independent film is important, though by the late 1990s, a clear and consistent definition of the latter became problematic. Traditionally, an independent film was a project that was financed, developed, and completed without involvement from any major Hollywood studio. However, by the year 2000, as one critic notes, "[t]he corporate complexity of the contemporary entertainment industry is such that many independent companies are, in fact, owned by the majors. For example, Miramax is part of the Disney empire; Fine Line and New Line are owned by Time-Warner; October Films has been absorbed by Universal/MCA."[2]

The independent film—whether a short film, feature, or documentary—has always been an avenue where black directors could find expression and gain experience. With its own history, which had a parallel development to the Hollywood industry, independent filmmaking provided black directors a viable storytelling medium, but to a smaller audience.

From approximately 1918 to 1948, black writers, producers, and directors created movies that targeted all-black audiences. Utilizing a cast of all-black performers, these movies sought to compete with Hollywood films, sometimes using similar stereotypes for characterization, but consistently presenting blacks in more varied images than seen in the Hollywood film. Through their very existence, these independent black filmmakers made a cultural and political statement that countered the messages presented by mainstream movies. The Lincoln Motion Picture Company, the Gate City Film Corporation, and Million Dollar Pictures were just three of the dozens of film businesses formed to make black independent movies. Some of those companies were black owned, while others had financial backing from white entrepreneurs. Outstanding among the black independents was filmmaker, novelist, and businessman Oscar Micheaux, a conspicuous success and survivor until the post–World War II period, when ethnicity became a marketable theme in Hollywood productions.

By the late 1960s and into the following decades, a new group of black independent filmmakers garnered critical attention for their short films, documentaries, and features. Offering alternative black images, they struggled to create "art" outside the Hollywood system with its formulaic predictability. Filmmakers such as William Greaves, Bill Gunn, and Ethiopian-born Haile Gerima have been lionized by critics and dedicated audiences, while directors Alile Sharon Larkin and Kathleen Collins have been revered as outstanding and influential independent voices. Other filmmakers with independent roots, such as Julie Dash, Charles Burnett, and Spike Lee, have been able to gain access to mainstream audiences, though their creative styles are evidence of their anti-Hollywood approaches.

What are the contributions black directors have made to Hollywood feature films?

Since the late '60s, black directors have helped to widen both the thematic focus and the visual style of American cinema. Thematically, black directors have explored neglected areas of African American experiences and culture. By doing so, they have encouraged audiences to look at American society in different and diverse ways, bringing fresh insights to movie characterizations, plots, and themes.

In regard to visual styles, black directors have come from backgrounds representing a range of storytelling skills and visual creativity—acting, photography, independent filmmaking, television productions, music videos, and the theatrical stage. Some black directors display a polished and unobtrusive mainstream style, while others demonstrate quirky and off-center styles that deliberately draw attention to technique and experimentation.

Whether they are pioneers like Gordon Parks, Melvin Van Peebles, and Ossie Davis, or whether they are current talents like John Singleton, Kasi Lemmons, and Carl Franklin, black directors of the Hollywood feature film are members of a remarkable group. Many have gained accolades for artistic achievement in a business where box-office receipts serve as the measure of a filmmaker's value. In a business often hostile to their presence, black directors have survived extensive pressures and politics to bring their projects to completion.

Black Directors in Hollywood examines those black directors who have had a narrative film distributed theatrically in America between the late 1960s and the winter of 1999. The goal is to consider the diverse pathways taken by the individual directors, while assessing the meanings and messages within their works. The hope is to appreciate the difficult task of black directors to adhere to the demands of the Hollywood system while remaining true to ethnic and cultural issues that exist inside and outside that system. In a critical and respectful approach, *Black Directors in Hollywood* recognizes and celebrates the visions and skills of black directors who have both sustained and transformed American commercial cinema.

CHAPTER ONE

The Pathmakers

Gordon Parks

After directing five motion pictures in Hollywood, I was still fascinated with its seductiveness and its challenges. Yet, sometimes I couldn't help but think of it as the grand illusion.[1]   Gordon Parks

In addition to his distinctive career as a professional photographer, Gordon Parks Jr. has also been a published poet, an author of three autobiographies, a novelist, a composer, and a Hollywood director. With an early life filled with racial oppression, restlessness, and violence, Parks could have ended up as so many other blacks did—hopeless, forgotten, and lost. But by his own admission his advantage "was the great love of [his] family—seven boys and eight girls, and a mother and father who cared about [him]."[2]

Without oversimplifying the importance of his family, Parks details in his autobiography, *Voices in the Mirror* (1990), the many experiences that he encountered from his birthplace of Fort Scott, Kansas—where he was born in 1912—to his travels throughout the United States, Europe, South America, and Africa. His background unfolded like a picaresque novel, and Parks grew to appreciate his privilege to know the people and places that he did. Both in and out of Hollywood, Parks was an unquestioned success. In particular, as a black director, he was a pioneer filmmaker of historical significance, and as an artist, his vision shaped a variety of films enjoyed by an international audience.

The first black photographer for *Glamour* and *Vogue* magazines, Parks landed an enviable position as a staff member of *Life* magazine in 1948. His first assignment was to cover gang confrontations in Harlem, the community that would later serve as the backdrop for his film *Shaft.* For over two decades, Parks' photographs won him acclaim and brought him in contact with numerous celebrities and politicians, including well-known blacks such as Sugar Ray Robinson, Richard Wright, Stokely Carmichael (Kwame Toure), Kathleen and Eldridge Cleaver, Muhammad Ali, and Malcolm X.

But it was in the late 1940s in Italy when Parks first contemplated directing films, as he photographed actress Ingrid Bergman and director Roberto

Rossellini. However, unable to attain an assistant's position with Rossellini, the opportunity to direct a feature-length movie did not arrive until the 1960s when, at the urging of actor-director John Cassavetes, Parks met with a Warner Brothers executive to discuss directing a movie based on Parks' novel *The Learning Tree.*

With his first film by the same name in 1968, Gordon Parks appeared intent on becoming an immediate black "auteur," as he served as writer, music composer, producer, and director on the film. Relying on Burnett Guffey as director of photography, Parks presented a film that used the natural vistas of the Midwest to tell the story of a small town and the narrow, racist thinking that affected both the black and white communities.

Set in Cherokee Flats, Kansas, in 1920, the story focuses on Newt Winger (Kyle Johnson), a fifteen-year-old black teen who must face the disappointments and dangers in life. One such danger occurs when Newt and his friends steal apples from a white farmer, and a confrontation erupts between the farmer and Marcus Savage (Alex Clarke), a troubled black boy who lives a tension-filled life with his father, Booker Savage (Richard Ward). When the boys witness Kirky (Dana Elcar), the white sheriff, shoot a black man fleeing from a craps game, Marcus' harsh assessment of whites seems to be true. But Newt's attention is soon drawn to Arcella Jefferson (Mira Waters), a black girl with whom he develops an innocent first love. Eventually, Marcus is sent away to reform school for beating the white farmer, and Newt plunges emotionally when Arcella becomes pregnant by the white son of the town's judge. Toward the end of the film, Newt witnesses the murder of the white farmer, killed by Booker Savage. Afraid that his revelation would begin a racial conflict in the town, Newt allows a white town drunk to be arrested and taken to court for the crime. However, Newt's moral sense wins out, and he confesses what he saw, resulting in the self-inflicted death of Booker Savage.

At the beginning of the film, with its languid, wide-angle shots of Newt walking carefree through meadows and near a lake, Parks suggests that this film will be a sensitive character study. With the title song performed by the smooth baritone of black vocalist O. C. Smith, the gentle tone of the film is underscored, a gentleness seen in both Newt and his family. The threat to that gentleness is shown through Parks' careful editing of sequences that hold both bitter and sweet experiences. Parks suggests that within the rural beauty hide the latent forces of destruction that hunt down black youth to destroy them emotionally and psychologically.

Parks also incorporates effective visual transitions from one sequence to another, unifying the film and shaping memorable images for the viewer.

In one scene, Newt looks through a microscope, focusing on the wings of a monarch butterfly. The image of the dark spot on the butterfly's right wing, resembling the dark pupil of a human eye, dissolves quickly into a close-up of the left eye of Marcus Savage staring into the camera. The camera pulls back, and Marcus stands defiantly before the judge who pronounces his reform school sentence. From the wonder of the butterfly, the camera thrusts the viewer into the angry, spiteful eyes of a young criminal. In another segment, Newt and his family gather at the dinner table, and as his father delivers grace the camera holds on Newt's hands, which are positioned in prayer. In a slow dissolve, the camera focuses on Newt's hands in the same position of prayer, but now as he attends a church service. In that moment, the minister admonishes young people to refrain from evil. Even as the minister speaks his words, Newt looks over flirtatiously at Arcella Jefferson.

Overall, *The Learning Tree* must be viewed as a success on many levels. It was a portrait of African American life in a serious and revealing manner, emphasizing a black teen's perspective. Significantly, it was a project where a black person controlled the creative process, including directing, screenwriting, and music score. More importantly to the interests of Warner Brothers studios, it was a film that completed shooting forty-eight days ahead of schedule.[3]

But despite the tender, dramatic portrayal of black life in *The Learning Tree,* Parks will be remembered more for his second film—the financially successful and controversial *Shaft* (1971). When *Shaft* made it to the theaters, some viewers, black and nonblack alike, saw an entertaining black hero in the James Bond tradition. Others, however, saw an exploitive black male stereotype thrown on-screen to increase Hollywood's profits. For those critics, *Shaft* defamed black culture—particularly the political and cultural expressions that were present in the late 1960s and early 1970s.

With Sidney Poitier's screen personas dominating the '60s, Richard Roundtree's characterization of John Shaft posed another kind of black masculinity. Unconcerned with integrating or being invited into a white home for dinner, John Shaft refuted middle-class concerns, sensibilities, and desires that lay at the foundation of the integrationist ideal. John Shaft was brash, clever, and sexual, and he was quite content to live in his Harlem community. There was no ambiguity about his politics, allegiances, or virility. He was *black*—in attitude, language, and psyche—and he constantly reminded other characters (and society) that they were *white* and subject to his wrath or sarcasm. He knew the codes of survival on the streets and was, possibly, one of the creators of the codes.

Despite the negative criticisms of John Shaft's image, Parks emphasized the positive in his film, which in his opinion was a movie that provided a younger black audience with a dynamic hero suited to the turbulent times. As for the critics' concerns about the wave of new black films, Parks concluded that "[i]t is ridiculous to imply that blacks don't know the difference between truth and fantasy and therefore will be influenced in an unhealthy way. . . . These movies are serving . . . [a] therapeutic function."[4]

Shaft is an action film that focuses on the cool-under-pressure titular black detective (Richard Roundtree) who is hired to return the kidnapped daughter of Bumpy Jones (Moses Gunn), a black mobster who runs Harlem's illegal activities. Jones perceives himself merely as a businessman, but Shaft reminds him that he is a destroyer of the black community. Shaft's loyalties are to black people, and when it becomes apparent that the kidnapping has been instigated by white mobsters, Shaft takes the case to avoid a violent gangster war in the community.

White screenwriter Ernest Tidyman generously peppered the script with the street expressions of the day, such as "funky," "right on," "dudes," "you dig," and "we're straight, baby." As the story follows Shaft, in his fashionable clothes and trademark black leather jacket, he moves between the white and black worlds. In his investigation of both worlds, John Shaft maintains a take-charge, no-nonsense approach as a matter of form. He bickers defiantly with white detectives; gives "the finger" to a white cab driver; indulges in recreational sex with black and white lovers; commands respect from white vendors and doormen; and stands confidently against white mobsters. But, then, despite his hard edge, Shaft gives money to a shivering black child sitting outside a Harlem apartment building, and he teams up with black revolutionaries as comrades-in-arms in their confrontation with the white mobsters—that is to say, the white power structure.

In his direction of the film, Parks reveals John Shaft's attitude, suaveness, and sexuality through camera shots that constantly frame Richard Roundtree's features and athletic frame. A former college football player turned model and actor, Roundtree's handsome looks, mischievous smile, voice quality, and abrupt emotional outbursts work well with Parks' camera. Whether long shots tracking Shaft along Harlem streets, medium shots during dialogues, or close-ups for the sake of catching Roundtree's dark features from different angles, Parks integrates Shaft into the environment, making him inseparable from the allure and edginess of the urban community.

Though slow-paced by the standards of a '90s action movie, Parks creates pacing by crosscutting between exterior shots with physical movement and interior shots in predominantly tight, confined spaces. There are no exploding cars or breathtaking stunts, but tension builds as Shaft charges into dangerous and unknown situations. At the same time, throughout the film, Parks remains aware of the effect that colors have upon the viewer. He deliberately chooses colors that are subdued, giving a preference to blacks, browns, and grays to match both the winter setting and the toughness of John Shaft's world. Then, in the climactic sequence, when Bumpy's daughter is rescued, the place of confinement has red-colored walls, which stand out in bright contrast as a setting for the battle of crashing glass and gunfire during the violent rescue.

Even more important than his pacing and production design, Parks respects the power of music in this film. He relies on the outstanding contribution of "Isaac Hayes's great theme music, which later won an Academy Award for best song—the very first for a black composer."[5] The signature theme for John Shaft becomes a basic ingredient to define the character's mood and energy. The music is full-blown like Shaft's ego, and it possesses an "in-your-face" arrangement, enticing and thumping with its rhythmic patterns of horns, synthesizer, wah-wah guitar, and percussion.

The ability to move from the rural, Midwest setting of *The Learning Tree* to the urban streets of *Shaft* demonstrated Parks' skills with visual storytelling. But for MGM studios, Parks proved something more crucial: he could direct a profitable film with black-oriented themes. On its $1.2 million cost, *Shaft* had grossed $18 million by the end of 1971.[6] Parks understood that with the financial success of *Shaft*, "Hollywood had the green light for black suspense films—and they [Hollywood studios] exploited them to a mercilessly quick demise with a rash of bad screenplays."[7]

Since Parks had turned such a profit with *Shaft*, an MGM studio executive sent Parks the script for the sequel—*Shaft's Big Score!* (1972). With Richard Roundtree secured to repeat his role as John Shaft and with another screenplay by Ernest Tidyman in hand, Parks completed a sequel that had a "paint-by-numbers" feel to it: all the elements were on the screen to fulfill the genre—action, sex, violence, and John Shaft's attitude. However, to his credit, Parks gave this installment of *Shaft* much more physical action than the first. Again, the action would not stand up by comparison to '90s carnage, such as that provided by directors John Woo (*Broken Arrow*, 1996), Michael Bay (*The Rock*, 1996), or James Cameron (the *Terminator* series), but for its time, the film presented some exciting sequences. And, importantly, at the center was always John Shaft, the black hero.

In the opening sequence, black businessman Cal Ashby (Robert Kya-Hill) is killed in an explosion before his scheming partner Kelly (Wally Taylor) can locate $250,000—money that Kelly has stolen to repay a debt to white mobster Gus Mascala (Joseph Mascolo). When Ashby is killed, Shaft is pulled into solving the murder because he respects Ashby (even though he and Kelly were running numbers in Queens) and because Ashby's sister, Arna (Rosalind Miles), has been Shaft's lover.

When Mascola muscles in on Kelly's business, Kelly goes to Harlem crime boss Bumpy Jones (Moses Gunn). Kelly plays the black mobster against the white mobster, and in the middle of it all, Shaft struggles to protect Arna and recover the money, while keeping the police under control. Along the way, Shaft has a tryst with Rita (Kathy Imrie), Kelly's live-in lover, and she later becomes Shaft's ally as he single-handedly defeats the white mobsters while wearing his trademark black leather outfit.

Parks returns to some favorite visuals in this sequel: the long static shots; a two-shot during dialogue with minimum crosscutting; extended slow-paced scenes; and extreme close-ups of Richard Roundtree's face. In this sequel, there appear to be more interior shots, particularly apartment interiors that are well lit and detailed in production design. In an opening pan of Shaft's bedroom, Arna's underclothes lead a pathway to the bed, and on his nightstand, Shaft has a copy of *Ebony* magazine. In other words, John Shaft stays black even in the bedroom and especially in his reading. Later in the movie, while in his living room planning strategy, Shaft goes to a bookcase filled with books. Before the viewer can read the titles in his small library, Shaft tugs at the shelves, removing the facade to expose his special assault rifle and ammo hidden within. In other words, John Shaft is prepared to read the last rites to any mobster who crosses him.

Although the winter backdrop in the sequel is similar to that in the original, here the somber tones do not dominate as much. The emphasis with the sequel seems to be action rather than suspense and emotional tension, and two sequences stand out as indicative of this action priority. The first occurs at a private club where Shaft goes to find Kelly. The club is owned by Mascola, and the entertainment features black women dancers, costumed sensually and exotically. In an alleyway in back of the club, several of Mascola's men corner Shaft and beat him severely. Parks crosscuts from the exotic dancers —their faces grimacing with ecstasy and pleasure—to the bloody face of John Shaft, as his beating unfolds in a strobe effect with jolting, abrupt movements. The physical intensity of the scenes contrasts in tone. The dance of pleasure in the interior is smooth and sensuous, while the dance of pain in the exterior fight is harsh and disjointed.

The second, at the film's finale, consists of an extremely long chase scene that begins on the street—Shaft drives a bright red sports car with a black racing stripe. From the street, the chase continues on foot, and then onto a speedboat that is shadowed by a helicopter. Reminiscent of the helicopter

Richard Roundtree, left, dons his leather and gun to corner a mob boss (Joseph Mascolo) in *Shaft's Big Score!*

chase scene with James Bond in *From Russia with Love* (1963), John Shaft, on foot, outmaneuvers a helicopter flying dangerously low to the water as well as in and around a vacant shipyard. Even here, Parks doesn't utilize numerous quick cuts or askew angles to heighten the chase. But, at one point, Shaft runs into an abandoned hangar, and as the helicopter pursues inside, it fires constantly. In a tracking shot, Shaft, in black leather, runs through the hangar, the spraying bullets sparking and ricocheting in the darkness, while the echoing gunfire reverberates loudly inside the empty hangar. The movement of man and machine in combination with the echoing din in the dimly lit hangar create a rush upon the viewer's senses. Then, unable to exit the closed end of the hangar, the helicopter reverses and goes out the same way it entered, but the elusive Shaft waits outside and brings the helicopter down explosively with his assault weapon.

Parks moved away from the black world of John Shaft with his next film, *The Super Cops* (1974). This film has to rank as Parks' weakest work, based on the lackluster critical reviews, as well on Parks' dismissive identification of it in his autobiography as a movie completed for MGM Studios.[8] Although the movie is based on the deeds of two real-life New York City policemen, one critic of the time dismissed the movie as "a loud and clumsy film about two [white] cops . . . who buck the system. . . . On the screen, though, their heroics look lame. We expect our cops to be either a good deal meaner . . . or at least stronger fantasy projections. . . . [H]ere [they] are neither real enough nor romantic enough."[9]

By contrast, Parks' next feature, *Leadbelly* (1976), attained a great deal of praise from film critics, but a peculiar rejection by its studio, Paramount Pictures. A victim of changes in leadership at the studio, *Leadbelly* received only minor marketing and support despite winning first place at the Dallas Film Festival, which prompted a Los Angeles critic to write: "You can't kill art. It is indeed a fine film, and it will live on."[10]

Leadbelly tells the story of famed bluesman, Huddie Ledbetter, a black musician who survives rough times in the early twentieth century and who writes popular folk and blues tunes, such as "Good Night, Irene," "Bring Me a Little Water, Sylvie," and "The Rock Island Line." Throughout the film, Parks blends areas that he explored in earlier films—the rural South, a true-life story, black music, and the theme of survival.

The film begins in 1934, as the shirtless, muscled body of Huddie Ledbetter (Roger E. Mosley) glistens sweatily beneath the sun as he breaks rocks in a prison yard. Then, interviewed by a white professor and his assistant who are collecting folk songs for the Library of Congress, Ledbetter is given a guitar and asked to sing his songs and relate his life into a recorder. Using a blurred screen to transition into the past, Ledbetter narrates his story, beginning around 1907. A country boy, he escapes to the city of Shreveport, Louisiana, and quickly falls prey to the bustling energy of Fanning Street and Miss Eula (Madge Sinclair), the madam of her own house of prostitution. Touching his hard stomach muscles, Miss Eula christens him "Leadbelly," and following a police raid, Leadbelly jumps a freight train and winds up in Texas, where he picks cotton, chases women, and composes music. Soon, he meets the musician Blind Lemon Jefferson (Art Evans); the two become friends and perform together on the road. Eventually, Leadbelly attempts to lead a stable life, but killing a man in a drunken fight leads to years on the back-breaking chain gang. After a short taste of freedom, Leadbelly stabs a white man in self-defense, which lands him back in prison, as the film lap dissolves back into 1934.

In addition to some fine performances, notably that of Roger E. Mosley as Leadbelly, Parks provides a story that has an effective balance of drama, humor, and musical energy. In one scene, Leadbelly arrogantly slaps down a ten-dollar gold piece and challenges anyone in a bar of black revelers to outsing or outplay him on the guitar. A drunken old man accepts the challenge, picking up a twelve-string guitar to match Leadbelly's six-string. In a sequence reminiscent of the "dueling banjos" scene in *Deliverance* (1972), Parks cuts between two-shots of both men playing and their individual hands on the frets and strings, as the old man gives young Leadbelly a public lesson.

And along with its captivating musical energy, the film possesses a number of artistic moments—tableaux that serve as aesthetic achievements in and of themselves. One such moment appears during a sequence following a country dance where Leadbelly has played his guitar and fought over his girl, Margaret (Dana Manno). A long, tracking shot follows Leadbelly and Margaret on horseback. Their figures, atop the horse, glide across the fields that are washed in the reddish-orange color of the sunrise. The light filtering hazily across the landscape is soft, and the mood is calm in juxtaposition with the frantic dancing of the night before. Later in the film, Parks' eye for still photography becomes apparent again. Immediately following a scene where Leadbelly has worked in a sun-drenched cotton field, the film cuts to the early evening—a wide angle shows gray-colored clouds filling the sky and, just beneath them, the lonely outline of a shanty on the horizon line. Then, from left to right, a solitary figure leads a horse across the horizon line toward the shanty, and with the muted grayness and open space in the foreground, the scene evokes a peacefulness and serenity. These types of images pepper the movie, reminding the viewer of the filmmaker's craft, but not detracting from the characters and the story line.

In fact, Parks does not allow the viewer to forget that Huddie Ledbetter is the focus of the film, as he dominates each scene from beginning to end. And as Leadbelly moves from scene to scene, from experience to experience, he comes to understand how his music and the hardships of his life as a black man—and as an unskilled laborer—are inextricably bound. In addition to the diegetic songs performed, Parks lays many of Leadbelly's songs over the action of the film, as the lyrics sung are connected to the events or characters in a specific sequence. The music, then, is used to show the various dimensions of Leadbelly's personality, as his music emanates from the character's nature, which is variously strong, weak, confused, and victorious.

At the same time that Parks delineates Leadbelly's individual story, he comments upon the larger racial and cultural stories of African Americans. In one case, as Leadbelly and Blind Lemon Jefferson travel together through the countryside in a car, Parks orchestrates a montage where the expansive fields and long dusty roads of the rural areas take on an alluring natural quality. But the captivating charm of the countryside clashes with the broken-down shanties and dirt yards where black people work and live.

And as the film ends, realizing his songs will be preserved in a library, Leadbelly returns to the rock pile, lifts his hammer, and swings it down upon the stones, declaring aloud: "You ain't broke my mind, you ain't broke my body, and you ain't broke my spirit." Parks freezes on Leadbelly's strong physique as he lifts the hammer high into the air to bring it down to break another rock. Here, Leadbelly cries out as an individual man defying the system that incarcerates him, but at the same time, he speaks as the voice for all African Americans whose spirits will not be destroyed or taken away.

After *Leadbelly*, Parks directed a television movie for the *American Playhouse* series, entitled *Solomon Northup's Odyssey* (1984), based on the slave narrative of the title character. From his most recent autobiography, Parks appears reflective and appreciative of his accomplishments, but not driven to attain further money or fame. Over his lifetime, he has been awarded twenty-four honorary degrees; the NAACP's Spingarn Medal in 1972; the National Medal of Arts at the White House in 1988; and accolades from dozens of his peers and filmmakers who followed him through the studio doors. He writes of himself: "I've been given several names—Mr. Dreamer, Mr. Striver, and occasionally Mr. Success. I've tried on all three for size. The first fit rather well; the third still has a slight feel of discomfort."[11] Whether prepared for it or not, Gordon Parks should accept the praise for the historical and cultural significance of his film directing, which has served as an exceptional model for black directors who have followed.

Melvin Van Peebles

One of the reasons I originally wanted to make films was that I got tired of what they [Hollywood filmmakers] were doing. . . . I knew I could do better. At least, I knew it wouldn't be hard to do better than that. . . . It took me ten years to get a chance to do it their way, and what I discovered at Columbia Pictures is that their way gets in my way. . . . I just did my best and got on with my own independent career.[12]   Melvin Van Peebles

It may be difficult to measure the extent to which Melvin Van Peebles shaped black filmmaking, and perhaps even more difficult to assess to what degree Van Peebles has inspired African American artists in general. Van Peebles has attained legendary status among creative people who view his success as a testament of perseverance and self-belief. At the very least, Van Peebles represents a pioneering independent vision that forced Hollywood studios to be aware of a new approach to the cinematic renditions of African Americans.

Born in 1932 in Chicago, Van Peebles went to Ohio Wesleyan University, receiving his B.A. degree in 1953. In 1955, he met Maria, a woman from a rich, white liberal family, and together they had three children, including a son, Mario. Van Peebles went into the air force and became an aviator, and after three years in the service he settled in San Francisco, where he began to make short films—one entitled *Three Pickup Men for Herrick* completed in 1958.[13] Finding that his talents were not welcomed in Hollywood, Van Peebles eventually made his way to Holland to study astronomy at the University of Amsterdam, where he studied acting as well. Facing marital problems, he journeyed to Paris, where he once again was drawn to filmmaking. Knowing he could get financial support from the government as a French filmmaker, Van Peebles taught himself French and wrote several novels to make a name for himself. His strategy worked, as he went on to make the French film *The Story of a Three-Day Pass* (1968), a film that received critical attention at the San Francisco Film Festival. From there, Van Peebles was able to make his way back to Hollywood.

Between 1968 and 1989, Van Peebles directed four feature films besides *Three-Day Pass*: *Watermelon Man* (1970), *Sweet Sweetback's Baadasssss Song* (1971), *Don't Play Us Cheap* (1973), and *Identity Crisis* (1989). The films offer a startling variety in tone, showcasing the contrasts between Van Peebles' work inside and outside the studio system.

The Story of a Three-Day Pass is a film that explores an interracial love affair between a black American serviceman and a white Parisian woman, emphasizing the racial consciousness of the black soldier and the racism of fellow white American soldiers. When the film was screened at the San Francisco Film Festival, it received some enthusiastic responses. One journalist acknowledged that "[s]ome of Van Peebles direction [was] good, especially where he gets across the idea that what people do and what they think may not run along the same lines."[14] However, other negative criticisms surfaced, and these mixed reactions to Van Peebles' first film were indicative of the oppositional responses he would continue to receive throughout his career, as critics, both black and white, have resisted Van Peebles' expressionistic, excessive visual style.

When Van Peebles completed *Don't Play Us Cheap* (1973), an adaptation from his own play, the response was lukewarm, as exemplified by one critic who concluded that "the film remains stagebound but engaging in sharing the ambiance of a Saturday night in Harlem."[15] This film remains one of Van Peebles' least-known works and was generally ridiculed by those reviewers who made the effort to evaluate it.

However, his three films *Watermelon Man, Sweet Sweetback's Baad-asssss Song,* and *Identity Crisis* are his most accomplished. The first movie, *Watermelon Man,* by its very title, prompts a reaction that taps into America's racial history and African American stereotypes. Scripted as a comedy by white writer Herman Raucher, the intention of the film was to provide a satiric look at the alleged liberal suburban notions of equality.

Van Peebles' sensibilities as an independent filmmaker are obvious in this film. Although *Watermelon Man* has a polished look in places, Van Peebles—serving as both director and music composer—consistently strikes a satiric chord with a heavy-handed experimenting in visuals and sound. The story centers on a white middle-class insurance salesman named Jeff Gerber (Godfrey Cambridge in whiteface makeup at first). Gerber, an outspoken racial bigot and sexist, awakes one morning to discover that he has turned black. In his shock and initial denial, Gerber believes that an overexposure to his sun lamp has caused the darkening of his skin; consequently, he uses extensive showers, bleaching creams, and even milk baths in futile attempts to regain the white complexion he worships. Inevitably, he endures a set of experiences with various white people in his life who display their hypocrisy, racial prejudice, and belief in racial stereotypes. After losing his family, job, house, and lifestyle, Gerber finally accepts his new blackness and all life's lessons that have come with it.

Unfortunately, the film contains awkward visual and aural expressions that weigh down an already vaporous script that relied too much on cutesy one-liners. The most memorable aspect of the film becomes the performance by Godfrey Cambridge. Required to pull off physical and verbal humor, as well as the pathos of an emotionally lost man, Cambridge is consistently radiant in a rather enigmatic role.

When looking for directorial areas to note, several are scattered throughout the film, even though the coherence of the entire film falters. One such area is centered in the visual metaphor of the "running black man." Van Peebles sets up this icon early in the film as Gerber goes through a daily ritual of jogging along the sidewalks in his suit and tie to beat the city bus to a distant bus stop. As he easily scurries past the bus, the bus's white patrons urge the black driver to hurry along to beat Gerber in his arrogant display

Jeff Gerber (Godfrey Cambridge, right, in whiteface) says good-bye to his wife (Estelle Parsons) in *Watermelon Man*.

of physical fitness. But when Gerber turns black and goes running through white neighborhoods, the reactions by whites alter—white women scream in fear, white men watch suspiciously, and eventually white police officers detain Gerber, believing he's running away from a crime scene.

The image of the "running black man" carries both a historical meaning (escaping slavery to freedom) and a political meaning (blacks running from racial hegemony). It works effectively in revealing the burdens imposed upon black men by a system that will always qualify and punish their blackness. This visual of the "running black man" surfaces again in a more jolting manner in Van Peebles' next film, *Sweet Sweetback's Baadasssss Song.*

When *Sweet Sweetback* was first released, it ignited outbreaks of discussions and arguments both within and outside the African American community. With an X rating for its elements of graphic sex, and with its nihilistic content, the film was either panned as cinematic trash by some or heralded as cinematic radicalism by others. And since its late-1960s release, the debate over the film's value has continued into the 1990s, and the film has assumed a cult status by young black filmmakers and the hip-hop generation.

Sweet Sweetback follows the exploits of a black man who demonstrates such exceptional skills during his preteen sexual initiation that his older lover anoints him with the name "Sweetback." His sexual prowess continues into adulthood, as he becomes a featured performer at an underground sex theater. But when he intercedes and beats two white policemen who were pummeling a black revolutionary suspect, Sweetback becomes a fugitive. He embodies the "running black man" who escapes the ghetto streets, to reach the rural countryside, and finally to reach and cross the Mexican border.

Given the historical context of Black Power during the late '60s and the growing Black Arts movement, the objectives of *Sweet Sweetback*—with its revolutionary messages and black hero figure—were appropriate and timely. However, the final film carries such provocative content and displays such an unusual visual style that it was doomed to controversy—a controversy that made it a financial success.

Black historian Lerone Bennett Jr. labels the film as "tasteless," suggesting its value was that it was "an obligatory step for anyone who want[ed] to go further and make the first revolutionary black film."[16] Augmenting that negative assessment, one black critic complains that the film "shows the moral decadence of some black folks, but never at any time does he [Van Peebles] reveal the social and political forces responsible for that decadence. . . . Van Peebles pictures sexual freakishness as an essential and unmistakable part of black reality and history—a total distortion and gross affront to black people."[17] From another viewpoint at that time, Huey Newton, a leader of the Black Panthers, would refer to the film as revolutionary black art,[18] echoing the praise that many viewers attributed to the film.

From a contemporary perspective, *Sweet Sweetback's Baadasssss Song* certainly stands out as an independent venture that became an impressive commercial accomplishment. Van Peebles raised $500,000 from his directorial earnings from *Watermelon Man* and various investors, and the film grossed over $10 million in its first run.[19] Even by today's accounting, that kind of twenty-to-one return can only be viewed as remarkable.

The final credit at the movie's end informs the viewer that the film was written, composed, produced, directed, and edited by Melvin Van Peebles. With hindsight, that accomplishment as a black auteur must be admired, but with that same hindsight, the goals that Van Peebles set out to achieve are not that perceptible. Without a doubt, the black man breaking his shackles and running for freedom connects Sweetback to his racial ancestors, as does the use of gospel music, blues, jazz, and the call-and-response chorus over the final sequences of the film. Van Peebles does a noteworthy job of linking the protagonist to a list of nameless black men who preceded him. In addition, Van Peebles emphasizes the ongoing friction between black men and police officers that surfaced again in the '90s with regard to Rodney King and O. J. Simpson.

The political messages of black unity, pride, and determinism falter, however, when weakened by the gratuitous and explicit sex in the film. Although the filmmaker wants to suggest the notion that sex has been the one province given to black men to display their competence, this notion itself is rooted within a racial stereotype nurtured during the slavery era. Van Peebles appears to be validating that sexual stereotype, even as he insists that other racial stereotypes are faulty. In particular, this sexual generalization carries another message in the film—black women are promiscuous. The filmmaker constructs black female characters that are either passive mother figures or lustful sexual figures, undercutting its proclaimed revolutionary dimensions. The latter images remain the most prevalent, assigning a rather narrow significance to black women and their place in the community and within any political activism. In four separate scenes, black women characters eagerly engage in sexual intercourse with Sweetback, suggesting, even if unintentionally, that black women are lascivious.

Even when the filmmaker attempts to present sex as a political weapon, the camera's lingering lens over naked flesh makes a different type of statement. In the sequence when Sweetback and the black revolutionary are fleeing the city, they are confronted by a gang of white bikers. When Sweetback is given his choice of weapons to challenge the gang leader in order to win his freedom, Sweetback chooses sex. The bikers' leader is a white woman—a blond Amazon—and as the woman and Sweetback strip and have intercourse in the circle made by the bikers, Van Peebles is obviously confronting the historical taboo of miscegenation. The scene is presented with frontal nudity and close shots of gyrating bodies until the white biker queen screams out Sweetback's name in orgasmic pleasure. Sweetback, and by association black men, has defeated the white bikers and the racial taboo, but the victory is only transitory, won through the phallus and not the spirit and intellect. Van Peebles reduces the political potency of the sequence to mere sexual potency. The black hero is just a black stud.

Nearly two decades after *Sweet Sweetback*, Van Peebles directed *Identity Crisis* (1989), based on the script by his son, Mario. The film presents the story of a deceased, gay French fashion designer who moves in and out of the body of a black rap performer. The gimmick here is that a street witch grants the request of the dying gay designer to live on, so his spirit is transferred into the body of the black rapper. The transformation is a bit incomplete, however, and consequently, whenever receiving a physical bump to the head, either the personality of the rapper or the designer dominates. Both the elder and younger Van Peebles understood that such a premise was outlandish and fantastical, as the film displays the tongue-in-cheek warning before the opening credits: "weird crap from Melvin and Mario." The film lives up to its warning as it parades a menagerie of characters: rappers, a nerd, Sikh drug smugglers, homeless witches, a dominatrix, a mute mud-wrestling Amazon, and a narrating cop who speaks in rhymes.

Other than the use of superimposition, when the narrating cop (Melvin Van Peebles) appears in a ghostly fashion over the action, or the use of black-and-white film images in various sequences, the elder Van Peebles does not distinguish himself as a director in this movie. Instead, the film appears to be a vehicle to showcase the screen presence of the younger Van Peebles, as Mario portrays both the streetwise urban rapper and the gay French designer.

Perhaps the most significant aspect of *Identity Crisis* within the collective works of Melvin Van Peebles can be found in the title itself. As with his earlier films, Van Peebles returns to the theme of identity—how complex it can be, but how simplistic and limiting when reduced only to race. He seems to be asserting that black people have survived those limitations, and that white people destroy themselves and others around them by maintaining those limitations.

In a notable fashion, Melvin Van Peebles has survived as a filmmaker despite the controversy and the limitations thrown at him. He appears to have shaped his film career in the same manner as a number of his films—elliptically, sporadically, but always with control. The quirkiness and frenetic energy of his visual style has influenced many directors that have followed him, and certainly his maverick and often radical approach to completing films has inspired just as many directors, regardless of their racial identity.

CHAPTER TWO

The Visionary Actors

Ossie Davis

Yes, I had enjoyed my stint as a director of *Cotton Comes to Harlem.* The exercise of power and authority was intoxicating, but I wasn't drunk. Directing calls for a vision and an itch, a dedicated focus, energy, the ability to be mean and stubborn if you have to, and at times, a little devious. Qualities I thoroughly understand, but do not have.[1]   Ossie Davis

Unlike Gordon Parks and Melvin Van Peebles, Ossie Davis came to film directing via a lengthy tenure as a writer and actor for the stage. In fact, by the 1990s, Davis had achieved a distinctive fifty-year career in theater and an overlapping forty years in film and television. Ossie Davis has been an artistic forerunner and an amazing example of talent and perseverance.

Davis' background has been highlighted in numerous African American biographies, as well as in his enlightening 1998 co-autobiography, *With Ossie and Ruby: In This Life Together.* Born in 1917 in Cogdell, Georgia, Ossie Davis was the son of religious parents, with his father serving as a preacher in their church. Upon completing high school, Davis attended Tuskegee Institute in Alabama, but unable to meet his financial obligations, he relocated to Washington, D.C., and stayed with relatives while studying at Howard University. The classroom, however, couldn't hold Davis and his ambitions to write fiction and drama. He traveled to Harlem, where he began acting with a black troupe in 1941. Joining the army to help the war effort, Davis was stationed in Liberia, West Africa, where he wrote and produced stage performances to entertain the soldiers. After the war, he returned to New York and continued acting, and in 1948, he met his future wife, Ruby Dee, while they performed the play *Anna Lucasta* with a touring company. In the 1950s, he added television and film acting to his repertoire, appearing in the films *No Way Out* (1950) with Sidney Poitier and *The Joe Louis Story* (1953).

By the '50s, Davis and Ruby Dee emerged as a couple who were both outstanding actors and politically active, targeting racial prejudice in their personal and professional lives. Together, they formed their own theater company, while visibly working for civil rights organizations. Davis' early theatrical triumph as both writer and actor occurred in 1961 with the play *Purlie Victorious*, which was later made into a film titled *Gone Are the Days* (1963) and a musical play titled *Purlie*. More television work followed in the 1960s, but it was in 1970 that he directed his first feature film, *Cotton Comes to Harlem*. He added to his filmography by directing *Kongi's Harvest* (1971), *Black Girl* (1972), *Gordon's War* (1973), and *Countdown at Kusini* (1976). Davis has also been credited with being one of the organizers of the New York–based Third World Cinema Corporation, a production entity that also trained filmmakers of color to work in feature and documentary projects; the company is credited with producing two black-oriented films— *Claudine* (1974), starring Diahann Carroll, and *Greased Lightning* (1977), starring Richard Pryor.[2] In the 1980s and 1990s, Davis continued to win accolades for his stage performances, and a younger generation of viewers has come to recognize his talents as a reappearing face in several Spike Lee films, including *School Daze* (1988), *Do the Right Thing* (1989), *Jungle Fever* (1991), and *Get on the Bus* (1996).

With the film *Cotton Comes to Harlem*, Davis, as director and coscreenwriter, developed a black-themed movie to be offered to a mainstream audience, helping to launch several years of films that would deliver black characters and settings that reflected the black cultural and political perspectives of the late 1960s and early 1970s. Based on same-titled book and black protagonists—Grave Digger Jones and Coffin Ed Johnson—created in the detective series by black author Chester Himes, *Cotton* is a black urban action comedy that parodies and celebrates black culture and the black community.

The opening credits appear under a song containing lyrics written by Ossie Davis—lyrics that state: "Ain't now, but it's going to be, black enough for me." The statement "Is that black enough for you?" resounds throughout the movie, a call that seeks a response about the substance and visibility of one's "blackness." This blackness of attitude, demeanor, and political convictions becomes central to the story line that connects the history of black Americans to the contemporary urban streets viewed during the opening sequence. Exploiting this "blackness" unashamedly, Deke O'Malley (Calvin Lockhart), a materially successful preacher, proselytizes for membership into his Back-to-Africa ship line. Although Deke possesses the potential to be another Marcus Garvey or Malcolm X, the movie's protagonists —Jones (Godfrey Cambridge) and Johnson (Raymond St. Jacques)—perceive O'Malley as the con man he is. As police detectives, Jones and Johnson serve as the controlling force in the community, as well as its protectors. When Deke O'Malley's outdoor rally is broken up by masked gunmen who steal $87,000 belonging to the African ship line, Jones and Johnson discover through Deke's woman, Iris (Judy Pace), that the good reverend had orchestrated the robbery himself. Deke's cohorts hide the stolen money in a bale of cotton that, during their escape, gets lost on the streets of Harlem—lost, that is, until a street junkman named Uncle Bud (Redd Foxx) collects the bale and eventually the money inside.

Most of the film follows the efforts of numerous characters to find that lost bale of cotton in Harlem. Car chases, shootouts, explosions, naked women, hip street language, trendy fashions, and an R&B/jazz-flavored musical score all come together as the basic aspects of this urban action genre. Yet, beneath the movie's comic tone, the director integrates messages about black culture and history. As an example, the director provides an obvious reference to Marcus Garvey's back-to-Africa movement of the 1920s through Deke's African ship line organization, but Davis goes further to highlight black history in a scene staged at the Apollo Theater before an enlivened black audience. Having obtained the cotton bale as a prop, a black woman dancer incorporates the bale into her choreography. Dressed in slave clothes and wearing the stereotypical pickaninny braids, she shuffles as a broken woman laboring around the bale; then, removing her slave attire and pickaninny wig, the woman dances atop the bale in liberation. Davis intercuts between the dancer and the black audience, showing the latter's comprehension and appreciation of the symbolic dance. Then, immediately following that performance, a gospel choir takes the stage to sing a traditionally arranged religious song.

Another cultural point comes at the end of the film, when Jones and Johnson have managed to expose and incarcerate Deke; they read a letter from Uncle Bud that is postmarked from Africa. Inside the letter is a color picture postcard with a photo of Uncle Bud, dressed in African attire, sitting regally with three black women attending him. As Johnson begins reading the letter, the still photo card, centrally framed in the camera, becomes a live-action sequence where Uncle Bud explains: "I am now a retired gentleman raising cotton on my own villa in Africa." The director shows the viewer that Uncle Bud, the symbol of the struggling, working black man, has gone full circle; he has taken advantage of the cotton bale to return home to control his own destiny and resources.

Whether or not white audiences evaluated the cultural messages, Davis generously included such messages for black viewers to contemplate. With the success of *Cotton*, which grossed over $6 million,[3] Davis could have continued in a similar vein. However, his passions moved him in a more dramatic direction. His next two films—*Kongi's Harvest* (1971) and *Black Girl* (1972)—were both based on material originally written for the stage.

Against the backdrop of the resurging feminist movement in the early 1970s, *Black Girl*, adapted from a play written by Ms. J. E. Franklin, is a film that explores the intricate and sometimes painful connections between mothers and daughters. Over the opening credits, the title song's lyrics ask the question: "Black girl, where do you think you are going to? Don't you know what can happen to a black girl who sets her eyes too high?"

As the story begins, Billie Jean (Peggy Pettitt), a black teen, rushes to her waitress job at a local club. Billie Jean's deep desire, however, is to dance at the club, as a way to make money to buy a house for her mother. Dancing is her passion, and when she does finally get the chance to dance on the club's stage, Billie Jean—like the Apollo Theater dancer in *Cotton Comes to Harlem*—performs an interpretive, African-style dance instead of a popular dance of the day. But Billie Jean's ambitions are hidden from her family, as she locks herself behind doors at home to practice her dancing in private.

At home Billie Jean shares a small home in a multigenerational household of women: Mu' Dear (Claudia McNeil), the grandmother; Mama Rosie (Louise Stubbs), the mother; and half-sisters Norma Faye (Gloria Edwards) and Ruth Ann (Loretta Greene), who constantly visit the house. As the film moves from a specific focus on Billie Jean to the other women in her life, the intense frustrations, anger, and desperation increase.

Mama Rosie, an obstinate woman, ridicules her daughters for their lack of achievement and fulfillment as she defines it. Constantly finding fault with her three biological daughters, Mama Rosie praises the accomplishments of her adopted daughter Netta (Leslie Uggams), a homeless girl she took in and raised. Netta, on the verge of graduating from college, remains the standard of excellence for Rosie, who hopes the educated daughter will return home to teach. Norma Faye (the oldest daughter), Ruth Ann (pregnant and a mother of two), and Billie Jean (who has quit school to dance) all share a resentment for Netta, as they struggle to find the favor of their mother. Oddly enough, Norma Faye and Ruth Ann, who are devious conspirators, also target Billie Jean as their emotional scapegoat because she has a different father and an ambition to dance.

At the same time, Mu' Dear and Mama Rosie have their own issues, as their often confrontational dialogue refers back to their troubled past. Additionally, Rosie also failed to love the men in her life, who have left her in her solitude of bitterness. When Earl (Brock Peters), one of her ex-husbands, returns to ask Rosie to go away to Detroit, the two find themselves unable to get past the problems of their former marriage. Earl (father to Norma Faye and Ruth Ann) has developed a successful shoe business, and he pleads for a new start with Rosie. Although Rosie is dissatisfied with her present life, she refuses to forgive Earl's infidelity that occurred eighteen years before.

Having faith in the script and his actors, Davis directs in a straightforward way that doesn't attempt to obscure the various story lines. From the cramped bedroom where Billie Jean rehearses her dancing, to the palpable tension among sisters, to the lighter sexual innuendos exchanged between Rosie and Earl—Davis moves the viewer between scenes and tones revealing the layers of emotions and flaws within each character. Davis avoids askew camera angles and erratic cutting as he peels back the surface of the characters to expose the frustrations simmering beneath.

In the interior of Rosie's house, Davis places his characters within hallway doorframes to emphasize the sense of incarceration that the women feel, limited and trapped by circumstances beyond their control. In a similar fashion, he uses space effectively, consistently placing Norma Faye and Ruth Ann together on one side of the frame with Billie Jean distanced on the other side. One of the strongest interior scenes occurs when the three sisters and Netta have a confrontation in the living room. Davis cuts from long shots to close shots, as the initial coldness toward Netta escalates into a dangerous moment when Norma Faye threatens Netta with a knife. Part of that escalation contains dialogue that shows the manner in which the two sisters use "femininity" as a weapon of choice. As Norma Faye and Ruth Ann deride Netta for attending a white college, they accuse her of being a lesbian because Netta does not have a man in her life. Norma Faye chides that Netta won't "disgrace this family by ending up funny [lesbian]." Ruth Ann adds disdainfully: "Raise up Netta's dress to see what the freak got. Didn't ever want to be seen naked—maybe she's a man . . ." Davis allows this impassioned scene to play itself out in a naturally intimidating manner without drawing attention to the camera and without any melodramatic music.

With the films *Cotton Comes to Harlem* and *Black Girl,* Davis shows that he can handle both comedy and drama handily, and he also displays an obvious respect for African American culture and community. And though *Black Girl* didn't raise the profits brought in by *Cotton,* the discrepancy in popularity rests more in the times than in any misdirection on Davis' part. Studios were perhaps unenthusiastic about marketing a film that explored emotional and psychological dimensions of black womanhood, and perhaps audiences were still hungry for the trendy black urban action films that dominated the period. But Davis gave notice that working-class black women—who were not prostitutes, drug users, or gun-toting heroines—had stories to tell that were provocative and relevant.

Davis' additional films did not attain either the critical praise or the wide audience of his first film, but in aggregate the films demonstrate the ongoing commitment to black cultural concerns that permeates Davis' position as a director. *Kongi's Harvest* (1971) was an effort to bring the Nigerian playwright Wole Soyinka's stage project of the same title to the screen. The film was independently financed but was unable to find an American distributor. With an all-African cast and shot in Nigeria, the film was, according to Davis, "a comedy of African politics [which shows] Africa as Africans see it."[4]

Gordon's War (1973) brought Davis back to the Harlem setting. The title character, a black Vietnam vet, returns to his urban home and organizes a war against the drug dealers pervading his community. With a mixed review, one critique praises the "sharp direction of Ossie Davis [who] catches the argot, the flavor and the sinister ambiance of the area," but concludes that the "picture is inconclusive, far from profound, and the urgency of the theme has been overly simplified to fit the action."[5] Davis' last film directorial effort — *Countdown at Kusini* (1976), costarring Davis with Ruby Dee — failed to find an audience and fared no better with the critics. The story, which Davis cowrote, is set in a fictional West African nation, and it explores the postcolonial struggles of a new nation as multinational corporations strategize to take the country over. One critic asserts that the film "wants to be 'serious' about African aspirations while also being entertaining. Though it tries hard, it's neither."[6] Still another reviewer ridiculed the project as the "sort of movie that illustrates what happens when achievement falls short of aims. . . . [T]his movie — filmed in and around Lagos, Nigeria — emerges as subpar adventure and less than lucid ideology."[7]

Having survived all of the less than favorable critical attention over the years for his directing, in the 1990s Ossie Davis continued to be a visible force in film, theater, and television. Apparently uninterested in dominating the spotlight, Davis has worked in a more quiet but consistent manner, bringing African American themes, issues, and experiences to mainstream audiences. And in those endeavors, his pride and confidence have always shone through despite obstacles and pejorative reception from many. With a seemingly extraordinary energy, he remains one of the few singular talents who has excelled in a variety of mediums and who has distinguished himself as a writer, actor, and director.

Sidney Poitier

I have a responsibility as an artist and because I am black, that artistic responsibility has a certain connectedness to the community of which I am a representative. . . . In order to influence the nature of the material you must first conquer any residual resistance there may be that says blacks can't make the money. . . . You therefore have to pursue those subjects that will satisfy a black community and that will seduce the white community purely on the basis of entertainment.[8]   Sidney Poitier

When Sidney Poitier won the Academy Award for Best Actor for his performance in *Lilies of the Field* (1963), he accepted the honor by referring to his historic career as being a long journey. Up to that point, he had accomplished an arduous task of defying a system that sustained itself by excluding people of color from positions of management and artistic control. Yet, following his Oscar win, over the next twenty-five years, Poitier would again prove his perseverance by directing nine films that ranged in genre and artistic achievement. Sidney Poitier won his way into film history based on his acting, but his acting allowed him to extend his influence and contributions behind the camera as a director.

Poitier chronicles his life in two revealing installments of his autobiography: *This Life* (1980) and *The Measure of a Man: A Spiritual Biography* (2000). Although reared in the Bahamas by his farming parents, Poitier was born in Miami, Florida, in 1927, when his parents traveled there to sell their produce. Formally uneducated Poitier moved to Miami at age thirteen to live with an older brother. Traveling to New York in the early 1940s, he supported himself by working in restaurants until joining the army at age sixteen. Returning to New York in 1945, Poitier responded to a newspaper advertisement by the American Negro Theater. But failing an audition due in part to his West Indian accent, he committed himself to improving his reading skills and learning to articulate clearly by mimicking radio broadcasters.

Although he failed another audition at the American Negro Theater, Poitier took a janitorial position there while studying to be an actor. As the decade ended, he gained a great deal of stage experience, and in 1950, he performed in his first feature film, *No Way Out,* portraying a black doctor accused of killing a white patient. For the next seventeen years, Poitier chiseled out a movie career as a black actor that still remains unequaled. Whether one labels him a role model or trailblazer, Sidney Poitier has portrayed an array of characters that have depicted the struggle, survival, and dignity of African Americans. His acting career peaked in 1967 when three films released that year carried his name as the lead actor—*To Sir, with Love, In the Heat of the Night,* and *Guess Who's Coming to Dinner.*[9] Between 1972 and 1990, he mixed an acting and film directing career, and in the '90s, he returned as an actor in dramatic features such as *Shoot to Kill* (1988), *Sneakers* (1992), and *The Jackal* (1997).

Over eight years, Poitier directed nine films, including *Buck and the Preacher* (1972), *A Warm December* (1973), *Uptown Saturday Night* (1974), *Let's Do It Again* (1975), *A Piece of the Action* (1977), *Stir Crazy* (1980), *Hanky Panky* (1982), *Fast Forward* (1985), and *Ghost Dad* (1990). Although Poitier has distinguished himself as a dramatic actor, six of the nine films he directed have been comedies. Perhaps, through his directing, Poitier has been able to find expression for that humorous side of his personality that remained locked behind the stern actor who served as role model for the black community for over two decades.

Poitier's directorial debut in *Buck and the Preacher* remains one of his strongest efforts. At first, Poitier's title role as Buck was the extent of his responsibility, but when "differences" surfaced with the initial white director, Poitier listened to the suggestion of his friend and costar, Harry Belafonte, and assumed the directing duties.

Set in the post–Civil War western frontier, the film follows Buck, a former soldier, as he guides black homesteaders into the open and free lands of the West. But a band of white riders, led by Deshay (Cameron Mitchell), claiming to be working as Labor Recruiters for the Planters Association of Louisiana, consistently burn out the black settlers' communities to force them to return to work on the white-owned lands. While escaping the white riders, Buck negotiates safe passage through Indian lands for his homesteaders and comes across the Preacher (Belafonte). Though antagonistic at first, the two men, along with Buck's woman Ruth (Ruby Dee), launch an offensive against the white riders who stole money from the black settlers. Buck and the Preacher kill Deshay and most of his riders, but unable to regain all of the stolen money, Buck, the Preacher, and Ruth rob a bank and find a temporary haven from a chasing posse among the Indians before rejoining the black wagon train.

The film presents a slice of black cultural history, integrating that history into the recognizable western genre with all of the expected conventions: gunfights, chases, a crude frontier town, an Indian village, and sweeping frontier vistas. Poitier, as director, makes certain to pay homage to the rugged beauty of the terrain, providing long shots and high-angle shots to highlight, in John Ford fashion, the natural wonder of rocky hillsides, desert scapes, and flowing plains overlapping one another.

But the film sparkles when Poitier explores those places where cultural and political lines cross. In one instance, Ruth shares dinner with Buck and the Preacher, as she pleads with the former to forget about heading west to join the black wagon train and instead go north to Canada. Ruth recognizes the reality of the times saying: "I ain't gonna live in this land no more. War ain't changed nothing and nobody. It's like a poison that's soaked into the ground. They ain't going to give us nothin' . . . no forty acres and a mule, no freedom either." In this scene three former slaves sit at a crossroads, all scarred in some way by the past and all seeking a new day of independence.

In an equally provocative scene, Poitier permits his camera to capture another simple, but potent exchange of ideas. In the Indian village, where Buck, the Preacher, and Ruth take refuge, Buck attempts to negotiate additional supplies and weapons from the Chief. Buck tells the Chief that the blacks and Indians have the same enemy. The Chief, through his wife who interprets, reminds Buck that he was once a sergeant fighting alongside the whites against the Indians. During the dialogue, Poitier places the black characters in a three-shot, cutting back and forth to the Chief and his wife in a two-shot. By framing them separately, their cultural lines and historical conflicts are emphasized. As the Chief goes on to bear witness about his vanishing nation, he tells Buck: "Tomorrow we will be like ghosts . . . but we will fight. . . . We need our guns and bullets for our own fight." Later, when Buck and the Preacher are cornered by the white posse, several Indian warriors intercede with their rifle fire, reversing the genre's cliche of "the cavalry coming to the rescue."

Despite the film's adherence to the Western genre and its noble cultural objectives, *Buck and the Preacher* struggled to find an audience. Notably, the film was hurt by competition from the dominant black images of the time — the black urban action images of Jim Brown, Pam Grier, Richard Roundtree et al. And though, in comparison, the depression-era film *Sounder* (1972) also ventured outside the urban setting, it attained critical praise and an audience that surpassed *Buck and the Preacher*. Perhaps, black cowboys and settlers were still too far removed from the traditional images of African Americans, and the sense of triumph suggested by the film's final freeze-frame — of Buck, the Preacher, and Ruth riding into the sunset — was too foreign a concept for audiences. Notably, in the late 1960s, the white male Western heroes prevailed in the genre, most notably in *Butch Cassidy and the Sundance Kid* (1969) or in films featuring Clint Eastwood's monosyllabic-speaking loner, including *A Fistful of Dollars* (1964), *For a Few Dollars More* (1965), or *The Good, the Bad and the Ugly* (1967).

Poitier's next feature was met with an even harsher reception than *Buck and the Preacher*. *A Warm December* is "the story of a successful black American doctor whose wife has died and left him with an eleven-year-old daughter; he goes to London on a vacation with his child and falls in love with an African princess."[10] Poitier attempted to fill a void in American cinema where romantic love between a black man and black woman was nonexistent. Furthermore, *A Warm December*'s relationship between an African American and a black African hooked into the era's celebration of the cultural connections linking the two. With these elements in place, the movie should have found an audience, but again the positive depiction of serious black romance was too alien a concept for Hollywood to promote.

A Warm December was Poitier's first feature under his deal with First Artists Corporation, a company formed to utilize four box-office actors as the artistic and money-making core: Poitier, Barbra Streisand, Steve McQueen, and Paul Newman.[11] And even though the film failed financially, Poitier's contract allowed him to have access to the $2 million needed to make his first comedy, *Uptown Saturday Night*—a movie made over the objections of the financial heads at First Artists and at the distributing studio, Warner Brothers.[12] No other black actor-director had that kind of power at that time—to have a financial flop but to demand a green light on his next film—and only a few blacks have enjoyed that type of power in the contemporary Hollywood system.

So, following the disheartening reception of *A Warm December*, Poitier turned to directing comedies. In fact, five of his next six films were comedies; the first three can be evaluated as companion pieces, due to their genre, the casting, and the similarity of themes and messages. In addition, those three films—*Uptown Saturday Night, Let's Do It Again,* and *A Piece of the Action*—reflected the changing audience. Black movie audiences began moving away from the black urban action formulas that emphasized the racist oppression of "the man," to a more traditional comedic structure that emphasized entertainment. In another consideration, those three films were more comfortable for nonblacks to watch as well. Although their settings remained within an urban black community, the middle-class black characters in those comedies were less abrasive integrationists, and thus evoked less guilt on the part of white viewers. At the same time, those three films show the development of Poitier as a Hollywood director. With his polished, straightforward style, Poitier was the ideal director to bring African American images to a mainstream audience during the post-Vietnam era. The political tensions and social eruptions of the late 1960s and early 1970s had created a mood that was best alleviated by the kind of comedies Poitier directed.

Uptown Saturday Night, scripted by black writer Richard Wesley, was a deliberate move away from the images of black superheroes, pimps, pushers, and prostitutes who had taken center stage in numerous black-oriented films during the previous five years. The movie presents two friends—factory worker Steve Jackson (Sidney Poitier) and taxi driver Wardell Franklin (Bill Cosby)—who become robbery victims while enjoying themselves at an illegal after-hours club called Madame Zenobia's. With numerous plot twists at the end, the black heroes prevail, and the gangsters are hauled away by the police.

In a departure from his better-known dramatic roles, Poitier takes the lead comedic role, but wisely pairs himself with the experienced comedian Cosby, who had also acquired a mainstream following due to his role on the '60s television series *I Spy*. Poitier appears a bit awkward in his comic persona, but he remains balanced by the more natural Cosby. But behind the camera, Poitier shows more confidence with the genre, allowing Cosby, Richard Pryor (as Sharp Eye Washington), and Flip Wilson (as the Reverend) to steal the scenes when necessary. And in a surprising role, Harry Belafonte, who parodies Don Corleone from *The Godfather* (1972), delivers an enjoyable performance as the eccentric mobster Geechie Dan. Similar to what he accomplished in his role as the Preacher in *Buck and the Preacher*, Belafonte demonstrates his ease and ability in stepping outside his romantic-handsome-singer image to create a convincing character.

Poitier shows in the film that he can work with actors, but he also crafts a movie that has structure and rhythm, even if some of the individual scenes appear sluggish in places. Moreover, he displays a keen ability to orchestrate effective chase sequences, which he builds upon in his later films *A Piece of the Action, Stir Crazy,* and *Hanky Panky.*

However, the black cultural elements that emerge in *Uptown Saturday Night* are just as noteworthy as the ones found within Poitier's Western, *Buck and the Preacher.* Poitier first of all reinforces the existence of black romance and love, as both Steve and Wardell are married to faithful, church-going wives. As with *A Warm December,* Poitier stresses the positive qualities of a committed relationship between a black man and woman, as he allows his camera to spend an extensive amount of time showing a teasing, loving dialogue between Steve and his wife, Sarah (Rosalind Cash), whom he calls his Queen. In another cultural statement, the black church appears in three sequences, including the closing credits, as various angles show the communal ties between the congregation, the Reverend (Wilson), and the choir that sings out traditional gospel songs. In contrast, when attending the club, Madame Zenobia's, subjective shots show Steve's and Wardell's observations of the fashionable and "cool" blacks who dance to the contemporary R&B music and display their jewelry, trendy clothing, cleavage, and sophistication. In all, Poitier's goal is to present the various dimensions of this black community, accentuating the monogamous, hardworking, pious men like Steve and Wardell as examples of the average black people making up that community.

That same communal element remains in *Let's Do It Again*, which "turned out to be twice as successful as *Uptown Saturday Night*," grossing $15 million by the year's end on its $3 million budget.[13] In regard to characters, the story resembles its predecessor, as it places two average, well-intentioned black men in overwhelming situations, and like the fictional Brer Rabbit from black folktales, the two male protagonists always find a way to survive the circumstances.

In Atlanta Clyde Williams (Poitier), a milkman, and Billy Foster (Bill Cosby), a factory worker, are officers of the all-black cultural organization called the Sons and Daughters of Shaka, led by the garrulous Elder Johnson (Ossie Davis). Clyde's faithful, prudish wife, Dee Dee (Lee Chamberlin), and Billy's faithful, sexy wife, Beth (Denise Nicholas), are also members and workers in the organization. With the threat of their building facing destruction by the city, Clyde and Billy develop a scheme to raise the necessary $55,000 to build a new hall. Under the guise of traveling to New Orleans with their wives for a vacation, Clyde and Billy place heavy bets on a boxing match with local black mobsters, Kansas City Mack (John Amos) and Biggie Smalls (Calvin Lockhart). Placing their money on a dubious challenger, Bootney Farnsworth (Jimmie Walker), Clyde assures their bet by hypnotizing Farnsworth to be an aggressive champion. They win, and return home to help the Shaka organization. However, six months later, Kansas City Mack shows up in Atlanta, and having figured out what occurred, he forces Clyde and Billy to return and hypnotize Farnsworth again for a rematch. However, Clyde and Billy outsmart the hoods by hypnotizing both boxers and placing their own bets that the boxers will knock out one another at the same time.

With another script written by black writer Richard Wesley, the film relies less on verbal humor than on broad slapstick and situational comedy. Many of the situations unfortunately are familiar—heroes caught outside on a high ledge; heroes caught in a strange woman's room by her lover; heroes dressed like flashy pimps when placing bets with mobsters; and heroes chased across rooftops, alleys, fences, and apartments. And though Jimmie Walker—who had gained fame as a television star on the show *Good Times*—encourages laughter as an anorexic-looking boxer going through his workout, Walker doesn't have the improvisational insanity intrinsic in characters portrayed, for example, by Richard Pryor.

Poitier maintains his same straightforward directing style in the film, not attempting any variations or experimentation with the camera or the film's structure. Other than using low-angle shots and slow motion during the boxing sequences, Poitier seems content to simply allow his film to follow a predictable development. Again, his visual style is secondary to the cultural messages of unity and his commercial message that black characters are financially appealing to a crossover audience.

With *A Piece of the Action*, Poitier was at his directorial best up to that point. With this movie, Poitier improves upon the comedy due to the fact that the humor emanates from dramatic situations. The characters, Manny Durrell and Dave Anderson, played by Poitier and Cosby, respectively, both have dramatic roots, and therefore the characters have an edge to them. The humor consequently comes from the dialogue and situations, not from broad slapstick or forced silliness that weakened the first two films in the comedy series.

Set in Chicago, *A Piece of the Action* begins with episodes of theft and hustles pulled off by Manny and Dave, respectively; investigating at each crime scene is Detective Joshua Burke (James Earl Jones). It is 1977 when Burke retires from the police force, roasted in the office by his friend and colleague Lieutenant Ty Shorter (Jason Evers), who has already been shown to have connection to the white mobster Vic Bruno (Titos Vandis), who is, incidentally, the target of the successful con game organized by Manny. Burke knows about Manny and Dave's illegal activities, and, remaining anonymous to them, Burke forces the two men to volunteer to work at the Benjamin Banneker Community Improvement Center, a neighborhood effort initiated by Burke's deceased wife. While Manny teaches the hardcore youth, Dave attempts to discover the anonymous person who has forced them into their situation. Just as they uncover the connection between Burke, his wife, and the Center, the mob boss discovers that Manny was the one who took him for the $475,000 con.

The key to making this movie work rests in Manny and Dave's likable nature. Shown to be smooth criminals at first, the hearts beneath their tough exteriors are slowly revealed. Manny's gentleness emanates first as he romantically interacts with his live-in girlfriend, Nikki (Tracy Reed), and then Dave's softness surfaces through his romantic involvement with the Center's director, Lila French (Denise Nicholas). The movie reinforces the significance of black romance—a theme Poitier underscores in his previous three directorial efforts—as "love" serves as a factor that transforms the hard criminal element within Manny and Dave. Basically, Manny and Dave are just two traditional, middle-class guys whose hard work happens to be on the other side of the law, but redemption arrives through their involvement in the black community and their romantic, monogamous relationships.

This affirmation of middle-class values appears important to Poitier, and he includes a scene between Manny and a distraught teacher, Sarah Thomas (Hope Clarke), as they discuss the challenge of their thirty Juvenile Court

In *A Piece of the Action,* hustlers Dave Anderson (Bill Cosby) and Manny Durrell (Sidney Poitier) are forced into respectable behavior by an anonymous caller.

youths. Manny soothes Sarah by criticizing the school system for failing the inner-city kids, but he assures her that being middle-class bears no shame. This sentiment surfaces again when Manny addresses the students in the Center's classroom. He motivates the students by giving each one half of a torn one-hundred-dollar bill as half their salary, to be paid in full if they work seriously at the job prep program.

Poitier remains cognizant of the black cultural messages he needed to convey to a black audience. In addition to the language (street but not gutter), hairstyles, clothing styles, and music of the day—Curtis Mayfield composes a score with songs performed by Mavis Staples—Poitier makes certain that certain points are emphasized. On one occasion, when Manny and Nikki accompany Dave and Lila for a night on the town, the four attend a performance of the Harlem Dance Theater. As they watch in pleasure, Poitier gives a wide angle that shows the all-black ballet company performing gracefully;

here, black culture and European culture merge harmoniously. In a more political manner, when Manny is taken to face the wrath of mobster Vic Bruno,
the white gangster consistently calls Manny "boy"—to which Manny insists,
as emphasized by his name, that he's a "man." And when it becomes evident
that Manny, a lone black man, has gotten the upper hand on five white gangsters by stashing copies of incriminating papers around the city, Vic Bruno
realizes he's been outsmarted and calls Manny a "man." As insignificant as
the distinction between "boy" and "man" might seem, due to the racial history and meanings of those words, Manny gains an important victory by the
end of the sequence.

After *A Piece of the Action,* Poitier shifts his thematic emphasis with his
next two films, *Stir Crazy* and *Hanky Panky.* With these two films, he trans-
fers his focus away from the inner-city black community, but continues to
display his facility at helming comedy films.

Stir Crazy works on the well-used premise of innocent heroes who are
mistakenly identified as criminals, and with this film Poitier relies on the
"interracial buddy film" formula popular in Hollywood at the time. Following up on the immense success of the Gene Wilder–Richard Pryor pairing
in *Silver Streak* (1976), *Stir Crazy* served as another entertainment vehicle
demonstrating Poitier's ability to bring in another box-office hit.

In New York City, Skip Donahue (Wilder), a playwright, and his friend
Harry Monroe (Pryor), an aspiring actor, decide to leave the fast-paced, stressful life of the city. While traveling across country to California, the two buddies stop off in Glenboro, Nevada, due to engine problems with their van.
Attempting to make money, they take a job to promote a local bank by performing together in bright costumes as live-action woodpeckers. When the
bank is robbed by two thugs wearing similar costumes, Skip and Harry are
mistakenly arrested and given a sentence of 125 years in the state prison.
As prison inmates, they get lucky when Skip proves to be an accomplished
rider on the Warden's mechanical bull. Warden Beatty (Barry Corbin) sees
his ticket to making a small fortune by betting against the rival prison warden in an upcoming rodeo. Skip and Harry agree to participate in the rodeo,
planning an escape with the help of several inmates they have befriended,
including the gay murderer named Rory (Georg Stanford Brown), a Latino
lifer named Jesus (Miguelangel Suarez), and a rotund mass murderer named
Grossberger (Erland van Lidth de Jeude). During the rodeo, the heroes make a
successful escape, only to find that they have been freed by the court due to
the efforts of their lawyer, Len (Joel Brooks), and his cousin Meredith (JoBeth
Williams).

Poitier opens the film with a montage of New York City scenes as Gene

Wilder's voice sings the lyrics to a song, titled "Crazy." The scenes beneath the titles exemplify the song's content: street people rummaging garbage cans, kids dressed in trendy fashions, congested traffic and sidewalks, a man and woman fighting over the same taxi, and a man getting slapped by a woman when he gets too friendly with his hands. But as he learned to do in his three previous comedies, Poitier permits his comedic actors to dominate the scenes. Sometimes, Poitier allows the scenes to go on far too long, but in those lengthy scenes of obvious improvisation, he often gets a strong payoff from Wilder and Pryor: when the two are first placed in a holding cell—the now-famous "that's right, we bad" sequence; when the two are first placed into prison, taking turns at having fits of insanity; and when the two are placed in the same small cell with Grossberger. Wilder and Pryor effectively bounce off one another's shtick in a natural manner, as both are verbal and physical comedians, and Poitier gives them room to explore their contrasting but complementary styles.

Poitier's efforts in *Stir Crazy* are appropriately polished, pulling together the kind of comedy that studios wanted to market—entertainment that would not offend or provoke the audience. And it would be easy to dismiss the film for the very reason that it accomplishes the goals that studios desired. *Stir Crazy* failed to win the praise of most critics, but it struck a note of admiration among audiences that made it the number three top-grossing film of the year, as well as the "second most successful comedy in industry history" at that time.[14]

Two years after *Stir Crazy*, Poitier completed the film *Hanky Panky*, again with comedian Gene Wilder. In this movie, Wilder buddies with his offscreen wife, Gilda Radner, in a story filled with government secrets and chase scenes. The story centers on a Chicago architect named Michael Jordan (Wilder) who, while visiting New York City, shares a short, flirtatious taxi ride with a mysterious woman, Janet Dunn (Kathleen Quinlan). After the encounter, well-dressed thugs kidnap, question, and drug Jordan; but escaping death, Jordan locates Dunn, only to have her die in his arms from a gunshot. Jordan is accused of the crime and runs from the law and the thugs, who are led by a crafty man named Ransom (Richard Widmark). Jordan connects with another mysterious woman, Kate Hellman (Radner), who helps Jordan secure a computer tape that everyone is searching for—a tape containing plans for the government's advanced weapons system.

Poitier displays his most eye-catching directing in the movie's opening sequence. With an obvious homage paid to Alfred Hitchcock, the beginning is pure cinema without dialogue, but accompanied by Bernard Hermann-esque strings that pluck and slide through minor chords, the camera holds close on a pair of waking eyes. From the subjective viewpoint, the eyes stare at a large wall painting that combines realistic objects, distorted designs, and bright colors. The angle widens to show that the eyes belong to a man and, cutting to his bare feet, to reveal red stains on his pants—perhaps blood, perhaps not? Descending the stairway, the man's elongated, ominous shadow flows along the wall, and once outside, he crosses the lawn to a barn. Climbing the rickety ladder to the loft, the man slips a secured noose over his head and jumps to a hangman's death. If the remainder of the movie had carried such a skillful marriage of visuals and sound, the end result could have been impressive. However, this movie is a comedy, and from this opening, it shifts to a tone that matches its rather fatuous title.

The humor in this film revolves around Gene Wilder's innocent-man-who's-caught-in-the-middle character. Wilder is funny at first when caught within the confusing circumstances of false accusations. But whereas in *Stir Crazy* Wilder had the opportunity to play off Richard Pryor's improvisation and performance, here, as the solo protagonist, his wide-eyed, open-mouthed, maniacal, catatonic antics eventually wear thin, leaving a film that is highlighted by no less than six chase sequences. Unfortunately, Gilda Radner's talents are minimalized by a characterization that lacks any contours or areas for her to develop comically, so she fulfills a thankless role as "the girlfriend" sidekick who must be rescued.

In 1985, Poitier took a different path in terms of genre, as he directed the musical *Fast Forward*. As with any musical, the movie at times calls for a suspension of reality, but at its heart, the film reaffirms the American myth that everyone—regardless of race, gender, or class—can fulfill their dreams if they remain true to those dreams. With its characters, plot, and tone, *Fast Forward* resembles two other films from the mid-1980s—*Breakin'* (1984) and *A Chorus Line* (1985). Similar to *Breakin'*, *Fast Forward* focuses on teens who express the vitality of popular street dancing, and like *A Chorus Line*, *Fast Forward* presents the aspiring dancer-singers who learn the torturous sacrifices that can be demanded in order to get through just one audition.

In the factory town of Sandusky, Ohio, eight high school dancer-singers calling themselves the "Adventurous Eight" complete a final rehearsal before sneaking off for a weekend trip to New York to participate in an annual competition, sponsored by the Sabol Entertainment Agency. Led by a handsome black teen named Michael (Don Franklin) and by a handsome white teen named Matt (John Scott Clough), the six other members of the group are girls—two white, two black, and two Latina. Hoping that a previous promise by Mr. Sabol (David White) will get them in the door, upon arriving in New York the eight discover that Mr. Sabol is dead, and the company rests within the control of a rather insensitive agent, Clem Friedkin (Sam McMurray). Friedkin tells the group that he'll give them a chance to audition when he returns in three weeks, which challenges the eight to find a way to survive until then. Despite the difficulties, the group survives, only to find Friedkin breaking his promise to them. Desperate, they find the widowed Mrs. Ida Sabol (Irene Worth), who, determined to maintain her husband's good name and to cast aside the boredom of retirement, decides to manage the group. Using her influence, Ida gets the eight onstage, where their performance wins the competition.

Working again with a Richard Wesley script, Poitier presents a group of wholesome adolescents who, due to their similarity of class, appear to have no conflicting racial issues. The two major conflicts in the subplot revolve around romance and dancing turf. First of all, though Michael and Valerie (Gretchen F. Palmer) and Matt and June (Tamara Mark) are romantic items, their romantic displays remain innocent, despite the fact that they are away on their own in the big city. However, when Matt becomes attracted to a rich girl, Susan Granger (Karen Kopins), who hires the eight to perform at her lawn party, the rift between Matt and June threatens to tear the group apart. However, by the final dance number, the Matt-June romance prevails. The second, and more interesting, conflict occurs when the eight decide to raise money by performing on the street, as they have seen done by a "break dancing" group. However, when this group, led by Caesar Lopez (Michael DeLorenzo), discovers they have rivals, the tension between the two sets of dancers makes for the movie's most exciting moments.

The choreography for the film is credited to Rick Atwell, who unashamedly borrowed from Michael Jackson's "Beat It" music video in providing the Adventurous Eight with their dance movements in the early portion of the film. For his part, Poitier does justice to the choreography by allowing space and wide angles to work together during the dance numbers. Unlike Richard Attenborough's directing of A Chorus Line, Poitier does not continually cut off dancers' bodies with medium or close shots, but allows the viewer to see the whole figures of the dancers. And at other places, Poitier is not afraid to move the camera with the dancers, rather than trying to force them into the framing of a static camera.

One sequence deserves special attention because Poitier gave it significant time in the movie. When June decides to leave because of Matt's infatuation with his rich girl, the other five women go after her in a show of solidarity. Although it is unlikely that six high school girls could go into a New York City bar and be served, the scene presents the young women drinking and sharing opinions about men and about their choices as women.

In a scene that presages the "black feminist" sequence in Spike Lee's *Jungle Fever*, the young women quickly agree that men are dogs and liars. But more complex are their observations about their mothers—women who remain in Sandusky, Ohio, married to men with beer bellies, trapped with too many children, and haunted by unfulfilled dreams. In this multiethnic, feminist session, Poitier evokes a recognizable teenage angst about growing older, but more importantly, he identifies the attitudinal changes among a younger generation of women who want more than what tradition demands they settle for.

Shifting to the last film directed by Sidney Poitier, *Ghost Dad*, the director returns to the familiar comedy genre, but unfortunately, despite the starring role of Bill Cosby, the film never materializes into an effective and memorable work. Part of the film's problem rests with its inability to define itself for an audience. Part-slapstick, part-fantasy, and part special visual effects, the film displays an unevenness in tone and intent.

The story follows Elliot Hopper (Cosby), a working single dad of three, who is obsessed with closing an international business deal. But Elliot's children feel neglected: Diane (Kimberly Russell), the high school daughter, and Danny (Salim Grant) and Amanda (Brooke Fontaine), the grade-school siblings. One day, while Elliot endures a heart-stopping taxi ride, the cab crashes through a guardrail on a bridge and into the water. Elliot emerges to find that he's a ghost, though his children can actually see him if the lights are lowered in the room. But Elliot learns that he is really a spirit and not a ghost; therefore, if he can find his body before it is destroyed, he can assume his old self again. Despite a few setbacks, Elliot succeeds, recommitting himself to his children.

Although Cosby works hard in various scenes to show the frustrations experienced by Elliot Hopper, those instances play clumsily when contrasted with the segments where his spiritual-self is played broadly to match the special effects. Cosby, whose comic behavior in earlier Poitier films emanates from realistic characters, attempts to work here from a one-dimensional premise. At the same time, Denise Nicholas, the romantic interest, can do very little with her underdeveloped character, and though the three youngsters are charming, their fresh faces and energy are unable to lift this sinking effort. *Ghost Dad* is devoid of the cultural messages, emotional contours, and light-hearted diversion of Poitier's earlier comedies. Like the film's title character, Poitier, as director, fails to resemble his old self in form, pacing, or social relevance.

Fortunately, when considering his contributions to film directing, Poitier will not be assessed by the disappointing showing of one film. Instead, his body of work demonstrates how he participated in shaping African American opportunities both behind and in front of the camera. He was uniquely successful in that he directed Hollywood films from a leverage point that he created by his own hard efforts as an actor. And though his directing credits will never surpass the historical and racial significance of his acting successes, Poitier remains, nonetheless, an impressive and invaluable asset in the legacy of black film directors.

CHAPTER THREE

Black Urban Action Films and Mainstream Images

The creative, pioneering efforts of Van Peebles, Parks, Davis, and Poitier were not just transitory occurrences that had no impact on the Hollywood scene. It wasn't that Hollywood was contritely endeavoring to make reparations for its legacy of African American screen images, nor was there a particular era of egalitarianism that white studio bosses were opening up for black filmmakers. By the early 1970s, it became a clear business strategy that black screen images offered a means for tapping into a large paying audience who found something compelling in those black images. The "good Negro" images may have played well in the previous decade, which saw the civil rights movement reach its height, but the political, economic, and cultural changes under way in America by the early '70s called for something new. The cultural images offered in black urban action films resonated with the times.

The black urban action film—deemed "Blaxploitation" at the time—became its own genre, and the genre proffered popular images of black men and women through traits of extraordinary cool, sexuality, and violence.

Black directors who obtained work in Hollywood at this time achieved varying degrees of success. Some made only one or two films, while others continued to work long into the 1980s and 1990s. Some worked only in films, while others directed projects for stage and television as well.

Gordon Parks Jr. was the outstanding black director of the seventies black urban action genre, fashioning movies that held a discernible political edge. With a black director such as Fred Williamson, the black action hero became a recognizable icon who, for better or worse, could be interchangeable with his/her white counterparts. At the same time, directors such as Ivan Dixon, Hugh A. Robertson, Ron O'Neal, Gilbert Moses, and Raymond St. Jacques all made a name for themselves in other creative areas before turning to directing films.

Gordon Parks Jr.

But remember, these two films [*Shaft, Super Fly*] brought out a new audience. They made money for shaky studios and launched new stars in Hollywood.[1]   Gordon Parks Jr.

At one point in his early years as a still photographer, Gordon Parks Jr. worked under the name of Gordon Rogers to avoid confusion with or exploitation of his father's name. But their names and professions would overlap in the early '70s as father and son both directed two of the most recognized black films of the era—*Shaft* and *Super Fly*, respectively.

Gordon Parks Jr. was born in Minneapolis, Minnesota, in 1934, and after attending the American School in Paris, he graduated from White Plains High School in New York state in 1952. He completed a two-year stint in the army before embarking on a career as a musician in the early '60s. But drawn to photography, he developed a convincing portfolio, eventually earning a position to shoot stills for the feature film *Burn* (1969). In 1969, he also won a position as a cameraman on the shooting of *The Learning Tree*, his father's first film. And again in 1972, he worked as a still photographer on Francis Ford Coppola's *Godfather* before getting the opportunity to direct his own film, *Super Fly* (1972). From there, Parks Jr. went on to direct three additional films—*Three the Hard Way* (1974), *Thomasine and Bushrod* (1974), and *Aaron Loves Angela* (1975)—before establishing his own film company in Kenya in 1979.[2]

Thomasine and Bushrod, perhaps inspired by director Arthur Penn's *Bonnie and Clyde* (1967), focuses on the titular black couple who are "stickup artists who roam the West after the turn of the century, shooting up citizens, falling in love (with each other) and distributing the plunder of the territorial banks among the poor folks. . . . They are pursued by a rabid white marshal, and naturally they meet a violent end."[3] With Vonetta McGee and Max Julien as the title characters, most critics applaud their chemistry, but the overall assessment of the film is less flattering. Black critic Donald Bogle concludes that the "movie has some mildly entertaining segments but is far too fragmented and sluggishly directed."[4] In a similar fashion, *Aaron Loves Angela* misfired in finding an audience. In his informative book, *Blackface: Reflections on African-Americans in the Movies*, black author, critic, and screenwriter Nelson George concludes that "*Aaron Loves Angela* is an at times refreshing look at love across ethnic lines as black Aaron (Kevin Hooks) falls for a Puerto Rican girl (Irene Cara)."[5] In the mid-1970s, a cross-cultural love story was too far removed from what studios were willing to market. So, despite any noble efforts on his part to explore more dramatic themes, Gordon Parks Jr. would be forever connected to the black action genre due to his controversial *Super Fly*.

Seldom has a film been praised and persecuted so extensively as Parks' *Super Fly*. The movie's story follows the protagonist named Priest (Ron O'Neal), a drug dealer and user, who decides to make one last score and then retire from the drug business. The title itself carries dual meanings. On the one hand, it refers to the street name given to extremely potent cocaine, and on the other hand, "fly" describes the successful combination of natty dressing and a confident attitude, with the superlative "super" emphasizing an outstanding achievement in that combination.

Parks opens the movie with an engaging juxtaposition of images. A high angle on two desperate junkies on a Harlem street corner contrasts with the initial presentation of the protagonist, Priest—sexually satisfied, snorting coke in bed with a nude white woman. As the two junkies walk the littered and populated streets of the city, the environment shows its harsh edges; then, as Priest, dressed in fancy clothes, rides the streets in his Cadillac, the congested and claustrophobic setting emerges even more. Over these images and opening credits, the thumping R&B music resounds repetitively, emphasizing the "cool" attitude that keeps Priest just above the quagmire through which he drives. Priest, unlike the junkies, is a survivor; his fancy clothes and hats, expensive car, black and white lovers, and arrogant attitude validate his triumph. At the end of the credits, when the two junkies attempt to mug Priest, the latter defends himself heroically—giving chase, catching, and beating one junkie in the interior squalor of a tenement building.

Throughout the movie, Parks appears to favor long, uninterrupted takes, which provide the scenes with a sense of real time and help to make the contrasting action sequences with their numerous cuts more exciting. In addition, these long takes give his sequences an awkward but natural quality, as characters deliver or improvise lines in an unhurried manner. Still, Parks delivers the expected elements of the genre—fights, shootouts, chases, sex scenes, and street language. Although the editing gets a bit clumsy, especially in the final fight sequence between Priest and several white thugs, Parks does offer a glimpse of visual freshness. For example, after Priest and his partner, Eddie (Carl Lee), decide to disseminate thirty kilos of cocaine, Parks cuts from live action to a sequence of still photographs. Jumping from long shots to close shots that fill the frame, Parks then divides the frame into three panels of photos, then four, and eventually six. Through these still photos, Parks shows how the cocaine is mixed and distributed among middle- to

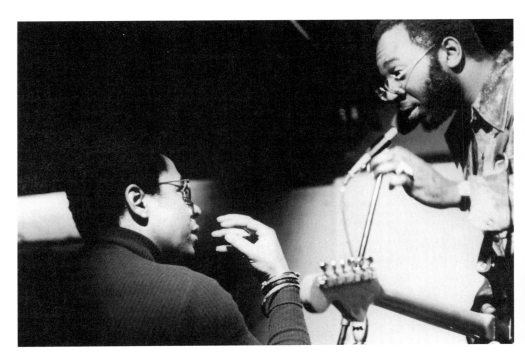

Preparing a nightclub scene in *Super Fly,*
Gordon Parks Jr., left, speaks with music
composer-performer Curtis Mayfield.

upper-class people, who are black and white, men and women. Over the visuals, the upbeat rhythm carries the lyrics to the song "Pusherman," a song that confirms that the people dealing the drugs can come from any area of life.

In fact, Parks uses music in a manner similar to that in other films of the era; he integrates music and lyrics that both add to the emotional content of a given sequence and provide exposition to character and/or plot. However, Parks struck gold when he integrated the catchy, memorable musical score composed by Curtis Mayfield. Already a familiar talent among R&B lovers, Mayfield created music and songs that masterfully evoked the contemporary musical tastes while capturing the thematic currents and pacing of the film.

But, beyond the music, the memorable and controversial aspect of the film was simply the character development of Priest—resulting from both Ron O'Neal's performance and Parks' direction. Priest emerges as an introspective, articulate, street-smart, independent, and skilled martial artist; he possesses those qualities admired in a heroic action character. And like other movie heroes, he appears to be a solitary man struggling against insurmountable odds—in this case, corrupt white officials and mobsters. With the help of his woman, Georgia (Sheila Frazier), Priest secures his money for a new life and has a final confrontation with the white Deputy Commissioner Reardon (Mike Richards) and his thugs. Priest tells the Commissioner that a contract has been taken out with the white mob to kill the entire Reardon family if harm comes to Priest. Priest announces defiantly: "I hired the best killers there are—white killers!" With that statement, Priest drives off to freedom, and the camera moves into a close shot of the Empire State Building—symbolically, a giant "finger" being "flipped" at the system and the city that would try to hold Priest down. By the film's end, Priest becomes a black champion who challenges the system and wins decisively.

Despite the various objections to the movie, *Super Fly* effectively actualized three goals: it fulfilled genre expectations, entertained a mainstream audience, and attained box-office profits. With a fragile budget of $500,000, the movie made $5 million in less than one year,[6] and in the 1990s, with a rerelease on videotape, the film has developed a cult following within the hip-hop generation.

Appearing two years later, *Three the Hard Way* contains some elements reminiscent of *Super Fly:* action sequences, violence, and integrated music lyrics. The film serves up three athletes turned actors—Jim Brown, Fred Williamson, and Jim Kelly—who also starred together in two other films, *Take a Hard Ride* (1975) and *One Down, Two to Go* (1982). With such an athletic trio, it becomes obvious that *Three the Hard Way* is heavy into depictions of black masculinity that existed in the early 1970s. First of all, a clear division is made between black and white male characters: the black heroes are united, sexually potent, confident, fearless, and resourceful, while the white male villains are inept, hypocritical, and psychotic.

The movie poses a plot centered on black genocide. An affluent white supremacist funds a white supremacist army, as well as the research of a white doctor to develop a formula that will, within a 72-hour period of time, kill only black people who ingest or drink it. At a hidden camp, experimentation with the formula has been occurring, using kidnapped black people for guinea pigs. One black man escapes and makes it back to the city to his friend Jim (Jim Brown). When Jim's woman, Wendy (Sheila Frazier), is kidnapped by the white racist army, Jim sets out to find her. Jim acquires the help of his friends Jagger (Fred Williamson) and Mister (Jim Kelly), and the three work together to save Wendy, as well as to foil the white supremacists' plans to release the genocidal formula into the water sources of three major cities.

Even before the opening credits, Parks gives warning that he wants the audience to be conscious of a plot that he believes is crucial. As the black escapee is being led by uniformed soldiers, Parks uses stop action, freezing the frame to force the viewer to take in the brutal treatment of the black man. Dramatic music is heard over the sequence, but it ends abruptly, leaving only silence as the escaping black man comes across the warehouse where he discovers layers of dead black men, their bodies stacked in the shadows. Later in the film, Parks utilizes the stop-action technique again to isolate the steel gray briefcases containing the genocidal formula. As the briefcases are being transported into the target cities by the racist couriers, the freeze-frame reminds the viewer of both the content and the lethal possibilities of the formula inside.

In the action segments, Parks situates the camera from various angles, always attempting to give the widest perspectives of the background environment and the heroes at the center of the action. There are chase scenes on foot, gun battles, martial arts fighting, car crashes, and explosions. Parks provides all the expected elements to the genre, allowing each one of his three urban action heroes to have his moment in the spotlight.

A notable sequence occurs at the film's end, as the three heroes rescue Sheila Frazier and destroy the compound and headquarters of the white supremacist organization. Shot at night, the darkness and shadows allow for a more exciting visual and aural experience, as firing weapons spark, shattering glass crackles, speeding jeeps rev their engines, and deafening explosions spiral colorfully into the sky. The three men take on the inept white army, who resemble Nazis in their khaki uniforms, emblems, and berets. The heroes symbolically fight both racist and anti-American forces at the same time. They are making the black community safe, but it's inferred that they are also saving America from being overrun by subversive and exploitive ideas. By their pronounced brotherhood, shared language, and ethnic pride, the black heroes are certainly committed to protecting black people, but as seen earlier, through their clothes, automobiles, boats, and apartments, these same black heroes believe in and have obtained material rewards in the American system.

When the film *Three the Hard Way* is placed together with *Super Fly, Thomasine and Bushrod,* and *Aaron Loves Angela,* the tendency may be to dismiss them all because they appear outdated and simplistic in regard to the elements of their genres. However, they represent the body of work of a director who met the expectations of the time, and a director who, particularly in the case of *Super Fly,* developed a characterization and visual look that was copied many times thereafter in numerous films.

Unfortunately, Parks would not be able to continue to entertain a popular audience or to debate his detractors. In 1979, while visiting in Kenya and preparing to direct another film, he died in Nairobi in a plane accident.

BLACK DIRECTORS IN HOLLYWOOD

Ivan Dixon

I would put simple, honest images of Black human beings in Black situations, Black human situations. There are human situations that people have regardless of color. . . . I just want to see it take place from the point of view of the Black ethos or social group.[7]   Ivan Dixon

Ivan Dixon, similar to Sidney Poitier and Ossie Davis, came to directing after gaining popularity as an actor. Dixon was a household name and face to millions of viewers due to his regular role in the late-1960s CBS television comedy *Hogan's Heroes.* Appearing as the character Sergeant Kinchloe, Dixon played a technical wizard who always remained the calm and thoughtful one among the American prisoners of war. As "Kinch," Dixon was the only black actor in an ensemble cast that made the Second World War popular and humorous; more importantly, Dixon's character gave an African American presence to the Allied military campaign against the Nazi regime.

Born in 1932, Dixon was raised in Harlem, and after his parents separated when he was a kid, he lived with his mother but worked as a delivery boy at his father's grocery store.[8] He traveled south where he attended North Carolina College, earning a B.A. in political science and becoming involved in drama groups. He was awarded a Rockefeller Foundation Scholarship and went to Case Western Reserve in Cleveland to work on a master's in theater arts.[9] However, he left the program and went to New York City, where he tried to break into Off-Broadway productions. His opportunity came when he got to be a stand-in for Sidney Poitier in the 1957 film *Edge of the City.*

Dixon's movie career included appearances in *Something of Value* (1957), *Porgy and Bess* (1959), *A Raisin in the Sun* (1961), and *A Patch of Blue* (1965), but his big-screen presence ignited when he won the lead role in the 1964 independent film *Nothing But a Man.* The film, still considered by many critics to be one of the most outstanding black male screen depictions, explores the odyssey of a southern railroad worker who faces and overcomes challenges to his dignity and manhood. Dixon's performance earned him the Best Actor award at the First International Festival of Negro Art in Dakar, Senegal.[10]

But Dixon's television work will be long remembered by most, and he excelled in that medium as well. In 1967 he was nominated for an Emmy Award for his leading role in the made-for-television movie *The Final War of Ollie Winter* (1967). Television also gave Dixon his entre into directing, with his credits including episodes of the shows *Palmerstown, U.S.A., The Waltons,* and *Baa Baa Black Sheep.*[11] But he got his chance at feature film di-

In *Trouble Man,* Robert Hooks, far right, is
"Mr. T," a well-tailored hero who opposes the
crooked duo of Chalky (Paul Winfield, center)
and Pete (Ralph Waite).

recting when the burgeoning black urban action genre opened the doorway
for him.

Similar to the many other black-oriented movies of the early 1970s,
Dixon's *Trouble Man* (1972) sets out to present a cool, tough, sexy, and
community-minded black male protagonist. The movie opens with Mr. T
(Robert Hooks) leaving a beautiful black woman lounging in a swimming
pool at a beach house in Malibu. After he straightens the creases in one of
the many suits worn throughout the movie, Mr. T drives his Lincoln into
the inner city to his office space at a billiards room run by his assistant,
Jimmy (Bill Henderson). When Mr. T is approached to provide security for
craps game organizers Chalky (Paul Winfield) and Pete (Ralph Waite), Mr. T
is set up by the two as the killer of local mobster Mr. Big (Julius Harris). But
Mr. T survives the pressures put on by the police and completes his revenge
by going after Chalky, Pete, and their thugs.

The best two aspects of *Trouble Man* are Robert Hooks' acting and Marvin Gaye's music. In the title role Hooks displays enough cool and machismo to rival his East Coast counterpart John Shaft. Like Shaft, Mr. T. is well known by everyone in the community, even the police who hassle him in hopes of breaking his confidence. Mr. T also possesses his counterpart's sexiness and skill with numerous women, though he has a steady woman friend, Cleo (Paula Kelly), who waits patiently for his attention. Mr. T also has a direct approach, and though he doesn't walk the inner-city streets like Shaft, Mr. T talks the street language that ingratiates him to blacks and shows his defiance to whites. Additionally, Mr. T owns an extensive wardrobe, as his suits are more appropriate for the Los Angeles heat than Shaft's leather jackets. Finally, Mr. T handles his enemies with the same lethal aggressiveness as Shaft, unleashing his wrath upon those who put him in a bad mood.

This last element of violence finds Dixon providing his more interesting sequences in the movie. The action scenes, particularly the final assault upon Pete's West Los Angeles high-rise condo, deliver the expected danger and gunplay of the genre. With a jazzy music score playing over, Mr. T outmaneuvers a gauntlet of thugs to close in and kill Pete in a showdown. Dixon seems intent on making his protagonist a thinking detective who, always well-dressed, triumphs despite being outnumbered.

Dixon's next movie, *The Spook Who Sat by the Door* (1973), maintains the element of violence, but its thematic focus has created controversial assessments concerning the value of the film. Based on the novel of the same title by black author Sam Greenlee, the story centers around Dan Freeman (Lawrence Cook), a black man who joins and trains with the Central Intelligence Agency. After five years of tolerating prejudice and inferior duties, Freeman quits and returns to Chicago. Observing the conditions of blacks in the ghetto, Freeman becomes a militant, recruiting and training other black radicals in the C.I.A. guerrilla tactics taught to him. But Freeman has a confrontation with a black friend, Reuben Dawson (J. A. Preston), who has become a police officer. Freeman stabs Dawson for his attack against the militants, but not before Dawson shoots and kills him, turning Freeman into a martyr as the revolution continues.[12]

Identifying *The Spook Who Sat by the Door* as a film that appeared at the crest of the black urban action film wave of the 1970s, authors James Robert Parish and George H. Hill conclude that "[t]here is a great deal going on in this film. The full spectrum of black society is presented, from the professional upper classes down to the skid row bums, and all angles of political thought from the 'Uncle Toms' to the ardent black activists and revolutionaries."[13] The movie failed at the box office, though some have suggested that it was intentionally pulled before it could find an audience.[14]

During the '70s, Dixon also moved back in front of the camera, taking roles in *Clay Pigeon* (1971) and *Car Wash* (1976). But his foray into the director's chair permitted Dixon to influence and challenge the expected mainstream images of African Americans. By adding his years of experience to an ongoing effort, he helped encourage studio opportunities for those black filmmakers who followed.

Fred Williamson

I wanted to make something dynamic in Hollywood, something true to myself, not just get a part and become an actor. So I started writing my own films and raising my own money. From 1970 to about 1976, the Black actor being the winner, being the hero was happening.[15]   Fred Williamson

Fred Williamson brought two important things to black filmmaking in the 1970s—a large, indestructible ego and entrepreneurship. With this combination Williamson stands out for his contribution to the international recognition of the black presence in commercial films. The objective for Williamson was not film as "art," but the commitment to film as the business of entertainment. His goal was not critical acclaim or awards, but to work in a business where he enjoyed both the control over his products and the profits from those products. One could obviously question whether Williamson acknowledged the political messages in entertainment films as they related to African American images, but one would have difficulty arguing that Williamson did not deal with Hollywood on his own terms.

Credited with making over fifty films—thirty of which he produced or directed—Williamson had a rather colorful odyssey to Hollywood.[16] Born in Gary, Indiana, in 1938, Williamson's athleticism earned him a track scholarship to Northwestern University. But once there, football coach Ara Parseghian recruited him onto the football team for an additional scholarship. Majoring in architecture at the university, Williamson put off his targeted profession when he was drafted to play professional football with the San Francisco 49ers in 1960.[17] He was christened with the nickname "The Hammer" because of the severe forearm blow he delivered to receivers coming at him in his defensive back position. After ten years of professional football—he also played for the Oakland Raiders, the Pittsburgh Steelers, and, in the first Super Bowl, the Kansas City Chiefs—he turned to architecture for his livelihood.[18]

From there, Williamson's escapades turned Hollywoodish in more ways than one. Claiming his indoor job as an architect made him restless, and after viewing episodes of the television show *Julia*, he closed up shop and journeyed to Hollywood to give acting a try. Bluffing his way into an interview with Hal Kanter, the producer of *Julia*, Williamson succeeded in winning a role on the show as Julia's steady boyfriend. In an interview, Kanter remarked of Williamson: "If we can find a bottle big enough to put his ego in . . . we'll need a redwood tree for a cork."[19] In addition to *Julia*, Williamson made other television appearances, and in 1970 he appeared in his first feature film, *M*A*S*H*, directed by Robert Altman.

The timing was ideal for Williamson's credentials, ambition, and physical attributes, as he went on to perform in a number of films of the '70s black action genre—films such as *The Legend of Nigger Charley* (1972), *Black Caesar* (1973), *That Man Bolt* (1973), *Hell Up in Harlem* (1974), and *Bucktown* (1975). He continued to be a screen presence in the '80s, and he revitalized his screen image for a younger audience in the mid-'90s with the films *From Dusk till Dawn* (1996) and *Original Gangstas* (1996).

As a director, Williamson completed numerous films in the 1970s and 1980s that display his cinematic approach—action-dominated, low-budgeted, and quickly shot movies. Peppered heavily with black and white women in sexually provocative roles, Williamson fostered movies where fighting, shooting, and explosions *were* the plot. Without apology, Williamson identifies the films he acted in and/or directed in the following way: "My pictures are action pictures. . . . A foot in the mouth translates worldwide. A joke does not translate worldwide. A punch in the jaw doesn't need a subtitle."[20]

A glimpse at just two of his films—*Adiós Amigo* (1976) and *One Down, Two to Go* (1982)—displays the visual style found in most of his films. The potential for quality exists in his movies, but Williamson's priority remained the finished marketable movie that would reach an action audience, without necessarily affecting that audience on any political level.

Adiós Amigo, which was written, produced, and directed by Williamson, is an action Western that follows a rather simple plot. A black outlaw named Sam Spade (Richard Pryor) consistently runs a con game on various characters, usually leaving his tough, fast-drawing amigo named Big Ben (Williamson) to take the blame. Actually, rather than having a plot, the movie is a series of vignettes, as Sam and Big Ben go from one predicament to the next, always after money and women.

The opening title song—which has a contemporary seventies feel to it—clashes with the nineteenth-century setting of the movie. Interlaced with the visual action throughout the film, the song works as an ongoing narra-

In *One Down, Two to Go,* Jim Brown, Fred Williamson (second from left), Jim Kelly, and Richard Roundtree join forces to battle their common enemies.

tion that attempts to hold together the threads of the vignettes. Additional unifying techniques are the detailed illustrations and/or tinted drawings that capture some aspects of the action in a given sequence. Working like a freeze-frame, the illustrations punctuate the end of a sequence and try to serve as a transition into the next live-action scene. At those places where the story jumps abruptly and elliptically, the drawings appear to be an attempt to fill in the void, suggesting problems with the film's editing.

In his role as Sam, Pryor does his best to give vitality to his scenes, and on occasion, he succeeds. Pryor's improvisations often infuse a wooden story with a sense of fun, but Pryor plays "Pryor"—a stand-up comedian caught in a Western. A similar situation rings true for Williamson. His open-shirt, cigar-chomping, tough exterior just happens to be in the Wild West setting; without the horse, the same image is projected in his other urban action films. The other performers in the movie pass back and forth in front of the camera, attempting to enliven their ineffectual lines of dialogue.

Eight years later, Williamson's directing did not change in any discernible way. In the movie *One Down, Two to Go,* Williamson is once again dealing with his favorite elements—fighting, shooting, women, and explosions.

The movie would appear to be worthy of attention as it pulls together, in one cast, four of the most popular black action heroes of the '70s—Williamson, Jim Brown, Richard Roundtree, and Jim Kelly. Williamson, Brown, and Kelly had worked together before in *Three the Hard Way* (1974), and Williamson, Brown, and Roundtree would later revive their union in *Original Gangstas*. Here, however, in *One Down, Two to Go*, the four stars give the movie a bit of "soul," but it contains little substance.

The movie begins at a full-contact karate tournament in New York, where Chuck (Kelly), a West Coast karate master, worries over the foul play aimed at his competing team. With the support of his friend and manager, Ralph (Roundtree), Chuck discovers that the white promoters of the tournament are attempting to fix the matches to hold on to the large $400,000 purse. When Chuck is shot by the promoters' thugs, Ralph puts in a call to some reliable friends, Mr. J (Brown) and Cal (Williamson). Mr. J and Cal arrive in limos to help their buddies, as fistfights, gun battles, and car explosions erupt. By the movie's end, the four friends prevail, and the thugs are dispatched.

Williamson both produces and directs this feature, giving it his trademark facets of an elliptical, sometimes confusing, story line connected by action sequences. The characters lack motivation in numerous places, and plot points dangle. Obviously shot quickly and without a variety of takes, the editing suggests desperation, as the music misses the opportunity to be as slick and "hip" as the four main characters.

In its attempt to capture the heroic images from a previous decade, *One Down, Two to Go* ignores the expectations of the audience of its day. By the early 1980s, black action heroes were needed to suit the burgeoning hip-hop generation and a mainstream audience attuned to the exploits of Sylvester Stallone (*First Blood*, 1982), Arnold Schwarzenegger (*Conan the Barbarian*, 1982), and Chuck Norris (*Missing in Action*, 1984).

If there was anything to commend about Williamson's direction in these two films, as well as others, it would be that he did work quickly and under budget. But those commendations don't address the aesthetics and/or cultural elements one might expect from a black director. However, Fred Williamson would probably be the first to insist that his objectives were strictly business and primarily entertainment. He would assess himself, not as an artist, but a savvy entrepreneur who worked on his own terms. Most critics would agree.

Hugh A. Robertson

My goal has always been to be a director. I decided to hold out, to use my reputation as an editor as a kind of lure. I sold things for my independence. . . . That way I could say no to editing jobs and still eat.[21]   Hugh A. Robertson

If one particular technical position were chosen as the best preparation for directing a film, it would be that of the film editor. Besides the physical organizing of a film's sequences, the editor must have a creative appreciation for the potential of the film, as well as a practical understanding of how to get the desired, maximum effect from the actual pieces of film that have been shot. Hugh Robertson came to film directing as an editor, having worked on the films *12 Angry Men* (1957), *The Fugitive Kind* (1959), *The Miracle Worker* (1962), *Lilith* (1964), and *Shaft* (1971). In 1960 he became the first African American member of the IATSE Motion Picture Editors Union after eleven years of applying for acceptance,[22] and he was nominated for an Academy Award for editing the film *Midnight Cowboy* (1969).

Born of Jamaican parents in Brooklyn in 1933,[23] Robertson began working in films when he was seventeen, studying at New York's New Trade Institute for Motion Pictures and the Sorbonne in Paris.[24] Though he gained some experience directing television shows, he used his editing on the film *Georgia, Georgia* (1972) as leverage to gain the opportunity to direct some of the additional footage on that film. MGM approached him with the script for *Melinda* (1972), and Robertson was more than interested. In this action piece, a black romance serves as one of the center points of the story, but beyond that point *Melinda*, by plot alone, serves as another example of the fare being offered during the early 1970s. The story follows a popular disc jockey, Frankie J. Parker (Calvin Lockhart), a swinging bachelor who ends a relationship with publishing executive Terry Davis (Rosalind Cash) to get involved with the mysterious Melinda (Vonetta McGee). When Melinda is murdered in Frankie's apartment, he becomes the main suspect for the killing. But more threateningly, Frankie becomes the target of a mob boss (Paul Stevens) and his thugs because Melinda has taped the mobster confessing to killing a union official. Having learned the martial arts from a local master (Jim Kelly), Frankie decides to go after the crooks himself to avenge Melinda's death. Along the way, Frankie and Terry connect again as a romantic item.

Shot in less than a month on a $650,000 budget,[25] the film grossed $5 million by the end of 1972.[26] Some critics saw it as a distinctive movie, while others placed it on the shelf with its action counterparts. In an off-handed praise for the filmmakers and the film, one critic remarked: "[T]hree of the most outspoken black talents around—director Hugh Robertson, writer

Terry Davis (Rosalind Cash) stands by her man, Frankie J. Parker (Calvin Lockhart), in the urban action drama *Melinda*. Courtesy of the Academy of Motion Picture Arts and Sciences.

Lonne Elder III, and actress Rosalind Cash—took one look at MGM's original script for *Melinda* and plunged into a battle that ended with the conversion of hopeless trash into stylish and diverting trash."[27]

Melinda was the only Hollywood feature that Robertson directed. In 1974, he moved to Trinidad, where he formed a film company that included a training program for young black filmmakers. While there, he directed a number of documentaries and two additional features for his company— *BIM* (1976) and *Obeah* (1987). At the age of fifty-five, he died of cancer in his adopted country.[28]

Ron O'Neal

When I was a child in the ghetto, I had no confidence or pride because no-body ever told me who I was or what I could do. Now . . . Black kids still have next to no self-image. . . . I'm hoping that the most inspiration will come from our success as filmmakers.[29]   Ron O'Neal

Having received acclaim for his stage acting, and for his signature role as Priest in the immensely popular *Super Fly*, Ron O'Neal was bound to draw attention to the first feature he directed. That movie, *Super Fly T.N.T.* (1973), was a follow-up to *Super Fly*, rather than a sequel. Although two major char-acters were repeated—Priest and his lover, Georgia (Sheila Frazier)—the set-ting, tone, and style of the two films differ significantly.

Born in Cleveland in 1937, O'Neal grew up in the city's black ghetto, and drifted toward acting when he was nineteen. He joined an acting work-shop in an interracial theater group called Karamu House, where over a period of nine years, he appeared in more than forty productions.[30] He at-tended Ohio State University,[31] but by the late 1960s, O'Neal was in New York, teaching acting in Harlem until he won a role in a summer stock pro-duction of *Show Boat*. Although his great ambition was to sing opera on the stage, he never auditioned despite four years of training. Instead, he re-mained focused on acting, and in 1970, his talent was rewarded when he won the Obie Award for his role in Charles Gordone's play *No Place to Be Somebody*.[32]

When O'Neal filled the movie screen as the drug pusher Priest in *Super Fly*, he became forever connected to that popular screen image, which helped him to direct his first film the following year. Following *Super Fly T.N.T.*'s failure at the box office relative to its namesake, O'Neal assumed diverse roles in films such as *The Master Gunfighter* (1975), *When a Stranger Calls* (1979), *The Final Countdown* (1980), *Red Dawn* (1984), and *Original Gangstas* (1996).

Unfortunately, as the director of *Super Fly T.N.T.*, O'Neal did not distin-guish himself. The story does contain its ambitious aspects, as it swings from political to existential themes. But somewhere between the story's efforts and the film's lethargy, the movie fails to be compelling.

Living in Rome with his woman, Georgia (Frazier), Priest attends a poker party where he snorts cocaine and gambles generously until the mysterious Dr. Sonko (Roscoe Lee Browne) solicits money for the liberation forces of Oumbia, a small West African country.

Meanwhile, Georgia meets another African American named Jordan

Gaines (Robert Guillaume), who is also living in Rome. When Gaines and Priest socialize at a restaurant, they strike up a friendship, both reflecting about the old days in the United States.

Eventually Dr. Sonko convinces Priest to invest in weapons for the African freedom fighters, and Priest travels personally to smuggle the guns into Africa by private plane. When Priest and the weapons are intercepted by the white military regime, Priest is imprisoned and beaten for information. He suffers, but doesn't reveal names, eventually beating his white guards and fleeing into the jungle where his black African brothers are waiting to help him. At the film's end, Priest, a changed and fulfilled man, returns to Rome, where Georgia awaits.

Despite the noble intentions to emphasize cultural awareness, black unity, and revolutionary zeal, *Super Fly T.N.T.* misses its potential. The script—written by Alex Haley—offers up flat characters and predictable plot points. Without any sustained action, the movie frequently breaks down into long scenes of philosophical dialogue that sounds artificial and forced. Toward the middle of the movie, Priest proclaims that in his vernacular the letters "T.N.T." stand for "T'aint Nothing To it." And by the movie's climax, this expression aptly describes the impression the movie leaves with the viewer.

Gilbert Moses

I feel like I'm a popularist. I take social conventions and turn them into art, popularize culture, give it a sense of proportion.[33]   Gilbert Moses

A successful stage and television director who died too early at the age of fifty-two, Gilbert Moses etched his name in the collection of respected black directors who could carry a project successfully through to fruition. Born in 1943, Moses grew up in a Cleveland ghetto, but he began acting at the age of nine, which perhaps ignited his love for artistic expression. Winning a scholarship to Oberlin College,[34] he studied German and French, though he saw himself as a sixties radical. He cofounded the Free Southern Theater, which toured the South in the 1960s for about nine years performing plays, such as *In White America* and *Waiting for Godot.* By the latter part of the decade, Moses was directing in New York, winning the Off-Broadway Obie Award for his 1969 production of *Slave Ship* by Amiri Baraka. He went on to direct *Ain't Supposed to Die a Natural Death* by Melvin Van Peebles and *Taking of Miss Janie* by Ed Bullins, with the latter winning the New York Drama Critics Circle Award for the best new American play in 1975. From

Title character in *Willie Dynamite*
(Roscoe Orman) wears his pimp
regalia when talking business with a
social worker, Cora (Diana Sands).

the 1970s to the 1990s, he also directed a number of television shows, such as two episodes of *Roots*, which gained him an Emmy Award nomination; *Benson*; and *Law and Order*.[35] For the big screen, Moses worked on two features of different tone, both set in urban environments: *Willie Dynamite* (1973) and *The Fish That Saved Pittsburgh* (1979).

Willie Dynamite is a film that is typical for its day in regard to the focus on black male characters negotiating the streets of an American city. Specifically, the film looks at the lifestyle of a successful pimp, named Willie Dynamite (Roscoe Orman), who refuses to give up his individuality or to join forces with his competitors to fight off the cops. But Willie is not only a proud man, he is a man who loves and respects his mother. When his mother discovers that Willie has earned his money as a pimp, she dies of a heart attack, an event that forces Willie to reform and go straight. Along the way Willie is also pressured to change his ways by the IRS, rival pimps, and Cora (Diana Sands), an ex-hooker turned social worker who struggles to get women off the streets and pimps out of their lives.

Although the film found an audience, strong criticism pierced at its images. A rather harsh assessment came from critic Ed Eckstine, who dismissed the movie pronouncing: "It is demeaning to me as a Black man to see such a statement of life and manhood as is projected in the film."[36] From another perspective, in his recent cult study of "blaxploitation" films, author Darius James looks back on *Willie Dynamite* with more praise: "*Willie Dynamite* is the hands-down winner of the all-out best blaxploitation movie of the seventies. With a metaphor not unlike the one found in Barry Michael Cooper's script for *New Jack City*, *Willie Dynamite* is a sly satire in the toast made on the impulses that drive corporate America."[37]

Not many critics, in the 1970s or 1990s, appear to support James' reverence for the symbolic value of *Willie Dynamite*. And though a younger, contemporary audience has rediscovered the film on video format, the movie's popularity comes from the humor found in its outdated styles and attitudes, and not from any breakthrough insight into society's economic structure.

Six years after *Willie Dynamite*, with *The Fish That Saved Pittsburgh*, Moses worked to bring a different kind of film to the screen, as by the late 1970s the super black urban images, along with trademark language and trendy styles, had become passé. *Fish*, instead, is a feel-good sports comedy that angles at entertaining with images of blacks that are more representative of the average guy sitting in the audience.

The movie's plot is simple and uncomplicated. It "is the story of a last-to-first place basketball team organized under the astrological sign of Pisces and helped along by coach Flip Wilson and real basketballer Meadowlark Lemon."[38] The movie also includes performances by Jonathan Winters, Kareem Abdul-Jabbar, and Stockard Channing, as director Moses confesses that "[t]here is a social statement in *Fish* and that is, if you believe in yourself you don't need any crutches and you can win; but it's very subtle and integrated in the piece."[39]

Although *The Fish That Saved Pittsburgh* fails to be memorable among the ranks of outstanding films, and though *Willie Dynamite* exists as a video novelty, the significance of Gilbert Moses as a director must be noted. As a stage, television, and film director, he added his remarkable talents to the widening of opportunity for black film directors.

Sadly, Gilbert Moses died in Manhattan in 1995 of bone marrow cancer.

Raymond St. Jacques

I think it is my duty to make the Black masses more discerning about films. I believe you can make entertaining films that are also enlightening.[40]

Raymond St. Jacques

Born James Arthur Johnson in Hartford, Connecticut, Raymond St. Jacques was raised in New Haven during his high school years. Unable to afford college, he went into the air force for four years, but eventually he attended Yale University.[41] He began a career as an actor at the American Shakespeare Festival in Stratford, Connecticut, and appeared in a 1961 Off-Broadway production of Jean Genet's play *The Blacks*, along with Roscoe Lee Browne, James Earl Jones, Lou Gossett Jr., and Cicely Tyson.[42]

St. Jacques was fluent in Italian and French, and it was from a French friend that he borrowed the name "Raymond St. Jacques" for his theatrical moniker because it sounded more exotic and impressive.[43] He put his skills and the name to good use as he went on to become one of the most recognizable faces and voices on the stage, on television, and in numerous feature films, including *Black Like Me* (1964), *Mister Moses* (1965), *The Pawnbroker* (1964), *Mister Buddwing* (1966), *The Comedians* (1967), *If He Hollers, Let Him Go* (1968), *Up Tight* (1968), *The Green Berets* (1968), *Cotton Comes to Harlem* (1970), *Come Back, Charleston Blue* (1972), and *Glory* (1989).

Book of Numbers (1973), produced by St. Jacques, sets out to explore the black community in a different manner from its contemporary productions. Blueboy Harris (St. Jacques) and his partner Dave (Philip Michael Thomas) organize a numbers-running business in the city of El Dorado, Arkansas, in the 1930s. Once they do, they come into conflict with a white crime organization that wants their competition eliminated. At one point, Blueboy and Dave are brought to trial, and Blueboy wears shabby clothes and does an "Uncle Tom" routine in order to get the white judge to throw the case out. But Dave, younger and more aggressive, becomes furious with Blueboy's strategy, despite its success. The relationship between the two becomes strained until Blueboy is killed, and Dave is consequently inspired to find a new motivation in his life.

St. Jacques realized that by focusing on criminals such as Blueboy and Dave, he risked elevating criminal behavior to a heroic level. But he clarified his objectives for the film in this way: "I didn't want to glorify the numbers racket per se. . . . Rather, I wanted to document the lifestyle of the 'colored' people of the period and relate it to the Black lifestyle of today, so that young people, and even older people, could have a visual understanding of the way things were in the past."[44] From his perspective, St. Jacques presents a small part of the community that offered some semblance of hope, though it was flawed and fleeting. Although the movie wasn't as popular as some of its contemporaries, one newspaper critic did find value in the movie, describing it as an "uncommonly well-balanced movie, intelligently directed, very cleverly edited . . . with an air of real enjoyment in what it is about."[45]

Dave Green (Philip Michael Thomas, left) comforts his dying partner, Blueboy (Raymond St. Jacques), in *Book of Numbers.*

When Raymond St. Jacques died of cancer in 1990, he was best known as an actor, but his single effort at film directing shows that not all sensibilities in the early 1970s were toward black superheroes. In addition, like Sidney Poitier and Ossie Davis, and later Bill Duke and Forest Whitaker, St. Jacques demonstrated that some black performers possessed skills to excel in front of the camera, but at the same time some black actors held a vision that needed to be launched from their presence behind the camera.

CHAPTER FOUR

Black Sensibilities and Mainstream Images

With black urban action films presenting the dominant images of blacks in the early 1970s, there seemed to be little room for any other depiction in mainstream entertainment. On the one hand, the prevalence of black superheroes, who were protecting the "community" against the "man" and drugs, provided an affirmation of black existence previously absent from the screen. Regardless of the flaws and redundancy of those black images, they revitalized the business motives of Hollywood studios.

Many of the black urban action films were in fact shaped by white writers, producers, and directors, often excluding African American filmmakers from the process. But despite the lack of control over depictions of their own people, a few black directors managed to chart out some movies that offered alternative ways of appreciating black culture. Collectively, these filmmakers—Berry Gordy Jr., Stan Lathan, and Jamaa Fanaka—presented images that displayed a more diverse black representation for the times. Unfortunately, the audiences for their films were not as vast as those for *Shaft* or *Super Fly*, but the content of their films deserves recognition as a concerted effort—with varying degrees of success—to show mainstream viewers other significant aspects of African American communities.

Berry Gordy Jr.

It [*Mahogany*] was one of the great thrills of my life . . . when I said "action" to begin the first scene I ever directed, everything and everybody started moving. . . . I'd been chairman of the board but never had the feeling of such power. It was incredible.[1]   Berry Gordy Jr.

Berry Gordy Jr.'s fame as a record mogul and music producer was well established by the early 1970s. He had spearheaded a remarkable business accomplishment by taking unknown talents and honing them into a self-contained empire that dominated the R&B music charts.

One of eight children, Gordy was raised in Detroit under the strict parenting of his father, a plastering contractor, and his mother, a teacher.[2] Although he did some boxing as a featherweight as an adolescent,[3] Gordy had a strong love for music even then, as his favorite musicians were Charlie Parker, Dizzy Gillespie, Miles Davis, and Erroll Garner.[4]

But with a wife and children to provide for, Gordy joined the ranks of many others in Detroit and obtained a job on an auto assembly line at Lincoln Mercury.[5] As he put trim and chrome around windows, Gordy struggled for opportunity as a songwriter. Eventually, one of the first songs that he wrote, "You Are You," made it into the repertoire of Doris Day,[6] and with $800, he established the Tamla record label, which in 1959 became Motown Records.[7] The first Motown hits included "Shop Around" by the Miracles and "Please Mr. Postman" by the Marvelettes;[8] decades later, in 1983, after achieving 110 number one hits, Motown Productions was the largest black-owned company in America, with revenues of $104 million.[9]

In the '70s, Gordy moved the company to Los Angeles and branched out into films and television as a producer. His first film, *Lady Sings the Blues* (1972), won a wide crossover audience and five Academy Award nominations,[10] but the film production side of Motown never reached the heights of success that the music side did, despite the company's involvement with the films *The Bingo Long Traveling All-Stars and Motor Kings* (1976) and *The Last Dragon* (1985). By the end of the '80s, Motown's dominance waned as the company's chief moneymaking artists—Gladys Knight, the Four Tops, Marvin Gaye, Michael Jackson—signed deals with other companies,[11] influencing Gordy's decision to give up control of Motown in 1988.[12]

When Gordy turned to film directing in the mid-'70s, he chose a black romance that examined the frailty of wealth and fame. *Mahogany* (1975) follows the odyssey of Tracy Chambers (Diana Ross), an aspiring fashion designer who's committed to achieving her dream of becoming internationally known and revered. Living in Chicago's inner city, Tracy works in a department store while attending evening classes in fashion design. She develops a romance with Brian (Billy Dee Williams), a black political activist committed to the community. When world-famous fashion photographer Sean McAvoy (Anthony Perkins) gives Tracy the opportunity to travel to Rome to work as a model and hopefully a designer, she follows her dream, becoming a popular model named Mahogany. McAvoy, dealing with sexual impotence, humiliates Mahogany at a fashion auction, but she is rescued by Christian Rosetti (Jean-Pierre Aumont), a wealthy Italian socialite.

When Brian arrives in Rome, he's unsuccessful in convincing Tracy to return to Chicago with him, so he warns her: "You may be a success, but you're all alone. . . . Success is nothing without someone you love to share it with." After surviving a car crash in which McAvoy is killed, Tracy is financially supported by Rosetti, realizing her dream at her gala opening of

In *Mahogany,* Tracy Chambers
(Diana Ross) chooses a romantic
relationship with Brian (Billy Dee
Williams) rather than a career as a
high-fashion designer.

her original designs. However, taking her bows, Tracy hears Brian's cautionary words in her head. Her fame is indeed empty, and the film ends as she
returns home to Chicago and to Brian, the man she loves.

The timing of this film's release had some significance in that the wom-
en's movement was influential in its popular appeal. The film's subject matter and its didactic ending definitely challenged some of the feminist ideas
finding expression at the time. Through the character Mahogany, the message was that a black woman's commitment to her man was synonymous
with a commitment to the black community, and that any consideration beyond that was nothing more than deluded selfishness. The enduring effect of
Tracy and Brian's romance revolved around their depiction of the ideal black
love and how it should fit into the black cultural tradition.

In weighing the story, the Tracy-Brian relationship, despite its political
message, gives the film much of its charm. As a first-time director, Gordy
allows the on-screen chemistry between Ross and Williams to work again
as it did in their previous pairing in *Lady Sings the Blues.* Ross' energetic
feistiness works well for Tracy's character, while Williams' relaxed suavity

thoroughly suits Brian's romantic allure. In their scenes of intimacy, Gordy gives the audience close-ups of kisses and embraces that come out of the old Hollywood style. Gordy constructs a subtle passion and does not push their "love" scenes into "sex" scenes, where the audience voyeuristically watches two naked people wrestling in the sheets.

Beyond the black romance, Gordy appears most comfortable in capturing the elegance of Mahogany's world of flowing gowns, catwalks, parties, and artistic excess. Gordy and Ross do an excellent job of making Tracy's ambitions and success believable, allowing just enough aspects of American racism to fuel Tracy's unquenchable aspirations. On the other hand, Gordy is not as convincing when structuring Brian's political world, despite the effort to keep the character's scenes primarily on the exterior streets. Gordy wants Brian to come off as a man of the streets and the community, but the vocal cadence, wardrobe, and dialogue of Williams' character doesn't ring true. Williams, as Brian, is certainly charismatic, but Gordy seems more intent on keeping the camera on close-ups of his actor's handsome features than on developing a street edginess to his character.

Mahogany is an entertaining film that offers a much needed contrast to the black urban action films that offer a steady and limited presentation of black romance and intimacy. The film also attempts to show the possibilities of following one's dreams despite the inner-city environment that all but suffocates those dreams. Significantly, it also underscores the efforts by committed black leaders to improve and maintain a black community through united determination. With those points, the film triumphs, but the resolutions at the end of the film tend to oversimplify life choices and to approbate traditional gender roles as the ideal.

Stan Lathan

I was directing theater in Boston and working at WGB[H], a public station. The station decided they needed a black director because they expected there would be rebellions that summer. We quickly put together a magazine show called "Say Brother" which gave a lot of African Americans their first shot at producing and directing.[13]   Stan Lathan

A significant creative presence in television since the late 1960s, Stan Lathan completed two feature films in the 1970s and 1980s that highlighted black cultural expressions. In the 1990s, he served as a producer on feature projects targeted toward the younger hip-hop audience.

Born in 1945 in Philadelphia, Lathan didn't pursue medicine as many other family members before him. Instead, he attended Penn State University and majored in liberal arts, a path that allowed him to follow his interest in entertainment. While doing graduate work at Boston University, he obtained a job at WGBH, the well-known PBS station. Lathan directed a weekly magazine show, entitled *Say Brother*, and he has had the skills and good fortune to be directing and producing ever since that time.

After Boston, Lathan went to New York, working as a director on the television shows *Black Journal, Sesame Street,* and *Soul.* Those projects earned him the directorial position on a feature-length documentary for Paramount titled *Save the Children,* which was filmed in Chicago. Gathering impressive television directing credits on shows such as *Sanford and Son, Cagney and Lacey, The Waltons, Hill Street Blues, Remington Steele, Miami Vice, Frank's Place, Roc, Martin, Moesha,* and *Russell Simmons' Def Comedy Jam,* Lathan also helmed the television movies *The Sky Is Gray, Go Tell It On the Mountain, Uncle Tom's Cabin,* and *The Child Saver.*[14] In the '90s, he has served as a producer on the feature films, *Gridlock'd* (1997) and *How to Be a Player* (1997); in addition, he has held the position of cochair of DEF Pictures.

Amazing Grace (1974), Lathan's first fictional film, is one of those movies whose aspirations exceed its accomplishments. Although possessing a bit of charm, the movie lacks those qualities that would make it memorable or outstanding. With its improbable plot, it comes across more as a fantasy than as the comedy the filmmaker intended.

The story opens at a train station, as black porter Forthwith Wilson (Slappy White), completing his last day of employment, meets Grace Tisdale Grimes (Moms Mabley), and the two become instant friends.

Once in Baltimore, Forthwith accompanies Grace to her home, where the two discover that the house next door has been purchased by Welton J. Waters (Moses Gunn), an insincere black mayoral candidate, and his alcoholic wife, Creola (Rosalind Cash). Grace threatens to expose Waters' schemes, if he and his wife refuse to conduct a serious campaign on behalf of the black community with Forthwith as the campaign manager. Faced with Grace's threats and her impassioned feelings about black unity and self-help, Welton and Creola commit themselves to the struggle. With Grace as the spiritual leader, Welton triumphs and wins the election.

To the director's credit, Lathan manages to give the audience some enjoyable moments within the movie, even though it remains top-heavy with its cultural and moral messages. First, he provides an appreciative glimpse at two of the screen's oldest and most maligned black performers—Lincoln "Stepin Fetchit" Perry and Butterfly McQueen. Perry portrays one of Grace's family members at the train station sequence. Later in the film, when Grace needs to find out who works in the mayor's office, she phones

Clarice (McQueen). In this brief appearance, McQueen pokes fun at the popular "Prissy" image from *Gone with the Wind*.

Not only does Lathan respect the screen contributions of Perry and McQueen, he certainly adores his leading lady, Moms Mabley. Playing her cantankerous, toothless, mischievous comedic character, Mabley serves as the film's focus. Her style—of witty comebacks, affected verbal delivery, and eyeballing—mixes effectively here with the soft-spoken, religious side of her character. She is at once adorably gentle, but just as suddenly she becomes an in-your-face, defiant pain-in-the-butt. Lathan obviously provides his leading lady the room necessary to improvise and to carry a scene in a particular comedic direction. There are scenes that benefit from Mabley's stand-up style, but, unfortunately, there are other scenes that seem desperately in need of tightening.

Lathan shapes a film that tries so hard to be positive and inspiring that it tends to oversimplify some of the real challenges facing an urban black community. In Lathan's amazing world, blacks have no conflicts in regard to communal goals or perspectives, despite gender and class differences. Lathan's Baltimore community is a monolithic group of black citizens who only need to verbalize their problems in order to find solution.

Lathan's visual storytelling is adequate for the film's tone. At places, there are instances of rough editing, rambling dialogue, and awkward silences, but Lathan is at his visual best during a montage sequence that shows Welton's campaign efforts, as he superimposes and intercuts the main characters canvassing the streets with newspaper headlines and community members talking about Welton. Beneath the uptempo music, the sequence has an energy and pace that's missing from other parts of the film.

It would be ten years later before Lathan would direct the feature film *Beat Street*, a venture that would be an entirely different genre for a definitively different audience. With *Amazing Grace* Lathan promotes his belief in community and black unity, but in *Beat Street* he takes a look at a distinctive, counterculture within the urban setting.

Set in the Bronx, where black and Latino groups intersect and sometimes collide, the rough streets serve as a character that seems intent upon crushing young dreams. In a neighborhood where young people are economically at risk, the significant factors in the lives of the central characters revolve around their creative talents and their friendships.

Two African American friends, Kenny (Guy Davis) and Chollie (Leon W. Grant), are close buddies with a Puerto Rican youth, Ramon (Jon Chardiet). Kenny and Chollie are deep into the hip-hop culture, while Ramon is a tagger whose moving canvases are the many subway trains that crisscross

Against a Bronx background, Chollie (Leon W. Grant, far left), Ramon (Jon Chardiet, third from left), and Kenny (Guy Davis, far right) attempt to survive the mean streets in *Beat Street*.

his neighborhood. Ramon is in love with Carmen (Saundra Santiago) and is also the father of Carmen's baby. He struggles to balance his need to create murals and his responsibility to Carmen and their child.

Added to this trio is Lee (Robert Taylor), who is Kenny's younger brother and a break-dancer who constantly explores new choreography with his dancing crew. His dancing catches the eye of Tracy (Rae Dawn Chong), a college student who is composing and conducting a combined modern dance and orchestral arrangement.

Following a subway fight that leads to Ramon's death, Kenny decides to use his one chance to deejay at an uptown club as the opportunity to give a tribute to Ramon. Organizing a New Year's Eve celebration where rap, gospel, modern dance, and break dancing are all mixed together, the film ends with the main characters participating in the tribute to their deceased friend.

Beat Street, coproduced by black singer-actor Harry Belafonte, is a well-intentioned movie that presents hip-hop culture to a larger mainstream audience. Director Stan Lathan works hard to show the music, dance, attitude, and language of a younger urban generation who find pride and release in new forms of expression. The script delivers the trendy vernacular of the streets and presents cameo appearances of then-popular performers, such as Grandmaster Melle Mel and the Furious Five, Afrika Bambaataa, the Treacherous Three, Tina B., and Brenda Starr. Appearing in the early years of hip-hop, the movie serves as a reminder of early rap before the gangsta rap domination of hip-hop in the '90s. Here, rap music is boastful, danceable, and critical of social ills, rather than a clarion call for homicidal behavior. Here, crews use break dancing to confront and outdo other crews, rather than breaking out automatic weapons and shooting indiscriminately. There's a particular innocence and charm to the movie that makes it watchable even years after its appearance date.

Lathan's direction in *Beat Street* appears more appropriate than in his previous film. He captures the street rhythms effectively during the opening credits as he cuts from boom box, to pop-locking street dancers, to vacant urban lots under the driving percussion of uptempo music. Interspersing still photos of black and Latino kids during the opening, he makes it clear who the focus of the story will be. From the vibrant faces of the teens to the graffiti and mural-decorated walls on building exteriors, Lathan pulls the viewer into a nonmainstream milieu. Actually Lathan scores best when he is on the streets, as he records the characters interacting with one another in the environment. In comparison, the interior sets lose some of the edginess that's maintained on the streets.

Stan Lathan has directed feature films that serve the purpose of entertainment well. Yet, they are salient examples of the director's objectives to impart African American culture to the larger society. He succeeds in that goal and, in doing so, demonstrates the manner in which mainstream movies can be both escapist vehicles and carriers of positive cultural messages.

Jamaa Fanaka

I did everything they said it takes to make it in the film industry. . . . They said you're [*sic*] got to have a hot film. I had three successful films. They said you need critical acclaim. I got rave reviews from the *Los Angeles Times, Variety,* the *Hollywood Reporter,* the *San Francisco Chronicle,* and the *New York Post.* What do you do next?[15]   Jamaa Fanaka

One of the more colorful and controversial personalities within the directing arena during the 1980s and 1990s, Jamaa Fanaka received perhaps more attention for his personal behavior than for his film directing. Acclaimed by some critics and dismissed by others, Fanaka still searches for industry validation and opportunities he declares are due him.

Born in 1949, Fanaka and his family moved from Mississippi to Compton, California, when he was twelve. He beat the odds and attended UCLA as an undergraduate and graduate student, and in the mid-'70s, two of his student films "were commercially released and got him some attention from critics."[16] But by the '80s, the director seemed to be colliding with the industry on various levels. In 1983, his deal to make *Street Wars* with Indigo Pictures, owned by Richard Pryor, fell through. In the press, Fanaka accused the parent company, Columbia Studios, of denying not only his film, but money promised to other black filmmakers as well. Then, in the late '90s, Fanaka was at war with the Directors Guild of America, with news-making incidents in 1997 and 1998 at various guild events. Accused of disrupting meetings, rude behavior, and using profanity against guild members, the DGA suspended Fanaka's membership for two years in October 1998 "for conduct deemed 'prejudicial to the welfare of the guild and unbecoming of a DGA member.'"[17]

As a filmmaker at UCLA, Fanaka's first film, *Welcome Home, Brother Charles* (1975), which he wrote, produced, and directed, has been described as a movie "dealing with a returning black Vietnam War veteran whose outrage at injustices on the home front lead to shocking, perverse results."[18] His next film, completed for his master's thesis, was *Emma Mae* (1976), a movie that "Fanaka considers a tribute to the strength and resilience of black womanhood."[19]

Fanaka's *Penitentiary* trilogy, however, comprises his best-known work. Collectively, the series of movies focuses on "the chronic problems of incarceration: the overcrowding, the hardened inmates misguiding the more innocent, the racial bigotry, and the rampant homosexuality."[20] After the success of the first movie in the series, *Penitentiary II* (1982) was dismissed by most critics and did very little business at the box office,[21] as it was cited for being "dreary and predictable" with "several irrelevant subplots that weave through the film without adding anything to it."[22] *Penitentiary III* (1987), though heavier with action than the first installment, came off as bizarre and over-the-top in characterization and situations. Its unevenness in tone, acting, and visual quality provoked mixed reactions and made it less than memorable.

Penitentiary (1979), the first in the trilogy, remains the most solid and accomplished of the trio of movies, all of which follow the experiences of the central character, Martel "Too Sweet" Gordone. In this film, a black drifter named Too Sweet (Leon Isaac Kennedy) hitches a ride with Linda (Hazel Spear), a prostitute who schedules her professional appointments over a CB radio as she drives her van along the barren highways. Too Sweet joins

Too Sweet (Leon Isaac Kennedy) is a fighting machine in *Penitentiary* and its two sequels.

Linda at a diner, where she approaches two white bikers as her prospective clients. A fight erupts and Too Sweet is knocked unconscious. He awakens as a prison inmate.

Behind bars, Too Sweet meets a menagerie of personalities: Lt. Arnsworth (Chuck Mitchell), the white officer in charge of the prison; Eugene (Thommy Pollard), a shy black inmate who eventually learns to stand up for himself; Jesse (Donovan Womack), an arrogant black cell-block leader; Half Dead (Badja Djola), a sadistic black inmate with ties to Jesse; Sweet Pea

(Wilfred White), a black homosexual; and Seldom Seen (Floyd Chatman), the elderly black inmate who becomes Too Sweet's friend and boxing trainer.

Too Sweet's pugilistic skills draw the attention of Lt. Arnsworth, who has an ongoing prison training camp to discover boxers that his brother-in-law can manage professionally on the outside. Arnsworth announces an upcoming boxing tournament where the grand prize is a conjugal visit. Too Sweet wins and discovers that his prize is Linda, the prostitute from the film's opening scene. She confesses to an angry Too Sweet that when he was knocked unconscious in the diner, one of the bikers attempted to rape her, so she stabbed him. When the cops arrived, they charged Too Sweet with the killing. As the film ends, Too Sweet wins a final boxing championship and is leaving prison, with the promise that Seldom Seen will also be paroled to work with him as a trainer.

As writer and director, Fanaka is intent upon weaving a tale of revelation that will open the viewer's perspectives on incarceration, particularly concerning black men in jail. He might have done this kind of exposé without the element of boxing as part of the story line, but its inclusion allows the director to connect to the popularity of the sport. After all, *Rocky* won the Oscar for Best Picture in 1976, and *Rocky II* was being released during 1979.

As for the boxing, Leon Isaac Kennedy possesses just the right mixture of good looks and cocky attitude to make him believable. With the taut, lean build of a welterweight fighter, the actor has quick moves and a style that mimics Muhammad Ali. Fanaka swings between long and medium shots to show the fights, which could use more polished choreography. Although he refrains from the quick cutting, editing, and sound design that are found in both *Rocky* and *Raging Bull* (1980), the various boxing matches do contain energy, if not the more crisp visual look of a big-budget film. On another level, the boxing serves as a metaphor for the struggle that Fanaka views as innate to black manhood. Too Sweet, as the story's protagonist, represents that black man who is battling the ongoing system where whites enjoy power, as well as those blacks who have been used and destroyed by that system. Boxing delivers a visual message about the black man's sociopolitical status in the larger society.

Interestingly enough, *Penitentiary* is the most powerful when it deals directly with the subject of manhood. For example, when Too Sweet proudly announces to Seldom Seen about the tournament prize of the conjugal visit, the elderly trainer dismisses the value of the sexual tryst. The older man tries to teach Too Sweet about valuing himself and about rejecting what the system gives him. Later, as Too Sweet is about to leave prison, Seldom Seen is reluctant to go along. In a sequence that presages Frank Darabont's *Shawshank*

Redemption (1994), the older man admits that he's afraid to leave prison because the inside provides a world that has meaning and in which he is respected. But the younger Too Sweet counters that inside the prison there's one thing missing—hope. Here, the younger inmate teaches the older convict that life beyond prison walls can offer a freedom and hope that can never exist behind bars.

Although the three directors here—Gordy, Lathan, and Fanaka—would not be the better-known film directors of the decade, they managed to give the black images of the 1970s something beyond the stereotypical fare of the black urban action genre. The three came to film directing via such different avenues, yet their films do connect to elements of African American culture that were being neglected during the '70s. Regardless of their critical reputations in the pantheon of filmmakers, Gordy, Lathan, and Fanaka deserve to be credited with reminding audiences, both then and now, that African American men and women have endeavored to find their dignity and significance in all milieus of American society.

CHAPTER FIVE

Michael Schultz: The Crossover King

In many films, I want to tell a story everybody can understand. But more importantly, I want an audience to come out of a film with more than what they went in with—thinking, feeling, laughing, crying.[1]   Michael Schultz

Between 1964 and 1985, Michael Schultz was Hollywood's major black director of feature films. Unlike other black directors, Schultz won acceptability and approval from the established studios, and he served as a formidable presence in stage and television direction as well.

Schultz was born into a working-class family in Milwaukee, Wisconsin, in 1939. With early dreams of becoming an astronautical engineer, he enrolled at the University of Wisconsin, but he later transferred to Marquette University and joined the Theater Arts Program.[2]

In 1964, he traveled to Manhattan and earned the position of assistant stage manager for the American Place Theater. Then he directed a number of Off-Broadway projects, before traveling to nearby New Jersey to continue gaining experience as a director. Schultz recalls: "I eventually found work at the McCarter Theater in Princeton which was a resident rep company that did eight plays a season. I directed three of them. That was my first real directorial experience."[3]

Soon afterward, he took a position as staff director for the Negro Ensemble Company, where he directed the play *The Song of the Lusitanian Boatman*, which won him the Obie Award for Best Direction for the 1968–1969 season.[4] Schultz continued to work for another two seasons at the company before going to Broadway. In 1969, Schultz directed the production of *Does a Tiger Wear a Necktie?* which brought him a Tony nomination for Best Director, and the play allowed him to direct his future wife, Gloria, as well as Al Pacino in his Broadway debut. Both Gloria (known then as Lauren James) and Pacino won Tony Awards—Best Supporting Actress for the former and Best Actor for the latter.[5]

Television directing followed in 1972, as Schultz took charge of the PBS version of Lorraine Hansberry's play *To Be Young, Gifted, and Black.* The project was shot in 16 mm film rather than the usual videotape, so the project gave Schultz his first film experience. His achievement with that play later landed him the directing position on the television adaptation of another play, *Ceremonies in Dark Old Men*, for which Schultz won the Christopher Award. In the 1970s he also directed a number of episodes of television series, including *The Rockford Files, Baretta, Toma*, and *Starsky and Hutch*.[6]

With these credits and experience, Schultz got the call to direct his first feature film, *Cooley High* (1975). The movie, obviously inspired by the success of *American Graffiti* (1973), presents the misadventures and challenges faced by inner-city black high school seniors. Similar to *American Graffiti*, *Cooley High* integrated a running sound track of songs contemporary to its period—specifically, the R&B music of the early 1960s, including artists such as the Supremes, the Four Tops, Stevie Wonder, the Temptations, Smokey Robinson, and others. But more importantly, the film provided a view of black youth not common at the time, and in so doing, it went a long way toward revealing the commonalities and the differences among black and white youth in their late adolescence.

Set in Chicago in 1964, the film opens with long shots of the city's business and riverfront areas, showing the urban splendor of the skyline; then, as the credits continue, the camera journeys across town, following an "el" train, to a less glamorous section of tenements and vacant, trashy lots. This montage of landscape tells the audience about class distinctions and racial segregation in the city, before introducing the two main characters of the story.

The story focuses on two senior friends: Leroy Jackson/aka Preacher (Glynn Turman) and Richard Morris/aka Cochise (Lawrence Hilton-Jacobs). Preacher, living at home with his mother and his sisters, is a fast-talking, risk-taking teen who possesses the sensitivity and talent of a poet beneath his garrulous veneer. Cochise, living with his mother, father, and numerous siblings, is the gifted athlete who prides himself on the tough, but smooth image he projects. Foremost in their concerns are "making out" with girls, socializing, and partying, and although Cochise appears to have more success with girls, Preacher does manage to eventually win the affection of his heart's desire—Brenda (Cynthia Davis), a young woman who succumbs to Preacher's poetry.

These black teens share escapades that lead them to the brink of trouble —ditching school, drinking alcohol, and joyriding in a stolen car. The latter leads to police confrontations and eventually to the death of Cochise. Losing his best friend, Preacher takes off for California to fulfill his dream of being a writer.

Displaying compassion for his teen protagonists, Michael Schultz delineates their stories with an effective balance of humor and drama. By showing the earlier '60s, when fistfights, drinking wine, and smoking marijuana were the most extreme forms of teen behavior, Schultz provides a glimpse of the decade before Black Power, feminism, and antiwar activism would permeate Chicago and other parts of the country.

Schultz does an outstanding job in the sequences with Preacher, Cochise, and the other male characters, as their natural dialoguing and physical posturing capture the nuances of adolescence. Likewise, the director demonstrates an easy control in developing the chase scene where Preacher wildly drives the Cadillac, with the young male teens inside, to elude two white patrolmen in a squad car.

At the same time, two scenes that stand out in their poignancy are those containing women characters as well. First, the relationship that develops between Preacher and Brenda follows the familiar "boy-eventually-wins-the-heart-of-the-girl-who-hates-him-at first" story line. After a montage of the young lovers holding hands as they walk the neighborhood to the Temptations' popular song "My Girl," Schultz presents the awkwardness of the teens as they become intimate. In the gentle sensuality of the love scene, Schultz allows the audience to experience the hurried groping that eventually becomes a nervous passion.

In another sequence, Preacher's mother comes home in the late evening tired and angry. She berates Preacher for being taken to the police station on the auto theft charge. She insists that while she works three different jobs, she depends on Preacher to set the leadership as the oldest sibling. She angrily instructs him to get his belt and prepare for his punishment, but when Preacher returns with the belt, he finds his mother has fallen asleep from exhaustion in the dining room chair. And as Preacher kisses his mother's forehead, the close shot of his expressive face shows both his pride in his mother and his shame at being arrested.

The popularity of *Cooley High* signaled a promising career as a Hollywood director for Michael Schultz. Completing a black-oriented movie that appealed to a wide audience made Schultz a likely candidate to become the premier black director at the time, as the early-'70s black urban action movies were beginning to lose their bankability. Remaining close to the comedy genre for his next film, *Car Wash* (1976), Schultz once again showed his confidence in presenting ethnic characters to a mainstream audience, as the movie mixes poignant dramatic moments and sometimes raucous humor.

With a script written by Joel Schumacher, Schultz presents an extensive set of characters in the tradition of director Robert Altman with films such as *M*A*S*H* (1970) and *Nashville* (1975). With thirty characters interacting during the course of one workday, *Car Wash* sets out to render the mundane, but humorous stories of Los Angeles characters from diverse ethnic, cultural, and class backgrounds. The plot—merely a series of loosely connected and sometimes overlapping episodes—reveals the dreamers, schemers, and in-betweeners, in a film that possesses opposing attributes: energetic but monotonous; fresh characterizations but yet stereotypes; and broad slapstick but poignant moments.

Of the numerous vignettes that function as extended jokes, two notable sequences exemplify the different types of humor within the film. The first example shows a verbal and satiric humor, as the director ridicules a parasitic preacher exploiting the black community. Similar to the parody that director Ossie Davis presented with his black minister/con man, Deke O'Malley, in *Cotton Comes to Harlem*, Schultz has Daddy Rich (Richard Pryor) riding his stretch limousine into the car wash, accompanied by four church sisters (the Pointer Sisters). Displaying his expensive clothing and jewelry, Daddy Rich magnetically attracts the workers to him—speaking nothing of substance, but saying what the workers want to hear. The more nonsense the preacher speaks, the more the workers love him. Eventually, a Black Muslim worker named Abdullah (Bill Duke) challenges Daddy Rich, stating that he "talks like a pimp." Abdullah correctly labels the preacher, but intoxicated with the presence of Daddy Rich, the workers defend him from Abdullah's criticisms. With Pryor at the center of the sequence, the segment works effectively as a comedic piece, but simultaneously, it connects to a larger political reality of exploited workers blinded by the lure of material gain.

A second sequence demonstrates the more prevalent physical and situational humor. Following the radio news story about a mad bomber, one worker, Hippo (James Spinks), sees a frantic man (Professor Irwin Corey) clutching a brown paper bag while his car is being washed. Hippo and his buddy T.C. (Franklyn Ajaye) stalk the man; heroically, T.C. grabs the paper bag and runs wildly throughout the establishment yelling that there's a bomb. Everyone gets caught up in the chaos, and when T.C. slips and the paper bag flies in the air, everyone ducks for cover. The bag falls, and the bottle inside bursts—the bottle carrying the frantic man's urine sample.

From that level of humor, *Car Wash* sometimes shifts to a serious tone—particularly shown in the relationship that develops between Lonnie (Ivan Dixon) and Abdullah. Lonnie, who has served prison time, is the most trusted employee at the business, as he opens up and closes the establishment on occasion. When Abdullah is fired due to his lateness and his attitude, Lonnie attempts to persuade the boss to take him back, defending Abdullah's obvious confusion. As the film ends, Abdullah returns with a gun to rob the cash register, and Lonnie pleads with him to put away his weapon, telling Abdullah: "Jails are full of thousands of young men just like you." As Abdullah breaks into tears from the overwhelming challenges of his life, Lonnie promises that he'll help him work things out. Here, one black man commits to helping another black man—not to save the money belonging to the establishment, but to save the potential of what Abdullah can become for himself and others.

Car Wash, marketed as a film where clowning and jiving prevail, might seem easy to write off as just a fluff piece, but the film possesses some valuable segments where it clearly exposes the very system of exploitation that it appears to accept. For his next two films—*Greased Lightning* (1977) and *Which Way Is Up?* (1977)—Schultz again utilizes the talents of Richard Pryor, the comedian who would become the dominant black film star of the late 1970s.

As told by the end captions of the film, *Greased Lightning* is based on the true story of Wendell Scott (Pryor), "the first black stock car racing champion in America." It's the mid-1940s, and when Scott returns from the war, the only work available for blacks is at the nearby factory. But Scott has his own dream of owning a taxi service to raise money to open his own auto garage and to marry Mary (a very subdued Pam Grier). But when the taxi business fails, Scott decides to drive deliveries for a bootlegger.

Eventually, Scott is captured by the police, but he's saved from jail by Billy Joe Byrnes (Noble Willingham), a white man who owns the local racetrack. Byrnes figures that blacks will come to watch a black car driver, and whites will come to watch the black driver get killed by the white drivers— a great business gimmick. The strategy works, but Scott survives and becomes a local hero to the black community. Despite the blatant racial prejudice, by 1955, Scott is winning races. Then, in a montage that covers the next ten years, Scott continues to make a name for himself at numerous professional venues. Even after a near-fatal track accident, Scott enters the grand nationals and wins, beating his longtime nemesis, white driver Beau Welles (Earl Hindman).

Schultz was able to keep Richard Pryor on his best behavior in this project, and going beyond his comedic persona, Pryor manages to give Wendell Scott a controlled confidence. Schultz, for his part, manages to provide the audience with a film that contains more action than his previous outings. In fact, during the early portion of the film, he spends *too much* time showing Scott maneuvering through the backwoods and eluding the country cops. From long shots to tracking shots—from interior shots within the moving vehicle to exterior shots focusing through the windshield at Scott—Schultz shapes the car chases and racing scenes effectively for both action and comedy. The action delivers visual excitement to assist the film's pacing, while the comedy stretches from verbal humor to sight gags. To make the racing scenes more compelling, Schultz successfully combines factual footage and fictional images to enhance the realism and spectacle of the professional racing circuit.

True to its objective, *Greased Lightning* pays homage to an African American pioneer who embodied what the civil rights era was about in terms of a black man gaining access to his dreams. In doing so, the film notes the prevailing racial barriers and the various attitudinal changes that occurred from 1946 to 1965.

For his next film, Schultz calls upon Richard Pryor again for the lead role. In *Which Way Is Up?* (1977), Schultz and Pryor take on a story that begins with strong political implications, but unfortunately, the story diminishes into a jumbled ambiguity.

Adapted from director Lina Wertmüller's *Seduction of Mimi* (1972), *Which Way Is Up?* follows the odyssey of Leroy Jones, who at first works as a farm laborer, living with his wife, Annie Mae (Margaret Avery) and their children. Inadvertently, Jones has his photo taken with a labor leader, and the company that owns the farmland send thugs to force Jones to take a one-way ticket to Los Angeles. Leaving his family behind, Jones flees to the city, where he falls in love, woos, and wins the affections of Vanetta (Lonette McKee), an activist for the farmworkers. Over the following year, Jones and Vanetta live together and have a child.

Through a set of accidental events, Jones is recruited by the company and is sent back to his hometown as a supervisor of the company's fruit-canning factory. Once Jones returns, he assumes a double life, both personally and politically. He resumes his married life with Annie Mae while, on the other side of town, he maintains his life with Vanetta and their child. In addition, he later becomes involved with the minister's wife, Sister Sarah (Marilyn Coleman). The humor, at this point, revolves around the manner in which Jones juggles his relationships with Annie Mae, Vanetta, and Sarah.

At the end, Jones is abandoned by all three women, who indict him for his lying, insincerity, and selfishness. Jones realizes too late the mistakes he has made, and after facing his fears with the Company, Jones walks alone down the highway—optimistic about beginning his life over.

Presumably, the film examines Jones' journey into manhood. From his earlier weaknesses, he grows into a self-respect that comes in the film's final moments. Disappointingly, the African American characters—particularly those portrayed by Pryor—come off as broad stereotypes. Consequently, despite any connections to political issues of labor and class, the shallowness of the black characters overwhelms the director's efforts to be satiric and insightful. The strongest recommendation for the film revolves around several performances—Richard Pryor in three separate roles; Margaret Avery as his transformed wife; and Lonette McKee as a political activist.

Furthermore, *Which Way Is Up?* fails to display any of the flashes of visual delight that Schultz achieves in the previous effort, *Greased Lightning*. In some sequences the lighting appears faulty, while in other sequences, the pacing is lethargic. The film possesses an unevenness about it, and Schultz relies too much on Pryor's characterizations to lift the various scenes to an engaging level. Pryor does shine in spots, but anchored to the problematic script, even *he* fails to make the film a consistently compelling work.

The situation gets no better with Schultz's next film, *Sgt. Pepper's Lonely Hearts Club Band* (1978). Trapped somewhere between fantasy and flimsiness, this movie is painful to watch. The director who enjoyed such a splendid debut with *Cooley High* in 1975, now three years later is doing mainstream fluff not worth the price of the popcorn that one would need to endure sitting through it.

Based on the title, songs, and loosely structured story of the same-titled Beatles album, this movie offers a mixture of American and British performers who sing their interpretations of the album's songs. The story—narrated by Mr. Kite (George Burns), the Mayor of Heartland—concerns young Billy Shears (Peter Frampton), the grandson of the famous musician-bandleader Sgt. Pepper who played magical instruments with the power to make people's dreams come true. Billy inherits his grandfather's musical instruments and talents and forms a band composed of his three childhood friends, the Henderson Brothers (the Bee Gees). With the support of his girlfriend, Strawberry Fields (Sandy Farina), and management by his stepbrother, Dougie (Paul Nicholas), Billy and the band become a hit. In Los Angeles, they record with a powerful music company, controlled by B. D. Brockhurst (Donald Pleasance), where they face big-city temptations, evil rock bands, and power-hungry villains. Fortunately, Billy and the band come to their senses, save the instruments from the evil villains, and consequently rescue the world from moral destruction.

With its $12 million budget, *Sgt. Pepper's*, at that time, was the largest film ever given to the control of a black director,[7] and unfortunately the film failed to be a box-office success. Part of the problem, as Schultz viewed it, was that the audience disapproved of Peter Frampton and the Bee Gees "impersonating" the Beatles.[8] Additionally, another weakness in the film revolves around the one-character voiceover and narration by the elderly Mr. Kite. The film's other characters do not deliver any dialogue, and the audience only hears their voices when they sing. The technique prevents viewers from connecting with individual characters, and the senior Mr. Kite is not the most appropriate narrator for a story targeted at a younger audience.

However, Schultz's direction of *Sgt. Pepper's* does warrant attention in that it confirmed him as a crossover director who could successfully bring African American experiences to a mainstream audience and who could complete Hollywood projects that bear no pronounced racial or ethnic focus. With the latter accomplishment, Schultz emerges as a predecessor to black directors who would later work on films that centered primarily on white characters—directors such as Bill Duke (*The Cemetery Club*, 1992), Thomas Carter (*Swing Kids*, 1993), Kevin Hooks (*Black Dog*, 1998), Forest Whitaker (*Hope Floats*, 1998), and Carl Franklin (*One True Thing*, 1998).

Of interest, producer Robert Stigwood had approached Schultz to direct the now-famous film musical *Grease*, with John Travolta and Olivia Newton-John; however, Schultz's schedule didn't allow him to work with Stigwood until the *Sgt. Pepper's* project. Why was Michael Schultz pursued as a director who could traverse the color line and excel in the popular milieu? No easy or singular response offers an answer. Part of the offer to direct *Grease* and *Sgt. Pepper's* perhaps revolves around Schultz's past experience with theater and television; he had already proven his directing skills in those popular mediums. Another consideration might have been his ability to obtain praiseworthy film performances out of Richard Pryor; if Schultz could bring out the actor in a stand-up comedian, perhaps the same would hold true with rock performers. A more provocative and revealing possibility, however, surfaces in a 1983 interview. When asked if his blue eyes, fair skin, and Jewish surname gave whites the comfortable feeling that Schultz was "more like themselves and therefore smarter and more trustworthy," the director replied: "That could be. And the name Schultz is always a shock to them. My experience at getting jobs all through my career has been that I got in the door because they didn't know I was black. . . . Now, whether or not the fairness of my skin or the color of my eyes or whatever helped them get over their own personal prejudices, well, that's possible."[9]

The box-office disappointment of *Sgt. Pepper's*, of course, provided ammunition for those naysayers who felt that black directors were not competent to handle mainstream material; but, as the movie found an audience in Europe, others concluded that Schultz was a pioneer. In a business that doesn't tolerate financial failure—particularly by people of color—Schultz managed to survive.

With his next movie, *Scavenger Hunt* (1979), other than to offer some visual sight gags and a long chase scene, Schultz appears content with doing a journeyman's job with the project. Because the sight gags are so numerous, they do manage to give energy to the movie, but many are predictable and thus largely forgettable.

Scavenger Hunt is one of those all-star comedies—similar to *The Cannonball Run* (1981)—that follows a formula found in all-star films of the era's disaster genre, such as *The Poseidon Adventure* (1972), *Earthquake* (1974), and *The Towering Inferno* (1974). The objective seems to be to gather stars, give them a common set of challenges, and allow them to overlap their characters' motivations and pursuits. Unlike the ensemble cast in Schultz's multicultural *Car Wash, Scavenger Hunt* presents more notable white celebrities in major and cameo roles—Richard Benjamin, James Coco, Ruth Gordon, Cloris Leachman, Roddy McDowall, Richard Mulligan, Tony Randall, Pat McCormick, Vincent Price, and, in an early screen appearance, Arnold Schwarzenegger. As for the actors of color, Cleavon Little and Scatman Crothers round out the cast.

With some twenty-five characters providing speaking roles that are integral to the plot, the motivations of the characters are too complicated to explore. The plot—as thin as it is—begins as millionaire eccentric Milton Parker (Price) dies, bequeathing his $200 million estate to those surviving family members and acquaintances who are able to collect the sundry items listed in a set of rules and clues. Some of these items, of course, are commonplace—a wedding gown, an inner tire tube, a toy bear—but others are unusual—a suit of armor, a live ostrich, a "fat" person. Different points are awarded for the various items, which, within a time limit, are to be placed in designated areas located on the estate grounds. Organizing themselves into five teams, the characters engage in their hunt, participating in many sight gags and vacuous dialogue along the way.

By the time the movie reaches its happy ending, a number of types have been targeted—overweight people, people who stutter, Native Americans, Asian Americans, corrupt lawyers, and biker clubs. If the writing had been penetrating and satirical, the allusions to these targets could have been more edgy and provocative. However, the film merely attacks these characters in broad, stereotypical fashion, resulting in insensitive and insulting depictions.

In a peculiar way, *Sgt. Pepper's* and *Scavenger Hunt* can be viewed as

Director Michael Schultz speaks with his actors, George Segal, left, and Denzel Washington, center, about a scene in *Carbon Copy*.

the two consecutive movies that comprise Schultz's bland period. As mainstream vehicles, the two stand as safe, harmless excursions, which sidestepped any serious exploration of dramatic issues of the day. In a striking departure, Schultz's next comedy, *Carbon Copy* (1981), possesses a smartly written script by Stanley Shapiro that presents a workable balance of humor and emotions without becoming either ludicrous or melodramatic.

The film follows Walter Whitney (George Segal), a successful corporate executive who has a beautiful home with all the trappings appropriate to his station in life: a lovely wife, Vivian (Susan Saint James); a domineering boss/father-in-law named Nelson Longhurst (Jack Warden); a resentful stepdaughter, Mary Ann (Vicky Dawson), who resents him; a close friend and lawyer, Victor (Dick Martin); and a dedicated Latina maid, Bianca (Angelina Estrada). Abruptly into his life comes Roger Porter (Denzel Washington), a young African American with an attitude and an accusation—Walter is his biological father.

After being convinced of their relationship, Walter attempts to help

Roger, whom he sees as a ghetto kid with no aspirations. But in that process of acknowledging and helping Roger, Walter discovers that his family and friends desert him. As credit cards are taken from him, and with no other resources, Walter joins Roger to stay in a less than desirable Watts apartment. Soon Walter discovers that the world offers him little sympathy, as he ultimately must take a job shoveling manure to earn a minimum wage. Surviving it all, Walter learns that Roger has graduated early from high school to attend medical school at Northwestern University. As the film ends, Walter decides to drive back with Roger to the Midwest with hopes that they can shape a father-son relationship.

Schultz handles this story effectively as he strikes convincing notes of humor that often overlap the biting satirical observations about race relations in America. The film carries a vigor in its pacing that matches its tone, and consequently Schultz doesn't allow the dialogue or the moments in the scenes to become too heavy-handed. Rather, the scenes reveal and confirm the old and painful truths of racial misconceptions and how they interconnect to class issues. In one of the early sequences in the film, Walter and Vivian converse in the lush greenery of their backyard as he attempts to convince her to adopt a black youth for the summer. Keeping her physical distance from Walter and waving a gardening tool like a weapon, Vivian defends the position of her affluent class: "If they [blacks] see a better way of life, they'll want it permanently." But Walter argues that given their financial status, they must help the underprivileged. Vivian impatiently asks: "When will we stop owing? They already have welfare, low-rent housing, special job programs, and four of their own television series. When will we stop owing and be even?"

Walter recognizes too much of his own weaknesses in his wife's perspectives, and he must directly come to terms with the sugar-coated racism of his boss/father-in-law. Nelson, who already knew of Walter's past relationship with a black woman, philosophizes that white corporate America is the "true minority" that keeps the country running. In his arrogance, Nelson critically reflects: "All power to the people? They had it once—it was called the stone age."

But at the heart of the film is the awakening and transformation that occurs within Walter as he gets to know his son and himself. In an early scene, Walter asks his lawyer-friend, "what does a father owe his son?" The answer to this question for Walter becomes clear as his initial resentment eventually grows into a respect for his son, Roger. The interplay between these two characters is structured carefully by Schultz, as their early acidity slowly moves to a mutual tolerance. In their roles, Segal and newcomer

Washington create a believable pair. Both actors are competent to pull off the necessary comedic touches, as well as the dramatic moments that play out at the end.

Given the strong points in *Carbon Copy*, Schultz's next outing, *The Last Dragon* (1985), is a disappointment. With the backing of Motown mogul and executive producer Berry Gordy, the film contains some mid-1980s dance and uptempo tunes that are appealing, but a story and characters that make a mediocre mix.

In the decade of martial arts popularity following the death of legendary Bruce Lee in 1973, the gimmick for the story appears marketable. After completing training with a martial arts Master (Thomas Ikeda), the protagonist Leroy (Taimak), a young black martial artist who lives in Harlem and who dresses in Chinese coolie attire, attempts to attain the highest level of knowledge by finding a higher master living somewhere in New York City. While pursuing this quest, the young hero crosses paths with two megalomaniacs—Sho'nuff (Julius J. Carry III), a self-proclaimed martial arts master of Harlem; and Eddie Arcadian (Christopher Murney), the owner of a video game empire. Leroy has an ongoing rivalry with Sho'nuff, but he becomes Arcadian's nemesis. As Arcadian maneuvers to kidnap Laura Charles (Vanity), the host of a rock-video television show, Leroy is luckily at hand to dispatch his thugs. While saving Laura and seeking the Master, Leroy must also win the respect of his family members, especially his younger brother, Richie (Leo O'Brien).

With this type of plot and cardboard characters, the tone of the film swings from the humorous to the silly. And though the inclusion of footage from a number of Bruce Lee films—such as *Fists of Fury, The Chinese Connection,* and *Enter the Dragon*—invigorates the action of the movie, even Bruce Lee is unable to save this movie from its erratic development. Adding to the over-the-top portions of the movie are Schultz's decisions to give many of his interiors a carnival-like atmosphere, through the use either of bright, pastel colors or of flat-looking dance-performance numbers set on soundstages.

The Last Dragon further suffers from inane dialogue and unbelievable characters that vacillate between fantasy and stupidity. One facet of the dialogue has Leroy speaking in a simplistic, broken English to emphasize his adaptation of Chinese manners. But the technique is too contrived and makes Leroy's character more wooden and unappealing. Leroy's articulation of mystical ideas and thoughts is aptly labeled by his rival as "mumbo jumbo." In general, the other characters in the film remain cartoonish and insipid, discouraging an audience to care about them to any degree.

Finally, one would expect Schultz to make up for the film's weaknesses with the action sequences. Though Schultz does an adequate job directing those moments, nothing dazzles in technique or in energy level. In some ways, the gimmick of showing actual Bruce Lee footage works against *The Last Dragon*. Although Taimak has a certain cuteness as the protagonist, he, of course, is no Bruce Lee. Even as the story calls for the character, Leroy, to copy the physical moves of his idol, Bruce Lee, the fight sequences of *The Last Dragon* remain only a dull copy of action seen elsewhere. Then, in the final showdown between Leroy and Sho'nuff, Schultz resorts to visual effects to show the power of "the glow" that Leroy achieves after realizing that he, from within, is already a martial arts master.

In *The Last Dragon* Schultz seems to be sleepwalking—going through the visual motions of putting together a story that lacks any passion or spirit of fun. Then, in that same year, Schultz helmed *Krush Groove*, a project that works as an ingratiating introduction to hip-hop culture for mainstream viewers. Unlike films before it, such as *Rappin'* (1985) and *Beat Street* (1984), *Krush Groove* utilizes the real-life artists to portray the movie's principal roles.[10] The initial idea, according to Schultz, was to shoot a concert movie of a traveling tour of rap artists, but with Warner Bros. Studios' success from Prince's *Purple Rain* (1984), the same studio was willing to take a chance on a low-budget film using actual performers.[11] Shot in only twenty-six days in Manhattan, the Bronx, and Queens on a $3 million budget,[12] *Krush Groove* is a musical film that delivers as an entertainment vehicle for a young audience across racial lines.

Based on the experiences of the now-legendary hip-hop mogul Russell Simmons, the movie has charm. As the story unfolds, an enterprising black youth named Russell Walker (Blair Underwood), working with his white partner, Rick (Rick Rubin), hustles to get his brother Run (Joseph Simmons) and his musical partners DMC (Daryll McDaniels) and Jam Master Jay (Jason Mizell) recorded and into the musical limelight. Calling their rap group Run-DMC, the performers have complete confidence in Russell to promote them and Kurtis Blow (as himself) to produce them. For funding, Russell takes a loan with Jay B (Richard E. Gant), a local, small-time hood. Along the way to success, Run is attracted to both the physique and musical talents of Sheila E. (as herself), a vocalist-percussionist who maintains a funk-R&B band and who holds little appreciation for rap; at the same time, Kurtis Blow, scouting new talent, becomes appreciative of the potential of three aspiring, heavy-set rappers who call themselves the Fat Boys (as themselves). As the settings move from clubs to concerts to stage contests, the audience is exposed to various rappin' styles and lyrical themes, from the political to the egotistical to a celebration of overeating.

Krush Groove displays an intoxicating energy and a tone to match. Schultz pulls the best from his performers in creating appealing screen personas. Allowing Blair Underwood to carry the strongest acting challenges in the film, the performers display their musical styles in a story that keeps them natural and believable. Kurtis Blow's "If I Ruled the World" is both egotistical and political; Sheila E.'s "Love Bizarre" and "Holly Rock" are explosive and salacious; and the Fat Boys' "All You Can Eat" is humorous and self-affirming. In one sequence showing a musical contest, brief camera time is also given to other aspiring popular groups, specifically New Edition, the Beastie Boys, and LL Cool J. Schultz also carefully includes some of the verbal expressions of the hip-hop culture, such as "def," "illin'," "frontin'," and "chillin'," to provide authenticity.

Krush Groove is not an intellectual journey through the burgeoning hip-hop culture, but it serves as a movie where fun and entertainment meet in a compelling manner. It is not surprising, then, that Schultz might continue to explore hip-hop culture in his next feature film, *Disorderlies* (1987).

The film features the then-popular rap group who had appeared in *Krush Groove*, namely, the Fat Boys—Markie (Mark Morales), Buffy (Darren Robinson), and Kool (Damon Wimbley). Despite any dynamic verbal qualities or energy in their music, in this movie their large physiques become the center of most of the childish humor. As the title suggests, the three work as orderlies in a Brooklyn nursing home that's cited as the worst in the country by a national newspaper. In Palm Beach, Winslow Lowry (Anthony Geary) is deep into gambling debts and needs to hasten the demise of his rich Uncle Albert (Ralph Bellamy). Geary hires Markie, Buffy, and Kool to attend his uncle, hoping that their ineptitude will finish off the ailing man. As Darren and Damon clumsily carry out their duties, Mark spends his time chasing Uncle Albert's pretty black maid, Carla (Troy Beyer). As the story progresses, Winslow's plan backfires, as Uncle Albert becomes rejuvenated by his "Boys"; the senior millionaire even begins to use hip-hop phrases, such as "step off, homeboy" and "stop illin'." As a final tactic, Winslow attempts to kill Uncle Albert, the Fat Boys, and Carla with explosives, but that too fails, leading to a happy ending.

No doubt, the story sounded interesting in development meetings as a vehicle for the rap group, but the resulting movie is predictable and irritating to watch. For all purposes, the Fat Boys are merely the Three Stooges in blackface; the humor never rises above the level of the familiar Moe,

Michael Schultz, far right, sets up a shot in
Livin' Large with T.C. Carson, far left, who
portrays protagonist Dexter Jackson.

Larry, and Curly. In addition to the consistent fat jokes, the movie thrives
on slapstick and sight gags—slapping, kicking, breaking furniture, falling
into swimming pools, falling off horses, and car stunts. All of these gags
have been viewed before and executed with more deftness and impact. The
only break in the silliness occurs when the music by the Fat Boys is played
over the action, particularly during the end credits when the movie merci-
fully ends.

In his next film project, Schultz begins *Livin' Large* (1991), similar to the
opening of *Car Wash*, with a high-angle view of a city, moving the camera
down closer into the urban maze, while credits roll and a hip-hop tune delivers the lyrics of the title song. The story presents Dexter Jackson (Terrence
"T. C." Carson), an African American broadcasting school graduate who
wants to break into television journalism and become a news anchorperson
like his idol Clifford Worthy (Bernie McInerney). Working at his family's dry
cleaning business with his sister, Nadine (Loretta Devine), and girlfriend,
Toynelle (Lisa Arrindell), Dexter carries his video camera with him as he delivers and picks up clothing around the city of Atlanta. After capitalizing on

an opportunity, Dexter is hired by the executive producer of the news program, Kate Penndragin (Blanche Baker), to do remote stories about the inner city. Kate, a heartless news exploiter, demands that Dexter refine his ghetto mannerisms and that he expose the scandalous side of the black community. In Dexter's obsession to reach his goal, he compiles stories that distort the black community and people whom he once called friends. Mysteriously, each time Dexter airs a story that hurts the black community, he notices that his appearance changes: his hair grows straighter, his complexion lightens, and his nose and lips become thinner. At one point, he even loses his ability to dance rhythmically, as he is unable to find the beat on a nightclub's dance floor. Eventually, Dexter comes to his black senses and is hired as the coanchor with his newscast idol, Clifford Worthy.

From the contemporary meaning of its title—living a life of material gain—to the final triumph of the protagonist, Schultz wants the audience to connect to one strong message: blacks must remain true to their ethnic selves. However, the upbeat ending still leaves unanswered a number of questions raised within the film. Can a person displaying distinctive ethnic attributes ever become accepted by the mainstream without "refining" or changing those attributes? If a person of color becomes successful financially, must he/she move out of the old neighborhood to complete the attainment of that success? Can blacks transform the media simply by becoming anchors in front of the camera, when the power and ownership behind the scenes remain in the hands of whites? Certainly, these questions are much too formidable for a comedy to tackle, but the film's ending remains unsatisfying due to these raised and unresolved issues.

As a director here, Schultz refrains from pushing beyond the expected and the acceptable in his filmmaking. After sixteen years of filmmaking, Schultz must have had an urge to give the story a certain visual complexity, but *Livin' Large* simply falls in line with his previous six films—"popcorn movies" that are filling until the viewer leaves the theater.

Michael Schultz offers a curious study of a black director in Hollywood. Undoubtedly a success as a Hollywood director, he worked steadily through three decades of shifting tastes in movies, and his contribution in that regard must not be reduced or dismissed. But somehow the promise and possibilities emerging from Schultz's first four films didn't become realized in his succeeding seven films. In particular, as the 1980s saw the emergence of a "New Wave" of young black directors, Schultz was in a position to serve as a veteran leader. But, instead, the younger filmmakers moved him toward the rear of the auditorium as they took center stage, and one is left wondering why and how that happened. Certainly, Schultz possesses the skills to direct provocative and memorable films, such as *Cooley High*, *Greased Lightning*, and *Carbon Copy*, that entertain but do not shy away from stimulating a viewer on a deeper political and cultural level. Hopefully, Schultz will emerge again and crown his mainstream career with the kind of films that reflect the artistic qualities that shaped his earlier works.

CHAPTER SIX

Spike Lee: The Independent Auteur

When I was becoming a filmmaker I knew it would be harder for me to be a black filmmaker. . . . But I realized that you just have to be two or three—four— times better. . . . This is just something you just know, growing up black. It's a given. The problem starts when people say that's a given and then use that as an excuse.[1]   Spike Lee

Between 1986 and 1996 Spike Lee completed ten feature films, and though this number does not qualify him as the most prolific black director ever in Hollywood, it would be impossible to deny that since the 1990s Lee has been the most visible and controversial black filmmaker. Lee's popularity has given him a recognition unequaled by other black directors. Due to his film directing, his presence in commercials, his outspokenness on racial issues, and his well-known courtside presence at New York Knicks pro basketball games—Spike Lee has become a celebrity. Yet, despite this celebrity status, Lee continually positions himself as a filmmaker first with a passion and commitment for telling various stories that clarify black experiences and explore interracial dynamics within American society.

Lee was born on March 20, 1957, in Atlanta, Georgia. Given the birth name Shelton by his father Bill, a jazz musician, and his mother, Jacquelyn, a high school teacher, Lee was labeled with the endearing name Spike be- cause his mother saw that he was a "small, wiry little boy."[2] Lee was only a couple of years old when parents moved the family to Brooklyn, New York, an environment that would provide an indelible influence on their closeness and on Spike's racial sensibilities, as the neighborhood provided him an early interaction with West Indians, Jews, and Italians.[3]

On graduating from John Dewey High School, Lee attended Morehouse College in Atlanta, as his father and grandfather did before him. Tragically, however, during his sophomore year at college, Lee's mother died of liver cancer.[4] This painful loss appears to have inspired the story line of Lee's later film *Crooklyn*, but Lee remained committed to finishing his degree at Morehouse, majoring in mass communications before returning to New York to attend New York University's graduate film school.[5] Living in the

New York area provided Lee the opportunity to be closer to his family, but a rift occurred between Lee and his father when the latter began dating a Jewish woman, whom he would eventually marry. Lee openly discusses his displeasure with his father's nonblack wife in later interviews,[6] and this animosity toward interracial love appears to have been referenced in a number of his films.

Lee spent three years in NYU's film school, where he made several student films including *The Answer*, a response to the 1915 film, *The Birth of a Nation; Sarah*, the story of a Harlem family on Thanksgiving Day; and *Joe's Bed-Stuy Barbershop: We Cut Heads*, his third-year master's thesis film. It was during the making of the last two films that Lee worked with fellow student Ernest Dickerson, the cinematographer with whom he would later collaborate professionally on several feature films.[7] With *Joe's Bed-Stuy Barbershop*, Lee gained considerable attention, winning the Student Academy Award, a 1983 screening at New York's Lincoln Center, screenings at international film festivals, and a contract with both ICM and William Morris.[8]

But work didn't flood in for a black director, even one signed to two of the best-known agencies in the film industry, so Lee worked at a film distribution house while trying to raise money himself for his first feature film, *The Messenger*. Unable to complete the movie, Lee moved on to another project—*She's Gotta Have It*, a film shot in twelve days, in 16 mm, and except for one sequence, in black and white.

She's Gotta Have It (1986) was one of the more auspicious and promising feature debuts in Hollywood's history. Stretching a humble budget of $175,000, Lee completed a project that dares to present a contemporary black woman as an independent, assertive person with an equally realized personal and professional life. As screenwriter and director, Lee gives audiences a protagonist who was singularly unique even as she voices many of the attitudes and concerns of women in the 1980s.

Nola Darling (Tracy Camilla Johns) is a layout and paste-up artist living in a Brooklyn loft. As she pursues her various interests in life, she enjoys friendship and intimacy with several, distinctively different black men: Jamie (Tommy Redmond Hicks), a no-nonsense intellectual; Greer (John Canada Terrell), a wealthy male model; and Mars (Spike Lee), an athletic jokester. Nola, remaining honest to all three, informs each about the others, as she enjoys the personality peculiar to each man. At first the men tolerate Nola's multiple partners because each wants as much time as possible, sexually and otherwise, with her. At the same time, Nola, befriending but rejecting the sexual overtures from a lesbian friend, Opal (Raye Dowell), proclaims her liberated heterosexuality. But soon, Nola's men increase their pressure on her to choose just one lover, inferring that Nola's behavior isn't normal. Nola, encouraged to be self-critical by her three men, decides that perhaps she does need to make a choice, and she chooses Jamie. But the night that Jamie comes over at her request, he believes she's admitting her love for him just for the sake of an evening's sexual pleasure and not as a commitment. Convinced that he alone knows what Nola wants, Jamie rapes Nola and leaves. After that tragedy, Nola tells a contrite Jamie that he still remains the one man she wants. But at the end, Nola realizes that Jamie was looking for a traditional life with her that doesn't appeal to her. So, she remains alone at the end, but satisfied that she has made her own choices and content to be herself.

She's Gotta Have It, though stylized, accomplishes a great deal, as the visual elements come together in an impressive marriage of style and content. To begin with, the black-and-white film, as well as still photos, imbue a documentary quality to the film, amplifying the confessional aspect of Nola's story. Then, in the middle of the film, as Jamie surprises Nola for her birthday, the film switches to color for a segment where Jamie and Nola are an audience of two for an interpretive dance staged for her birthday present. The color is startling, yet warm, as it suggests the sincere emotions that exist between Jamie and Nola. Out of all of her men, it is Jamie whose efforts to please Nola appear to confirm true love.

Throughout the film, Lee allows his characters to "break the fourth wall," as they look into the camera and speak to the audience. This also augments the documentary-like nature of *She's Gotta Have It*, but it also draws viewers nearer emotionally to the characters. Each character provides a different point of view, but one that overlaps or contrasts with the others', giving the audience a chance to look into the nature of the characters and the issues involved.

Lee also moves his camera generously, including both the handheld technique and the circular pan. The handheld technique suggests the cinema verité used by French filmmakers of the 1950s and by American feature director John Cassavetes in the 1960s. This technique gives a jerkiness to the frame, as well as a distinct rhythm and energy to the film. In another way, the technique encourages the viewer to be conscious of the fact that a film is being viewed and to intellectually engage a given scene and the film as a whole.

When Lee incorporates the circular pan, as he does when Greer announces to Nola that he will be the model on the cover of *GQ*, he creates a heightened focus on the two characters who are centered in the frame. In this scene, the rapid movement enhances their emotions and punctuates their exclusion of the world around them, which spins haphazardly. In this same sequence, as Greer and Nola remove their clothes and climb into bed, their intimacy is not based on an inner passion but purely on physical pleasure. To underscore this, Lee places his camera above the bed to keep viewers at a distance, and from that high-angle shot, he speeds up the action, showing Nola and Greer's coupling in various positions in a quick, humorous pace, as he nullifies any semblance of committed love in their union.

With this stylized approach to telling Nola's story, Lee runs the risk of alienating mainstream viewers who have been conditioned to appreciate fluid, polished, color filmmaking where stories maintain a certain chronology. Instead, Lee challenges the viewer to experience a black-and-white story that suggest both factual and whimsical elements, both traditional and experimental camera techniques. To his credit, Lee is successful due to the nature of Nola's story and its contemporary late-1980s setting. Unfortunately, a questionable aspect in Nola's story does surface—specifically, the rape scene that prompts Nola's declaration of love for the man who raped her. Up to this point in the film, Nola exhibits an admirable independence, and her honesty with all three lovers speaks of her integrity. Jamie's assault of Nola not only demonstrates his exercise of power over her, but his insistence—though he claims to love her—that Nola is nothing more than a piece of property, a body, to him. As Jamie sexually dominates Nola, he questions her: "Whose pussy is this?" Nola responds, "Yours." With such a horrific event occurring between the two, an independent Nola would certainly reject Jamie after that point. Black feminist and cultural critic bell hooks, takes exception to this rape scene in no equivocal terms: "In this instance, rape as an act of black male violence against a black woman was portrayed as though it was just another enjoyable sexual encounter. . . . [T]he sexist assumption that woman as desiring subject, as active initiator, as sexual seducer is responsible for the quality, nature, and content of male response."[9] For hooks, the sexist notion that the woman causes her own sexual victimization is intrinsic within the scene.

Regardless of critical responses, *She's Gotta Have It* propelled Spike Lee to the forefront of discussion regarding black directors as well as independent filmmakers. The film was shown at the San Francisco Film Festival, and it received the "Prix de Jeunesse" Award at the Cannes Film Festival; more importantly for Hollywood, the small budget project went on to make more than $7 million.[10]

With his next film, Lee made an unexpected choice of subject—the cultural, political, and personal interactions at a small, all-black college. And due to the large cast and demands of the musical numbers, costuming, and set designs, the film demanded a higher budget than *She's Gotta Have It.* Consequently, Lee wound up leaving a smaller distributor for a traditional studio—Columbia Studios. With a $4 million budget and menagerie of technical and creative talent, Lee moved from being an independent filmmaker to being a director with a mainstream studio backing.

School Daze (1988) offers filmgoers a look at a fresh topic to American cinema, as it exposes some *intra*racial issues seldom seen. Set on the campus of the fictional Mission College, *School Daze* displays a mixture of tones— parts drama, comedy, musical, and fantasy. Due to this, the film appears uneven at places as some of the shifts in tone occur abruptly. Nonetheless, the film stands out as a creative articulation to a black audience with scenes that sometimes criticize that same audience.

Even before the Columbia Studios logo has disappeared from the screen, the sounds of a boat creaking on the ocean can be heard. Then, as a chorus sings the gospel song "I'm Building Me a Home" over the titles, under the titles the frame is filled with the diagram of the bottom of a slave ship, where Africans were stacked for the dread Middle Passage. Then, through a series of black-and-white stills, Lee provides an overview of African American history, including images of slave quarters, black workers, Frederick Douglass, Booker T. Washington, Mary McLeod Bethune, Joe Louis, Stokely Carmichael, Martin Luther King Jr., and Malcolm X.

From there, the story begins during Homecoming Weekend at the college, as Dap Dunlap (Laurence Fishburne) speaks at a rally demanding that Mission College divest its money in the then apartheid-based South Africa. Dap, the campus radical and political voice in the film, insists that students should protest, disrupt classes, and even shut down the school until full divestment occurs. Interrupting the rally, Julian (Giancarlo Esposito), the leader of the Gamma Phi Gamma Fraternity, opposes Dap's political efforts. This conflict between Dap and Julian continues throughout the story, smoldering in intensity until it flares up at the film's end.

As the weekend proceeds, another ongoing conflict simmers as well—the dislike between the fair-complexioned women students called the Wannabees and the dark-complexioned women students called the Jigaboos. Using complexion and hair texture as qualifiers of acceptability, the two groups declare and physically demonstrate their common disdain. Later in the film, another type of opposition emerges—the college men versus the local working-class black men. Clashing at a fast-food restaurant, Leeds (Samuel L.

Jackson) blames Dap and his buddies for the lack of jobs in the town, claiming that college men are "niggers" just like them. Dap defuses the altercation by insisting that none of them are "niggers."

All of the characters, events, and issues culminate early Sunday morning, following a night filled with Homecoming festivities and the successful pledging by Half-Pint (Spike Lee) and others into the Gamma Phi Gamma fraternity. When Julian forces his girlfriend, Jane (Tisha Campbell), to have sex with Half-Pint to prove her love for Julian, Jane reluctantly does so. But after she does, Julian accuses her of misunderstanding his instructions and breaks up with her, which was his original intention. When a proud Half-Pint rushes over to brag to Dap that he is no longer a virgin, Dap, angry at the debasing arrangement, runs to the campus's center, ringing the bell and demanding that everyone on the campus "Wake up!" These final words become a clarion call for all the blacks to open their eyes and look at who they are and what they are doing to each other.

In this film, where the title "daze" informs us of the filmmaker's plan to critique confusion, Lee spares little in his exposure of what he perceives to be flaws among some African Americans. The fraternity serves as a blatant example of duplicity as the oft-used word "brother" rings hollow. Julian, intoxicated with his power, disconnects himself from Dap's political activism against apartheid, while he maintains his elitist position in the fraternity and on campus.

In the "Wake up!" montage, cinematographer Ernest Dickerson gives Lee an impressive golden fuzziness that mirrors the confusion of the black community on campus. As Dap is highlighted in extreme close-ups, slow motion, and Lee's distinctive "isolation" shot, his character takes on a symbolic status as the connecting voice to all those voices of black leadership suggested by the opening black-and-white stills. Dap serves as the voice of black consciousness that helps the fuzziness to dissipate, and by the end of the montage, as all the characters congregate into the frame, the images are sharper and clearer as they hear Dap's inspiring statement.

Lee's "isolation" shot is an expressionistic technique where he places a character or characters at the center of the frame in a medium shot, and then, the characters are "pulled" forward toward the camera on a moving dolly. This self-conscious technique appears to be an effort to highlight the introspective nature of the single character, or to emphasize the significant dialogue between two characters. Often intrusive and annoying, the shot nonetheless forces viewers to be conscious of the technique, impressing on them the importance of that moment in the story. This technique is employed in most of Lee's succeeding films as well, becoming one of what black critic Nelson George refers to as "Spikeisms—devices sprinkled throughout the feature that stop the narrative yet reinforce the film's theme."[11]

Lee also uses other techniques that will surface again in later productions. For example, the extreme slow motion—similar to what Martin Scorsese overused in *Raging Bull* (1980)—that captures and extends a moment, noting the significance of one character from the subjective viewpoint of another, or punctuating the emotional intensity of the character centered in the frame. In another editing technique, several characters are shown in succession and are connected because they speak the same mode of ideas. Specifically, in the scene when Half-Pint attempts to get a date, he goes to the girl's dormitory lounge and delivers a flurry of pick-up lines. Half-Pint speaks to one girl; a cut back to Half-Pint, who delivers another line; then a cut to reveal that he's speaking to another girl; and a cut back to Half-pint, and so on. The editing demonstrates Half-Pint's insincerity, and as four women all reject his crass efforts—one woman portrayed by Kasi Lemmons, the later director of *Eve's Bayou* (1997)—the scene becomes humorous due to Half-Pint's futile machismo. Lee utilizes this editing technique even more effectively for purposes of character revelation in his later film *Mo' Better Blues.*

With all the stylization occurring in the film, Lee winds up doing an impressive job of presenting more conventional, polished musical numbers, which is somewhat surprising given all the emphasis on political issues. Three of the songs occur at the Homecoming festivities: Jane and three Gamma Rays perform a sultry number, "Be Alone Tonight," in full makeup and evening gowns; Keith John sings Stevie Wonder's "I Can Only Be Me"; and the late Phyllis Hyman performs the jazzy "Be One." Lee allows each piece to be performed in its entirety, maintaining the integrity of each song, even as the musical numbers connect to some aspect of the film's numerous themes. In a bit more exploitive vein, as the camera gazes upon numerous female derrieres, Lee also highlights the contemporary group EU, which performs a song entitled "Da Butt," as the Mission College students wear appropriate bikinis and swim trunks for the dance's beach party theme.

However, the most elaborate and abrupt musical number is the beauty salon sequence in which the previously mentioned Wannabees and Jigaboos break into dance while singing "Straight and Nappy," a song commenting on "good and bad hair." The beauty salon number is a throwback to the traditional Hollywood musical where characters break from the realistic tone of the film and perform an integrated song that functions as an extension of the film's theme. The piece tackles the issue of surface beauty and "aesthetics" as it demonstrates how pervasive surface appearances can be even among blacks.

This color consciousness within the black community reappears later in a dialogue between Dap and Rachael, as she questions whether her dark complexion fits in more appropriately with Dap's posture as a black political leader. Then, again, during the Homecoming coronation sequence, the Queen and her court are all fair-complexioned women. Lee develops this area as an issue that demands as much attention as apartheid, the educational system, class differences, and personal relations.

The following year, Spike Lee widened his visual canvas, taking on the complex issues of interracial and interethnic conflict in *Do the Right Thing* (1989). Set within the Bedford-Stuyvesant area of Brooklyn on the hottest day of the summer, Lee develops a story that is both critical of and sensitive to the various ethnic peoples sharing a small urban maze. In places theatrical, spontaneous, or expressionistic—the film delivers the political sensibilities of its director, who does not flinch in using his art form to present a number of messages about the urgency of interracial understanding, respect, and dialogue.

From the opening credits, the film explodes with an energy absent from other contemporary films. With the rap group Public Enemy uncoiling their aggressive style in the tune "Fight the Power," choreographer-actress Rosie Perez performs a solitary dance routine that's edited carefully with brilliant colors and urban sounds to show the anger, attitude, aggressiveness, and sexuality of the hip-hop generation. The visuals and sounds overwhelm the senses, pounding out the frustration and volatility that lie simmering within the urban neighborhood that serves as the film's focus. When the opening credits and choreography end, the first words spoken in the film, by deejay Mister Senor Love Daddy, are the final words spoken in Lee's previous film—"Wake up!"

With its ensemble cast, *Do the Right Thing* emphasizes the interaction of numerous working-class people: Mookie (Lee), a rather self-absorbed African American man who's obsessed with making money, while neglecting his son and his son's Puerto Rican mother, Tina (Perez); the Italian family, consisting of Sal (Danny Aiello) and his two sons, who own a pizzeria; Radio Raheem (Bill Nunn), a proud black who struts the neighborhood as his boom box blasts his anthem, "Fight the Power"; Buggin' Out (Giancarlo Esposito), an impulsive black man who attempts to organize a black consumers protest against the pizzeria; Da Mayor (Ossie Davis), an elderly survivor of personal pain who seeks companionship with Mother Sister (Ruby Dee), the elderly matron of the block; Smiley (Roger Guenveur Smith), the stuttering black man who sells cultural posters and pride; Mister Senor Love Daddy (Samuel L. Jackson), the black deejay who fills the airwaves and the streets with soul, rap, and R&B; and the three black men on the corner who observe and critique the life of the neighborhood—Sweet Dick Willy (Robin Harris), ML (Paul Benjamin), and Coconut Sid (Frankie Faison).

Working again with director of photography Ernest Dickerson, with his father, music composer Bill Lee, and with production designer Wynn Thomas, Lee—serving as writer, actor, producer, and director—completes a memorable movie that utilizes and incorporates a bevy of camera angles, musical forms, and visual textures to accomplish his most ambitious film to that point. The film carries a dedication to Michael Stewart and Eleanor Bumpurs, two black people who "died at the hands of NYC police in separate controversial incidents."[12] Then, at the film's end, the postscript provides two opposing statements about the nature and use of violence—one by Dr. Martin Luther King Jr. and the other by Malcolm X. With these captions at the end, along with the interracial clashing within the film, Lee smacks the audience in the face with a didactic movie that grabs the emotions.

Two sequences are outstanding in their exploration of the futility of racial bigotry and their demonstration of Lee's creativity. The first begins with a two-shot that reveals the dialogue between Mookie and Sal's oldest son, Pino (John Turturro). Having called Mookie a "nigger," Mookie challenges Pino to identify his favorite athlete and entertainer—both of whom are black; Mookie pushes the point that Pino admires black celebrities who must be, logically, "niggers" as well. Stuttering a response that tries to defend the absurdity of position, Pino becomes offensive, launching a derisive attack upon black leaders. From that point, their dialogue breaks down into racial name-calling on the part of both characters. Immediately following, Lee presents an expressionistic montage which further shows the silliness of racial name-calling and stereotyping. Zooming in, from a long shot to a close shot, in turn, on four separate characters, Lee has each one break the fourth wall and spout off a litany of racial generalizations: Pino derides blacks; Mookie defames Italians; a white police officer criticizes Latinos; and a Korean grocer berates Jews. Then, abruptly, Senor Love Daddy bursts forward toward the camera, calling: "Time out . . . you got to chill that shit. . . ." Senor Love Daddy, the voice of reason who earlier urged everyone to "wake up," now pleads with the characters, and the audience, to cease the stereotypical attacks on one another. The sequence is tinged with humor, but it scorches with the truth that stereotypes often dominate one's interactions with others.

The second noteworthy sequence occurs toward the end of the story, as the long day of racial tensions finally explodes. In a skillfully structured cacophony of personalities, sounds, music, and colors, Lee fills the screen with one of the most stirring riot scenes ever filmed. At the center of the storm are Sal, Radio Raheem, and Buggin' Out—the last two having clashed earlier in the day with Sal at his pizzeria. When Radio Raheem and Buggin' Out join forces and confront Sal at closing time, Sal responds with anger, and flailing a baseball bat, he destroys Radio Raheem's treasured boom box. Like dominoes toppling, Sal and Radio Raheem's physical grappling begins to affect everyone around them, and a brawl ensues, spilling outside the pizza parlor and onto the streets. When the police arrive, their determination to restrain Radio Raheem results in a choke hold that kills the young man on the spot. The cops, putting both Radio Raheem and Buggin' Out into squad cars, make a hasty exit from the neighborhood.

In the aftermath, in the eye of the storm, as Sal and his sons face the multiethnic crowd that gathers, Sal's lack of remorse for Radio Raheem's death infuriates the people who see the same pattern of white cops killing blacks as in other neighborhoods. Then Mookie, unable to contain his frustration at the day's events, throws a garbage can through the window of the pizzeria, and the storm erupts again. As Da Mayor ushers Sal and his sons to a safe distance, the multiethnic crowd release their pent-up tensions by destroying the pizzeria.

Although most critics praised the efficacy with which Lee presents the riot sequence, some debate the manner in which Mookie plays such a pivotal part in such a politically charged event. It seems clear that by tossing the garbage can, Mookie merely demonstrates his class rage, but not any cultural or racial leadership. Mookie, who works as a delivery man for the pizzeria, is both the supporter and the victim of the capitalist system, in which his ethics and income are inextricably bound. However, in the filmmaker's defense, it is this very flaw in Mookie's character that appears to be emphasized throughout the movie. Mookie emerges as a tragic figure in that he *cannot* separate "getting paid" from his sense of manhood, and in his confusion of priorities, he is no better than others, regardless of race, who always place money and property over the value of human dignity.

In contrast to the large and diverse ethnic canvas of *Do the Right Thing,* *Mo' Better Blues* (1990) displays a more confined story that functions as a moralistic tale of self-awareness and redemption. The more intimate nature of the story emerges in the opening credits as the camera, in extreme close-up, moves down and along a glistening trumpet in a sensuous manner. From the trumpet, the camera catches the face of a musician, a woman's neck-

In *Mo' Better Blues,* Left Hand Lacey
(Giancarlo Esposito, left), Giant (Spike Lee,
center), and Bleek Gilliam (Denzel
Washington) prepare for a jam session.

line, and then a woman's hand caressing the musician's hand. As key lighting strikes hands, face, and instrument against the dark, a moody tone is
evoked, preparing the viewer for the impending emotional conflict between
a musician-artist and the women in his life.

The film opens in Brooklyn in 1969, as the camera pans across treetops
and down to the urban street where four young boys gather beneath the open
window of an apartment, yelling for young Bleek Gilliam to join them in
playing baseball. However, Bleek busies himself indoors with his trumpet
lesson, forced to keep practicing by his mother, Lillian (Abbey Lincoln), and
encouraged by his distracted father, Big Stop (Dick Anthony Williams). As the
young boy plays, the transition is made to the adult Bleek (Denzel Washington) who now, some twenty years later, is playing before an adoring crowd.

Joining Bleek onstage are the members of his jazz quintet: sax player
Shadow Henderson (Wesley Snipes), pianist Left Hand Lacey (Giancarlo Es-
posito), upright bass player Bottom Hammer (Bill Nunn), and drummer
Rhythm Jones (Jeff Watts). While Bleek plays his music, he appears to be

secure and happy, his only problems stemming from Shadow's rather long solos and the mediocre management by his friend Giant (Spike Lee).

The major difficulty in Bleek's life revolves around his intimate relationship with two women who love him—the long-suffering Indigo (Joie Lee) and the aspiring vocalist Clarke (Cynda Williams). Caught between the two and unable to give to either woman the kind of commitment that she wants, Bleek chooses his music in the manner of a self-centered artist. However, when Bleek attempts to rescue his buddy Giant, who suffers a brutal beating because of unpaid gambling debts, Bleek is struck viciously in his mouth, both scarring and ultimately destroying his upper lip as far as his music is concerned. Although after a year he attempts to play again onstage before a crowd, he is unable to control his notes, and he leaves the stage, broken and ashamed. In the aftermath, he goes to Indigo—Clarke having meanwhile developed a relationship with Shadow—and he begs Indigo to marry him, to give him something of value in his life, and to save him from his emptiness. She does, and they have a son. As the film ends, the opening sequence is replayed as their young son practices his trumpet. When the son's friends come to ask him to play ball, Bleek allows his son to go outside to enjoy something other than his trumpet.

In the hands of a less skillful director, this film could have become just a melodramatic story about a love triangle. Lee, however, sets his sights on something grander and more stimulating. He invites the audience to look at a flawed character whose sexist machismo is deplorable, but whose dedication to his music is intriguing. In fact, along with the films *Paris Blues* (1961), *Round Midnight* (1986), *Bird* (1988), *Kansas City* (1996), and *The Tic Code* (2000), *Mo' Better Blues* presents one of the most respectful and extensive inclusions of blues and jazz music in a feature film. Lee does not cut off most of the songs performed onstage, but allows them to the play fully, providing high angles, close shots, and fluid movements to match the tone of a given song. The music actually becomes a character in the film, as multidimensional and vital as the human characters interacting within the story. The title itself underscores this integral aspect about the music. In one scene Bleek tells Clarke that "Mo' Better" is a euphemism for making love, and the conventional meaning for the "Blues" suggest something painful or sorrowful. So, here in the title mix sexuality and music, pleasure and art, freedom and commitment.

In the film Lee displays some camera techniques that he uses in other films. The circular pan that he incorporated in *She's Gotta Have It* is utilized again in this film. On one occasion, Bleek faces the camera, alone, practicing his instrument. As he moves into the spell of the instrument, Bleek actually moves in a 360-degree circle as the background fades to dark; then, when the doorbell buzzes, the spell is broken and the lights come up in the background, showing his frustration with being interrupted. Here, the technique works well to emphasize Bleek's journey into the music and away from the world around him.

Lee also introduces a trucking shot here that he will use again in *Jungle Fever*. At one point, Bleek and his group exit the stage and move toward the dressing room, along a twisting narrow corridor. As they walk directly toward the camera, it moves backward allowing the sequence to develop in real time in one, long take. The challenge of successfully negotiating the long, narrow corridor is impressive, even as the movement of camera and characters provides an alluring kinetic energy.

Lee also returns to the handheld camera, used effectively here during a scene when the quintet rehearses and the members initiate an argument about money. As Left Hand Lacey walks in late again, the camera follows him in the room, catching the physical spacing and the emotional outbursts of the characters in a natural way without cutting from shot to shot. At the same time, Lee also nurtures color and tone as he did in *School Daze* and *Do the Right Thing*. A number of interior shots, again to the credit of cinematographer Ernest Dickerson, appear washed in beautiful ambers and luscious tans, often juxtaposing brightly lit interiors with darker emotional textures. For example, in one scene Lee uses colors and framing to punctuate the shadowy nature of two of his characters. Moe and Josh Flatbush (John Turturro and Nicholas Turturro, respectively) are the brothers who own the "beneath the underdog" Club where Bleek's quintet performs. In a scene where darkness and light play against one another, the brothers are seen on the left side of the frame, which is split by the vertical doorway; to the right of the doorway, on the wall, are framed photographs of black musicians including Duke Ellington. Visually the scene emphasizes the manner in which the two white businessmen—who are separated by class and culture from blacks—exploit the black talent for their personal profits. As they discuss whether or not to give Bleek and his group a raise, they rationalize the reasons as to why they should keep more themselves.

Lee shows his sharp visual style in yet another sequence, as he exposes Bleek's frailties and confusion in his love triangle. While being intimate with Clarke, Bleek kisses her, but in a smooth edit, as he lifts his head, Clarke has visually become Indigo; similarly, in the same sequence as Bleek caresses Indigo, she suddenly becomes Clarke. The editing demonstrates Bleek's growing disorientation that culminates when, in the middle of a passionate moment, Bleek calls Clarke "Indigo"; then, with a quick edit, he immediately speaks to Indigo but calls her "Clarke." Bleek eventually is shown in a medium shot looking from one woman's face to the other, seemingly unable to tell them apart. So, as the angry voices of the women rain down on him, Bleek reaches for his trumpet and plays, finding his peace in the instrument.

In an interesting swing of the pendulum, Lee returns to the controversial areas of interracial relationships in his next film, *Jungle Fever* (1991). Specifically, he journeys head-on into the still contentious issue of interracial sex and romance. With the opening credits to *Jungle Fever*, Lee presents some energetic visuals beneath the upbeat title song performed by Stevie Wonder. The names of the cast and production crew are printed on the various street signs found in and around New York City, particularly those two neighborhoods—Harlem and Bensonhurst—that serve as home to the film's characters. The signposts and cityscapes suggest the interconnection among the black and Italian urban dwellers; unfortunately, the similarities are lost on the characters, who continue to racially isolate themselves.

Jungle Fever takes on the long-standing social taboo of miscegenation and interracial romance. Other films that preceded it, such as *Pinky* (1949) and *Imitation of Life* (1959), gave a cursory look at interracial couples, and two films in the 1960s—*One Potato, Two Potato* (1964) and *Guess Who's Coming to Dinner* (1967)—focused on interracial marriage between a black man and a white woman as their central story lines.

In *Jungle Fever*, Flipper (Wesley Snipes), a married man with a daughter, confronts a pair of bigoted white bosses who refuse him a partnership in their architectural firm. Flipper's friction with the pair intensifies when they hire an Italian American temporary secretary, Angie (Annabella Sciorra), rather than hiring an African American as Flipper requested. Angie's naïveté annoys Flipper at first, but eventually when they both begin working late hours, they discuss their personal lives and connect—not as boss and assistant, but as a man and woman. But their affair is doomed, as family and friends discover their relationship and as segments of the public ridicule and harass their closeness.

If Spike Lee had focused on this central story line with better-defined characters, this film might have been a milestone regarding race relations. However, the filmmaker attaches an obvious bias regarding the issue, and he interweaves subplots that detract from the main story rather than strengthen it.

The bias surfaces during the opening credits with the title song that contains the lines: "I've gone white girl hazy, she's gone black boy crazy . . . we're in love." The lack of genuine affection between black and white emanates from these lyrics, shaping the sentiment of simple racial curiosity as the fundamental attraction. Later in the film, when Flipper confides his affair to his best friend, Cyrus (Spike Lee), the latter articulates the filmmaker's viewpoint in more direct terms when he states: "You's got jungle fever, that's all."

As the screenwriter, Spike Lee neglects to fully develop Flipper's and Angie's motivations. For example, the film opens with one of the hottest, most explicit love scenes Lee has ever directed. Flipper and his wife, Drew (Lonette McKee), enjoy an obviously passionate, uninhibited intimacy. In their afterglow, they are both satisfied physically and emotionally—in what is alluded to as one of many such occasions. Consequently, when Flipper has sex with Angie at the office, it seems too manipulative and abrupt. "Sexual-racial curiosity" or jungle fever would hardly be strong enough to match the deep passion Flipper displays toward Drew. Later when Flipper and Angie receive insults from his pious father, Reverend Purify (Ossie Davis), at dinner, Flipper handles the criticisms even-temperedly, and in another instance, when the two are offended by a black waitress (Queen Latifah) in a restaurant, Flipper demands to see the manager to seek satisfaction. But ironically, when the police harass Flipper on the street—placing a gun to his head—because they think he's assaulting Angie, Flipper, in the aftermath, blames Angie for telling the cops that they're lovers and thereby jeopardizing his life. Certainly, a black man of his intelligence comprehends the historical conflict between black men and the police system. In the aftermath of such a confrontation, his anger would be directed at the cops, not at the woman. However, a more striking contrast is Angie's motivation. Unlike Flipper, she does not explain her attraction to him as being racial curiosity. A working-class woman living in an oppressive home where she cares for her father and two adult brothers, Angie is suffocating in an environment of both sexism and racism. Her attraction to Flipper remains intertwined to her efforts to break away from that world. If she were only interested in Flipper because of his race, no doubt her curiosity would have been fulfilled after their initial intimacy. Angie appears to be a character searching for something more than simply surface satisfaction.

In addition to the confusion regarding the import of "jungle fever" to Flipper's and Angie's characterizations, Lee as writer and director includes two subplots that detract from the central focus of the film. First of all, he adds the story line revolving around Flipper's brother, Gator, a crack addict who enjoys being high. Gator (Samuel L. Jackson) exploits the love of his mother (Ruby Dee) to gain money to buy drugs. Teaming up with his equally addicted girlfriend, Vivian (Halle Berry), Gator moves in and out of his family's lives as the quintessential black sheep of the family. This antidrug theme is so prominent that it intrudes on the Flipper-Angie story line.

The second subplot that serves to detract from the central story line concerns the burgeoning relations between the Italian American vendor, Paulie (John Turturro), and the African American customer, Orin (Tyra Ferrell). Paulie is connected to Angie by growing up in the same neighborhood, and like Angie, he's a caretaker for his father, Lou (Anthony Quinn). And though Paulie and Angie date—more from having grown up together than from any romantic attraction—Paulie is attracted to Orin, who makes her daily visits to buy newspapers and to encourage Paulie to apply to college. At one point, Paulie asks Orin if she would ever consider going out with a white guy. Orin responds honestly that she's not sure. But rather than simply seeing each other as sex objects from another race, the two weigh the racial issue before dating. Perhaps this couple appears as a balance to the Flipper-Angie affair, and perhaps Lee is suggesting the possibilities of an interracial coupling. However, with Flipper and Angie's relationship taking the dominant position in the film, the filmmaker strongly underscores his bias against interracial relationships.

Although the film delivers two torrid sex scenes, Lee seems more comfortable directing scenes of conflict in this movie. The movie takes on another level of intensity, for example, when Drew throws Flipper's clothes into the street; when Paulie and his café buddies argue; when Angie's father physically beats her; and when Gator confronts his father. Lee's direction becomes sharper and more precise in such scenes of confrontation.

Jungle Fever could have been a remarkable film if given a fuller touch in the writing. Perhaps in this case, Lee would have done better simply to direct and to allow another writer to tackle the development of the central story line. Interestingly enough, one of the most memorable sequences of the film was actually improvised—the "black feminist" segment where Drew and her black women friends discuss, complain, and testify about the disappointments with black men in their lives. For this sequence, Lee uses simple high-angle shots, close-ups, and two-shots, allowing the women's dialogue and body language to connect to the audience. In this segment, less is better—less of Lee as a screenwriter and less obtrusive camera work.

Regardless of the weaknesses that surface in *Jungle Fever*, Lee accomplishes a unique motion picture with his best work, *Malcolm X* (1992). With this film, Lee not only took on his most costly project, but he tells the story of a controversial twentieth-century leader who has assumed a position as a mythical hero to many black and white Americans.

Bringing *Malcolm X* to the screen was Spike Lee's labor of love, and based on the $20 million or so put into the film by Warner Bros., Lee understood that he had to make a film that would have a considerable crossover appeal in order to be a box-office success. He eventually raised about $30 million in total by borrowing from a number of black celebrities such as Michael Jordan, Oprah Winfrey, and Janet Jackson as investors to complete the film.[13]

Lee decides to tell this three-hour-and-twenty-minute story in three sections, relying on his familiar production team—Monty Ross as coproducer, Ernest Dickerson as cinematographer, Terence Blanchard as music composer, and Wynn Thomas as production designer. The first section chronicles the criminal phase of Malcolm's life, with flashbacks fleshing out his background. The second section focuses on his prison time, where he educates himself and converts to the Nation of Islam. And the third section highlights his religious leadership, his political perspectives, and his assassination. Each section has its share of powerful moments, and each demonstrates the impressive growth of Malcolm's character as skillfully portrayed throughout by Denzel Washington.

One of the bolder aspects of the first section occurs at the beginning, when Lee uses the infamous news footage of the attack on Rodney King by Los Angeles police officers. These early images punctuate the documentary nature of the bio-drama and suggest that the contemporary status of black men in 1992 was not so far removed from the earlier decades of the 1940s–1960s covered within the film.

But one of the more dynamic relationships of the first section is that of Malcolm and West Indian Archie (Delroy Lindo), the king of the numbers who assists Malcolm in learning the trade. Lindo has a dynamic presence that complements Malcolm's eager gangsterism in this early phase of his life. Another important relationship develops between Malcolm and his sidekick Shorty (Spike Lee), who have a humorous but revealing episode with "conking" or straightening their hair, noting the then-popular endeavor of blacks to seek the hair appearance of whites. This hairstyle, along with Malcolm and Shorty's zoot suit apparel, befit Malcolm's early years when he was lost to his own cultural history and legacy. On the other hand, Malcolm and Shorty's intimacy with white women allows Lee to touch again upon the interracial taboo highlighted in *Jungle Fever*, as he gives the taboo its historical significance in the 1940s. The film suggests that the seven-year prison sentence Malcolm receives was due not to his burglary but to his conspicuous connection to white women.

The prison scenes carry a duller look to them—the warm colors and polished visuals of the first section have faded to a weary grayness. But this section brightens up through the character of Malcolm himself due to his en-lightenment as a self-educated man and as a religious convert. As Malcolm learns the power of words and reading, his insolent attitude modifies, and Washington shows the changes through nuances in voice, posture, and facial expression. The audience can actually see and hear the transformation from petty criminal to a thinking, purposeful man. At the same time, the prison scenes show Malcolm's attraction to the Nation of Islam as Baines (Albert Hall) leads Malcolm to a knowledge of the religion. Although criticized by some as an example of Lee's mishandling of factual issues—Malcolm was in reality led to his conversion by his bother and sister—the role of Baines symbolizes the successful efforts of the Nation of Islam in saving black males from crime-ridden pasts.

The final section holds a number of scenes that display the mature Malcolm, as Denzel Washington fills the camera with the dynamism of his performance, the forceful cadence of his voice, and the emotional strain of moving from religious follower to political leader. Although the sequences between Malcolm and his wife, Betty (Angela Bassett), hold warmth and sensitivity, the filmmaker is at his best with the larger scenes that cover Malcolm's speeches to ever growing crowds, his leading of the Fruit of Islam before the New York Police Department, his life-changing journey to Mecca, and his dignified courage when facing his impending death.

Lee directs the impressive sequence that presents Malcolm's journey to Mecca in a romantic but reverent manner. The crowded streets, the vistas of desert and dunes, and the dutiful praying of the hundreds of Muslim worshippers are showcased in a montage of images where softness and gracefulness match the tone and sincerity of Malcolm's odyssey. And, admirably, Lee's control as a director emerges in this section, as the filmmaker avoids some of his more self-conscious camera techniques to allow the film's content to take the priority. Rather than distract viewers from the main character and his story, Lee permits the viewer to come close to the title character and, in an empathetic way, to view his flaws and triumphs. Although Lee does utilize his isolation shot—a medium of Malcolm moving slowly toward the camera as he sits on a dolly—showing a thoughtful Malcolm on his way to the ballroom where he will be assassinated, Lee maintains a less obtrusive approach throughout the film. And in the bloody assassination, Lee refrains from showing Malcolm's death in a slow-motion ballet of sentimentality. Instead, through quick shots between Malcolm, his killers, and the chaotic crowd, Lee captures the brutal quickness and pain of Malcolm's final moments. Lee chooses to end the film with a reality-based sequence similar to that with which he began the film. Integrating documentary footage of Malcolm's actual funeral and a tribute by Ossie Davis, Lee then presents black South African leader Nelson Mandela speaking to a classroom of children about Malcolm.

Although Lee's labor of love received only two Academy Award nominations—for Denzel Washington as Best Actor and for Best Costumes[14]—and though it won neither one, Spike Lee had once again demonstrated a determination to complete a film project *his* way. And despite the fact that it was not a Hollywood blockbuster and that it received a mixture of critical reviews, Lee demonstrated that he could make an epic film as skillfully as an experimental film.

In contrast to the telling of the story of a public and cultural figure such as Malcolm X, Lee took the opposite direction in his next film, *Crooklyn* (1994). Returning to his familiar Brooklyn setting, in the early 1970s, Lee —cowriting with family members Joie Lee and Cinqué Lee—presents one of the few feature films that weighs the significance of the emotional and psychological shaping of a preadolescent black girl's life.

Troy Carmichael (Zelda Harris) is the only girl in a family of five children. That position provides her a special relationship with her father and mother, while guaranteeing an ongoing sibling hostility with her brothers. Carolyn (Alfre Woodard) is a mother who works outside of the home full-time, while trying to maintain the household's schedule and finances. Woody (Delroy Lindo), the father, has committed himself to the artistry of his music, not wanting to sell out by becoming a performer of popular tunes. Troy serves as a central consciousness in the film as the events are sifted through her young eyes and sensibilities. The urban neighborhood and its motley characters, the stress-filled marriage of her parents, the suburban ethics of her southern relatives, and the death of her mother—all of these major areas and events are framed by Troy's process of maturation, as she moves from a bratty kid to a responsible preteen.

Troy's world is a tough urban one, where children live without the benefit of clean air, green lawns, quiet evenings, and bicycle paths. Yet, her world is rich with multicultural voices, a sense of community, and a cohesive family. Although the mixture of African American, Latino, and Italian often presents clashes and arguments, there remains a sense of community in which Troy and her family are known and recognized. The kids who play on the streets possess different complexions, hair textures, and languages, which sometimes become a source of criticism; yet, an awareness of friendship and protection exists among the kids. In a related way, throughout the film, Lee overlays a continuous sound track of popular music of the historical time—the R&B, funk, reggae, and rock that forever flows from radios and singing voices. By integrating all of the multiculturalism and pop culture icons, Lee tells the audience that Troy is not deprived and alienated from the society around her. Despite the drugs on the street and the economic stress in her home, her life is still enriched by diverse people and shaped by some of the same ideologies as her white counterparts' lives might be. In other words, to be an urban black child does not necessarily mean that one is born into degradation; on the contrary, Lee suggests that Troy's concrete world is superior in numerous ways to the suburban, upper-middle-class environment that she visits in Maryland.

This contrast between the Brooklyn and Maryland environments is effected specifically by a visual distortion that makes the screen images appear elongated. Here, Lee is taking a rather bold approach to telling his story. Much more than just inserting a single stylized shot or short scene, Lee changes the aspect ratio for a long segment of the film, forcing the viewer to spend more than twenty minutes with the special effect. In essence, Troy's normal, enriching urban world has been replaced by an aberrant, confusing suburban setting. This segment of *Crooklyn* has been criticized the most by critics and moviegoers alike, as being too abrupt and overdone. However, it does work effectively as a successful blend of form and content, challenging the audience to engage the film on an active, intellectual level.

When Troy returns to Brooklyn, the aspect ratio returns to normal, as Troy confronts the tragedy of her mother's hospitalization and death by cancer. In this final segment of the film, Lee provides the most poignant moments while showing the transformation of Troy from a girl to a young woman. The funeral sequence, Troy's nightmare, and Troy's sitting in her mother's chair—all of these images work together in proclaiming Troy's coming of age.

Lee follows the intimacy of *Crooklyn* with a didactic saga of the urban mean streets in *Clockers* (1995). Lee had certainly emerged as one of the obvious choices of directors to do such a story about New York, and here he tells a story coscripted with Richard Price, the white author of the same-titled novel on which the film is based. The title comes from a term that "is slang for a small-time drug dealer who hustles around the clock,"[15] and the filmmaker's intent is to present the exploitive, violent, and dead-end life of teenage clockers. This intention is both the noble objective and, at the same time, the flaw in this overworked message film.

The opening credits of the movie are intentionally disturbing—color photograph stills of dead black youth, showing the bloody, bullet-ridden corpses in numerous crime scenes. As he does so effectively in his 1998 documentary film *4 Little Girls*, Lee tells a visual story filled with the sad truths of wasted young black lives. The opening alone carries such a powerful message that more restraint in what follows would have been better; instead, Lee attempts to top his initial images with the most graphic and violent film that he's made to date.

Strike (Mekhi Phifer) sits in an urban park listening to several teenagers debating the merits of sex and violence in rap music. Impatient with the frivolity of the conversation, Strike urges everyone to get back to work, and it becomes obvious as they take up appointed positions and attitudes that these teens are selling drugs. Strike, who suffers from ulcers, is ambitious, however, and he wants to get off the streets. Rodney (Delroy Lindo), the main dealer and father figure to the group of clockers, offers Strike the chance to leave the streets if he will kill Daryl (Steve White), the fast-food manager who has been cheating Rodney out of some of the money for drugs sold through the restaurant. Strike, however, is not a killer, and he attempts to get in touch with a hit man through his older brother Victor (Isaiah Washington), an emotionally stressed man working several jobs to support his wife, Sharon (Lisa Arrindell), and their children.

When Daryl winds up dead, two homicide detectives enter the story—Larry (John Turturro), a jaded Italian, and Rocco (Harvey Keitel), a Jewish-Italian cop who still professes values and a belief in the possible goodness of people. After a particularly grisly investigation of Daryl's body—where there are close shots of brains oozing from a cracked skull, bloody bullet holes, and a bullet lodged in the teeth—Rocco is determined to solve the murder.

Added to all of this, Strike befriends Tyrone (Pee Wee Love), a preadolescent boy who worships him despite the warnings of his mother (Regina Taylor) and Andre (Keith David), a black cop who dedicates himself to working with the neighborhood youth. In two pivotal twists in the story, young Tyrone shoots and kills a local thug, Errol (Thomas Jefferson Byrd), and Victor's mother (Frances Foster) proves that Victor's confession of killing Daryl is true. Rocco shapes Tyrone's killing as an accident, and he accepts Victor's plea of self-defense, allowing both black males to return to their families. For his part, Strike leaves the urban life of a clocker, riding away on a train, apparently off to see the world.

Clockers is a movie that *should* work effectively because it possesses some impressive elements—a superb cast, a gritty realism, and a contemporary story of triumph. Yet, despite the captivating cinematography by Malik Sayeed, the movie moves sluggishly and suffers from heavy-handed visuals that fail to enhance the story.

One of the first weaknesses stems from Strike's continual ulcer problems. In addition to drinking chocolate milk and downing over-the-counter medicines, the character Strike spends much of his time doubled-over in front of the camera as he spits out blood. The symbolic point of the ulcer is apparent early on, but Lee maintains such a stream of bloody coughing by Strike that it becomes disgusting to watch by the middle of the film.

A similar lack of subtlety is shown by Lee in a number of scenes where technique becomes distracting. One such scene occurs when Rocco is attempting to intimidate Strike in his park location for drug selling. As Rocco interrogates him, the camera holds them in a two-shot as it continually moves in a semicircle—from right to left, then from left to right, and back again. Although the camera movement is meant presumably to imply that Rocco is closing in on Strike as his prey, the resulting effect is seasickness. The camera movement intrudes on the dialogue and preoccupies viewers with the technique, rather than the scene's content.

A second example of a distracting camera happens later in the film, as Rocco shapes Tyrone's confession of killing Errol. As the young boy mumbles a motivation for the shooting, Rocco precedes to place words into Tyrone's mouth to structure a viable confession. As he does so, the camera cuts from the interrogation room to the park, where Rocco is also present. As he speaks directly to the audience, dictating the circumstances leading up to Errol's death, Rocco moves in a circle in the foreground while various clockers are shown in the background. It is a dizzying shot that calls attention to itself more so than to Rocco's words. Then, in the same sequence, a tracking shot gives a close profile of Tyrone riding his bike, but Rocco, still breaking the fourth wall, is attached by a seat to the moving bike. The result is a moving shot of both Tyrone and Rocco at the same time, though the former is in the past time and the latter is in the present. It is a creative shot, but its peculiar execution is abrupt and almost humorous.

Even though *Clockers* suffers from its imposition of form over content, the film's antidrug message provides it with a redeeming quality of good, albeit overbearing, intentions. However, with Lee's next film, *Girl 6* (1996), one is hard-pressed to discover a compelling reason to recommend the film. In spite of the remarkable performance by Theresa Randle in the lead role, the selected songs by Prince, and once again, the engaging cinematography of Malik Sayeed, *Girl 6* remains a muddled marathon of misery.

The script, written by black writer Suzan Lori Parks, tells the story of Judy (Randle), an aspiring black actress in New York who meets formidable barriers to working on the stage and in film. In the opening scene, despite her deft acting of a dramatic monologue, a New York film director (Quentin Tarantino) wants her to show her breasts as a part of the audition. Disgusted with the experience, she hurries from the office, passing a long line of black actresses waiting for their turn at the audition. Judy's agent (John Turturro) berates her for walking out of such an important audition, as does her acting coach, but Judy has principles and ambitions to be recognized for her acting talents. At her apartment building, she shares her frustrations with her next door neighbor and friend, Jimmy (Spike Lee), who supports her efforts. Needing a well-paying job, Judy interviews at two phone-sex services. The first one, located in an office building, is run by a take-charge black woman named Lil (Jenifer Lewis), and the second service is actually a home-based business organized by another boss (Madonna). Lil's service contains numerous women of different ethnicities and ages who, given numbers as names, conduct their fantasy-phone-sex conversations from their cubicles within a secured building. The other service requires Judy to phone from her apartment, engaging in more uninhibited fantasies and desires.

Up to this point, the film has been distinctive as both a chronicle on the extreme difficulties that black actresses face in gaining work in their field and the lure of a fantasy-sex business where women remain in control at all times. The juxtaposition of the two worlds speaks to the sexist standards in society: namely, black actresses remain powerless in the acting world where men dominate, while women maintain power in a world of sexual fantasies.

Judy, who shows intelligence enough to keep a distance from her shoplifter ex-husband (Isaiah Washington), falls victim to her own addiction to fantasies. In fact, the concept of falling pervades the movie. At one point, Judy's acting coach instructs her to "drop into the pain" to show emotions; similarly, when Judy first interviews with Lil, the latter is attempting to complete a crossword puzzle by finding a word that means "that falling feeling"— vertigo. Then, to further punctuate the concept of falling, the story contains a subplot about an eight-year-old Harlem girl, Angela King (Jacqueline McAllister), who falls down the elevator shaft of her tenement building. Judy becomes obsessed with this ongoing news story, and at various places as she sinks into her delusions, a cutaway shot shows the camera falling through an open elevator door and down into the darkened abyss.

Judy, for no apparent reason, stops going to auditions and begins to enjoy "acting" in the various phone-sex fantasies. Taking on the name of "Lovely Brown," Judy soon loses a grasp on reality and plunges into the phone character, who begins to dominate her life. Then, in another subplot, Judy, as Lovely Brown, becomes intrigued with a steady phone caller who is identified as Bob Regular (Peter Berg). At first, they talk about Bob's mother, who suffers from cancer, but eventually, they talk about seeing one another. They make a date to meet at Coney Island, and dressing up for the occasion, Judy waits all day for Bob, who never shows up. This fall into desperation makes the character appear rather stupid, though the first thirty minutes of the film have shown her to be principled, intelligent, and street-smart.

At the same time, another type of fantasy plays a significant part in Judy's life—specifically, her fantasy of being various black film and television personalities. In three separate sequences, as Judy stares at herself in the mirror, a freeze-frame occurs with her voiceover announcing her vision of being a well-known black woman character. First, she sees herself as Dorothy Dandridge portraying Carmen Jones in the 1954 film of the same title. The second daydream shows Judy as "Foxy Brown," a superheroine character from the 1970s "blaxploitation" film. Then, in a third fantasy, Judy becomes "Thelma," a character from the popular '70s television show *Good Times*. For some inexplicable reason, however, Thelma interacts with characters from another show of the same era—*The Jeffersons*. The problem with these three fantasies is that they do not move the story forward, particularly the third one that's based on television characters. Consequently, the sequences are not necessary, since such daydreams and whims could have been alluded to in Judy's dialogue with other characters. The most relevant fantasy would be the Dorothy Dandridge image because of the direct bearing it would have on Judy's efforts to break into film acting; consequently, the symbolic value of Dorothy Dandridge could have been interlaced throughout the film.

Toward the end of the film, Judy's fantasy world comes crashing down into a dangerous reality. Choosing to work for Madonna's home-sex business, Judy becomes embroiled with a sadistic caller (Michael Imperioli), who verbally abuses her and terrorizes her with his constant calls. At one point, when Judy reaches the bottom of her fantasy world, as she endures an emotional breakdown, the sadistic caller forces her to repeat his demeaning statements about her value and worth. Having lost control of the fantasy and become its victim, Judy is shown in Lee's distinctive isolation shot—a close view of her as she moves forward into the camera, along a narrow hallway washed in reds and greens, that suggest her confusion between stopping and going.

The movie should have ended at this juncture. However, as Judy is leaving the city, her ex-husband arrives, and standing in the middle of the street, they embrace and kiss passionately. During this lengthy and unexplained kiss that's shown in a long shot, numerous telephones fall from the sky onto the street around the couple—pink, blue, and white in color. What does it all mean?

Then, in Los Angeles, a director (Ron Silver) is impressed by her reading, but casually asks her to remove her top. Essentially, Judy has gone full circle, and she walks out of the audition. And in a final shot, Judy steps over the sidewalk star of Dorothy Dandridge on Hollywood Boulevard, as she crosses the street to the Mann's Chinese film theater, where the marquee shows that the film being shown is *Girl 6*.

Lee obviously wants his audience to make a certain leap in viewing *Girl 6*, and, no doubt, he believes he is offering an interesting journey into the emotional and psychological arenas of a contemporary black woman following her dreams and fantasies. But with the incoherence of the film and the inconsistencies in his protagonist, the filmmaker is off target and ineffective.

Fortunately, Spike Lee finds material that is more suitable for his talents in his next film, *Get on the Bus* (1996), which is one of Lee's most outstanding works. The film contains themes and characters that find completion in Lee's sensibilities as an independent filmmaker. Ironically, it has become one of his least seen feature films, as its theater run elapsed quickly despite the film's timely focus.

With a script by black writer-director Reggie Bythewood, the story presents the bus journey made by about twenty black men from Los Angeles to Washington, D.C., in order to attend the 1995 Million Man March. As the characters make their way across America, the audience takes an odyssey through the lives of sixteen of these men who present a variety of perspectives, proving that there are commonalities and differences among black men. With an ensemble cast of black actors, anchored by the veteran Ossie Davis, Lee manages to explore a plethora of issues that have no simple solutions for the men on the bus or, by inference, for society at large.

During the opening credits, the camera slowly moves among close shots of a black man in manacles, as the song "Put Your Heart on the Line," written by Kenneth "Babyface" Edmonds, is sung by Michael Jackson. The poignancy of the song coupled with the visuals of a chained man work effectively to emphasize the fetters the American system have imposed upon black masculinity. From there, the film opens with a father literally chained to his son as they argue about getting onto the bus. Evan Thomas (Thomas Jefferson Byrd), holding a court order to keep his son, Junior (De'Aundre Bonds), tethered to him for a 72-hour period, insists that they will be making the trip together across the country, regardless of the teen's angry resistance. These two serve as an important symbol beyond their father-son relationship; as other men on the bus comment on Junior's chains, they question both the legitimacy of the disciplinary action and the power of the legal system to order such a restraint.

A number of historical, political, and cultural issues echo throughout the film, as the other characters are eventually revealed. George (Charles S. Dutton) is the bus supervisor and the spiritual drum major of the men; Flip (Andre Braugher) is an egotistical, misogynist, and homophobic actor; Gary (Roger Guenveur Smith) is a biracial L.A.P.D. officer; Jamal (Gabriel Casseus) is a former gang member turned Muslim; Kyle (Isaiah Washington) is a gay Republican just emerging from the closet; Randall (Harry Lennix) is educated and Kyle's former lover; Xavier (Hill Harper) is a university film student who is videotaping the trip; Craig (Albert Hall) is the assistant bus driver, who isn't allowed to complete the trip to the March; Wendell (Wendell Pierce) is a loud-mouthed Republican businessman who sees only the negative in black people; Jay (Bernie Mac) is a young, struggling small businessman; and Rick (Richard Belzer) is the Jewish bus driver reluctant to drive a busload of black men to a March supported by Black Muslim leader Louis Farrakhan.

But at the center of this group is the eldest member, Jeremiah (Ossie Davis), who is the griot and heart of the men. One key connection occurs between Jeremiah and Xavier, as Jeremiah teaches him how to finger the African drum. Having provided a cultural significance to the drum by telling its oral history, Jeremiah educates the university student in the affection that one must bring to the drum in order to allow the drums to speak. Like the Evan-Junior relationship, the Jeremiah-Xavier bond serves as a metaphor for the history and continuation of African American culture and community. Jeremiah passes along the drum—an instrument of cultural communication, musical expression, and personal expression—to the younger student.

While being videotaped, Jeremiah explains his reasons for making the trip. Having decided to miss the 1963 March on Washington in order to be a good "Negro" who worked hard for his company, Jeremiah found himself being passed over for promotion. After thirty-three years and a pink slip, he begged to retain his job at a 30 percent pay cut. But when a corporate takeover occurred, during the resulting downsizing Jeremiah became jobless— leading to alcoholism, a lost family, and a lost life. For Jeremiah, the Million Man March becomes the miracle he needs to change his life—a final atonement and redemption that will connect him to his inner self and to other black men. In his own words, Jeremiah is seeking a miracle. Ironically, Jeremiah never makes it to the March, dying of heart complications on the way. Jeremiah's death and the written prayer he leaves behind link the men as a community rather than the collection of individuals they were at the start. Going to the Lincoln Memorial, they hold their own vigil, remembering Jeremiah and, as George urges, remembering the responsibility that each must take to transform himself and the black community upon returning home.

After their vigil, at the foot of the Lincoln statue, the camera lingers on the chain-tethers that have been left behind by Evan and Junior.

To his credit, Spike Lee gives notable portions of the film to dealing with the homophobic attitude among the men. At first, a collective sigh of rejection of the gay characters is shared among the men, but through Flip's continual wisecracks and demeaning statements, the vulgar gay bashing becomes intolerable to most of them. Both Kyle and Randall respond to Flip's taunts, each asserting various perspectives that call attention to their double bind—being discriminated against due to their race and their sexual orientation. By the time Kyle and Flip engage in a physical fight at a rest area, everyone is cheering for Kyle to defeat Flip and all the prejudice that he represents.

In another topical area, one issue discussed revolves around the exclusion of black women from the Million Man March. Lee, a director often accused of presenting flawed women characters, appears to be conscious of addressing this point in the film. When the audience first meets Gary, he is arguing with his girlfriend because she opposes his attending a sexist event. But Gary emphasizes the need for black men to examine themselves before assuming a future leadership role in the family and community. Later in the film, at a rest area in Little Rock, Arkansas, two African American women converse with Gary and Flip, where one also takes offense that black women have been excluded. The other woman, however, recognizes the need for black men to attend the March for personal improvement and male unity. Like other issues in the film, one simple response does not answer all questions, but the acknowledgment of diverse responses affirms the vital need for further discussion.

One of the challenges of shooting the film is that much of it takes place in the interior of a moving bus. The confined space runs the risk of being claustrophobic, but by using an abundance of natural light, close-ups, two-shots, reverse angles, and askew angles, Lee prevents a tediousness from setting in. Lee also juxtaposes key lighting in an impressive manner in one particular sequence. Early on in the film, the day's natural light and the evening's streetlights bathe the interior of the bus, but later, when the bus is pulled over by two white Tennessee highway patrolmen at night, the lighting changes dramatically. Coming aboard the bus with a drug-sniffing dog, the white patrolmen aim the bright flashlight on each individual's face in the bus, a spotlight suggesting suspicion of criminal activity and the exercise of control by the white officers. Even when Gary steps forward, identifying himself as a police office by showing his badge, the patrolmen reject any code of fraternity as law officers and reduce Gary to the level of everyone else—all black "boys" and subsequently all potential criminals, who must follow orders of the white officers. In the aftermath, as the bus pulls away in the shadowy, diffused light, the viewer can see the anger and disgust of the black men following their humiliation.

Lee is just as successful with integrating both recorded and performed music in the film. As the bus leaves Los Angeles, George pops in a cassette tape of James Brown singing "Papa Don't Take No Mess," and all the men join in a unified burst of male affirmation. Then, at the end, when they finally arrive in Washington, D.C., having endured the emotionally draining experiences along the way, Curtis Mayfield's "We're a Winner" blasts over the quick cuts capturing the crowded highways of black men in vehicles carrying banners and statements of pride and unity. Additionally, Lee adds vigor to the film by incorporating the collective singing of the men on the bus. Rough and awkward—the men's singing injects a sense of "realness" and raw energy to particular scenes. For example, in the early stages of the film, the men share a "roll call" song, where a nonsense chorus is sung followed by an individual crooning an emotionally expressive rhymed verse. Similarly, when the bus breaks down, Gary pulls out his acoustic guitar and delivers a spontaneous verse about the incident; in turn, several of the men take a turn and contribute a rhymed verse.

The aspects of improvisation, documentary, and factual events merge effectively in a contemporary exploration of African American men. Lee balances the messages and the medium in an engaging manner, while presenting an ensemble of characters who possess their individual qualities and their communal concerns. Lee obviously believes in the redeeming aspects of this film, seeing in the various stories of the black male characters the many emotions and sensibilities present among all people.

Spike Lee has accomplished a number of significant things with his film career. First of all, he has provided mainstream audiences with examinations of black cultural life and interaction across ethnic and racial lines. In addition, Lee single-handedly established a repertory company of actors who would come to be appreciated for the depths and diversity of their skills —Denzel Washington, Laurence Fishburne, Giancarlo Esposito, Samuel L. Jackson, Wesley Snipes, Isaiah Washington, Delroy Lindo, John Turturro, Bill Nunn, Roger Smith, and Thomas Jefferson Byrd. At the same time, despite his limited parts for women characters, he still provided mainstream audiences with some of the freshest faces of talented women of color, such as Tracy Camilla Johns, Rosie Perez, Halle Berry, Cynda Williams, Joie Lee, Tisha Campbell, Annabella Sciorra, Tyra Ferrell, and Theresa Randle. To Lee's credit, he has also provided some veteran actors with roles that have highlighted their remarkable abilities—Ossie Davis, Ruby Dee, Danny Aiello, Lonette McKee, Al Freeman Jr., Dick Anthony Williams, Frances Foster, Charles S. Dutton, Alfre Woodard, and Harvey Keitel.

However, Lee's greatest influence behind the camera has been the manner in which he has helped to open the possibilities for other black directors. Never losing his perspective on the necessity of having black directors at the helm of a film project, each time Lee has fought for control of his film, he has been fighting for the opportunity for other black directors to have their chance to enter the tightly closed doors of Hollywood. Always an advocate for black filmmakers—sometimes to the point of irritation—Lee has maintained an integrity and vision that have resulted in a body of films that have, collectively, made an impact upon Hollywood's depiction of black culture and the industry's recognition of the black director.

CHAPTER SEVEN

Keeping It Real (Reel): Black Dramatic Visions

Among the thirty-five or so black directors whose work has appeared in the 1990s, about thirteen have made dramatic films that call attention to the serious content, as well as the technical merits, of their works. The extent of the box-office appeal and the storytelling success varied among the thirteen directors, but their films, collectively, address the vital need to assess African American culture, experiences, and characters in ways that recognize black people as complex human beings.

Charles Burnett

I have no interest to do cars banging into each other; I don't have the talent to pull off that sort of thing. . . . Most of the films I like to do aren't very commercial. They're not high concept. They're hard to pitch to executives. They're character-driven and theme-driven. I mean, I'm not trying to be sophisticated, but my movies are not designed for 18-year-olds.[1]

Charles Burnett

In many ways, Charles Burnett does not belong in a discussion concerning Hollywood films. For Burnett, a seasoned and experienced filmmaker, his preference for low-budget, independent films has given him a distinguished status as an artist. Unfortunately, his lack of visibility among mainstream audiences, both black and nonblack, has kept his work in the shadows of '90s films that examine black experiences.

Although he grew up in Watts, Burnett was born in Vicksburg, Virginia, in 1944. While studying theater arts at UCLA, he made a student film in 1969 titled *Several Friends* and a fourteen-minute graduate-level film, *The Horse*, completing the university's film school as one of several black independent directors, such as Haile Gerima and Larry Clark, and later Julie Dash and Sharon Larkin.[2]

As writer, director, and cinematographer, his independent first feature, *Killer of Sheep* (1977), was "the powerful story of a slaughterhouse worker who tries to make more of his life than merely a waiting room for death."[3]

There was no commercial distribution, but the film received enough critical attention to help him win a Guggenheim Fellowship.[4] The award money went into completing his next independent feature, *My Brother's Wedding* (1983), "a tragic comedy that . . . focuses on a young man who hasn't made much of his life."[5]

In 1988, Burnett won the coveted MacArthur Foundation genius grant, which awarded him $275,000 for five years,[6] allowing him to pursue his kind of filmmaking without the usual fiscal worries. He applied some of his money to making his first commercially released feature, *To Sleep with Anger* (1990).

In addition to the fictional films he directed, Burnett served as writer and cinematographer on the independent film *Bless Their Little Hearts* (1984), and he cowrote and directed the documentary *America Becoming* (1991), which looked at the cultural diversity of immigrants arriving in the United States.[7] Then in 1995 Burnett wrote and directed his most recent commercial film, *The Glass Shield.*

With his first commercial feature, *To Sleep with Anger*, Burnett presents a rather enigmatic film that connects with an audience in tune with mythological and symbolic storytelling. One film scholar suggests that the film explores the "twin themes of innocence and ambiguity" where "masked evil" enters the life of a middle-class black family.[8] These particular themes are not new to Hollywood films, but certainly Burnett's writing and his visual techniques make this unconventional story inaccessible to a mainstream audience.

The opening credits exemplify Burnett's unusual handling of the visual story. Under the written text and a bluesy gospel song, a fifty-ish black man, later identified as Gideon, sits at a table rather stiffly in a white suit and shoes. The table bears a small bowl of fruit, and in the background above the table is a portrait of an elderly black woman. The camera pans from Gideon to the portrait and down to the bowl of fruit. Suddenly inside the bowl a flame appears, burning conspicuously but not consuming the fruit. Then, there's a cut to the table legs that begin to burn in flames, and over to Gideon's shoes that are also caught in flames. Panning up to a medium shot, the flames appear across Gideon's chest, as he closes his eyes to sleep. A dissolve shows Gideon sitting in a backyard, where he's barefooted and wearing jeans and a T-shirt.

Without any characters named or any established connections, this opening seems eccentric and confusing, particularly with the burning flames that don't consume. With the dissolve to Gideon, it appears the character has been dreaming the opening sequence, but it's unclear. The aspects of uncertainty, mystery, and complexity permeate the film, making it intellectually engaging but cold and ponderous.

In general, the story looks at a black middle-class family in Los Angeles, where the southern-rooted parents, Gideon (Paul Butler) and Suzie (Mary Alice), interact with their adult sons, Babe Brother (Richard Brooks) and Junior (Carl Lumbly). The rivalry between the brothers becomes apparent, as Babe Brother and his aloof wife, Linda (Sheryl Lee Ralph), prefer money to the southern ways and family traditions. Junior and his pregnant wife, Pat (Vonetta McGee), blend in more easily, shunning materialism in their closeness to Gideon and Suzie. Into this already troubled scenario comes an old southern friend, Harry (Danny Glover), filled with memories of the old days, but he slowly ignites friction and animosity among family members and numerous friends. Harry is both superstitious and devilish as he brings a negative spirit into the lives of the other characters. The family and their friends suffer various traumas—for example, Gideon's stroke and the near-fatal fight between Babe Brother and Junior—but as the film ends, Harry dies in a freak accident as he slips on some discarded toy marbles. Unable to get rid of Harry's body, the family must maneuver around the corpse, which cannot be moved, due to the city's bureaucracy, for several days as it lies in the doorway of the kitchen. Yet, the family does carry on, and it survives despite the evil that Harry brought with him.

In *To Sleep with Anger* the writer-director is urging the audience to examine the inner workings of multigenerational, familial relationships in a different way. At the same time, the story utilizes certain southern traditions and superstitions to highlight particular black cultural elements—some that should be remembered but not necessarily applied to modern black life.

But the film is most effective when focusing on the family, and one of the strongest sequences occurs when the family's confrontation peaks. During the scene, a storm rages outside, as Babe Brother, Junior, and their families come to visit the ailing Gideon. When Junior discovers that Babe Brother refuses to assist Suzie in moving Gideon's bed, the brothers engage in a hostile argument. Jumping from medium shots to tight shots where characters fill the frame, the argument escalates into a physical fight, and Babe Brother pulls out a knife. But Junior's anger dominates, and as he is about to force the knife into his brother's chest, the women rush in, and Suzie grabs the knife by the blade to prevent one brother from killing the other. In that moment of terror, Burnett holds on to the two brothers atop the kitchen table, surrounded by the women who try to pull them apart. Every face strains with pain until a shocked Suzie realizes the knife cutting into her hands.

Later, at the hospital, Suzie manages to smile triumphantly as she watches the brothers talking and laughing with one another again. The layered meanings and powerful images in this segment are captivating, yet this degree of coherence isn't maintained throughout the film. This inconsistency diminishes the possible greatness of the film, leaving more frustration than satisfaction for the audience.

Four years later, Burnett completed another feature that manages to weave a more open and political story. *The Glass Shield* (1995) looks at the culture of law enforcement and how its immoral and racist practices can destroy those who swear to uphold the law, regardless of their ethnicity or good intentions. Basing his script on another screenplay of a true story, Burnett develops characters and situations that force viewers to take a side on various issues, making it impossible to hide behind a neutral position.

At the center of the story, JJ Johnson (Michael Boatman), a new recruit into the Edgemar Sheriff's Department, dreams of being a peace officer, and his girlfriend and later fiancée, Barbara (Victoria Dillard), patiently supports his efforts, though she has some reservations. Another new recruit, Deborah Fields (Lori Petty), being a woman and Jewish, warns JJ of the problems she has already faced at the Edgemar police station, but JJ, a bit of a sexist himself, brushes off her cautionary statements. But as the white watch commander, Clarence Massey (Richard Anderson), comes down hard on JJ for any petty mistakes, and as two white detectives, Gene Baker (Michael Ironside) and Jesse Hall (M. Emmet Walsh), constantly exhibit their arrogant resentments about blacks and women, JJ senses that an inner circle of hatred definitely exists. But to be one with his fellow white officers, JJ refrains from questioning the suicide of a black inmate and looks the other way when arresting officers allow a police dog to attack a perpetrator. JJ even lies in court to back up a colleague, Deputy Jack Bono (Don Harvey), when a black youth, Teddy Woods (Ice Cube), is charged with killing a white woman in a foiled carjacking.

Discovering that Detectives Baker and Hall have altered reports and the serial number of the handgun belonging to Woods, JJ conducts an investigation of the Edgemar station, anonymously feeding information to James Locket (Bernie Casey), the black lawyer representing Teddy Woods. Woods wins his freedom, bringing a crackdown on the Edgemar station, but not before Deputy Bono informs the D.A.'s office that JJ perjured himself. Bono gets immunity, but JJ faces a trial as the film ends. With the clear and honest criticisms from his fiancée, Barbara, JJ painfully realizes that his positive action in exposing the racism and corruption at the sheriff's department could not absolve him from his decision to commit perjury.

Charles Burnett, center, orchestrates a shot for his protagonist, JJ
Johnson (Michael Boatman, far right in uniform), in *The Glass Shield*.
Courtesy of The Museum of Modern Art/Film Stills Archive.

Burnett's hard and unflinching look at the racial, economic, social, and moral issues in this film make it an outstanding work. Burnett and Boatman provide the JJ character with admirable, if naive, qualities that make his fall into conformity painful and believable. JJ's passion to become a uniformed officer distorts his perceptions of the situations around him. He refuses to believe that after working hard and making it inside the system that that same system will not fully embrace him.

One of the many sequences that work effectively occurs after JJ appears in court to admit to the corruption that he's seen. Wearing his deputy uniform, he gives his testimony proudly. Then, when Watch Commander Massey takes the stand, his testimony, with its resentment against affirmative action, is juxtaposed with a quick cut to the men's room. There, still in his uniform, JJ sees the word "nigger" written in large letters across the mirror. Then, a cut back to Massey shows him talking about the integrity of the Edgemar station. It is a simple but powerful moment for both JJ and the audience.

Burnett's films demonstrate that he doesn't shy away from presenting themes based on cultural and political issues. At the same time, he has no reservations about tackling those issues in a style that might not be digestible by a mainstream audience. From his years as a documentary filmmaker, Burnett has, no doubt, learned that the audiences for his films might indeed be smaller. But regardless of who is in that audience, Burnett will encourage viewers to experience the film with their intellect as well as emotions.

John Singleton

American films serve to take black people and dehumanize them . . . to make black characters who are one-dimensional. But everything I do is in opposition to that. I try to make all the characters in my movies multi-dimensional.[9]

John Singleton

The impact of John Singleton as a black director in Hollywood has been remarkable. On the strength of his first feature, *Boyz N the Hood* (1991), Singleton became the first black director to be nominated for an Academy Award. Such a tribute makes a statement about his impression upon the established Hollywood community.

Born in Los Angeles in 1968, Singleton was nine years old when his father took him to see the film *Star Wars*, an experience that convinced the boy he wanted to grow up and make movies.[10] Since his parents were unmarried, Singleton spent time living with both. When he turned twelve, he moved in with his father, a mortgage broker, whom Singleton describes as similar to the Furious Styles character in *Boyz N the Hood*. In high school Singleton began to take an interest in writing, so that when he entered the film school at the University of Southern California, his scriptwriting was his strongest talent. While still in college, he obtained internships, working first as a production assistant on the television children's show, *Pee-Wee's Playhouse*, and then as a directing intern of *The Arsenio Hall Show*. But it was his internship at Columbia Studios that enabled him eventually to get his script of *Boyz N the Hood* to the studio head, Frank Price. With Price's support, Singleton was also able to negotiate directing the film even though he had little experience behind the camera.[11]

Boyz N the Hood remains one of the most reviewed and discussed films of the 1990s. The success of the film can be measured in a number of ways, even as the major weaknesses of the film stem from the same flaw found in other Singleton films—his flat characterizations of women. The timing of the film's appearance, on the heels of Spike Lee's opening of the Hollywood doors, was advantageous. With Lee's New York focus in his films, Singleton offered an inner-city vision of Los Angeles that had not been previously shown.

Emphasizing the relationship between a father and son, *Boyz N the Hood* shows the positive results when a father figure remains present throughout a male's adolescence. The preteen protagonist, Tre, is taken by his mother to live full-time with his father, Furious (Laurence Fishburne). Furious, a mortgage broker, cherishes the responsibility of laying down the rules and limitations for his son. Tre's good friends are brothers who live across the street—Doughboy (Ice Cube) and Ricky (Morris Chestnut). Doughboy, who is eventually arrested for stealing, does not receive the same affection from his mother, Mrs. Baker (Tyra Ferrell). And always lurking as a formidable character interacting with all three boys is the street environment, where dead bodies, gang members, and hostile neighborhoods prevail. The story jumps forward when the three boys are in their late teens: Tre (Cuba Gooding Jr.) holds a job and plans to go to college; Ricky, a father himself now, is an outstanding athlete and hopes for a college scholarship; and Doughboy is an experienced thug who sells drugs.

Tre's life is a balancing act between adhering to his father's teachings, hanging out with his friends, and attempting to be intimate with his girlfriend, Brandi (Nia Long). When Ricky is shot and killed by gang members, both Tre and Doughboy desire revenge. Disobeying his father's orders, Tre sneaks out and joins Doughboy and other homies to drive the city streets in search of Ricky's killers. But despite his anger, Tre knows that to seek revenge is wrong. Tre gets out of the car, but Doughboy and the others eventually find and kill the shooter. With a rift between him and his father, Tre knows he'll have to earn back the trust that he once had, and as the film ends, Doughboy encourages Tre to go to college, even as Doughboy realizes his short future is there on the streets of the inner city.

As a director, Singleton takes viewers not only into an inner-city neighborhood that he knows well, but into the language, confusion, and difficulties of the teenage years. One notable section presents the teens all hanging out in their cars, socializing and showing off their rides and male bravado. The friction that occurs erupts into violence as gunshots go off and chaos takes over the avenue. In another scene, Tre returns to his house from a cookout, and abruptly he's confronted by a car of black males, one of whom aims a shotgun at Tre, before the vehicle moves on. The tension happens quickly and frightfully, as the viewer senses how volatile the neighborhood can be.

Some of the more memorable scenes happen between Tre and Furious, as father and son talk about numerous topics. The love between the two is evident, and the emphasis on such a positive bond is rare in recent films. However, one questionable segment with the two occurs when Tre lies to his father about losing his virginity. In a visual montage that uses Tre's voice-over, viewers see Tre meeting and then bedding a voluptuous young black woman, until he's forced to flee through an opened window. The sequence, though Tre's fantasy, seems out of place and unnecessary, adding again to a criticism that the black women characters seem to be rather shallow as either sex objects or emotionally abusive mothers. Granted, Brandi as an exception to the other women characters does have her specific ambitions to avoid pregnancy and go to college, but her eventual decision to become sexually intimate with a distraught Tre suggests that she's having sex to comfort him and not for her own benefit as well.

Some of the critical comments aimed at Singleton's women characters no doubt reached the director's ear, because in his next film he tries to rectify the situation. *Poetic Justice* (1993) ventures forth to explore the passions, strengths, and longings of a young inner-city black woman.

The protagonist, Justice (Janet Jackson), playfully fights off her aroused boyfriend as the two sit in the front car seat at a drive-in movie. When the boyfriend returns from buying food at the concession stand, he's shot in the head, presumably by gang rivals. After that loss, Justice places all her emotions into her poetry, and focuses on her job at a hair salon, where the owner, Jessie (Tyra Ferrell), serves as her friend and older sister. Jessie tells Justice to move on with her life and find a new love, as does Justice's best friend, Iesha (Regina King).

A young mail carrier, Lucky (Tupac Shakur), busily puts the moves on Justice without any success. With the friendship of Chicago (Joe Torry), Lucky deals with more serious problems—hassles on the job and conflicts with his former drug-addicted lover with whom he's had a daughter, Keisha (Shannon Johnson).

A hairstyling show and a mail delivery run to Oakland bring the four main characters together: Chicago and Isha are involved, while Justice and

Lucky are reluctantly paired. The journey from Los Angeles to the Bay Area sizzles with scatological arguments and physical fights. But along the way, Justice and Lucky connect emotionally. Separated after an argument in Oakland, eventually Lucky comes around, bringing his daughter to the salon to meet Justice. As the film ends, Justice begins to style Keisha's hair, exchanging promising smiles with Lucky.

In the '90s, it was the exploration of black manhood that was the norm in movie after movie, and unfortunately, in *Poetic Justice* Singleton's writing fails to authenticate the female protagonist. Justice, never fully developed, eludes our understanding. There are references to a benevolent grandmother and an alcoholic mother, and there are moments when she reflects upon going to college. But the middle portion of the film presents her as such a screaming, cussing, strident woman that her qualities are muddled, and we cannot grasp her motivations.

In all fairness, there are those places where Singleton's writing and directing merge well. After the killing of Justice's boyfriend, Singleton presents an effective montage that combines emotions and social awareness. As Justice's voiceover reads a poem, entitled "Nobody can make it out here alone," she visits a cemetery, attends a cosmetology class, drives a graffiti-sprayed street of the inner city, and walks along a sidewalk where cops harass black teens. These images show Justice's inner-city world, as well as the importance of her poetry as a survival tool. With the poignant poem being read over, viewers can sense her inner emotions and her growing wisdom.

Later in the film, as the four characters make their contentious journey to Oakland, they are drawn by the aroma of barbecue to the "Johnson Family Reunion," where Lucky pretends to be a distant cousin. In this section, poet Maya Angelou makes a cameo appearance as Aunt June, bemoaning the "kids today" and their lack of parental teaching and knowledge of what is "right." It is also here at the reunion where the ice breaks between Justice and Lucky; the two begin to open up and communicate. But the symbolic value here, as Singleton's camera gives glimpses of the reunion, exists in the sense of family that has been alien to the four characters. Here in the rural setting, the four urban youth attempt to blend into something that has been missing from all of their lives—a kinship with others who care for and extend themselves to one another.

Singleton's directing appears much more proficient in *Poetic Justice* than his writing. This same observation holds true for his next film, *Higher Learning* (1995), an ambitious but enigmatic film. In *Higher Learning* Singleton focuses on another environment that he knows well—the American university, where undergrads of diverse backgrounds and varied levels of emotional maturity are thrown together.

In California, at Columbus University, a number of students begin the academic semester: Malik (Omar Epps), a black track runner; Kristen (Kristy Swanson), a white suburbanite; Deja (Tyra Banks), an ambitious black track star; Remy (Michael Rapaport), an emotionally confused youngster from the Midwest; Taryn (Jennifer Connelly), a white feminist activist; Fudge (Ice Cube), a black politically minded upperclassman; Monet (Regina King), an easygoing black co-ed; and Wayne (Jason Wiles), a good-hearted white liberal. At the center of these disparate students is Professor Maurice Phipps (Laurence Fishburne), a caring, but demanding political science instructor. The story focuses mostly on the lives of Malik and Kristen, but in several quick shifts, the film tries to develop the experiences of all the other characters mentioned. The result is a film that seems disjointed at some points and elliptical at others. Just when viewers might want more detail about one character, the emphasis moves to another character. Then, when the characters connect due to their status as classmates or roommates, the script still withholds certain information from the audience, leaving far too many unanswered questions.

In a crucial part of the movie, an intoxicated Kristen is raped by a white fraternity brother. She returns to her dorm and confesses what happened to Monet, her roommate. The white fraternity brother phones, insisting on speaking to Kristen, but when Monet refuses, he calls Monet a "black bitch." Monet goes directly to Fudge, who leads a black posse, with Kristen and Monet in tow, to crash the white fraternity party. Kristen points out the fraternity brother who raped her, and Fudge and the posse drag him outside onto the lawn, forcing the frightened white student to apologize to Monet for the name-calling. Somewhere in the fray, however, Fudge and the posse seem to have forgotten that Kristen was raped. The white fraternity brother was guilty on two counts, but the film implies that the most serious was the name-calling.

Another problematic situation revolves around Professor Phipps, who interacts with both Kristen and Malik, though more so with the latter. Throughout the film, viewers never gain insights into the professor's personal life; he appears to live in his office or the classroom. Does he do research or work in the community? Does he have a family? Does he spend as much time counseling his own children as he does his students? The character functions as an intellectual voice, a political voice, and a fathering voice all at once, and certainly Laurence Fishburne lives up to the task of all three.

Unfortunately, the story keeps his character on a shelf, bringing him out when needed to drop some thoughtful ideas whenever the movie loses pace.

Singleton is at his best with two visually stimulating sequences where just the camera and images provide the clearest messages. In one montage, Kristen finds herself romantically attracted to both Taryn, the feminist, and Wayne, the liberal. In a tight two-shot, viewers see the two women embrace and kiss; then Taryn leans back out of the frame, and when Kristen moves forward for another kiss, she now kisses Wayne. As the two become naked under the covers, the faces of the lovers change again so that Kristen is beneath the covers with Taryn. This smooth editing is done in a lyrical manner that maintains the same intensity of desire for both lovers. In other words, though Kristen seems torn between Taryn and Wayne, she holds a similar affection for them both.

Later, in a climactic sequence, Singleton focuses on a peace rally held on the quad and attended by the major characters. Remy, who has left school and joined a neo-Nazi group, perches himself on a building's rooftop with a rifle. Amid Kristen's speech about peace, Remy opens fire, and the crowd scatters chaotically. From various angles, cutting from Remy to the unarmed crowd, Singleton captures the horror of the violent moments. In the barrage Deja is shot, and dying in her own blood, she screams, "Why?" With a sound effect, her voice amplifies, reverberating the disturbing question across the quad area.

Higher Learning flows from the director's didactic motives, as he, no doubt, wants to present a serious look at the challenging issues confronting university students. His questions about race, gender, class, and personal identity are weighty concerns that definitely deserve a cinematic treatment. His tight shots of the American flag in the opening and closing of the film indict the entire society. The word "unlearn," which is typed across the screen over the American flag in the final shot, punctuates the director's urging for peaceful coexistence. But a film that raises question after question, without moving the characters in a clear way toward some answers, becomes exasperating.

In 1997 Singleton completed his most impressive film to date—the intense historical drama *Rosewood.* The film provides a version of the actual incidents surrounding the 1922–23 racial conflict in Florida between the black citizens of Rosewood and the white inhabitants of the nearby town of Sumner.

Coexisting in their contiguous but segregated worlds, blacks and whites pursue their separate lives. The Carrier family—a black extended family including Sylvester (Don Cheadle) and his mother Sarah (Esther Rolle)—serves

Sylvester (Don Cheadle, left) contemplates a survival strategy with Mann (Ving Rhames) in *Rosewood*.

as the center of the Rosewood community. Sylvester is a teacher, while his mother does domestic duties for whites, including the Taylors, a young married couple. Significantly poised between both black and white communities is John Wright (Jon Voight), a white businessman whose general store resides in Rosewood. Early on, Wright, a married man, enjoys an affair with Sylvester's cousin Jewel (Akosua Busia) and enjoys business success among his black customers.

Then, amid the notice that an escaped black convict may be in the area, a black stranger with a bold attitude and money rides his horse into town. This stranger, named Mann (Ving Rhames), is charismatic, direct, and self-assured—an obvious problem for a number of whites, including Mr. Wright, who discovers that Mann is competing with him to buy several acres of property. Added to this mix is the emotionally troubled Fannie Taylor (Catherine Kellner), a white woman who's unsatisfied with her marriage and life. After she's beaten by her white lover—an incident witnessed by Sarah—Fannie makes up a story that a black man attacked her. Hearing Fanny's accusations, the white community explodes into violence and destruction which lasts for several days, leaving over 150 people dead, according to the film's postcaptions.

Once the film evolves into the heightened racial hatred of mob justice over Fannie's alleged rape, the pacing and tone of the film shifts to another level. Singleton overwhelms viewers with frenetic, intense sequences that expose the madness and brutality of the mindless lynchers: burnings, beatings, hangings, shootings, and torture. Singleton presents humanity at its basest, showing the extremes to which racism plunges human behavior. Similarly, he provides heroes, particularly black heroes who, despite fear and being outnumbered, stand fast against a tide of violence.

One sequence offers a look at both the rhythm of the film, as well as the heroic qualities of Sarah and Sylvester. During a second night of violence, Singleton crosscuts between the mob's growing frenzy on the exterior and a youngster's birthday party being held at the Carrier house in a brightly lit interior. The angry, torch-bearing lynchers contrast sharply with the frightened cries of unarmed children taking cover on the floor. As Sylvester gathers his weapons to confront the mob alone, Sarah steps onto the porch to address the men. Between the porch and the fence is the front yard, a visual chasm between the white and black worlds. And even as Sarah informs the mob about the white lover, the bloodlust increases, as Sarah is gunned down. Sylvester drags his dying mother inside, sends the children and women into the swamp, and returns to face the mob.

Later in the film, Singleton presents his most carefully rendered action sequence. After working out a dangerous plan of escape together, Mann and Mr. Wright get the children and women from the swamp onto a small train late in the night. As the small locomotive gathers steam to take off, the mob bears down on horses and wagons to deliver its death sentence. Mann scoops up a straggling black youngster, before firing at the mob. As the train speeds away, the mob continues its chase, and suddenly dozens of black men hiding in the woods run out and desperately try to board the freedom train. Singleton crosscuts from the train, to the chasing mob, to the running black men, in a rapid succession of images, creating a visceral montage.

Though the typical upbeat Hollywood ending can not feasibly conclude the film, Singleton makes a point of providing a final segment that suggests hope. Within the film Duke (Bruce McGill), a white leader of the lynch mob, teaches his son the lessons of racial hatred—namely, the inferiority of blacks, the ways of tying a hangman's noose, the beauty of a raging fire, and the suppression of tears when seeing the dead bodies of black babies. By the movie's end, the son, about twelve years old, has heard and seen enough. With his belongings bundled over his shoulders, he leaves his father declaring, "I hate you. You ain't no man. I don't know what you are, dad!" Clearly, the son rejects the father's prejudices and runs away from the white supremacist legacy that his father wants to pass along to him.

As a director, Singleton has demonstrated his courage in staying true to what he knows, as in *Boyz N the Hood* and *Higher Learning,* while taking a risk to explore some areas more distant but still engrossing, as in *Poetic Justice* and *Rosewood.* Despite any weak box-office showings with *Poetic Justice* and *Higher Learning,* Hollywood appears to be willing to give him an ear, which is certainly more than many other black directors can expect. Singleton's best work may still lie ahead. He clearly has the directing talent and experience, and from all indications, a considerable amount of confidence.

Matty Rich

I think you have to be born with the talent to know how to communicate and deal with people. I think anybody can direct a movie, but I think the best directors are communicators. They can get what they want, not by screaming or forcing people to do things, but by making it a team. I just had to do it, and I had to believe in myself.[12]   Matty Rich

One of the youngest black filmmakers to garner Hollywood's attention in the 1990s, Matty Rich stepped into the director's spotlight without having gone through the experiences of film school, music videos, television production, or stage performances as had many other '90s directors. Like the title of his debut film, he was straight out of Brooklyn and catapulted, perhaps too quickly, to the heights of newest black director of the "hood."

Born in Brooklyn as Matthew Satisfield Richardson, he was raised in the same environment of the Red Hooks housing projects that served as the key setting for his first film. At age ten, he felt anxious that his life wasn't as materially rich as the family he saw on *The Brady Bunch,* so with his mother's urging, he began reading books to learn about moviemaking. But at thirteen, after seeing several friends shot and one killed, Rich resigned himself merely to finish high school alive. He took a three-week writing class at New York University, and using his mother's and sister's credit cards, he put together an eight-minute film about his life. Getting himself time on a local black radio station, Rich then begged for investors, and $77,000 later, he went on to shoot his feature, *Straight Out of Brooklyn* (1991), completing it at the age of 19.

Straight Out of Brooklyn opens with exterior shots of Brooklyn tenements during the day and then at nightfall. The buildings are hard, tall, ominous, and surrounded by bare trees. Over these visuals, the strains of a poignant piano and woodwinds can be heard, until the scene cuts to an interior bedroom where a black teenager, Dennis Brown (Lawrence Gilliard Jr.), lays awake listening as his father, Ray, verbally and physically abuses Dennis' mother.

The remainder of the movie takes the viewer deeper into this bleak environment, where Dennis' dropout friends, Larry (Matty Rich) and Kevin (Mark Malone), are equally disappointed with their young lives. Although Dennis receives encouragement from his longsuffering mother, Frankie (Ann D. Sanders); his sister, Carolyn (Barbara Sanon); and his waitress girlfriend, Shirley (Reana E. Drummond), he scoffs at spending years in college or working at a low-paying job. Dennis convinces himself that any future opportunities, as well as an end to his parents' abusive marriage, will only come from making big money immediately and crossing over into the Manhattan skyline that looms in the background. With an ill-conceived plan to rob a local drug dealer, Dennis organizes Kevin and Larry to pull off the armed heist. But wearing no masks, the teens are easily recognized and hunted down by the dealer, Saledene (Joseph A. Thomas) and his supplier, Luther (Ali Shahid Abdul Wahhad). Following the night when Frankie is hospitalized because Ray beats her severely, Ray is recognized as Dennis' father and shot dead by the drug lords. At the same time, Frankie dies in the hospital from her injuries, leaving Dennis and his sister fated to a hopeless future.

In *Straight Out of Brooklyn*, the story surfaces as the most pertinent area of discussion. Technically, the film has too many conspicuous flaws in sound, lighting, and editing to evaluate it for its cinematic elements. Further weighed down by long, static takes and overwritten speeches, the movie might be dismissed, if not for the passion within the story and the strong performance by Lawrence Gilliard Jr.

Certainly, Matty Rich knows and understands the urban tenements and presents the obvious challenges and the resourceful people who inhabit the environment. He criticizes the prevalence of drugs, killers, and economic pressures, affirming that the projects are indeed tough and that, as indicated in the on-screen postscript, "[t]raditions pass from one generation to the next. We need to change." But Rich also makes a point of showing the potential to achieve through characters such as Shirley and her boss–restaurant owner, Mrs. Walker (Doris Black). As the two women dialogue in one scene, Mrs. Walker states, "To go straight out of Brooklyn, you have to earn it." Shirley hears the truth in Mrs. Walker's observations, but unfortunately for Dennis, he never gets that message. To Dennis, obtaining money without weighing the consequences appears to be the best way to change a desperate

Matty Rich, right, outlines a scene with Larenz Tate, who plays Drew, in the coming-of-age story *The Inkwell*.

situation. The folly of his youth endangers him as much as the hostile streets that he fights to survive.

Straight Out of Brooklyn brought Rich much praise and helped establish his production company, Blacks N Progress. Rich then turned to writing for a period of time. He was offered a number of directing projects that focused on gang and urban life. But Rich changed courses and chose to direct *The Inkwell* (1994), which was "a coming-of-age story . . . set among upper-middle-class blacks on Martha's Vineyard."[13]

In the movie's plot Drew (Larenz Tate), at sixteen, is an introverted youth who communicates more with his toy doll than with his parents, Kenny (Joe Morton) and Brenda (Suzanne Douglass). Drew's father, a former Black Panther Party member, hates his son's weak nature and dreads the upcoming trip to the island resort of Martha's Vineyard to vacation with the Phillipses, his upper-class in-laws. Once there, both Drew and Kenny are uncomfortable—Drew dislikes the beach and forced socializing, while Kenny disdains the conservative, Republican attitudes of their hosts—Spencer (Glynn Turman), Frances (Vanessa Bell Calloway), and Junior (Duane Martin). Frances and Brenda are sisters, but with the added presence of their mother, Evelyn (Mary Alice), conflicts often arise.

Drew eventually befriends an older married woman, Heather (Adrienne-Joi Johnson), and develops a crush on a spoiled flirt, Lauren (Jada Pinkett).

Later, he has an intimate moment with the former and survives a broken heart from the latter, growing emotionally from both experiences.

The movie finds its most arresting moments through the acting of Larenz Tate and Joe Morton. Tate turns a blurry, disturbed character into a focused teen, whose growing maturity is given shape in gestures and vocal tonality. Tate, an often underappreciated black actor in Hollywood, gives substance to the script's gaps, creating a character who walks the tightrope between boyhood and manhood. Morton, for his part, takes a mythical figure—the older, bitter black radical—and imbues a cardboard type with warmth and intelligence, as well as anger.

As for Rich's directing, the film has an inconsistency about it; at places, it appears that two movies are being made. On the one hand, Rich pushes the humor to an over-the-top excess, and on the other, he seems seriously to explore black teenage angst, as well as black political viewpoints. The result is a movie where the tone and pacing are erratic at best.

The Inkwell may remind some viewers of *Summer of '42* (1971) with its affair between an adolescent male and an older married woman, but the former has among its goals a more extensive story about class and politics within black culture. Matty Rich can be applauded for his attempt to render this more complex story, but he appears more at ease with the streets of *Straight Out of Brooklyn.* With both films, he's a director who exhibits talents, but one who seems to be still looking for his particular style. By 1998, Rich had been involved with some television projects, one of which was writing a script based on the life of rapper Tupac Shakur for HBO. With the experiences he has gained in writing and directing for television in the late 1990s, Rich will hopefully find his stride soon and fulfill the promise of his first film.

Mario Van Peebles

As a director I was making films I was compelled to make. Films that might not have been made if I didn't direct them. . . . I was there and took up those causes and we got some pictures green-lit that otherwise might have gone unproduced.[14]   Mario Van Peebles

Mario Van Peebles managed to make a debut as a film director with one of the most financially successful box-office hits of the 1990s—*New Jack City* (1991). Shot in thirty-six days on an $8.5 million budget,[15] the film made $50 million within the year,[16] making it the year's most profitable film for Warner Bros. studios.[17]

Son of famed black director Melvin Van Peebles, Mario seemed destined for his own turn in the spotlight. Like his father, Mario has been an actor, producer, and director, and as the son, Mario has never hesitated to give his father praise and credit publicly for his access into the entertainment business.

Born in Mexico City, Mario lived in Europe as a youngster until he returned with his father to the United States to live in San Francisco and then Los Angeles.[18] Attending Columbia University in New York to study economics, Mario entered a career in business, working for an investment firm, the commodities exchange, and later as a budget analyst with the City of New York during the administration of Ed Koch. But his interest in entertainment drew him away from the business sector, and he studied acting in New York with Stella Adler.[19] Returning to Los Angeles, he eventually earned some appearances on television shows, most notably his recurring role on the first year of *L.A. Law*. Over the years he also gained roles in television movies, such as *A Triumph of the Heart: The Ricky Bell Story*, *Children of the Night*, and *Stompin' at the Savoy*, and feature films, such as *The Cotton Club* (1984), *Heartbreak Ridge* (1986), *Jaws: The Revenge* (1987), *Highlander: The Final Dimension* (1994), *Gunmen* (1994), and *Solo* (1996).

He was able to gain directing experience through television, as he helmed some of the segments of his own detective series, *Sonny Spoon*, as well as episodes of *Wiseguy*, *21 Jump Street*, and *Top of the Hill*. For his direction of the CBS After School Special *Malcolm Takes a Shot* in 1990, he was nominated for a directing award by the Directors Guild of America.[20]

New Jack City (1991) served as an impressive announcement that Mario Van Peebles had arrived as a director. Thematically, the film touches upon a number of issues that would dominate political discussions in the United States during the decade of the '90s: the pervasiveness of the drug business in the nation's inner cities; the multicultural fabric of American society; the responsibility for community safety; and the use of police violence to combat criminal violence.

Based on a script written by Thomas Lee Wright and Barry Michael Cooper, *New Jack City* takes the viewer into the contemporary inner-city world where hip-hop meets the established gangster genre. The title itself alerts the audience to the influence of the times; "New Jack" in hip-hop argot identifies "street smarts" and "street knowledge and survival." In the "New Jack" inner city where people are enmeshed within a struggle to survive, there has to be a "New Jack" cop who can infiltrate and destroy the criminal element within that jungle. Van Peebles interlaces genre conventions, music video techniques, hip-hop music and language, and slick visuals to attract a young multiethnic audience.

From left to right, Detectives Park (Russell Wong), Stone (Mario Van Peebles), Peretti (Judd Nelson), and Appleton (Ice-T) commit themselves to battling vicious gangsters in *New Jack City.*

In the impressive opening sequence beneath the credits and the hip-hop version of "For the Love of Money," the camera looks down on the buildings and streets that entrap its inhabitants. It moves in to a close shot of a man being held upside-down over a bridge railing, where crime boss Nino Brown (Wesley Snipes) berates a drug dealer before ordering his henchman, Duh Duh Duh Man (Bill Nunn), to drop the man to his death in the river below. Nino's power and callousness is established, just before the introduction of his eventual nemesis, an undercover cop named Scotty Appleton (Ice-T). Scotty sets up a drug bust by taking down a street dealer named Pookie (Chris Rock), an arrest that is completed after an exhilarating chase sequence along city streets, stairways, fences, and train tracks.

While introducing these characters, Van Peebles creates pacing and rhythms that thump with energy in tempo with the opening tune performed by Queen Latifah. Using a fluid camera, askew angles, and extreme close-ups, Van Peebles gives an in-your-face look at the street scene with its accompanying chaos and volatile aspects. This frenzied feel continues as Nino and his gangster cohorts take over an apartment building for drug production; as Detective Stone (Mario Van Peebles) works the bureaucracy to put together his "New Jack" squad; as the gangsters take out the competition in the hood; and as rival mobsters from outside the hood threaten Nino's rise to power. Oddly enough, the film slows its pace when the antidrug theme gets an emphasis, as Scotty recruits the dealer-turned-junkie Pookie as an undercover spy. Forcing Pookie into a rehabilitation program, the montage of Pookie's painful journey to sobriety is didactic and cumbersome. And though the message is important, the film collapses into a languid mode that contrasts with the energy of the previous sequences.

But Van Peebles allows the film to recover, and upon Pookie's self-destructive relapse and his death by Nino's thugs, the interplay between Nino and Scotty finally occurs, creating a new tension in the film and recapturing the rhythms of the earlier part of the film. Scotty, assuming an undercover role of a drug supplier, befriends Nino and plants seeds of mistrust between Nino and his partner Gee Money (Allen Payne). Although Scotty's true identity is revealed during a drug deal, the aftermath leads to Nino's killing of Gee Money and Nino's capture. The Scotty-Nino tension escalates into the courtroom where Nino manipulates the system to get a lesser sentence that will place him back onto the streets in a year. Fate intercedes, and the Old Man (Bill Cobbs), an activist from the neighborhood, shoots Nino as he exits the courtroom.

As the director, Van Peebles achieves some measurable results when using the camera to reveal both the story and the nature of his characters. For example, during a wedding scene, as Nino and his cohorts are leaving with other guests along an exterior stairway, the rival Italian mobsters attempt an assassination. Presented in slow motion and alternating points of view, the scene recalls the interior train station shootout in Brian De Palma's *Untouchables* (1987), which was itself an homage to Sergei Eisenstein's *Potemkin* (1925). In both De Palma's and Eisenstein's films, as a shootout occurs on the steps, an innocent child in a baby stroller rolls down the steps toward its death. But in *New Jack City*, Nino grabs a young girl and lifts her before him as a human shield until he can take cover. In Nino's world there are no innocent children, only consumers to be used one way or another. Nino's blatant effort at self-preservation complements the early scene at the bridge, and it reveals his total disregard for anyone else. In another reference to De Palma, while basking in his power at home, Nino watches the video of De Palma's *Scarface* (1983), in which the protagonist-gangster, Tony Montana, revels in the mantra "The world is mine."

At the film's climax, Van Peebles augments his effective character revelations. As Nino exits the courtroom, he sarcastically reminds reporters that his sentencing is an example of American justice being served, but the Old Man arrives to deliver his own street justice. In a slow-motion sequence the camera cuts among Nino, the Old Man, Scotty, and Scotty's "New Jack" white partner, Peretti (Judd Nelson). As the bullet pierces his chest, Nino goes stiff and falls head-over-heels across a second-floor railing, reminiscent of the death of the dealer at the bridge at the film's opening. Nino's physical fall serves as a metaphor for the gangster's world: life at the top of the criminal heap soon leads to the final plunge into death. As Nino falls, Scotty replaces his sunglasses to move undercover again into the streets, while Peretti smiles triumphantly, obviously glad that Nino couldn't beat the justice of the streets.

Van Peebles accomplishes a great deal in *New Jack City*, but with *Hoodlum*, *The Godfather*, *Scarface*, and other gangster films it shares a major shortcoming: basically, the women characters, who are rather problematic in their motivations, are presented superficially. In *New Jack City* Keisha (Vanessa Williams) is a violent, gun-toting gangsta who serves Nino; Selina (Michael Michelle) is an intelligent, strategy-planning member of Nino's group who also loves Nino; and Uniqua (Tracy Camilla Johns) is a gangster groupie who plays lover to Nino to obtain the party life. All three of these characters possess some interesting dimensions, but they are never explored or revealed in detail.

Following the box-office success of *New Jack City*, Mario Van Peebles decided to move to a different genre. On the boot heels of the critically praised revisionist Western *Unforgiven* (1992), Van Peebles took a turn at retelling the involvement of African Americans in developing the late-nineteenth-century American frontier. *Posse* (1993) is Van Peebles' treatment of the actual prominence of black settlers and cowboys, and the omission of those black pioneers in history books and Hollywood movies.

Posse opens with an Old Man (Woody Strode) who talks directly into the camera about weapons of the frontier and the vagaries of history in omitting the truth about black westerners. The Old Man finishes his history lesson by referring to a photo of a group—or posse—of riders, including five blacks and one white, who were led by the black desperado Jessie Lee (Mario Van Peebles). After stealing gold from Colonel Graham (Billy Zane) during the Spanish-American War in 1898, the posse takes off for the United States, drifting westward toward the frontier. Once in the West, the posse discovers a black youngster stranded in the desert, and they add him to their group as well.

By the time the posse arrives at a black town called Freemanville, Jessie Lee's past falls more into place for the audience and his posse. Jessie Lee is welcomed by his former love interest, Lana (Salli Richardson); her father, Papa Joe (Melvin Van Peebles); and the town's newly appointed black sheriff, Carver (Blair Underwood). A confrontation between Jessie Lee and Bates, the white sheriff, erupts, with the latter supported by the arrival of Colonel Graham and his men who are tracking the stolen gold.

Jessie Lee prevails, and as the story ends, the camera returns to the Old Man who opened the film, revealing that he's actually telling the story to two black filmmakers in the 1990s—Reginald and Warrington Hudlin. Then, it becomes clear that the Old Man is the black youngster who had been rescued from the desert by Jessie Lee and his posse.

The complexity of the plot and the large ensemble cast—twenty actors are named in the opening credits—are indications of *Posse*'s ambitiousness, which provides both its charm and its flaws. Mario Van Peebles seeks to direct an epic drama that highlights multiethnic participation in the West. Throughout the film, the audience observes Native American, Chinese, Spanish, black, and white characters all interconnecting in lives of desperation and triumph. But at the center, Van Peebles lays out the story of African Americans, who are varied in their education, background, and motivation, but who all play a part in the theater of the western frontier. Linking well-known historical elements such as slavery, the KKK, and black economic struggle with lesser-known factors, such as black soldiers in the Spanish-American War and Bishop Turner's back-to-Africa movement, Van Peebles offers an extremely large canvas of black culture.

That complexity at times weakens the story. The director seems to be squeezing so much information into the movie that it takes on an episodic, vignette quality about it. The character Jessie Lee serves as the connecting thread that binds all the locales and characters together, but his stoic, Eastwoodian demeanor sometimes fails to provide an emotional level that one would expect from a passionate man such as Lee turns out to be. The Clint Eastwood–antihero type works effectively for the necessary gunfights and battles, but there are other moments when Jessie Lee needs to become more expressive.

Another weakness stems from the setting and time of the story. Although Jessie Lee and his posse leave behind the war of 1898, they appear to ride into a frontier that's more appropriate for the late 1870s–1880s. The sparse frontier look of the towns and the laying of railroad ties by Chinese and black laborers appear to be from that earlier time. In addition, the locales of Cutterstown and Freemanville are missing certain facets, such as wooden sidewalks, telegraph lines, and churches, that might mark a western town near the turn of the century.

However, praise must be given to Van Peebles' directing of invigorating action sequences. With Dutch angles, tight framing, zooms, slow motion, and quick cutting, the movie's fight scenes and sepia-toned flashbacks are alluring. Van Peebles shows more proficiency when telling a visual story that's not required to integrate dialogue and exposition.

With his next film, Van Peebles stays with his role as a film griot of black history. Just as *Posse* sought to blend forgotten facts with an entertaining story, *Panther* (1995) takes on a similar task. With a script written by his father and based on his father's novel of the same title, Mario Van Peebles reaches out for that same hip-hop audience that found *New Jack City*, attempting to school them to the recent past of the late 1960s.

Panther opens with documentary footage showing various people and events significant to the civil rights and human rights struggle in America. The black-and-white footage sets the mood of the times and the dramatic nature of the film to follow. From there, the story opens in Oakland, in 1967, as a young black boy on a bicycle pedals through the neighborhood eyeing the people and activities that abound. As he does, an older male's voiceover emerges, which cleverly leads the viewer to think the young boy and the older narrator are the same. But, in an abrupt twist, the young boy on the bike is struck by a vehicle and killed at an intersection—an intersection where the narrator, Judge (Kadeem Hardison), who's a Vietnam veteran, lives nearby with his mother, Rita (Jenifer Lewis). Judge goes on to explain how the efforts to get a traffic light placed at the intersection to prevent further deaths actually opened the way for the organizing of the community.

Two young men from the community, Bobby Seale (Courtney B. Vance) and Huey Newton (Marcus Chong), turn their energy to organizing young black men to protect their community from police, drug dealers, and apathy. Calling themselves the Black Panthers, they eventually decide to carry guns, which is legal at the time, and to patrol the community. Needing Judge's military expertise in weapons, they succeed in their nightly patrols, as well as their morning breakfast programs for neighborhood children.

The film follows the rise of the Black Panther Party and the now-infamous people belonging to the party, such as Eldridge Cleaver (Anthony Griffith), and those infamous people opposing the party, such as FBI Director J. Edgar Hoover (Richard Dysart). A subplot that has Judge pretending to be a spy for the authority's front man, Inspector Brimmer (Joe Don Baker), adds tension to the story when another Panther member, Tyrone (Bokeem Woodbine), believes that Judge actually *is* a spy.

When the FBI finds that their tactics of intimidation and violence fail to break up the Panthers, they move to their ultimate weapon: the strategy of dumping heroin into the black community. This plan comes to the attention of Judge, who, along with Panthers Tyrone and Alma (Nefertiti), blows up a warehouse storing a load of drugs. However, the victory is hollow because the Panther leaders are dead, jailed, and/or exiled. Viewers are reminded through the closing captions that drug addiction spilled over into other communities as well: in 1970 there were "300,000 drug addicts in the United States," and in 1995 there were "3 million drug addicts" in the country.

Although *Panther* has a more focused story than *Posse*, the former still suffers from the same overambitious intent as the latter. The story attempts to tell too many stories and to integrate too many historical facts and people. Judge does work well here as the central character who connects the various plot points, but since his character is not privy to the inner office discussions among police and FBI authorities—as well as the arrangement between the authorities and the Mob—there are conspicuous places where an omniscient point of view takes over, leaving Judge's story offscreen. This sometimes creates abrupt shifts when viewers would otherwise prefer to remain with the major characters. In addition, Van Peebles does paint a rather romantic view of the Black Panther leaders, Seale and Newton. Because they are constantly "doing good" for the community and the Black Panther Party, the audience never gets a sense of their private lives—who they were when they took off the black leather jackets and berets. Their on-screen concerns and commitment come off as being genuine, but there isn't enough of a back story to suggest the reasons why they were so motivated.

In *Panther* Mario Van Peebles has developed a visual storytelling that is as polished and energetically paced as any Hollywood film. Van Peebles knows how to engage an audience and to effectively blend action with exposition. In the sequence, for example, where the Black Panthers patrol the neighborhood and intercede as police prepare to attack a black suspect, the director fuses dynamic acting, crisp dialogue, quick cutting, and throbbing music to make the suspense palpable. As the Black Panthers, holding their weapons ready, stand face to face with white policemen with their weapons drawn, the black crowd gathers and looks back and forth in both fear and pride. And as the Black Panthers triumph by citing the laws that justify their actions, the white cops can only move away in defeat.

After *Panther*, Mario Van Peebles returned to acting on the big screen, stepping from behind the camera to develop crossover roles in the action films *Gunmen* and *Solo*. But in the future, he will certainly maintain a presence on both sides of the camera, because like a number of other black directors, Van Peebles appears at ease with the total filmmaking process. And, like Bill Duke or Carl Franklin, Van Peebles knows how to present a story about black culture in a framework and manner that American mainstream audiences have become accustomed to watching.

Ernest Dickerson

Cinematography is a craft that sometimes rises to the level of art. . . . As a cinematographer I'm able to paint . . . the emotions of a story, through color and camera angles and lighting, light and shade. Being a director, I'm not as concerned with that as much as I am with telling the story with actors. . . . I think every film should have its own look, and as a director I can set it in the right course.[21]   Ernest Dickerson

Most critical moviegoers are quite familiar with the name of Ernest Dickerson. As a cinematographer, he added a visual excellence to numerous films that has earned him a much-deserved admiration for his considerable skills. Coming to directing via his work as a cinematographer provided Dickerson with an experienced eye and attitude for working with actors and technical personnel as well.

Born in 1952, Dickerson grew up in Newark, where his father was a grocery store manager and his mother a librarian. Attending Howard University, he majored in architecture and minored in photography.[22] But his interest eventually steered him into filmmaking, as he attended New York University. It was there that Dickerson met Spike Lee, and the two paired together on several student films, as well as a number of feature films.

Although as early as 1983 Dickerson had cowritten a script, *Juice*, with Gerard Brown III, and he entertained aspirations for directing, he put these aside as cinematography work came his way. In addition to shooting the Spike Lee films, Dickerson was the cinematographer on numerous films, including John Sayles' *Brother from Another Planet* (1984), Michael Schultz's *Krush Groove* (1985), Robert Townsend's *Eddie Murphy Raw* (1987), and Peter Wang's *Laserman* (1990).[23] Dickerson also did camera work on the first season of television's *Tales from the Darkside*. In 1989 he won the New York Film Critics Circle Award for cinematography for *Do the Right Thing*, and in 1991 he was honored for his body of work by the San Francisco International Film Festival.[24] In the '90s Dickerson directed a variety of film genres for television and theatrical release, but the feature film *Juice* emerged as his most impressive drama during the decade.

On the set of *Juice,* director Ernest
Dickerson, center, plans a scene with his
young actors, Omar Epps, left, and Khalil Kain.

Basing *Juice* (1992), his directorial debut, on interviews conducted with
young African American men in Harlem, Dickerson explores the manner
in which adolescence, ambition, and anger all combine to shape the choices
made by the story's major characters. Set on the Harlem turf, four friends
since elementary school have made it to their high school years sharing a
close bond. Q (Omar Epps) dreams of being a hip-hop deejay; Raheem (Khalil
Kain) serves as leader of the four and peacekeeper; Steel (Jermaine Hopkins) eats constantly; and Bishop (Tupac Shakur) simmers with anger. Skip-
ping school, they spend a typical day together—hanging out at the pool hall,
owned by Trip (Samuel L. Jackson); betting on arcade games; walking the
streets; and "chillin'" at whomever's house has food.

Q finds solace from his boredom through his love for music, and through
the older divorced woman, Yolanda (Cindy Herron), with whom he's intimate. Working an evening shift as a nurse, Yolanda seems a voice of reason
in Q's often confusing life. Out of the four, Bishop emerges as the most restless; he wants more money, more respect, and more power—that is, "juice,"
on the streets.

After a violent store robbery, Bishop shoots Raheem, threatening the lives of Q and Steel if they reveal the deed. Bishop, a self-proclaimed crazy killer, tells Q unequivocally that he doesn't care about anyone, claiming: "I ain't shit and ain't never going to be nothing."

Finally, Q faces Bishop unarmed, and the two eventually carry their fight to a rooftop where a party is in full swing. In their struggling, Bishop slips over the edge of the roof and, despite Q's attempt to save him, falls to his death. Numerous people from the party have been watching the fight and Bishop's death, and one tells Q, "You got the juice now, man." Q shakes his head in the negative, and the film holds on a freeze-frame of his face.

In its focus on urban black males, *Juice* bears a similarity to two films that preceded it—*Boyz N the Hood* and *Straight Out of Brooklyn.* Although the three movies have different settings, the themes intersect and expose the daily pressures placed upon African American youth. But at the heart of the cultural and sociological issues, *Juice* seeks to caution society to be conscious of those who remain on the edges of acceptability. Bishop's longing for "juice" results from a confusion and frustration with the definitions of manhood and respect. And the film implies that there are far too many Bishops in America who have given up on striving for "tomorrow" because they have no belief in "today."

As a director, Ernest Dickerson brings his experienced eye to the film, serving up a visual story that never stumbles in capturing the look, pulse, sounds, and smells of the Harlem world of the four major characters. He can give legitimacy to the proud and arrogant attitudes of the four friends as they strut the neighborhood streets, and at the same time, Dickerson effectively records the adrenaline-filled chase scenes between the four friends and the cops.

One of the more subtle, but arresting, sequences occurs after Raheem's funeral. Bishop, who actually killed Raheem, shows up at the mournful gathering of family and friends, comforting Raheem's distraught mother with promises of finding Raheem's killer. As Bishop consoles the mother with a hug, he looks over and finds Q staring at him. In the crosscutting between their stares, the revelation of Bishop's evil nature is evident. Q recognizes what Bishop has become, and understands that, despite their many years of friendship, they can now only be enemies. It's a noteworthy moment that's accomplished by acting, situational irony, and the crosscutting of close-ups.

Dickerson's directing is solid throughout the film, but the script is not without flaws: The characterizations of the minor characters lack detailing—for example, the parents of the four teens and Trip, the pool hall owner.

But by far, the most problematic supporting character is Yolanda, Q's older girlfriend. The two enjoy an obvious emotional and physical connection, but from whence does it come? Viewers are never given any clue as to how they met or why an older professional woman would be involved with a high school teen still living at home with his parents. Q emerges as the most ambitious and thoughtful of the four young friends, but would those qualities be enough to attract Yolanda into a steady, and seemingly monogamous, relationship with the youth?

Dickerson waited almost a decade to be able to direct *Juice,* and the passion that he has for the material is evident in the careful attention he gives to presenting his four main characters in a genuine way. Although they belong to the same "crew" and share the same language, music, and attitudes, he manages to give each a voice and singular personality. After *Juice,* Dickerson directed movies for the video audience—*Surviving the Game* (1994) and *Demon Knight* (1995); for theatrical release, the action-comedy *Bulletproof* (1996); and for television—*Blind Faith* (1998), *Ambushed* (1998), *Futuresport* (1998), and *Strange Justice* (1999).

Albert and Allen Hughes

People are so stuck in the three-act structure. . . . We want to get out of that. We want to make a movie one day where there are no rules at all—something like Pink Floyd's "The Wall" or Disney's "Fantasia," all of these crazy things. Some crazy non-linear movie that deals with anything you want.[25]

Albert and Allen Hughes

Anointed by critics as the filmmakers to watch in the future with the debut of their first feature, *Menace II Society* (1993), twin brothers Albert and Allen Hughes display a dynamic cinematic style even as they deliver rather burning criticism of their fellow filmmakers. Young and confident, the brothers show both the boastful attitude and media awareness of the hip-hop generation.

Born in 1973 in Detroit, their father was black and their mother Armenian. As a single parent, their mother moved them to Pomona, California, a city about forty miles east of Los Angeles, where she developed a business while sending them to suburban schools. They were making home movies at twelve years old, and by high school began taking film classes. After graduation, Albert attended film classes at Los Angeles Community College, inspiring him and his brother to make two short films, which enabled them to obtain an agent. Their professional directing careers began with music videos, completing thirty videos in six months, working with hip-hop performers, such as Digital Underground, Tone-Loc, KRS-One, Too Short, and Yo-Yo. Then, at age twenty, they got the opportunity to direct their first feature, *Menace II Society*, which on a $3 million budget ended up grossing close to $30 million. The film was a remarkably successful film debut, and it premiered at the 1993 Cannes Film Festival and received Best Picture honors at the 1994 MTV Movie Awards.[26]

Working as a complementary team, "Allen focuses more on the actors and Albert more on cameras as the technical side, but both emphasize that the division of labor is only a vague one."[27] To maintain control over their film works, in 1993 the Hughes brothers organized a production company called Underworld Entertainment, which includes a division called Underworld Records that's connected to Capitol Records, allowing the brothers to develop new musical acts and to produce sound tracks.

Menace II Society opens in Watts in 1993, when black teenagers Caine (Tyrin Turner) and O-Dog (Larenz Tate) enter a small market run by a Korean couple. When hurried by the two grocers to make their purchases, the two teens respond with verbal anger. Then, as Caine drinks his beverage, O-Dog robs, shoots, and kills the male cashier. After securing the security tape, he also kills the Korean female grocer. Caine's voiceover, which will be heard throughout the film, confesses how such an unpredictable tragedy was typical of his inner-city life.

Exposed to drugs as a kid, the teenage Caine sells drugs at school while living with his elderly grandparents. A boy/man, Caine remains committed to an imprisoned homie, Pernell (Glenn Plummer), and to protecting Pernell's girlfriend, Ronnie (Jada Pinkett), and their son. But associating with O-Dog and other neighborhood thugs, Caine barely escapes death from rival gang members and from police confrontations. Caine's grandparents try to guide him. His friend Sharif (Vonte Sweet), who has turned Muslim, attempts to influence him. And Sharif's schoolteacher-father, Mr. Butler (Charles S. Dutton), seeks to counsel him, warning: "Being a black man in America ain't easy. The hunt is on, and you're the prey. . . . All I'm saying is survive."

Eventually, Ronnie convinces Caine to leave with her and travel to Atlanta where she has been promised a job, but Caine's past catches up with him, and he's killed in a drive-by attack. In a final voiceover, viewers understand that Caine throughout the movie has been speaking from the grave, realizing too late that he wants to live.

The film contains a number of strong messages, but to the credit of effective filmmaking, the messages do not overwhelm the story. Instead, with a script by Tyger Williams that presents intriguing characters and through direction that pulls strong performances from the actors, *Menace II*

Society distinguishes itself as a successful marriage of story and cinematic technique.

The movie possesses a mix of simple, emotional moments that are juxtaposed with powerfully visceral sequences. Framed with energetic pacing and a meticulous detail to period music, the movie captures and holds the viewer's attention. One of those brief emotional segments occurs when Caine and Ronnie visit Pernell to inform him that they are leaving for Atlanta. Pernell, on one side of a glass barrier, has difficulty conversing with Ronnie. Their conversation through the phones remains strained and awkward, as they inhabit two different worlds. But when Caine takes the phone, he quickly connects with Pernell, and though the barrier is still there, the two men are linked in spirit. As they speak, the directors cut back and forth between close-ups of the two, lowering all of the ambient noises to further emphasize the closeness of the characters. Only their voices exist as they reach through the barrier and link together, and in a final instruction, Pernell tells Caine to "take care of my son. Teach him better than I taught you."

The final sequence, however, strikes a different chord. Crosscutting— between Caine, Anthony, Sharif, and O-Dog as they pack the van for the Atlanta departure on the one hand and the arriving vehicle carrying the drive-by shooters on the other—creates a palpable tension, as slow motion is contrasted with real action. And when Caine is shot and lays dying, his amplified heartbeat is synchronized to the flashing of images from his past. This visual passing of life before the character's eyes is seen under the voice-over that acknowledges that the value of life is learned too late. The sequence is compelling and merges a number of visual and aural techniques at once, exemplifying a creative approach that recognizes the power of such assimilation.

For some, however, the film's graphic violence is a detracting element. Indeed, the movie contains its share of both shocking and bloody shootings. Black scholar Henry Louis Gates comments: "[T]he violence seems both over-the-top and unremarkable—and above all, real. You don't know whether you're watching a nightmare or the nightly news."[28] The objective in *Menace II Society* does not appear to be to overwhelm viewers, but rather to show the reality of the world in which Caine and his homies exist. The Hughes brothers use violence as a storytelling tool, but don't allow the violence to dominate the story.

Graphic violence escalates in the Hughes brothers' next film, *Dead Presidents* (1995), which follows its protagonist into the Vietnam War. Supplying images of the violent chaos of battle and its effect upon the soldier, the Hughes brothers punctuate the horror of the battlefield by including bloody

After a flawed robbery, Cleon (Bokeem
Woodbine, far left), Jose (Freddy Rodriguez
in whiteface), Anthony (Larenz Tate in
whiteface), and Kirby (Keith David, right) find
themselves stranded on tough streets in
Dead Presidents.

body parts, castration, and decapitation. The war sequences in *Dead Presidents* are difficult to sit through, forcing viewers out of their comfort zone and into the on-screen horror zone.

In 1968, in the northeast Bronx, the protagonist, Anthony (Larenz Tate), and his high school friends, Skip (Chris Tucker) and Jose (Freddy Rodriguez), work the early morning milk delivery run to make money. Anthony finishes his deliveries by stopping at the house of his girlfriend, Juanita (Rose Jackson), and her younger sister, Delilah (N'Bushe Wright). The story jumps ahead one year to disclose that Anthony runs numbers to make money, working out of the pool hall owned and run by Kirby (Keith David), a gruff man who has a fatherly affection for Anthony.

By 1971, Anthony is running through the jungle of Quang Tri Province, as bombs explode around him. On his second tour of duty in Vietnam, he looks older and weary. His homeboy Skip has been drafted and winds up in the same squad that includes a wild black soldier named Cleon (Bokeem

Woodbine). Cleon, a preacher's son, has survived four years in Vietnam, his insanity apparent as he carries a souvenir head taken from an enemy soldier.

Returning to the Bronx in 1973, Anthony finds the neighborhood has changed, but he connects with Kirby and Joe, who was also in the war. Anthony goes to visit Juanita and his daughter born while he was away, and he also sees Delilah, who has now become a black revolutionary.

Anthony tries to make a family with Juanita and their daughter, but the little money he makes at a butcher's shop isn't sufficient. So Anthony plans to heist an armored vehicle carrying bundles of old money—the "dead presidents"—to a repository. With a crew—of Kirby, Skip, Joe, Delilah, and his war comrade Cleon—Anthony leads the assault. Camouflaged in whiteface and knit caps and bearing automatic weapons, the crew looks ghostly and lethal. In the process of the heist, Delilah is killed, and while escaping, Joe meets his end. Eventually Cleon is arrested, turning in the rest of the group. Found guilty at his trial, Anthony is given fifteen years to life. The film's final images show Anthony riding in a correctional facility's bus, being taken off to prison.

Anthony's story is tragic, not just on the level of losing his freedom, family, and friends, but in regard to losing his failing ideals. At the beginning of the film, Anthony talks about joining the military in glowing patriotic terms. And when he speaks to his father, a Korean War veteran, Anthony asserts that entering the service will help him become a man. Clearly, the young Anthony searches for a means of fulfilling himself, and little is offered by his environment. And after coming home from the war, Anthony's inability to establish a new life is exacerbated by his family and Juanita, who are ignorant of what he sacrificed in the war. During one argument about money, Juanita tells Anthony, "Ain't no free meals here like in the marines. This is the real world." And on the day of his judgment, the white judge, who announces that he is a veteran of World War II—"a real war"—shows no compassion for Anthony's dilemma.

The visuals and music are deftly interwoven, as in the sequence when Anthony and his crew rob the armored vehicle. Their whiteface makeup speaks directly to the issue of people of color feeling like clowns in American society. Their faces become white masks that show both the sadness of their economic desperation and the denial of white society to see them as human beings. At one point in the segment, Anthony, in white mask, looks up through a grate to watch the white officers from the armored truck. From a high-angle shot, the image—of the black man in whiteface caught behind the "bars" and looking up at the white men above him—punctuates the economic and political conflicts. Cutting to a wider shot, the American flag bil-

lows in the edge of the frame. Then, as the robbery is botched and the exploding armored truck is consumed by flames, the individual "dead presidents"
rain down over the streets as the robbers watch. Like an image from Dante's
Inferno, the flames of hell burn around the crew hurrying to save the money
they believe will save them from their economic hell. The scene reveals the
irony and futility of their situation.

The Hughes brothers exhibit a comprehension of the power of the image,
and they do not hesitate to place an image, regardless of its graphic display, in
the faces of the viewers. Their style reflects their work with music videos and
the cinematic influences of filmmakers such as Martin Scorsese and Brian
De Palma. The Hughes brothers capably serve up a commercial style that examines the experiences of African American males whose spirit and potential are nullified by an indifferent society. By doing so, they distinguish themselves as two of the most important black directors who excel by Hollywood
standards, while maintaining their ethnic edge.

Doug McHenry

We don't want to minimize the fact that there is institutional racism in Hollywood, as there is any place else in our society. . . . What is different is that we
have to focus on our attitude about it. George [Jackson] and I are a team. . . .
[W]e really focus on a strategy of how to win. We think there's an enormous
opportunity in the kind of pictures that we do.[29]   Doug McHenry

Very few black directors have come from the educational and professional
background that Doug McHenry earned for himself. A graduate of both Harvard Business and Law schools, McHenry could have followed a more comfortable and secure life, but his itch for success in the film business led him
to scratch his way to Hollywood.

Born in 1952, McHenry grew up in Richmond, California, and attended
Stanford University, where he studied economics,[30] before traveling east to
Harvard.[31] Working as a lawyer, he became involved with producers Robert
Rehme and Peter Guber, working as the latter's assistant before moving on
to Casablanca Filmworks. At Casablanca, McHenry took positions as both
a business affairs executive and then a production executive, becoming involved in the films *Thank God It's Friday* (1978), *The Hollywood Knights*
(1980), and *Foxes* (1980). Later, when he went to AVCO/Embassy Pictures as
a creative executive, he was connected with the making of *Scanners* (1981)
and *Escape from New York* (1981). In 1985, McHenry teamed up with black
producer George Jackson to complete the film *Krush Groove.*[32] By 1996,
McHenry and Jackson had become a successful Hollywood duo, producing

nine films together,[33] including *New Jack City* (1991), *House Party 2* (1991), *Jason's Lyric* (1994), and *A Thin Line Between Love and Hate* (1996).

Jason's Lyric, McHenry's first solo directing effort, strives to combine two categories of film—the romance and the contemporary urban black drama. Using the familiar framework of the Cain-versus-Abel relationship, the story begins with happier times during the childhood of brothers Jason and Josh, playing in tranquil fields with their father, Maddog (Forest Whitaker), and nurtured by their loving mother, Gloria (Suzanne Douglass). But when Maddog returns from the Vietnam War a broken man, a domestic fight leads to his shooting death, which sends Josh to jail for the crime.

Living in Houston as an adult, Jason (Allen Payne) works at a television repair shop, and Josh (Bokeem Woodbine) finishes a stretch in the penitentiary. But the brothers are still close, with Jason taking the leadership in providing emotionally for both his brother and mother. When he meets Lyric (Jada Pinkett), a local woman who lives with her hustling brother, Alonzo (Anthony "Treach" Criss), Jason and Lyric develop a romantic relationship, while Josh adapts a gangster lifestyle, first selling drugs and then carjacking. Josh's behavior ultimately leads to a split with Jason, who plans to leave town with Lyric and to leave behind the ghosts of the past. As it turns out, on the night that Mad Dog was shot, Jason was the one who actually pulled the trigger. At the height of their standoff, Josh accidentally shoots Lyric, but Jason carries her away from the violence. Left alone, Josh shoots himself. As the film ends, Jason and Lyric ride the bus together into their new future.

Besides the solid performances by Payne, Pinkett, and Woodbine, *Jason's Lyric* presents the audience with a romantic love story between a black man and woman seldom seen in the '90s. Sex between black partners had been evident in other movies, but in this film, McHenry wants to focus on how the romance and affection culminate into both a physical intimacy and commitment. In this aspect, the film finds its strength. The film allows a delicate but effective balance between a traditional cinematic romance and a romance rooted within certain ethnic and class realities. For example, Lyric is not a woman who is quickly whisked away into intimacy by flowers or good looks. She makes it clear to Jason that she has avoided "dating guys in the ward because [she] was tired of wondering if [she were] going to find them in a body bag." For Lyric, she needs a black man who can meet her on her own terms— someone who dreams about the future and who risks taking the initiative to change. Unlike her close friend Marti (Lisa Nicole Carson), who settles for a relationship with Alonzo solely for the sake of having a man in her life, Lyric seeks something more of substance. Lyric helps Jason to see his world and

Jason's Lyric highlights the hopeful love between Lyric (Jada Pinkett) and Jason (Allen Payne).

his possibilities in a different way, and as she becomes his lover, she figuratively becomes his lyric—his song of change and freedom from the past.

McHenry takes time to develop the closeness between Jason and Lyric in a passionate manner. Rather than simply providing sensationalized sex scenes, the director is intent upon weaving the coupling of the characters into the story by having their intimacy result from their deepening relationship. This intimacy, however, was the stimulus for the marketing restrictions from the Motion Picture Association of America (MPAA), as the graphic nature of the coupling met with barriers. But McHenry directs for sensuality and not just sexuality in the film, and consequently the movie deserves a different kind of consideration as opposed to a film such as the graphic *Basic Instinct* (1992).

McHenry appears less effective, however, in telling the gangster story. His action scenes, some violent and bloody, possess a clichélike quality. Although commercially viable for the mainstream audience, the action fails to evoke tension or excitement. Perhaps part of the locus of disappointment is within the script, where the action sequences revolve more around the character of Josh, who is the less successful characterization of the two brothers. Josh, unlike Jason, emerges a one-dimensional character, whose motivation and nature remains obscure. When Josh becomes the main focus of a given sequence, that flatness of characterization weakens that segment.

On another interesting note, McHenry included in *Jason's Lyric* the bizarre, but interesting, character of a street person, a nameless man who breaks the fourth wall and preaches to the audience. Disconnected from the other characters in the story, this self-appointed griot, in close-up, delivers his toothless perspectives. His tirades about tragedy and love become simultaneously humorous and thought-provoking. Although this character only appears twice in the film, perhaps his presence could have been more integrated into the story.

Doug McHenry's success as a producer has been validated by the box-office returns of such films as *New Jack City* and *House Party* sequels. But *Jason's Lyric* demonstrates McHenry's potential as a director, and perhaps future projects with stronger and more focused content will provide him the materials needed to distinguish himself behind the camera.

David Clark Johnson

There's definitely a universal theme in the film [*Drop Squad*], one that cuts across all cultural levels. I think everybody can relate to people who deny their heritage because they feel it's not chic to have an accent or a poor background. . . . [W]hat America is about is being able to achieve while still maintaining your identity.[34]   David Clark Johnson

Born in Baltimore, Maryland, Johnson was a graduate of Howard University, and after college he eventually made his way into writing, working for ABC News, CNN, and PBS's *Sesame Street*. With his writing and producing partner, Butch Robinson, Johnson put together a short film, entitled *The Session*, which he also directed. Entering the short movie in a number of film festivals, Johnson was able to gain the attention and interest of producer-director Spike Lee. With Lee becoming involved as an executive producer, Johnson was able to develop *The Session* into the feature film *Drop Squad* (1994).[35]

It's obvious that the concept for *Drop Squad* must have been quite eye-catching to Lee. The story has the elements of satire and political drama, as well as ethnic and cultural messages targeted directly to members of the black community. It suggests a cinematic canvas that would allow some provocative images and ideas to be presented to that audience.

Under the movie's opening credits, the content of a radio talk show can be heard. The radio voices discuss the possible existence of an activist group called the "Drop Squad," a possibility confirmed when a black politician who has just received a bribe is kidnapped and rushed away in a black van.

Immediately, the scene shifts to a neighborhood restaurant where a black woman is trying to contact the Drop Squad. She suspects that the man she is speaking to, Garvey (Ving Rhames), may be that contact, and she explains that she wants her brother, Buford (Eriq LaSalle), picked up. Later, Buford is taken from the streets and secretly delivered to the Drop Squad headquarters, where the aforementioned black politician is being held, as well as a local drug dealer, named Fat Money (Tico Wells). But the central hostage in the story is Buford, and soon, the audience learns what he discovers. The Drop Squad, a clandestine organization led by Rocky Seavers (Vondie Curtis-Hall), has been working underground for over a decade to deprogram blacks who have conceded their ethnic identity to obtain mainstream acceptance or material gains. At the heart of the organization is an effort to reconnect errant blacks to their roots within their families and community.

As Buford undergoes the intense questioning and cultural exorcism at the secret headquarters, cutaways to Buford's past disclose the details of his racial betrayal: the shame he has for the folk/country manners of his family and friends, as well as the racial stereotyping he supports at his advertising agency job. And ultimately, Buford's most harmful action springs from his refusal to help his childhood friend, Flip (Afemo Omilami), to get a job at his ad company. Finally, Buford is shamed into contrition, when Rocky brings Flip to confront Buford as the last step in the deprogramming.

At its best, *Drop Squad* examines issues of racial identity and consciousness similar to those that formed the thematic core for the film *A Soldier's Story* (1984). And similar to the confused character of Sgt. Waters in the latter film, Buford has to confront the emptiness of his choice to live for and be like white people. But *Drop Squad* isn't written as deftly as *A Soldier's Story*, nor does it have the effectiveness of tone and structure. And, unfortunately, *Drop Squad* maneuvers itself into a dangerous ethical corner. By posing the as-

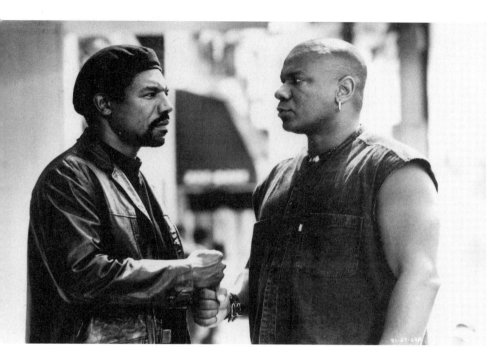

Rocky Seavers (Vondie Curtis-Hall, left) and Garvey (Ving Rhames) are comrades in an underground Afrocentric group in *Drop Squad*.

sumption that confused blacks can be deprogrammed to become real blacks again, the film implies that there exists a certain perspective and set of standards that one must have in order to be "black." The movie implies that there is one black aesthetic or black ethos that encompasses all blacks across class, religious, and geographic lines.

Perhaps this question is too philosophical and inappropriate for a film like *Drop Squad*, which has its best moments when presenting satire. For example, in one sequence, at a family barbecue, Buford proudly shows his new videotaped commercial for a fried chicken chain. The commercial, which includes a cameo by Spike Lee, incorporates numerous racial stereotypes— heavy-set gospel-singing black women; mammy-style cooks; grinning coontypes; and loud-talking, chicken-loving blacks. Buford proudly points out the parody in the advertisement, but his family members, who are supposedly less sophisticated than Buford, angrily chastise him. What Buford fails to recognize is that, for the sake of his job and money, he has exaggerated and distorted black individuals into stereotypes that can only serve as cartoonish statements about the black community.

When Johnson, as cowriter and director, keeps the story on the satirical edge, the film sails effectively through narrative waters. But when he ventures into more dramatic currents, the movie capsizes clumsily. On the whole, the director attempts to accomplish too much with *Drop Squad*, and in the process, he doesn't satisfactorily deliver a coherent and memorable film.

Preston A. Whitmore II

The brothers I met in the service were such heroes to me that I wanted to pay tribute. . . . Previous films about the Vietnam experience have portrayed black servicemen as either cowards, buffoons, or background characters. This film [*The Walking Dead*] is different, not only from other war movies, but also from other films about African American men.[36]   Preston A. Whitmore II

Preston A. Whitmore II, born in Detroit, began his writing career by penning song lyrics. He worked for the legendary music team of Holland/Dozier/Holland, and along the way studied law, before making a transition into screenwriting. His major breakthrough as a screenwriter was with his script for the action-thriller *Fled* (1996), which aided him in the getting his first directing project, *The Walking Dead* (1995), to the screen. Especially vital to the latter film were the three years that Whitmore spent in the marines before coming to Los Angeles in 1985.[37]

The Walking Dead bears a striking resemblance to the war sequences in *Dead Presidents* by the Hughes brothers. Intent upon telling the stories of the Vietnam War through the experiences and reflections of black soldiers, the film focuses on four infantrymen from a variety of backgrounds.

In South Vietnam in 1972, a white commanding officer welcomes new men to the platoon, as he describes the mission to evacuate a prisoner-of-war camp near the North Vietnam border. Later, when dropped at the zone miles south of the POW camp, many of the men are killed, and the platoon members are separated. Four black soldiers survive in one squad and decide to complete the mission, hoping to find a radio at the POW camp to call for help. Sergeant Barkley (Joe Morton), a spiritual man, leads a motley group that includes Hoover (Eddie Griffin), an irreverent, loud-talking soldier; Cole (Allen Payne), a no-nonsense career soldier; and Joe (Vonte Sweet), an insecure, naive soldier. Each of the men has a past, which is revealed through flashbacks as they make their way to their target.

Following enemy confrontations, as well as fights among the four, they arrive to find the POW camp already evacuated. They radio headquarters only to find that the camp will be imminently bombed. Escaping into the

Director Preston A. Whitmore II, center, arranges a scene with actors Vonte Sweet, left, and Allen Payne for his war drama, *The Walking Dead.*

bush toward the landing zone, Joe is shot dead, while Cole and Barkley are wounded. And in an act of courage, Hoover saves Barkley, as they're lifted out of the battlefield by a helicopter.

Although well intentioned, *The Walking Dead* can't survive wooden dialogue, elliptical flashbacks, and technical deficiencies. The dialogue is consistently stilted, as it tries to be symbolic in some scenes and realistic in others. In particular, the dialogue between the men and women in the flashbacks never rings true; instead, the words, sentiments, and expressions seem forced and unintentionally vague. The flashbacks provide another weight to the film, as they neither move the story forward nor provide particularly interesting perspectives on the four major characters. The flashbacks, confusing in time and setting, slow down the story and break the tension created in the battle scenes. Technically, the editing becomes clumsy, and the continuity gets lost. For example, in one sequence Barkley and Hoover's arguments evolve into a medium shot of a physical fight in a jungle clearing. In the middle of their fight, the scene cuts to a wide angle of both men flying high in the air following an explosion and of them landing in a river. The awkward cutting begs several questions. Who threw the grenade at them?

How did they get from the middle of the jungle to a river location? Why weren't they both killed, or wounded, from the explosion that was powerful enough to lift them in the air, flinging them yards away from the clearing?

The Walking Dead fails to really exhaust the characters' war story, and at the same time, it neglects to present fully realized back stories of the individual men through the flashbacks. Somehow, Whitmore, as writer and director, doesn't quite fulfill either position effectively. He seems tentative in completing the story in detail and unsure about directing the visual story. The objective to tell the Vietnam War from the perspectives of black soldiers remains important, but *The Walking Dead* is not the vehicle that accomplishes that task successfully.

Tim Reid

I can sit on my butt and wait for Hollywood to have some warm change of heart and I'd starve to death. . . . I'm not going to do that. I'm going to hustle and do what I always did as a black in the segregated south. We survived. We were entrepreneurs.[38]   Tim Reid

Similar to director Ivan Dixon, Tim Reid gained a national visibility via his role on a television network comedy. Reid's subsequent success has been a testament to a fighting spirit that seems missing from some of his younger contemporaries. Born in 1944 in Norfolk, Virginia, Reid was reared there and went on to attend Norfolk State College. After completing a B.A. in business, he worked in marketing for DuPont, but his interest in entertainment led him to partner with white comedian Tom Dreeson to develop an act that they performed at clubs and, eventually, on television talk and variety shows.[39] As a solo act, Reid opened for singer Della Reese before getting a recurring role on *Easy Does It*, a short-lived summer replacement show. But with other guest-starring roles following, Reid was cast as Gordon "Venus Flytrap" Sims, a member of the ensemble cast of the comedy *WKRP in Cincinnati*, which ran on television from 1978 to 1982.[40]

Reid negotiated his successful years on *WKRP* into regular roles in later television shows, including *Simon & Simon, Frank's Place*, and *Sister, Sister*. For *Frank's Place*, which he coproduced, Reid received an Emmy nomination for Outstanding Lead Actor in a Comedy Series.[41] He appeared in two feature films—*Dead Bang* (1989) with Don Johnson and *The Fourth War* (1990), directed by John Frankenheimer—before forming his own production company, United Image Entertainment. The company produced the television film *Race to Freedom* and the film-to-video project *Out-of-Sync*.[42]

In 1996, Reid moved from being a producer to directing his first feature

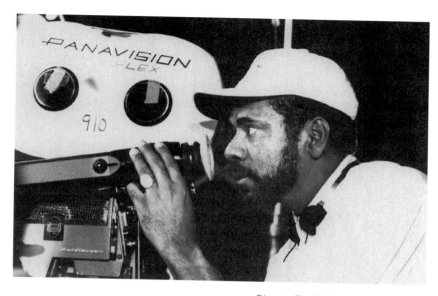

Director Tim Reid puts a shot into focus. Photo by Robert Houston; courtesy of Tim Reid Productions, Inc.

film, *Once Upon a Time . . . When We Were Colored.* The next year, along with his wife, actress Daphne Maxwell Reid, he joined with two Virginia businessmen to open New Millennium Studios, a television and film production facility established on a 62-acre site near Richmond, Virginia. Reid hopes to attract filmmakers to his site as an alternative to the Hollywood environment, since the business contains a 15,000-square-foot soundstage, two back-lot sets, and a recording studio.[43] In addition to producing *Linc's,* an original Showtime dramatic-comedy for adults, in 1999 Reid was chosen to receive the Producers Guild of America Oscar Micheaux Award for outstanding achievement in film and television production.[44]

Once Upon a Time . . . When We Were Colored shines as a small, independent film that achieves what it seeks to do. The movie, based on the autobiography of black author Clifton L. Taulbert, explores the extended family and the black community that nurtured and shaped the protagonist from birth until adolescence. It is at once a period piece, showing the stringent racial polarities in Mississippi in the late 1940s and 1950s, and a coming-of-age story that simmers with the cultural, spiritual, and ethical elements that fashion a black boy's life.

Under the opening credits, slow languid pans of the delta, an old plantation, the countryside, and rural roadways establish the pace and setting for the film. Added to that, a voiceover belonging to the adult protagonist, who is reminiscing about his past, gives a documentary feel to the film. Moreover, Reid's decision to concentrate on the emotional and psychological impact imbues the film with a sensitive and noble quality.

In the story Cliff, the young black protagonist, is literally born in a cotton field in 1946, in Glen Allan, Mississippi, surrounded by black workers who are related by family or friendship. From there, he learns about the generosity of affection of his extended family and the racial boundaries and etiquette of his southern home. A number of events and people make an indelible mark on his psyche. His great-grandfather, Poppa (Al Freeman Jr.), shows him a dignified strength and leadership; a Ku Klux Klan parade reveals racial hatred; his older cousin Melvin (Leon) comes home from Detroit to testify to the possibilities waiting in the North; his Aunt Ellie, nicknamed Ma Ponk (Phylicia Rashad), raises and cares for him like her own son; Miss Maybry (Polly Bergen), the white employer, helps him develop his love for reading; and Cleve the Ice Man (Richard Roundtree) shows the courage and perseverance of being a black businessman. What Cliff realizes through all of these surrounding characters is that he never faces hardships alone. The unity of his family and community offers him a foundation on which to erect a positive self-image and the means to survive a hostile society. And as his dreams and ambitions take him away from his small town at the end, Cliff carries a self-confidence that will allow him to succeed.

Reid chooses the subtle approach in making this film, not intruding or complicating the story with rapid cutting or experimental camera shots. Subjective and reverse-angle shots serve well to suggest the world as it was being seen by the protagonist. Long shots give the viewer the sense of community, the physical nature of the small town. In a number of sequences, Reid opts for long takes, suggesting both "real time" and a slower rhythm, perhaps to make the sequence more impressionable on the viewer.

In one sequence, however, he does rely on some basic crosscutting to emphasize the need for maintaining family connections. Ellie takes in a boarder, Nila (Iona Morris), a black woman who works as an exotic dancer in a traveling carnival. Disliking the hick town with its country people, Nila condescends to everyone. But eventually Ellie and Nila, who are about the same age, share their pasts with one another. Ellie chose not to join a traveling choir when she was younger, but remained at home, close to her ailing mother and other family members. On the other hand, Nila hurried away from her small Alabama hometown to follow her dreams of show business, leaving behind her angry mother who forbade her to go. When Nila provides passes for Ellie to come to the show, Ellie, a good Christian woman, scoffs at first, but eventually that night goes to see the exotic performance. As Ellie watches and perhaps reflects upon her own missed dreams, Reid crosscuts to the house where Ellie's mother is dying and where family members are gathering. He moves back and forth between the loud, raucous show, where white men whistle in delight, and the solemn stillness of Ellie's mother's deathbed. When Ellie reaches home and discovers that her mother died while she was at the show, she's overcome with guilt because she wasn't at her mother's bedside—a guilt she'll carry for the rest of her life. In the ensuing scene, Ellie warns Nila to go back to Alabama and make up with her mother before it's too late. Ellie tells her, "Go visit your mama, baby, because time's too short and life too precious!"

But ultimately this film is about Cliff and the numerous lessons that he learns, and in that way it reminds one of the protagonist, Kyle, in Gordon Parks' *Learning Tree*. The spiritual survival and cultural pride of Kyle and Cliff offer a discernible contrast to the characters Caine in *Menace II Society* and Q in *Juice*. Despite the varying time periods, economic challenges were there for all four young men. Was it merely the rural versus the urban environment that made the differences in their outcomes? Were the black directors of these four films suggesting, even unknowingly, that the small-town community instills more hope than the large inner-city neighborhoods? Certainly, the fulfillment of Cliff and Kyle weighs heavily for arguing the benefits of the rural environment, as opposed to the contemporary, urban setting that usurps hopes for young African American males. And with *Once Upon a Time . . .* director Tim Reid leaves viewers with the optimism that individuals can overcome barriers and can create their own possibilities in life.

Robert Patton-Spruill

I found out the hardest thing to do is to deal with someone *after* they've given you a lot of money. . . . [I]n film, you need three things to do it right. The first is the ability to write it yourself. The second is the business savvy of an MBA. The third is to get the attention of the guys with the money.[45]

Robert Patton-Spruill

Born in 1969 and raised in Roxbury, a predominantly black section of Boston, Patton-Spruill made his way to Boston University, where he majored in film studies.[46] While teaching acting at Boston's Dorchester Youth Collaborative, an antiviolence media arts center for teenagers, he wrote the script for what would become his first feature film, *Squeeze*. Raising initial funding from friends and family to do a short film, he eventually used the short to pull together $350,000 from investors.[47] When he completed the film and earned a screening at the Los Angeles Independent Film Festival, the door opened for Patton-Spruill to receive a $1 million worldwide distribution deal from Miramax.[48]

Although *Squeeze* (1997) covers familiar urban ground in terms of subject matter, the film becomes noteworthy due to its creativity and hopeful spirit. *Squeeze*, which sometimes has a documentary feel, reaches out to viewers with disturbing situations and empathetic characters. Based on stories by Emmet Folgert, Patton-Spruill wrote the script with an obvious nod to the French New Wave film, *The 400 Blows* (1959), directed by François Truffaut.

The story follows three teenagers of various ethnic backgrounds who form a much-needed friendship: Tyson (Tyrone Burton), an African American; Hector (Eddie Cutanda), a Puerto Rican; and Bao (Phuong Duong), a Vietnamese. In a complex plot, the three friends are enticed into illegal activities and are targeted by local gang members. After getting busted in a stolen car, Bao gets caught while Tyson and Hector escape, but when Hector's drug-addicted mother shoots herself, both Tyson and Hector vow to work for another week and then leave for New York. But Tyson is caught by gang enemies, who beat and torture him, pushing the teen into a nervous breakdown. For his part, Hector gets a gun for protection, but seeing Tyson's emotional condition, Hector turns over his weapon and drugs to authorities, indicating his effort to start a new life.

Squeeze succeeds in taking away the glamour of street life and showing the fear and confusion of fourteen-year-old boys moving into manhood. Patton-Spruill does a commendable job of showing the vulnerable and tough aspects of Tyson and Hector. These characters, though spunky enough to survive the streets by their wits, are in need of discipline and love. They are at once innocent and guilty, trying to hang on to lofty dreams of becoming professional athletes and the simple dreams of having a family. They are wanna-bes, who assume macho attitudes and strive to make money quickly as a cure to all of their problems, not yet mature enough to see the flaws in their decision making.

Patton-Spruill incorporates a number of effective techniques that help shape the meaning of his story: slow wipes, freeze-frames, long uninterrupted takes, use of a fisheye lens, subjective viewpoints, and rotating cameras. In a noteworthy manner, in three back-to-back sequences, the director triumphs in his connection of visual style to story. First, when Tyson suffers a beating and torture from his enemies, Patton-Spruill rotates his camera around Tyson, who, seated in a chair, is the unfortunate prey of the teenage predators. As they beat Tyson and burn cigarettes into his chest, his painful cries are mixed with his subjective shots of his tormentors. The fisheye lens shows the manner in which Tyson sees the world, distorted and night-marish; the vocal taunting of the crew is exaggerated and terrifying as they complete their sadistic acts. Following that sequence, the film cuts to the exterior as Tyson is thrown onto the sidewalk from the crew's moving van. Tyson, hurt and frightened, collects himself on the busy, indifferent streets where he's surrounded by traffic but all alone. Then, cutting to the interior bathroom at his house, Tyson tries to collect himself, staring in the mirror at his bruised face and the burn marks on his chest. In his rage he lashes out at the shower curtains and wall shelves, exploding uncontrollably. But as he does so, Patton-Spruill keeps him inside the small, confined bathroom, which further emphasizes his entrapment. The tight framing is claustropho-bic, underscoring the character's inability to break beyond his immediate environment—even his released anger has nowhere to go but against walls that he can't break down.

Squeeze deserves the attention it received at the Los Angeles Indepen-dent Film Festival, and it deserves to be acknowledged as an outstanding ex-amination of the inner city with all of its consequences and possibilities. As writer-director, Patton-Spruill announces himself with a debut movie that signals some great work to come. Whether he will stay close to his Boston environment and independent filmmaking sensibilities or be lured by Holly-wood cash and flash remains the usual question to be answered. Hopefully, the director will choose a pathway that will allow him to continue to ex-plore African American issues with the same level of skills and passion he displays in his first feature.

Darin Scott

If you don't really love movies, stay out of the business. It's very torturous, and you could put the same amount of agonizing work and angst into a more stable, normal business, and probably make more money. You can work hard and do all the right things and still not be successful if you have bad luck. You need a break. You need a couple.[49]   Darin Scott

Darin Scott was born and raised in southern California, in the city of Ingle-wood, which perhaps prompted him to do his college studies at the Univer-sity of Southern California. After graduating with a B.S. in chemical engi-neering, Scott worked for a while at Proctor & Gamble. But his love for movies led him to cowrite a low-budget horror film entitled *The Offspring* (1987), which he also produced. When the movie's "modest success was noted . . . Scott was brought in to develop and produce another thriller, *Stepfather II* (1989), the sequel to the original cult hit."[50] His other producing credits include such diverse movies as *To Sleep with Anger* (1990), *Menace II Society* (1993), and *Fear of a Black Hat* (1994).

In 1998 Scott moved to the position of director on a contemporary urban black thriller, titled *Caught Up*. The best thing to admire about *Caught Up* is the two major actors—Cynda Williams and Bokeem Woodbine. Unfortunately, however, for both of them, neither one delivers a performance that comes close to their abilities. Williams, who was hypnotic in *One False Move* and dazzling in *Mo' Better Blues,* never finds her stride in this film, though she certainly gives the movie its more sensual and erotic moments. Woodbine, who was a forceful presence in *Jason's Lyric* and *Panther,* never really finds his character, as he often overacts in an attempt to create substance for a flat character.

The thing that hurts both of these actors, as well as the movie in general, is a flawed script, which was written by Darin Scott. This story, though filled with ample plot twists, never provides fully realized characters or polished and effective dialogue. The dialogue, in particular, misses its target, or worse yet, doesn't seem to know what the target is. At various places, the dialogue is poetic, streetwise, wordy, elliptical, and goofy. As a result, the movie's tone is confusing, as the story shifts from drama, to satire, to thriller, to comedy—sometimes all in the same scene. This postmodern style has worked appropriately for other movies, but not here in this particular thriller.

Through his opening voiceover, protagonist Daryl Allen (Woodbine) warns the audience that his story is a bizarre but true account of his life. After spending two months in jail for dealing drugs, Daryl is ready to lead a straight life with his woman, Trish (Williams), and their son, Jerome (Shedric Hunter Jr.). Daryl wants to open his own nightclub, and he's shocked when his homeboy Trip (Damon Saleem) robs a bank for start-up capital. Trip wounds the white security guard (Jeffrey Combs) and is killed while escaping. Unfortunately, Daryl gets five years in prison for being an accomplice.

When Daryl emerges to begin the life of an ex-con seeking a job, he discovers that Trish and their son have moved away. By chance Daryl meets a beautiful woman in a diner who bears an exact resemblance to Trish. This woman, Vanessa (Cynda Williams), is a psychic, and leaving the restaurant together, the two are shot at by a masked gunman. Mutually surviving the violent attack leads the two into a sexual interlude, and consequently Vanessa arranges a job for Daryl with a transportation-for-hire service. Working as a driver, Daryl meets other hired ex-cons, including Herbert (Clifton Powell), who later reveals himself as undercover Detective Frank Lowden.

After Daryl and Vanessa are attacked a second time, Vanessa confesses that she's hiding from a former boyfriend, Ahmad (Basil Wallace), from whom she stole numerous diamonds. After a night of passion, Daryl wakes up to find Vanessa dead beside him in the bed, a knife driven into her chest. Daryl eventually discovers that the dead woman in the bed was actually his former girlfriend, Trish, and not Vanessa.

At an abandoned house, Daryl catches up with Vanessa and her accomplice—Detective Lowden—as they are about to exchange the diamonds for millions with a low-life fence. But Ahmad and his henchmen appear, and in a wild gun battle in the darkness, all of the characters, except for Daryl, are killed.

In a final revelation, Daryl is confronted again by the masked gunman who earlier stalked him and Vanessa. The gunman turns out to be the revengeful white security guard who was wounded in the groin years before at the bank robbery pulled off by Trip. Daryl survives the guard's attack, and in the end, finds his son.

No doubt, Scott was able to sell the idea of this movie on the numerous plot twists and bizarre characters. But he neglected to make certain that there was sufficient substance to balance the narrative convolutions. Other than one well-shot chase scene and a couple of lyrical montages using superimposition, the visual appeal of the film is slight. The viewer is forced therefore to spend the most energy attempting to figure out where the movie wants to go. Should the viewer laugh or be impressed by Daryl's poetry recitations when he first meets Vanessa? Should the audience take seriously the sudden and abrupt superstitious nature that Daryl develops when Vanessa reads his future via tarot cards? Or have pity for or laugh at the white security guard who quotes lines from Shakespeare as he takes his revenge on Daryl? These are just a few of the questions that surface while watching the movie. Unfortunately, writer-director Scott doesn't quite present a clear and convincing story that could provide possible answers. Certainly, the director's goal was to entertain, but most viewers hope to be entertained without paying such a painful and confusing price.

Hype Williams

I'm hoping to translate the things I've learned here [in music videos] into doing films that one day have a look and feel that no one has ever seen. . . . [O]n the one hand a lot of films I like are really simple. But on the other, I love what happens here in Hollywood; I love the size and the ability to create a world that is truly my own.[51]   Hype Williams

Born and raised in Queens, New York, Williams studied in the film program at Adelphi University in the late 1980s, taking a job at Classic Concept Pro-

Shooting *Belly*, Hype Williams, left, discusses
a scene with characters Tionne (Tionne
Watkins, center) and Kisha (Taral Hicks).
Courtesy of the Academy of Motion Picture
Arts and Sciences.

ductions, where music videos were being shot. In 1993 he put together his
own company to make music videos, seeking out lesser-known acts at the
time such as Brandy and Usher. But beginning in 1994, he was working with
better-known hip-hop performers, such as the Wu-Tang Clan, the Notorious B.I.G., Tupac Shakur, LL Cool J, Sean "Puffy" Combs, Will Smith, and
Mariah Carey.[52]

As the writer and director of *Belly* (1998), his first feature film, Williams
brought his music video techniques to the big screen. Although limited in
its release, the film found a hip-hop audience, if not extensive critical acclaim. *Belly* is indeed visually stunning, and in its last twenty minutes it
attempts to deliver a thoughtful message. However, as far as the message is
concerned, it may be too much too late.

Under the confessional narration of one of the central characters, named
Sincere (Nas), the story follows several gold-chained members of a crew who
enter and rob a nightclub in a storm of gunfire. Sincere and his childhood
friend Tommy "Buns" Bundy (DMX) have been leading their crew on such

robberies, but Buns wants to move into the more profitable arena of drug dealing. Buns—with a live-in girlfriend, Kisha (Taral Hicks), and an underage girlfriend on the side, Kionna (Lavita Raynor)—becomes obsessed with making the big money. Sincere, living with his girlfriend Tionne (Tionne "T-Boz" Watkins) and their son, desires something more out of life than simply hustling the streets and making money.

But Buns connects with a Jamaican drug supplier named Lennox (Louie Rankin) and floods drugs into Omaha, Nebraska, via an associate called Knowledge (Power, i.e., Oliver "Power" Grant). Moving in a different direction, Sincere reads the writings of Reverend Savior (Minister Benjamin F. Muhammed), a charismatic religious leader. After Knowledge is apprehended and Lennox is killed, Buns winds up behind bars also. Sincere bails him out, and Buns is pressured by federal agents into becoming a spy within Reverend Savior's organization with the goal of assassinating the minister. But Buns becomes affected by the Reverend Savior's message, and when the opportunity arises, Buns is unable to kill him. In the final scenes, Sincere and Tionne have decided to leave the United States and to try a new life in Africa.

The movie, from the production design to the cinematography, is a stylized sensory feast. With strobe effects, extreme slow motion, handheld cameras, and extreme angles—along with high energy music that samples jazz, hip-hop, and Caribbean styles—*Belly* grabs the viewer's attention from the opening sequence. The stumbling blocks lay in the story's lumpy dialogue, the exploitive presentation of women, and its heavy-handed ending. Although the latter was well intentioned as a cautionary technique to emphasize antidrug and self-improvement messages, the earlier focus on the materialistic rewards of the gangster life obscures those messages. *Belly* possesses the slickness of *New Jack City,* and then it attempts to declare the spirituality of *Malcolm X.* It pays homage to the first film but neglects to capture the power of the second. And, ultimately, *Belly* comes down to being another film that offers violence as entertainment, and a hip-hop sound track as the predetermined value of the film.

The African American directors who have fashioned dramatic works in the 1990s have demonstrated a variety of approaches and sensibilities as filmmakers. While some have been embraced by studios, audiences, and critics, others still remain in relative obscurity. Yet, each individual has added an important voice and style to the increasing wave of talent that continues to shape the artistic and commercial shores of visual storytelling.

CHAPTER EIGHT

And Still They Rise: Black Women Directors

The dearth of women directors in Hollywood has been emblematic of the extensive sexism and patriarchy within the studio system. The celebrated white women directors of the 1930s and 1940s, specifically Dorothy Arzner and Ida Lupino, led the way for others—many of whom obtained work and prominence in the 1980s and 1990s, such as Amy Heckerling, Martha Coolidge, Nora Ephron, Penny Marshall, Kathryn Bigelow, and Jane Campion. According to critic Christine Spines' aptly titled essay "Behind Bars," "in 1997, women made up only 12.2 percent of the [Directors] guilds members."[1] Of the many factors preventing women directors from gaining projects, Spine cites the preferred leadership role of male directors; the perception that an on-screen focus on women's experiences equals box-office failure; and the reluctance to trust big budgets to women.[2]

Confronting both racial and gender biases, black women directors of feature films remain an anomaly, although the talent of black women directors surfaces at film festivals and within television projects. Significantly, black women have been more visible outside of the Hollywood studio system, primarily in independent films, documentaries, and videos. But due to the lack of popular appreciation of those forms, those women directors have reached a smaller audience and received less critical attention. In her informative article "Independents Day," Tara Roberts observes that many black women directors sidestep the frustrating studio system and complete low-budget projects because "they know that some people in the country yearn to see depth and beauty and range of Black women's faces, bodies, and lives on the screen."[3] Roberts' collection of notable black women directors includes Jennifer Haskins-O'Reggio, Stacey Holman, Nandi Bowe, Shari L. Carpenter, Alison Swan, and Bridgett M. Davis, among others.[4]

Despite the formidable challenges posed by the Hollywood system, some black women directors got the opportunity to work in the '90s. By that decade, a number of factors finally influenced the studios to grant a nod toward a select number. First of all, as noted, the history of the pioneering work by women directors, both black and nonblack, had cracked a few doors. Secondly, by the mid-'80s black *male* directors had demonstrated that black perspectives and experiences were fresh, acceptable content for mainstream film audiences. The box-office success of black male directors chipped away a bit more at the barriers excluding directors of color.

A third factor was the increased publication of black women authors beginning in the mid-'70s and into the '90s. The inextricable relationship between literary characters and film images has always been measurable in Hollywood, and the emerging political, cultural, and feminist/womanist dynamics prevailed in the writings of Maya Angelou, Toni Cade Bambara, Nikki Giovanni, Gayle Jones, Audre Lorde, Paule Marshall, Toni Morrison, Gloria Naylor, Ntozake Shange, and Alice Walker, to name some of the more successful. Over the years, some black women writers have had their works turned into feature films, most notably Lorraine Hansberry's *A Raisin in the Sun* (1961), Kristin Hunter's *Landlord* (1970), Alice Walker's *The Color Purple* (1985), and Terry McMillan's *Waiting to Exhale* (1995) and *How Stella Got Her Groove Back* (1998).

A fourth factor was the increasing frequency of black women's appearances in movies, television shows, and television commercials beginning in the 1970s, which collectively gave visibility to black women in American society. Quantity certainly did not equal quality, as far as the collective roles for black women: on the one hand, superheroes such as in *Cleopatra Jones* (1973) and *Coffy* (1973) or, on the other hand, hookers, drug addicts, and victims. But occasional images began to appear that suggested the complexity of black women's experiences, providing a humanity to their visibility, as in the films *Sounder* (1972), *Claudine* (1974), *The Color Purple*, and *She's Gotta Have It*, to cite a few.

Finally, as mentioned earlier, black women independent filmmakers were seizing the camera as an extension of both their visions and voices. They gathered experience through film schools, on television shows, as movie interns and productions assistants, and on made-for-television movie projects. In the latter case, two black women directors in particular have distinguished themselves—Neema Barnette and Debbie Allen. Black women have prepared and are continuing to prepare themselves for feature film directing. They are well aware of the machinations of the Hollywood system, and they are sacrificially committed to the battles that await them. By the end of the 1990s, nine black women stood out as examples of the efforts and varied achievements in feature filmmaking: Euzhan Palcy, Julie Dash, Leslie Harris, Darnell Martin, Kasi Lemmons, Millicent Shelton, Troy Beyer, Cheryl Dunye, and Maya Angelou.

Euzhan Palcy

People say it is very difficult to do films. Yes. And more difficult when you are a woman. Yes, that is true. But if a woman loves film, if a woman wants to be a director, she must fight hard, very hard, to do that, because I think that women have another point of view, *un autre regard,* than men. It is very important, urgent, that women make movies.[5]   Euzhan Palcy

Euzhan Palcy was the first black woman to direct a Hollywood feature film. Financed by MGM, *A Dry White Season* (1989) was a brave film that explored the oppressive system of apartheid that strangled South Africa while honoring the active resistance to that regime.

Born on the island of Martinique in 1957, Palcy studied in France and made her first film when she was seventeen. Later she worked in Paris as an assistant director on various films, and eventually she met the French director-critic François Truffaut, who helped her raise funding for *Sugar Cane Alley* (1983), her first feature-length film.[6]

Sugar Cane Alley was presented at the Venice Film Festival, and consequently Palcy came to the attention of Hollywood producers. Set in Martinique on a colonial plantation in the 1930s, the film focuses on a young boy's experiences with poverty, colonialism, and racial oppression.[7]

It was her next film, *A Dry White Season,* that found an American audience and critical praise, with its marquee white actors—Donald Sutherland, Marlon Brando, Susan Sarandon, and Jürgen Prochnow—and its impressive supporting black cast, including Zakes Mokae and Winston Ntshona.

The central white character, Ben du Toit (Sutherland), enjoys a privileged life with his family, just as other whites do in South Africa. Possessing a naïveté, or at best an indifference, about the status of blacks, du Toit scoffs at the accusatory claims of his black gardener, Gordon (Ntshona), that his son and other black children have been tortured and killed by the police. But when Gordon's wife, Emily (Thoko Ntshinga), informs du Toit that Gordon has been arrested and later found dead, du Toit's personal investigation becomes an odyssey into the truth of apartheid and its destructive core.

Ben du Toit's journey is a costly one, as he loses the support of his wife, daughter, and friends through his growing skepticism toward and questioning of the police. When du Toit is challenged to assume a responsible role by Stanley (Mokae), a black activist, du Toit attempts to use the law to strike against the system's vicious racial oppression. A white human rights lawyer, Ian McKenzie (Brando), leads the courtroom battle, and despite the incriminating evidence against the Secret Police led by the ruthless Captain Stolz (Prochnow), there's no victory or justice. With the help of his son and a

Director Euzhan Palcy prepares a scene with Donald Sutherland, who plays the politically transformed schoolteacher Ben du Toit in the tense drama *A Dry White Season. Courtesy of Euzhan Palcy.*

concerned journalist, Melanie Bruwer (Susan Sarandon), du Toit delivers revealing and indicting documents to the press for publication, but du Toit is murdered by Captain Stolz. Then, at the end, Stanley takes out his personal revenge and completes a political objective by gunning down Captain Stolz.

In the opening sequence, under the credits, Palcy shows two young boys —one black, one white—playing together on a grassy lawn. Their play is filled with the laughter, physical energy, and innocence typical of such activity. But as the film begins, these boys—sons of Ben du Toit and Gordon Ngubene—are forced to deal with the burden of racial politics. Palcy contrasts the lives of her black and white characters more distinctly as the film continues, crosscutting quickly between the comfortable, spacious, brightly lit environments of the white characters and the poverty-stricken, congested, stark homes of the blacks.

Early in the film, Palcy's handling of an attack sequence establishes the film's tension and presents the brutality of the apartheid system. As dozens of unarmed young black people, some preteens, march in protest, they are confronted by armed police who fire and kill at will. Palcy presents shots in a rapid succession, showing children scrambling for safety and helping one another, as they are shot, beaten, and pulled away into waiting police wagons. In this, which is by far the most jolting sequence, her camera details the inhumanity of the officers and the helplessness of the children. The tone is sobering and heart-rending, and Palcy has structured images that plainly display the two confronting worlds of black and white, the collision of liberation and oppression.

Palcy also uses cutaways impressively to enhance the emotional impact of certain sequences. For example, when Stanley arrives to tell of Emily's fate, the visual story of Emily's mistreatment is shown while Stanley narrates. Stanley's words over the images of Emily blend together to deliver a forceful blow to the viewer's senses. And at the end, when Stanley waits to shoot the unsuspecting Captain Stolz, Palcy's camera moves in slowly for a close-up of Stanley's face; as it does, intercuts of Gordon, Emily, and Ben provide the personal motivation for Stanley's actions.

Some critics of the film disliked the focus on the white protagonist, du Toit, particularly since his personal loss and death attribute to him certain heroic qualities. But those critics miss the mark and the reasoning behind Palcy's use—as both screenwriter and director—of du Toit's character. Placing the character of Ben du Toit at the center serves as an effective method for showing the responsibility whites *should* assume in order to catch up to the freedom fight already waged by black women and men. Du Toit is not a white martyr, but a victim of his own ignorance and indifference. Even as the story emphasizes his transformation, it condemns who he was, and ultimately his murder isn't a plot device to elevate his actions, but a final statement about the cost of freedom already paid by numerous blacks. To dwell on the white male protagonist in this case is to overlook the powerful story and the impressive directing that make *A Dry White Season* a moving film.

The 1976 setting of *A Dry White Season* is updated by the 1989 facts captioned at the film's end, informing the audience that children as young as eleven had been detained without any formal criminal charges. But the driving passion behind the filmmaker's efforts was expressed in the final sentence of the caption: "This film is dedicated to the thousands who have given their lives and to those who carry on the fight for a free and democratic South Africa." With the political changes toward democracy that occurred in South Africa in the early 1990s, perhaps Palcy's film was one of the numerous factors that brought attention to the genocide in that country.

Julie Dash

Film is hypnotic. When you go into a cinema you extend your belief for hours. . . . I think that for a lot [of] white males, and black males too . . . [t]hey get to go there and assume the personality of the characters on screen. . . . A lot of people couldn't do that for *Daughters of the Dust*. . . . I mean, I've seen men run out of the theater.[8]   Julie Dash

In contrast to the political canvas used by Euzhan Palcy, Julie Dash presents a black cultural quilt in her *Daughters of the Dust* (1991). Like Palcy, Dash completed a number of short films before her major work, but unlike Palcy, Dash's roots were planted in the independent filmmaking tradition. Such a background served Dash well because the barriers to completing *Daughters of the Dust* were overwhelming and, unfortunately, typical for an independent filmmaker.

Born in New York City in 1952, Dash studied film production at the City College of New York and studied directing at the American Film Institute and the University of California, both in Los Angeles.[9] An earlier short film, *Illusions* (1982), set during World War II, included black actress Lonette McKee in the role of a black woman who passes for white to work as a movie executive.[10] In this film, Dash presents the element she would develop in more complexity in *Daughters of the Dust*—the black woman as protagonist, emphasizing, in particular, the significance of physical appearance, collective cultural identity, and personal autonomy.

Daughters of the Dust, set in the turn of the century in South Carolina and Georgia's Gullah islands, presents the celebration of a black family prior to their journey to the North. Central to the family and the film's story are the numerous black women characters—young and old, prostitute and mother, Christian and spiritualist, living and unborn. During a day of picnicking, picture taking, and beachcombing, members of the Peazant family talk about the importance of African myths, family legacies, personal tragedies, and spiritual strengths. Dash carefully examines a complex portrait of a black family—culturally, historically, and emotionally. Moreover, the central women characters in this family monopolize the viewer's attention, and Dash reveals what no other Hollywood filmmaker had done in the past—namely, that black women possess physical and spiritual beauty, as well as a psychological diversity.

Dash serves as screenwriter and director of the film, providing two major narrative voices for the audience to follow: Nana Peazant (Cora Lee Day), the elder of the family, and the Unborn Child (Kai Lynn Warren), who will be born into the Peazant family. Through Nana's voice and character, the importance of the ancestors and their existence among the living is emphasized. Through the Unborn Child's voice and character, the connections between the family's past and its hopes for the future are presented. Visible to only the audience at times in the film, the Unborn Child understands her place in the ongoing legacy; she comprehends her importance in convincing her father, Eli (Adisa Anderson), that she is indeed his child and not the offspring of the rape of Eula (Alva Rogers), the wife and mother-to-be.

Although a linear story is hidden within the film, the evolution of the day's events is actually developed in stunning images, music, and voiceovers that are interwoven, layer upon layer, forcing the viewer to take in a more intricate presentation. With its tapestry story—at places elliptical and at other places profound—*Daughters of the Dust* requires the audience to suspend commonly held notions about narrative films and to absorb a visual storytelling that is as unique as the 1902 Sea Islands setting. At one point Nana explains to Eli: "I'm trying to learn you how to touch your own spirit . . . something to take north with you along with your big dreams." In a similar way, Dash, as director, is inviting viewers to touch that spiritual side of themselves as they experience her film.

Whether the story provides satisfaction or not for the viewer depends on the viewer's willingness to open up to a different experience. However, few viewers can come away from the film without being affected by its captivating images. From aerial shots that provide an expansive natural meeting of ocean and sky—to intimate shots where black women cluster in twos or threes, their physical closeness and touching underscoring their affection—Dash places visual pearls before the viewer. Each frame looms autonomously in careful composition, where textures and hues blend harmoniously, yet each sequence builds upon the previous in either deepening or contrasting emotional tones.

For example, early in the film Iona (Bahni Turpin), the teenage daughter of Haagar (Kaycee Moore), reads a letter sent to her by her Cherokee Indian lover named St. Julian Last Child (M. Cochise Anderson). As Iona's voice reads the letter's content, which expresses affection and hope of her staying behind, the camera opens on a close shot of the Native American and then, pulls back slowly showing him sitting in the center of a large moss tree. The images stress both the letter's content and the feelings between the two. Like the man in the tree, their love is encompassed with a natural innocence and beauty; their feelings remain unspoiled in their raw simplicity. At the film's end, when Iona jumps off the family boat, leaving Haagar crying after her, the Cherokee lifts her onto the back of his horse and the lovers disappear into the forest. Beyond the romantic aspect, the two sequences link together and visually make a statement about the purity of young love, intercultural connections, family ties, and the profound choices one makes in life.

In another example, when Eula is fully pregnant, she reveals aloud the story of Ibo Landing (her home) to her Unborn Child. She tells the story of the Ibo people brought to the islands by force to be slaves, and how they looked around the new world with their powers and saw the tragedies that were to come. Then, without hesitation, while still manacled, the Ibo turned and walked on the ocean, all the way back to Africa. While Eula, in the foreground, speaks this myth, Eli, in the background, walks out into a cove, seemingly walking on top of the water as his ancestors had done, and he retrieves an African figurehead floating there, a remnant from a slave ship abandoned generations ago. The weathered African figurehead bears the same dark colors as Eli's skin, and as he cradles it, there is a marriage of sight and sound. The masthead, the shadowy water, the human forms, and black history all come together as Eula's voiceover connects the present and past.

In several sequences, Dash allows pure cinema to touch the audience, as she cuts among scenes with different characters without the intrusion of dialogue. In some segments, she incorporates a slow motion, which looks more like a strobe effect, to punctuate an emotionally charged moment or to draw attention to a character's powerful presence, as when the Unborn Child moves among her family. At other places, Dash utilizes the freeze-frame, suspending the moment and creating a photo—a memory to be carried away and recollected by the viewer.

With *Daughters of the Dust*, Dash creates a film where art, culture, politics, and the marketplace could meet. She reminds an audience that black people belong to a rich and still unfolding history. Unlike most filmmakers, who isolate black experiences to either the southern plantation or the urban plantation (ghetto), Dash encourages viewers to see another history that's less told and celebrated. And in a memorable way, Dash invites an audience to appreciate black women for their depth and complexities.

Leslie Harris

My idea of success is not to go out and direct a film that has white characters in it. My vision of success is to go out and direct a film that has *good*
characters in it and a *story* that's good.[11]   Leslie Harris

In an industry where teenage girls are traditionally shown as white, as
screaming victims, or as precocious vamps, a movie focusing on a black
teenage girl would be doomed to resistance. Movies such as *Clueless* (1995)
and *The Craft* (1996) were more typical of what Hollywood was willing to
market, where white teenage girls were comical, trendy, teasingly sexy, and
latently dangerous in their clumsiness. In those films and others, a black
teenage girl could be a sidekick supporting the white female protagonist, or
in other films a love interest and extension to the teenage male, as in *Boyz
N the Hood* (1991), *Menace II Society* (1993), or *Zebrahead* (1992), but certainly not the focus of the movie—until Leslie Harris' *Just Another Girl on
the I.R.T.* (1993).

Born in Ohio in 1959, director Leslie Harris studied both art and film in
college, receiving a master of fine arts. Moving to New York, Harris worked
in advertising, but found more creativity in writing her screenplay.[12] Like
Julie Dash, Harris received a plethora of negative feedback about her efforts
to make a movie with a black woman at the center, and like Dash, Harris
obtained partial financial support from New York's Women Make Movies,
Inc., an organization assisting women filmmakers.[13] With partial funding
Harris still faced defeat, and at one point she "ran out of money and had no
food, only film, in her refrigerator." Finally, she obtained funds to finish the
project through Miramax Films, the National Endowment for the Arts, and
the Jerome Foundation.[14]

In an early scene in *Just Another Girl*, the seventeen-year-old protagonist, Chantel (Ariyan A. Johnson), breaks the fourth wall explaining: "I'm a
Brooklyn girl . . . don't let nobody mess with me. I do what I want when I
want." In this bold announcement is both the strength and weakness that
Chantel possesses. On the one hand, she is a smart, independent young
woman who plans to be a doctor and to make a way out of her limited environment. On the other hand, she is selfish, impatient, and more of a talker
than a doer—very much the essence of her peers, who worship material pos-
sessions and immediate gratification.

Popular with her homegirls, Chantel enjoys hanging out and talking with
them about family, dreams, schoolwork, sex, and boys. Hounded by Gerard (Gerard Washington), who lives in her tenement building, Chantel keeps
him at a usable distance until she meets Tyrone (Kevin Thigpen) at a house

Even though she's *Just Another Girl on the I.R.T.,*
Chantel (Ariyan A. Johnson) seeks a better life,
which mistakenly includes an intimate
relationship with Tyrone (Kevin Thigpen).

party. Tyrone is cute, but more importantly he has a vehicle and money
enough to take Chantel to a restaurant; subsequently, she succumbs to his
advances, engages in unprotected sex, and becomes pregnant.

Hiding the pregnancy from her parents and seeking help at a clinic where
she meets a black counselor named Paula (Chequita Jackson), Chantel pro-
crastinates about terminating the pregnancy and frivolously spends the $500
Tyrone gives her for an abortion. But one night, while alone with Tyrone,
the baby comes early, and the pain and chaos force Chantel to get instructions over the phone from Paula. After the birth, Chantel frantically orders
Tyrone to get rid of the newborn baby girl, a final effort to avoid the "trap"
of motherhood. Tyrone carries the baby in a plastic bag to the street and approaches a nearby trash can, but he can't bring himself to abandon the child.
In the concluding sequence, Chantel breaks the fourth wall and confesses
the sacrifices made for her child, as she lives at home and attends a community college. But with Tyrone's support for the child, Chantel displays her
determination to keep pursuing her goals.

Harris accomplishes a challenging feat in *Just Another Girl*—honestly presenting a black teenage girl's urban world, while exposing the character's flaws that are partly caused by the environment and partly generated from the contradictory aspects of the character's age. If mishandled, the film could be seen as an indictment of the character and, by association, black teenage girls. However, the director presents her protagonist as a person with varying levels of competence. Chantel is a work-in-progress as a girl on the brink of womanhood, where one mistake could change her life. But Chantel is not a loser, and, ironically, even as she savors peer popularity, she doesn't want to be like everyone else in her neighborhood.

Harris takes care in showing the world of Chantel and her peers, specifically in the party scene where cool attitudes, uninhibited dancing, flirting, being seen, and thumping hip-hop music preempt all other considerations. However, one of the more successful scenes that captures the adolescent thinking of the times occurs when Chantel and two friends sit on a park bench. Using a stationary camera to provide a three-shot, the girls discuss sex with both authority and misinformation. Seeking "real men" rather than boys, they share distorted facts: you can't became pregnant if you have sex while standing up, and AIDS is a disease that attacks only gays and IV drug users. The scene is humorous, authentic in its language, but sad in the ignorance of the streetwise girls.

Perhaps the most intense scene occurs at Tyrone's apartment when Chantel's baby arrives. In the hysteria of the situation, the characters move from the bed, to the adjoining bathroom, and back to the bedroom—there's no escape. While Chantel's screams increase in decibels, Tyrone searches the medicine cabinets and then a medical book for a quick remedy to end the experience. But there is no quick fix, and amid the hollering and blood, the baby forces her way into the world. Chantel and Tyrone are obligated to work together, accepting the weight and fear of the moment, just as, together, they engaged irresponsibly in sexual intercourse.

Just Another Girl on the I.R.T. deserves a much larger audience than it has received. Harris' insights into teenage life, peer relationships, and environmental pressures are skillfully rendered. Harris presents a protagonist who is thoroughly convincing and memorable in both her mistakes and her triumphant spirit.

Darnell Martin

I love directing, but I hate the business end; hate's not even a strong enough word. . . . [S]tudios are very important, they buy and sell films, but they're not filmmakers. . . . I don't like it when executives tell me, "I've made a number of successful films." If they haven't made your film, they can't help you.[15]

Darnell Martin

Similar to *Just Another Girl on the I.R.T.*, Darnell Martin's *I Like It Like That* (1994) suffered a short screen life, though it received its share of critical acclaim. Although burdened with a banal title, the film featured content that covered some fresh and pertinent areas: the gender roles in a Latino community, the individual versus community identity for a Latina; the significance of parents as role models; and the connection between self-esteem and a fulfilling job.

Born in 1964, Darnell Martin grew up in the Bronx, the setting for her film, and she attended Sarah Lawrence College, where she discovered an interest in filmmaking.[16] Rejected from the film schools she applied to, Martin worked at a camera store. Through her job she met Ernest Dickerson, who was working as a cinematographer for Spike Lee, and Dickerson helped Martin attain a position as a production assistant on Lee's *Do the Right Thing*. In turn, Lee assisted her in gaining entrance into the New York University Film School.[17]

The short films Martin made at film school provided her the means of attending the Director's Workshop at the Sundance Film Institute. From there, she managed to get New Line Cinema and Columbia Pictures interested in her script *Black Out*, which became *I Like It Like That*. By the late 1990s, Martin made her way to the small screen, directing episodes of HBO's tough prison series *Oz*.

With its comedic tone, *I Like It Like That* has an energetic rhythm as it follows its focus on Lisette Linares (Lauren Velez), who's "just another Latina" in her Bronx neighborhood. Lisette—Catholic, biracial, a young mother of three, and dedicated to her children's father—acquires an overdue maturity when she becomes financially self-sufficient and emotionally stronger in order to parent her children.

In the opening sequence, Lisette and her husband, Chino (Jon Seda), are making love in their bedroom as neighbors listen below an opened window. The major personality defects in the two characters appear in this scene: Lisette and Chino are in bed together physically, but competing—Chino struggles to hold back an orgasm, while Lisette labors to make him have one.

When Chino steals a television during an energy blackout, he's caught and sent to jail, leaving Lisette and their three children in a quandary. Unable to raise bail money, Lisette follows the advice of her brother, Alexis (Jesse

Lisette (Lauren Velez) and husband Chino (Jon Seda) struggle with their marriage and with cultural expectations in *I Like It Like That.*

Borrego), and seeks a job. Although a simple quest for some women, Lisette's search for a job takes her out of the neighborhood, out of tradition, and out of the shadow of her man. But as Lisette moves out of that shadow, she becomes estranged from Chino and more absorbed in her job at a record company and begins to neglect her children. So, for the sake of her children, she arranges a coparenting agreement with Chino, who has obtained a job as a security guard.

After Lisette and Chino face their infidelities during their separation, Lisette finally gets Chino to realize that he has been selfish, something she has already admitted about herself. During the closing credits, Lisette works at her job, assisting in a music video, and Chino and the children are with her. Although far from an ideal couple, after much pain and confusion, they have finally reached a point where they communicate with one another.

Of the numerous things that Martin does effectively as the director, she displays a proficient handling of exterior crowd scenes. In confrontations between various characters, where voices are booming in anger and no one is listening, she captures—through long shots, tilted angles, high-angle shots, and medium shots—the street-corner chaos of lives on the edge and lives filled with frustrations. The street fights are charged with the volatile aspects of cultural clashes, economic desperation, and destructive gossip.

At the same time, Martin is just as successful in visualizing Lisette's individual angst early in the film. Unable to raise money for Chino's bail, Lisette locks herself in the bathroom, attempting to figure out some solutions. Her children pound incessantly at the door screaming for their father; the neighbor lady downstairs beats on her ceiling with the broom to call attention to the upstairs noise; and Lisette counts her few dollars, hoping to make it more. The noise and the financial stress overwhelm her, and in a burst for escape she turns up the radio, sings at the top of her voice, and dances wildly with a mop, striking out at the tub and basin. From a high-angle, overhead shot, Martin shows Lisette in the middle of the small bathroom; she's enclosed, spinning around in circles, and trapped. The only way out is through the same door she entered, where she'll have to confront and somehow handle her children, her husband's incarceration, and her financial burdens.

Receiving strong critical praise for the film, it's surprising that Columbia didn't carry on a more pervasive marketing effort to attract an audience. Certainly, there was much to appeal to Latino and black viewers, and with its concerns for contemporary love relationships, young parenthood, and self-esteem, there was much for a wider audience as well. Once again, Hollywood missed a major opportunity to be both progressive and profitable, but hopefully in the near future, Darnell Martin will bring her considerable talents back to the big screen.

Kasi Lemmons

I wanted to create a piece that was visual and lyrical with characters speaking in the rhythms that I remember from my childhood. . . . [S]ince it was personal . . . I could be totally free with the questions I was asking myself . . . like: what is reality? What is the nature of memory?[18]   Kasi Lemmons

Before directing *Eve's Bayou* (1997), one of the most original films of the 1990s, director Kasi Lemmons had gained experience on movie sets as an actress. She was born in St. Louis in 1963 and spent occasions in Tuskegee, Alabama, at her grandmother's house, giving her exposure to the southern environment. She attended New York University, UCLA, and the New School of Social Research in New York. But having done some acting as a child, she eventually found herself auditioning for a part on *The Cosby Show.* She used the audition to gain a writing job, where she received her first script-writing credit.[19]

As her efforts at acting continued, she was able to win roles in a number of films, including *Vampire's Kiss* (1989), *The Silence of the Lambs* (1991), *Candyman* (1992), *Hard Target* (1993), *Fear of a Black Hat* (1994), and *Drop Squad* (1994).[20] But her goal of becoming a feature film writer urged her on to complete the script for *Eve's Bayou,* and with the encouragement of her actor-director husband, Vondie Curtis-Hall, she began the arduous process of shopping the script around Hollywood. After many rejections, Lemmons, through an agent, finally got her script to a receptive Caldecot Chubb, who had produced the more unconventional movies *To Sleep with Anger* (1990) and *The Crow* (1994). When Lemmons asked to direct *Eve's Bayou* herself, Chubb agreed if she, as a new director, would first direct a short film version, which became *Dr. Hugo* (1998), starring Vondie Curtis-Hall and Michael Beach.[21]

Eve's Bayou presents the visions of Eve Batiste (Jurnee Smollett), a ten-year-old girl named after an ancestor who possessed a gift of clairvoyance. But at her age, Eve doesn't quite comprehend the possible powers she possesses, nor does she understand that what she sees and hears may not be the "truth" of what is. In the 1962 summer setting of the movie, Eve observes her family interacting with one another: her father, Louis (Samuel L. Jackson); her mother, Roz (Lynn Whitfield); her aunt, Mozelle (Debbi Morgan); and her older sister, Cisely (Meagan Good). Eve loves each, but discovers aspects about all four that are at times unclear: her father's house calls on women patients, her mother's strict rules, her aunt's mystical powers, and her sister's accusations of sexual advances by their father. On the fringe of her family, Eve discovers another perplexing figure—Elzora (Diahann Carroll), the voodoo practitioner who becomes a last resort when Eve needs to wield control over her father.

The complexity of this film makes it both alluring and elusive. Although there is a story line that's accessible, the real center of the film is the various relationships where characters both connect with and combat one another. First of all, there is a sister-to-sister link between Eve and Cisely that runs the gamut from a rivalry for their father's attention to the sharing of secrets through verbal and silent gestures. Lemmons does a remarkable job of pulling forceful performances from her two young actors, who, particularly Smollett as Eve, must show innocence, precociousness, moodiness, and evil all within the compressed time period of the story. Another sibling connection is the brother-sister relationship between Louis and Mozelle, both

Director Kasi Lemmons, left, considers a shot with crew members on the set of *Eve's Bayou.*

of whom are similar in that they both are in professions in which they attempt to help others. As a doctor and adulterer, Louis addresses the physical needs of his clientele, and as a medium, Mozelle heals the spiritual and emotional ailments of her customers. But the two clash over Louis' infidelities, and ironically, Louis risks losing the family he has while Mozelle—widowed three times—yearns to have a family.

However, beyond the relationships mentioned, there exists a visual layering as well, as Lemmons shows the overlapping between past and present, the tenuous aspect of truth, and the imposing nature of visions. The melding of past and present begins in the opening images of the film, as the swamps, moss-covered trees, and eerie landscape confirm the weight and tangible facets of a southern history that plays a palpable role in the present. As the characters move across the landscape, they become entwined in the moods created by that exterior. A more striking mix of past and present occurs when Mozelle is telling Eve about her lost loves from the past. Lemmons shrewdly uses lighting and mirrors to physically show the three men lost to Mozelle, as Mozelle turns and interacts with them in the past, while still telling her story in the present time. The technique is simply executed but forceful in its impact on the viewer's sense of time and place, transporting the audience into an ethereal world where Mozelle's reality and memory merge.

The elusive qualities of truth receive attention early in the film, when a sleeping Eve wakes up undetected and observes her father and Matty Mereaux (Lisa Nicole Carson) having sex in the shadows of the carriage house. Eve tells Cisely, who insists that Eve's perception was blurred by explaining what Eve actually saw. Lemmons gives the audience a visual sequence that matches each girl's account of the incident, leaving Eve and the audience questioning what indeed happened. Later in the film, following Cisely's accusations against her father, Lemmons again provides two sequences of the same event, each bearing the narration by a different character. Louis' memory of the incident recalls Cisely's advances to kiss him and subsequently his violent pushing away of his daughter; Cisely's version recounts a drunken Louis who pulls his daughter into an intimate embrace. Again, both Eve and the audience have to deal with two versions of a truth that each character professes.

Thirdly, Lemmons delivers visual sequences that show the prophetic visions seen by Mozelle and the dreams experienced by Eve. These sequences are shown elliptically in amber shading, often without clarity. The images hint at what has happened and what will happen, empowering Mozelle to understand events and people, while confusing Eve as to what to believe and hold true.

Kasi Lemmons has achieved a compelling film with *Eve's Bayou*, and with the work of her cinematographer, Amy Vincent, Lemmons has accomplished a visual style that is difficult to resist. Along with the production design by Jeff Howard, editing by Terilyn A. Shropshire, and music by Terence Blanchard, the resulting film pulls the audience deep into its rhythms and moods, evoking a haunting and memorable experience. With this first feature, Lemmons has crafted a work that exists somewhere between an art house film and a period piece that speaks to a smaller Creole community within the larger African American culture. With all the different elements—cultural, thematic, and visual—that are addressed within the work, it serves as a unified affirmation of the writing and directing talents of Kasi Lemmons.

Millicent Shelton

Part of the struggle of being a woman and being black—but more being a woman—is it's hard for people to see you. You have to work harder. I would have liked to have done my first film by 26. But that's all right. I'll be around longer."[22]   Millicent Shelton

Millicent Shelton was born in St. Louis in 1967, and she later graduated from Princeton University. She was able to gain filmmaking experience in 1988, serving as a production assistant on Spike Lee's *Do the Right Thing* (1989). She gained a production assistant position on *The Cosby Show* before going on to study in the graduate film program at New York University. Her time at NYU was supported by paying jobs she obtained on music video shoots, and the experience led to her directing the music video *Expression* for the hip-hop group Salt-N-Pepa. Shelton added to her music video experience by directing projects for Mary J. Blige, MC Lyte, R. Kelly, Aaliyah, Heavy D, and others.[23] With her first feature, *Ride* (1998), Shelton relied on personal experience for the story, following the challenging assignment she had of getting thirty Harlem kids to Miami by bus to be extras in a music video for music producer Teddy Riley.[24]

Shelton's *Ride*, a movie that would certainly fit into the category of films shaped by hip-hop sensibilities, carries the setting, language, sexuality, attitude, and music sound track to appeal to a younger audience. With Warrington and Reginald Hudlin as the movie's producers, there is a similar energy level as their earlier hit *House Party* (1990), but unfortunately, the comparisons end there. Despite its good intentions, *Ride* is an unappealing journey into a tedious and jaded story.

As the opening credits roll, the hip-hop tune "Let Me Ride" plays over footage of actual hip-hop and R&B performers in studio sessions, interviews, and concerts. A voiceover by Leta Evans (Melissa De Sousa) informs the viewer that having grown up on MTV and BET, she aspires to be a music video director. But after finishing at New York University Film School, she finds herself taking on a job as an assistant to well-known video director

Aspiring video director Leta Evans (Melissa
De Sousa) keeps control of teenage extras
with the help of Poppa (Malik Yoba) in *Ride*.

Bleau Kelly (Downtown Julie Brown). Trying to negotiate an opportunity to direct her own video, Leta agrees to take a group of inner-city youth from New York to Miami to be extras at the shooting of the new video by the famous performer Freddy B (Luther Campbell). Leta discovers that, in an effort to relieve the budget, the trip will be on a dilapidated bus, driven by two questionable rascals, Roscoe (John Witherspoon) and his brother, Bo (Cedric the Entertainer).

Even worse, Leta finds that the youth are a wild group, kept under control only through the efforts of a community activist called Poppa (Malik Yoba), who is helping his friend Freddy B in exchange for financial support for a new community center called "The Rites of Passage." Leta admires Poppa's altruism, but she has more concerns about the motley group traveling on the bus.

The group of malcontents survives one another, as Leta and Poppa become closer romantically. When the bus breaks down, they all realize they will share a common fate if they don't reach Miami on time for the video.

Luck and some stolen money gets them there, but Leta is fired after defending her group's fun-loving behavior. But, unified, the group refuses to work on the video until Leta's back on the job, and as she's rehired, the video is shot as the movie ends.

As writer and director, Shelton mixes elements of the films *Fame* (1980), *Bustin' Loose, House Party,* and *Get on the Bus.* In addition, there is obvious homage to a number of Hollywood movies whose titles or content are referenced throughout the film. The opening of the movie works well, as the footage of rappers and Leta's voiceover create expectations of insightful and perhaps satirical examination of music videos and filmmaking in general. The movie's script, however, never delivers. One of the major problems is the protagonist, Leta. Actress Melissa De Sousa does an admirable job with only the skeleton of an inconsistent character. Having lived in the New York area to attend NYU Film School, Leta would certainly be more street-smart and savvy when dealing with the youth in her charge. Since she manages to talk her way into a position working with Bleau, the top video director, why does she become so inept when handling the kids and the various problems arising along the journey to Miami? Sometimes, Leta is smart and experienced, as when she speaks with Tuesday (Kellie Williams) about the latter's unwanted pregnancy and emotionally abusive boyfriend, Brotha X (Sticky Fingaz). Yet, she appears flustered when making small talk with the kids or taking a leadership role. And if Leta was capable of graduating from NYU Film School, why does she only aspire to direct music videos?

Another character suffering from the script's vagueness is Poppa. Malik Yoba, one of the most talented black actors in the business, can't dignify a character that remains no more than an idea. With all of his unselfish activism for the community and playing big brother, Poppa fails to be real and three-dimensional. The scenes that include him never appear to be complete, but are truncated after he delivers a line of dialogue that functions as a message.

Shelton's direction also seems unsure, as if she's uncertain how to tell the story. The movie develops like a string of non sequiturs. The elliptical story that results can not be the director's objective, since the incoherence and flatness hurts both the pacing and significance of the narrative. It's difficult for a viewer either to care for the characters or to be satisfied with the weary plot.

Another weakness is the film's attempts at comedy; the movie too often relies on bathroom humor or flatulence jokes. At the same time, there are no clever quips or dialogue to provide an engaging verbal humor. The comedic elements do not punctuate the scenes, nor do they build up as the movie progresses.

Other than an effective use of freeze-frames and Leta's voiceover when first introducing the youth to the audience, the visual work is uninspired. Along the way, the viewer can spot cameos by Fred Williamson, Doctor Dre, and Snoop Doggy Dogg, but their appearances can't save the movie from the lethargy that plagues it.

Shelton misses a chance to slice into two rather interesting issues. At the beginning of the film, when Leta first goes to the video production office for a job, she is lost within a bevy of beautiful black women waiting to audition for videos. Leta asserts to one woman that she would never peddle her flesh for a music video, and the woman only gives her a disdainful look until she learns that Leta is a director. Immediately, the woman, and several others nearby, force their headshots into Leta's hand. Who are these women? Why do they settle for being flesh toys in music videos? How does a woman director approach sexuality differently in music videos?

A second issue revolves around the rap duo Indigo (Guy Torry) and Casper (Reuben Asher). The former is black, and Casper, who speaks and dresses "black," is white. He has an additional reason for journeying to Miami—to find his missing father. Casper believes that although his mother is white, his father must be black, because Casper considers himself black. He resents the group's teasing and calling him Vanilla Ice; from Casper's perspective, his blackness is not in his skin color, but in his ethos. When he does trace down his father, Casper, to his disappointment, finds a white man. Is Casper correct in suggesting that "blackness" exists in the mind and not in the complexion? Is blackness a cultural and political identity that isn't restricted to complexion?

These last two issues were obviously too serious for Shelton's goals—one of which, no doubt, is to have a marketable hip-hop sound track. With this last goal, she succeeds, and in many ways the movie functions as a music video itself, sampling pieces and notions of other films in hip-hop fashion. But if Millicent Shelton was able to get this film made, she obviously has the potential and connections to do more as a filmmaker. Perhaps, her voice will come through with more clarity and force in her next project.

Troy Beyer

I think the main thing I hope everyone will realize is that, although we experience things in our life alone, we're not alone in our experiences. As unique and original as we may think they are, they're really quite universal.[25]

Troy Beyer

Troy Beyer has been in front of a camera since she was a child, and her accumulated credits for television shows, commercials, movies, and videos would be the envy of many an aspiring actor. However, in the 1990s, she added directing to her résumé, proving again her versatility and resilience.

Born in 1965 of an interracial marriage, Beyer was raised in New York by her black mother after her parents divorced. Dealing with financial difficulties, her mother took the suggestion of a next-door neighbor—choreographer Alvin Ailey—and took Beyer to a casting agency.[26] At the age of four, she received a major role on *Sesame Street*, remaining in the cast for seven years.[27] Desiring a break from the business, Beyer left her mother and moved to live with her white father in Caldwell, Idaho, where she stayed through her high school years.[28]

Beyer returned to New York to attend the College of Performing Arts, and lucked into a small part in *The Cotton Club* (1984), albeit in a scene that was lost to the editing room floor.[29] Moving to the West Coast, she signed with the Wilhelmina Talent Agency in Los Angeles, appearing in twelve commercials in a year. She went on to do a five-part guest-starring role on the series *Knots Landing*, and appearances on the shows *T.J. Hooker* and *Murder One*.[30] But it was in 1986–87 that she became popular again with a two-year stint on *Dynasty* as Jackie Deveraux, the daughter of the character played by Diahann Carroll. Beginning in the late '80s, she acted in a number of movies, including *Disorderlies* (1987), *The White Girl* (1990), *The Five Heartbeats* (1991), *Weekend at Bernie's II* (1993), and *Eddie* (1996).[31] She also worked at developing a writing career, finally selling her first screenplay, *B*A*P*S* (1997), which was directed by Robert Townsend.[32]

The first twenty minutes of Beyer's feature *Let's Talk About Sex* (1999) is a winning mixture of script and directing. Beyer, serving as actress as well, pushes the viewer into a contemporary situation and premise, but after the first third of the film, the script can't maintain quite the same crisp edge as the directing.

When Jasmine "Jazz" Hampton (Troy Beyer) discovers that she needs to submit a completed video for consideration for a television production job, she enlists the help of her two housemates, Michelle (Paget Brewster) and Lena (Randi Ingerman). Approaching women on the beaches and streets of Miami, as well as at numerous parties, the three friends tape several of them—varied in age, ethnicity, and sexual orientation—recording their responses to questions and issues about sexuality, relationships, and men. As they compile a range of attitudes, ideas, and experiences, Jazz, Michelle, and Lena also reflect upon their own lives and relationships. Jazz ponders her broken engagement with Michael (Joseph C. Phillips), which she eventually

Voicing the concerns of contemporary women in
Let's Talk About Sex, Jazz (Troy Beyer, center)
sparks an honest evaluation of relationships for
her friends Lena (Randi Ingerman, left) and
Michelle (Paget Brewster). Courtesy of the
Academy of Motion Picture Arts and Sciences.

mends. Michelle weighs a strategy of using men before they hurt her by walking away. Lena confronts the truth of her sexual exploitation by her selfish
lover, Scott (James Hyde).

After editing a finished version of the video, Jazz relies on Michelle to
deliver the only copy to the television station, but the latter loses the tape,
and with it Jazz's hope of getting the job. In the disappointing aftermath,
Jazz realizes that her effort to be creative and give life to the television program was her sublimating way of making up for infertility. As the film closes,
Michael proposes again, and Jazz accepts, inspiring Michelle and Lena to
make honest decisions in their personal lives.

Beyer's *Let's Talk About Sex* is on one level a film within a film, as the
footage of conducted interviews becomes a major portion of the larger film.
Keeping the feel of spontaneity with the women on videotape, their state-

ments about sexual preferences and dislikes are both refreshing and diverse. For a change, women assert their viewpoints on sexuality, which run from conservative to kinky, showing that women's attitudes and appetites vary considerably. Beyer taps into a host of perspectives, while presenting an ethnically and culturally diverse set of women characters. At the same time, she doesn't hesitate to cross the line of sexual orientation, as a subplot highlights a loving lesbian relationship that undergoes some of the same emotional tugs-of-war as the heterosexual unions portrayed.

Paralleling the documentary aspect of the videotaped interviews, in the larger film Beyer effectively utilizes some of the standard aspects of independent films—handheld cameras, extreme close-ups, natural lighting, and a visual quirkiness. At places the movie shifts and becomes lyrical, as the camera revolves around subjects, creating long scenes in real time with a minimal amount of cutting.

One technical aspect of the movie that fails, however, are the cutaways to sequences that visualize a particular woman's anecdote. These sequences, which are not differentiated through visual effects, are sometimes abrupt and confusing; more importantly, the director's choice to visualize some experiences but not others is unclear. For instance, it makes sense to visualize Jazz's long, passionate kissing with Michael as she—while being videotaped—is happily describing this orgasmic experience; both Jazz and Michael are vital to the main story line. But when a store clerk confesses her disappointment with a lover's behavior following sex, a sequence shows the two in bed with accompanying dialogue to punctuate the male lover's rudeness. The two characters are not vital to the main story, so why is their situation worthy of portrayal?

If Beyer could have sustained the magic achieved early on in the movie, she would have had an outstanding work. Although a very watchable film, *Let's Talk About Sex* might prove to be most satisfying for the liberation and validation that it gives to women's perspectives. Moreover, in a promising manner, it indicates that Troy Beyer, as a director, has the experience and potential to do some significant and eye-catching work on the big screen.

Cheryl Dunye

I make independent independent film, not Hollywood independent film. . . . I consider myself a filmmaker, an artist and an activist. My strategy has been to use the 16 mm format to get a message across about the multiplicities that are inside all of us, the kind of cultural schizophrenia we either accept or pay tons of therapy money for.[33]   Cheryl Dunye

One of the major emerging talents in independent filmmaking in the late 1990s, Cheryl Dunye directed her first feature, *The Watermelon Woman* in 1997. Its subject matter and visual style never drew long lines at suburban cineplexes, so it had a short life on very few American theater screens. Unfortunately, the viewers have lost out, since the film brings provocative and fresh perspectives on interpersonal relationships, historical myths, and the politics of filmmaking.

Dunye was born in Monrovia, Liberia, in 1966; her father was West African and her mother an American from Philadelphia.[34] Raised in that city, she embraced her lesbian orientation in her early teens,[35] which was no doubt a considerable challenge as a young black woman negotiating life within a black community. Attending Rutgers University, she went on to make short films and videos, such as *She Don't Fade, Vanilla Sex, The Potluck and the Passion,* and *Greetings from Africa,* that have garnered praise and attention.[36] In 1993 her videos were honored with a showing in the Biennial Exhibition at the Whitney Museum of Modern Art in New York City.[37]

Her feature *The Watermelon Woman* developed as a result of "the real lack of any information about the lesbian and film history of African-American women,"[38] and the film has won praise at film festivals and with critics. Yet, despite the accolades, the film has endured a host of negative voices; in 1996, when it was discovered that grant money from the NEA partially funded her film, Dunye was accused by some members of Congress of exploiting taxpayers' money to carry out a gay and lesbian agenda.[39] However, Dunye has been championed as vehemently as she has been criticized. According to black feminist Michelle Wallace, "Dunye is to be considered a leading figure . . . in the latest generation of black feminist artists and intellectuals. These extraordinary women have thrived upon the accomplishments of a highly developed realm of black feminist cultural production, most of which is still a secret to mainstream arts audiences."[40]

Presented in a documentary fashion, *The Watermelon Woman* follows Cheryl (Cheryl Dunye), a struggling filmmaker, who becomes fixated on a 1930s black actress named Fae Richards (Lisa Marie Bronson), who was known by the Hollywood nickname "The Watermelon Woman." Cheryl decides to make a documentary film about her efforts to discover the background of Richards, as well as the reactions that various people have toward her screen image. Cheryl conducts her research and video shooting while holding down a job at a video store, working alongside her friend Tamara (Valarie Walker), an outspoken black woman with a taste for black porn films. Both lesbians, Cheryl and Tamara share personal and political perspectives about race and gender, but they collide when Cheryl begins a relationship with a white lover, Diana (Guinevere Turner).

As Cheryl uncovers more details about Fae Richards, Cheryl discovers that the latter was also a lesbian who had a white lover, and becomes fascinated by the parallel between herself and Richards. But as Cheryl becomes committed deeper into her film project, her friendship with Tamara becomes cold and, eventually, she loses Diana. But Cheryl perseveres, and as the film ends, Cheryl presents her film-bio of Fae Richards to the audience. The footage shows the burden of the "mammy" roles that Richards endured; her efforts to redefine herself as a singer in the 1940s; and her drift into an obscure personal life in the 1950s, living with a black lover until her death. As the movie ends, Cheryl explains to the audience that for her—in spite of stereotyped roles and being forgotten from the annals of cinema—Fae Richards, as a black actress and a black lesbian, represents hope, inspiration, and possibilities for success.

Dunye creates a clever and engaging story with *The Watermelon Woman*, inviting viewers to contemplate the manner in which numerous black actresses were constrained to limited screen images in the 1930s and 1940s without having their talents recognized or their personal lives respected. She further highlights the importance of movies with all-black casts that attempted to offer black performers a variety of roles absent from Hollywood movies. At the same time, Dunye's film invites viewers to take a closer look at lesbian communities comprised of various ethnicities, political viewpoints, and individual ambitions. As the viewer journeys from the lesbian clubs and sexual intimacy in Cheryl's contemporary life to the lesbian connections of the past in Fae Richards' life, Dunye presses the point that such relationships have as much history as the cinema she uses to present her historical search.

In its mock documentary structure, Dunye permits herself and other characters to break the fourth wall and comment on Richards or the image of "The Watermelon Woman." Some of the characters being interviewed are fictional, portrayed by actresses, as well as real-life authors and historians. One of the best-known speakers is Camille Paglia, the white feminist critic who articulates her theory about the significance of the "watermelon" and the "mammy" that has been misunderstood by both black and white historians. Her statements are controversial as always, and watching her stylistic delivery on film suggests that she's doing a parody of herself.

Dunye's visual style again gives a nod to documentary filmmaking, as well as to the low-budget foundation of the project. Using a host of techniques—including wipes, fades-to-black, title cards, handheld cameras, 16 mm film, uninterrupted long shots, awkward lighting, and elliptical cutaways—Dunye aims for a movie with a different feel and look about it. Rejecting the polished, fast-paced Hollywood approach, the movie begs to be pondered in both its form and content. It leans toward an experimental mode, but remains entertaining with its story-within-a-story structure.

The Watermelon Woman offers a vision that may not be for everyone, but it serves as a work for those who seek a distinctive emotional, intellectual, and cinematic experience. It has been the type of movie that evokes either favorable response or harsh rejection; there's little room for fence-sitting. But, regardless, with this movie, Cheryl Dunye has established herself as an artist who uses film for her canvas and an activist who gives a voice to women largely absent from mainstream films.

Maya Angelou

I spoke to the cast and crew and said: "This is your world. I write books. If you see something you don't think is right, call me aside in private, take a walk with me and tell me. And I will do the same thing with you."[41]

Maya Angelou

Maya Angelou made her way into celebrity status as a writer of autobiography, poetry, children's books, and screenplays. Then, in 1999, she moved behind the camera to direct her first feature, exploring family relationships and the healing power of self-love.

Born Marguerite Johnson in St. Louis, Missouri, in 1928, Angelou lived her early life in Stamps, Arkansas, where she was raised by her religious grandmother. By sixteen, Angelou was living in California with her biological mother, and dealing with her first pregnancy. She eventually pursued acting, dancing, and singing, but then became active in the Southern Christian Leadership Conference and the civil rights movement. She also worked as a journalist, spending time in Africa in both Egypt and Ghana.[42] Angelou made her initial impact as a writer with the popularity of her five-volume autobiography, beginning with the 1970 book, *I Know Why the Caged Bird Sings.* In the 1970s and 1980s, she also penned children's books and volumes of poetry, and in 1972 her screenplay *Georgia, Georgia* was made into a film, followed by the television movie scripts *I Know Why the Caged Bird Sings* (1978), and *Sister, Sister* (1982), and by *Blacks, Blues, Blacks* (1979), a public television miniseries. In 1993 she distinguished herself as the first African American poet to write and read an original work—the poem "On the Pulse of Morning"—for the inauguration ceremonies for a U.S. president.[43]

Director Maya Angelou leads her stars, Alfre Woodard and Wesley Snipes, into their next scene in *Down in the Delta*.

Down in the Delta (1998) announces in an emphatic manner the considerable talents of Maya Angelou as a filmmaker. With a script by Myron Goble, and a production team that cites Wesley Snipes as one of five producers, the movie is a character and family study with no apologies for its sometimes elliptical story. With exceptional performances by Alfre Woodard and Al Freeman Jr., the movie confirms the significance of the extended family, as it praises the advantages of the southern rural environment over the northern urban setting.

In Chicago, Rosa Lynn Sinclair (Mary Alice) works hard to support her despondent and unemployed daughter, Loretta (Alfre Woodard), while protecting her grandchildren, Thomas (Mpho Koaho) and Tracy (Kulani Hassen), from a neighborhood of violence and drug dealers. Loretta, with no work skills and a minimal education, finds solace in alcohol and marijuana, until Rosa Lynn pressures her to take the kids and visit Mississippi for the summer. The plan is to work for and live with Rosa Lynn's brother, Earl (Freeman). To purchase bus tickets, Rosa Lynn pawns a silver candelabra that she and Earl call "Nathan."

Once in the South, Loretta endures her daily routine of living in a dry county and working as a sausage stuffer at Earl's business—the "Just Chicken" restaurant. Eventually, Loretta adjusts to the locale, helped along by three factors: her friendship with a local woman, Zenia (Loretta Devine); her growing importance at her waitress job; and her realization of the improved life for her children. When Earl's son, Will (Snipes), pays a visit with his wife, Monica (Anne-Marie Johnson), and their two sons, family tensions emerge. Will, a corporate lawyer in Atlanta, doesn't take the same kind of pride in his roots as does Earl, yet Loretta and Will, despite their class differences, find a way to connect and to respect one another.

With Will's legal help, Loretta assumes a leadership role in organizing the locals to purchase the closing chicken factory. She discovers a new life and purpose in the South, where she and the kids decide to stay. Loretta returns to Chicago in order to buy "Nathan" from the pawnshop, and as the movie ends, she tells Thomas the full story about the candelabra and its importance to the family history.

The story of "Nathan" revolves around Earl's great-great grandfather, Jesse, who was a little boy when he saw his father, Nathan, sold away in exchange for a silver candelabra. After the Civil War, Jesse steals the candelabra and goes searching through the South to find his father. Unsuccessful, he returns home, names the stolen candelabra after his father, and passes the item down to the members of the black Sinclairs, making certain the story of the auction is passed along as well.

With the solid performances in the major roles, Angelou's work is made much easier in this debut film. Angelou aims for a lyrically structured story that moves along at a leisurely pace, particularly in capturing the casual atmosphere of the southern setting. With the frequent use of dissolves and fades-to-black, the gentle rhythm of the movie works effectively. In many ways, the movie strikes a more authentic chord when it's set in the South, as the northern, urban sequences at the beginning of the movie lack the same intensity.

Another area of weakness stems from the impression that in places information appears to be left out; specifically, Will and Monica remain rather vague and flat. To his credit, Wesley Snipes shapes an interesting personality from a script that seems content to keep him a shadow. Unfortunately, Anne-Marie Johnson, here in a dramatic role, has little to work with in the story. There's a line of dialogue that mentions marriage trouble, but Monica's discomfort when visiting her in-laws doesn't receive any development.

But Angelou's obvious focus here is with the character Loretta and her journey to self-esteem. The generous close-ups of Woodard and the improvisational feel of the scenes centering on Loretta suggest the director's passion for the character. Just as significant, however, is the supporting story of slavery and "Nathan," and in those sequences that show the historical segments, Angelou favors amber tones and soft lighting to punctuate the past. Though no dialogue is spoken during the historical sequences, the voice-overs of Earl and Rosa Lynn work well in connecting the contemporary to the past via the oral tradition.

In retrospect, the nine black women directors discussed here provide a distinctive range of thematic concerns, cultural issues, political perspectives, and cinematic styles. Most wrote *and* directed their films, which testifies to their skills as multidimensional filmmakers, and all of them weathered the Hollywood system overwrought with genre formulas and repetitive plots. Importantly, audiences, both black and nonblack, deserve to experience the films of black women directors who will certainly entertain, but who will also provoke thought and a reevaluation of the possibilities of commercial cinema.

CHAPTER NINE

Not without Laughter: Directors of Comedy and Romance

Hollywood films that have presented comedy and romance, or a combination of the two, have been an industry staple for decades. Comedies, of course, entertain by providing the audience an escape from the formidable problems of the real world outside the theater. For their part, romances plunge headlong into the emotional turmoil that surrounds relationships, exploring the dynamics of failing intimacies or shaping the facets of happy-ever-after unions.

African American images have been a part of the comedy genre since the silent era, and throughout the studio years, Hollywood's approach to black people was that they were certainly good for a laugh. African Americans have always fit well into the areas most recognized in movie comedies: physical, verbal, and situational humor. For blacks, the physical comedy usually has been played with broad exaggeration, such as slapstick, that is, violent hitting and falling in a clownish manner, or visual shtick such as eye-rolling, an overly nervous demeanor, or eccentric body movements. Verbal humor has revolved around malapropisms and broken English, while situational humor has allowed blacks to be depicted in various stages of confusion, fear, inadequacy, and ignorance.

In contrast, romance has been a different challenge for blacks in Hollywood. Traditionally, romance, affection, and matters of the heart were off-limits for black characters as the major focus of a film. Certainly, Hollywood has shown blacks who have been married and blacks who have engaged in sex, but the more amorous and sensuous aspects of those unions were seldom explored until recent years.

Building on the directorial work of Ossie Davis, Sidney Poitier, Berry Gordy, and Michael Schultz, African American directors in the 1980s and 1990s have presented cultural experiences and comic traditions in movies that have reached out to audiences that have comprised various racial backgrounds. Some of the movies have been outstanding in showcasing blacks' talents and cultural expressions, while others have been mediocre in their renderings. Collectively, the black directors of comedy and romance are indicative of the range of accomplishments and disappointments of these decades. Some of these directors demonstrate ways in which genre elements take precedence over ethnic and cultural issues, while others display a strong consciousness about the use of traditional genres to reveal particular dynamics that spring from black experiences.

Oz Scott

The theater is fresh. And fun. It has a great deal of freedom. The advantage of movies, however, is that you can say, "This is it. That's what I want." That's what's up there forever; it doesn't change. Plus, I love what you can do in the editing room.[1]   Oz Scott

Oz Scott made his mark in theater before he stepped behind the camera to direct for television and film. Born in Virginia, he went to New York to study at New York University, where he remained until receiving his master of fine arts. While attending the university, he obtained a job working with Joseph Papp, the producer of the city's public theater.[2]

But it was in 1975 that he became recognized for his stage direction of Ntozake Shange's *For Colored Girls Who Have Considered Suicide When the Rainbow Is Enuf.* The enormous popularity of the show earned him the call to direct his first feature, *Bustin' Loose* (1981).[3] In addition to this film, Scott also went on to direct television shows for both network and public television, but his film debut was noteworthy as he worked with two veteran performers—Richard Pryor and Cicely Tyson.

Bustin' Loose begins in Philadelphia, where thief Joe Braxton (Pryor), scores petty heists. Joe winds up in court, given years of probation under the control of a black parole officer, Donald Kinsey (Robert Christian). Joe receives the chore to drive Kinsey's romantic interest, Vivian (Cicely Tyson), and eight homeless kids by bus to live on a farm near Seattle. Joe rebuffs the job, especially when he meets the eight children, about eleven to fourteen in age, who all have peculiar problems. For instance, Samantha (Kia Cooper) is a black girl with an obsessive attachment to a teddy bear, Anthony (Edwin Kinter) is a pyromaniac, and Harold (Jimmy Hughes) is blind and fixated on driving moving vehicles. As the motley group travels across country, they clash and irritate one another, but slowly develop a sense of caring. But once they reach the farm, Vivian runs into a stumbling block—back taxes and late payments on the farm have put it into receivership to a local bank.

Having fallen in love with Vivian and the kids, Joe scams the needed money from Professor Renfrew (George Coe), a local con artist who is run-

Stuck on a bus with troubled kids,
Vivian (Cicely Tyson) and Joe
(Richard Pryor) find a rare moment
of enjoyment in *Bustin' Loose*.

ning a pyramid scheme. In the meantime, the eight kids have befriended the
bankers, who agree to help. By the end, Joe, Vivian, and the kids have formed
a family, and Kinsey sets Joe free to remain with them.

Oz Scott seems to do his best directing when Joe, Vivian, and the kids are
on the road trip. The movie maintains a brisk pace as the audience gets to
know the individual personalities of the characters. Without using any visual
tricks, Scott brings the characters closer and closer to roundness, stripping
away their individual tragedies. Scott pulls good, though sometimes overly
emotional, performances from his children actors, and he allows the relationship between Joe and Vivian to come slowly toward affection without
sacrificing the stubbornness in both characters.

It is during the final thirty minutes, as the group reaches the farm, that
the script and the direction slip. The plot twist regarding the bank payments
is too contrived, and it diminishes the intelligence and resourcefulness displayed earlier by Vivian. After defying a number of formidable challenges,
Vivian becomes distraught and helpless when the bank fails to give her a
loan. The other plot twist concerning Professor Renfrew and the pyramid
scheme is too convenient. Joe, as he forlornly walks the town's streets, just

happens to see the flyers announcing the "Dare to Be Rich" seminar, and then, selling the bus, he appears at the seminar wearing a cowboy outfit and speaking in a down-home accent. None of the whites attending the seminar seem upset that a fast-talking black cowboy takes over the seminar and begins handling thousands of dollars that have been collected.

Aside from the story defects, Scott wisely allows Pryor to dominate the scenes where a mixture of slapstick, sight gags, and verbal humor unfold. Perhaps the best-known sequence of the film is also the most successful in achieving both humor and social commentary. After the bus becomes stuck in mud following a rainstorm, Joe's tight-lipped anger is barely contained as he tries to push the bus with Vivian at the steering wheel. Falling face down in the mud, Joe orders Vivian and the kids to remain in the bus as he slips away to get help. Mumbling angrily through the woods, Joe is suddenly surrounded by a group of torch-bearing Ku Klux Klan members in traditional white sheets and hoods. At that point, the Richard Pryor persona takes over, as Joe leads the Klan back to the bus. Joe convinces the Klan leader that all the children on the bus are blind, and are being taken to "the Ray Charles Institute for the Blind." The Klan leader agrees to help, Joe gives him a fretful kiss on the cheek, and the Klan members push the bus out of the mud, falling into the slop as the bus speeds away.

Oz Scott seeks to provide an entertaining vehicle with *Bustin' Loose,* and some marginal success is achieved. The multiethnic casting of the children and the affirmation of the nontraditional family structure emerge as strong aspects of the movie. But in the final assessment, this is a film whose most effective parts begin and end with Richard Pryor. When he's allowed to burst free with his character, the movie does well, but when he's strapped by awkward plot twists, it slows down to nothing more than a humdrum comedy.

Topper Carew

I want to do things that bring joy and enlightenment and vision into people's lives. . . . That is the agenda.[4]   Topper Carew

Born Colin Carew in Boston in 1943, Topper Carew lived and worked in Washington, D.C., for more than ten years. He began his college education by attending Howard University, where he received a B.A., but he went on in 1970 to earn a master's in architecture at Yale University. He continued his advanced education by attending Union Graduate School, completing his Ph.D. in communications at that institution, before going on to study broadcast management training at Harvard University's Graduate School of Business.[5]

Although he later taught architecture and urban design at Yale,[6] his creativity drew him toward television, and in 1980 he became the producer of the PBS series *The Righteous Apples*, a show that focused on four teenagers working together in a racially mixed rock band.[7] He continued to work as a television producer over the next decade and a half on various comedy shows: *Bustin' Loose* in syndication, *Homeroom* for ABC, and *Martin*, with Martin Lawrence, for the Fox network. He also produced the 1983 feature film *D.C. Cab*, and then served as the executive producer and director of the 1991 film *Talkin' Dirty After Dark*.[8]

In his first feature effort as a director, Carew takes an interesting focus — similar to that of the movie *Punchline* (1988) with Sally Field and Tom Hanks — that affirms that the personal lives of stand-up comedians contain an inordinate mixture of chaos and drama. *Talkin' Dirty After Dark* focuses on several black comedians who deliver scatological jokes and sexually oriented routines before a live, late-night black audience: Terry (Martin Lawrence), an opportunist who romances the club owner's wife to get more stage time; Aretha (Phyllis Yvonne Stickney), whose stage success is threatened by a violent, jealous boyfriend; Jackie (Marvin Wright-Bey), the emcee who tries to win true love while surrounded by groupies; Percy (Darryl Sivad), an out-of-town comic trying to break into the Los Angeles scene; Roach (Dwayne Kennedy), a pseudo revolutionary who will do anything for fame; and Kwame (Lance Crouther), an African-garbed brother who goes with the flow. Of all these comic characters, Terry receives the most screen time, as his strategy of wooing Rubie Lin (Jedda Jones) speeds toward disaster when her husband, Dukie (John Witherspoon), suspects their hanky-panky. Most of the movie's time line occurs during one night when all of the aforementioned comedians and others take their turns onstage while dealing with wild events occurring backstage.

Some of the craziness springs from Rubie Lin and Terry dashing into the linen closet and meat locker to fondle and kiss, while other zaniness develops when the two Bad Girls (Vanessa Hampton and Robin Montague) try to entice Jackie from his date, Kimmie (Renee Jones). Then more chaos results from Dukie's attempts to seduce Aretha, which trigger the explosion of Aretha's jealous boyfriend, Bigg (Tiny Lister Jr.), who proceeds to tear the club apart.

Despite the potential of the premise, the movie never gets beyond a lackluster effort. Carew, who wrote and directed the movie, certainly provides enough energy to the film, but it's an energy that never takes the audience to anywhere worthwhile, in terms of either humor or character revelation. Even the possibility of using the stand-up routines as a humorous through-

In *Talkin' Dirty After Dark,* suspicious club owner Dukie (John Witherspoon, left) strikes a threatening pose next to stand-up comedian Terry (Martin Lawrence).

line is never realized; the stand-up jokes by the comedians are more crude and graphic than funny. Similar to the HBO comedy showcase *Def Comedy Jam,* the humor here is just a bit above locker-room creativity.

The other aspect of the film that fails to please is the manner in which Carew allows awkward breaks in numerous scenes that have no sense of closure. A situation is set up, but then is never completed before going to the next. This disjointed feeling happens conspicuously toward the end of the movie. After the raucous fight at the club caused by Bigg, Terry—who has just escaped death after being caught with Rubie Lin by a gun-wielding Dukie—stops the fight when he hits Bigg over the head with a frying pan. In the very next scene, Terry drives Rubie Lin to her home in his old car. But why? Obviously, the near-death experience at the club would have persuaded Terry to keep his distance. But even more confusing is the fact that Dukie is there waiting at the house in his pajamas and robe and with Dobermans. Did he leave the club, which was in disarray, before Rubie Lin and Terry, and if so, why would Terry drive Rubie Lin home? The next scene is the following morning, and Terry and Rubie Lin wake up in bed together at his apartment, and when the phone rings, it's Dukie, asking her to return. Abruptly, Terry's voiceover—which is heard for the first time in the movie—now comes over a visual montage to explain how the lives of various characters worked out. Why were Rubie Lin and Terry still together in his bed given the trauma of the night before? Why is there suddenly a voiceover, and why is it Terry's? Carew seems to have reached the end of a story that he had no closing for, and so he tacks on an intrusive voiceover and a montage to quickly and not-so-tidily tie up the loose ends.

Carew is a producer who had gained a great deal of experience by the time he made *Talkin' Dirty After Dark*. However, it seems that as he took on the duties of both writer and director of the movie, he wasn't quite sure of what he wanted to present and whom he perceived as his audience. Consequently, the potential of the movie disintegrates into an ineffective comedy that contributes little to the genre or to the depiction of African Americans.

Richard Pryor

The project [*Jo Jo Dancer*] was my own creation, my own madness. Certainly, it takes a degree of madness to produce, direct, cowrite, and star in a movie. By the time I took all that damn film in the editing bay, I felt like a snake charmer slowly being strangled by his own charming pet viper.[9]

Richard Pryor

Considered by many to be the most recognized and influential black comedian ever, Richard Pryor endured an early life blemished with hardships and tragedies that seem stranger than fiction. Born in 1940 in Peoria, Illinois, Pryor lived a childhood of neglect by his parents, while being raised by his grandmother. Living in a house that served as the family-owned brothel, Pryor was exposed to sexuality, gambling, alcohol, and drugs as a boy. He was expelled from a Catholic school when his home life was discovered, and he was raped at the age of six, a secret he carried with him for years. Of his childhood, Pryor reflects: "Growing up was a minefield. I had to watch every step, but it was hard to remember all the time."[10]

In 1958 he began two years in the Army, and once out, he drifted toward show business, which seemed suited for his high energy level, as well as offering his two major life interests at the time—drugs and women.[11] Stand-up routines led to television appearances, and by the late '60s, Pryor was on the big screen. His ascendancy to stardom was remarkable, and as critic Donald Bogle notes, by the end of the '70s, Pryor was "the most important black actor working in American motion pictures."[12] His fame carried its downside, with a number of failed marriages, a heart attack in 1977, and a suicide attempt in 1980 when, influenced by a cocaine delirium, Pryor "doused himself with cognac and ignited it with a lighter."[13] Then, while filming *Critical Condition* in 1987, he began to suffer dizzy spells, weight loss, and physical immobility, which was eventually diagnosed as the early stages of multiple sclerosis.[14]

On the screen, between the late '60s and the late '80s, Pryor was the comedic king in more than two dozen films, including *Lady Sings the Blues* (1972), *The Mack* (1973), *Car Wash* (1976), *The Bingo Long Traveling All-Stars & Motor Kings* (1976), *Silver Streak* (1976), *Which Way Is Up?* (1977), *Greased Lightning* (1977), *Blue Collar* (1978), *Stir Crazy* (1980), *Bustin' Loose* (1981), *Jo Jo Dancer, Your Life Is Calling* (1986), and *Harlem Nights* (1989).

Behind the screen, he also made his mark, particularly in 1983, when he signed a five-year, $40 million deal with Columbia Pictures to produce several low-budget movies under the aegis of his Indigo Production Company. Unfortunately, even with actor-athlete Jim Brown as the production executive at Indigo, the company never really fulfilled all of the expectations that many had for it, and Pryor himself suggested that "Indigo was a fiasco, something much bigger than I could handle. I didn't know how to run a company, and, come to think of it, I didn't even want a company."[15]

Pryor also made a step behind the camera as director in 1986, helming his autobiographical movie, *Jo Jo Dancer, Your Life Is Calling*. To his credit, Pryor tries some unconventional elements in rendering his story. The structure is nonlinear, visual effects are used to simulate Jo Jo's dual personalities, and Jo Jo's alter ego—also played by Pryor—moves across time lines and interacts with various characters in the past and present.

Although the movie swings back and forth through decades as the Alter Ego appears and engages in various discussions, the fabula of the story is the following. Growing up in a brothel, where his mother (Diahhne Abbott) works as a prostitute and his father (Scoey Mitchell) as a handyman, Little Jo Jo (Elon Cox) finds love and understanding in the presence of his grandmother (Carmen McCrae). As an adult, when Jo Jo tells his father he plans to be a comedian, he is met with negativity—a physical beating from his dad and abandonment by his young wife, Alicia (Tanya Boyd). Jo Jo takes off for Cleveland and hits hard times, until he sneaks into the dressing room of Satin Doll (Paula Kelly), the headline stripper at the Club Shalimar. With Doll's support, as well as that of the other blacks at the club, Jo Jo begins to develop as a comic, until he clashes with his mobster boss, who refuses to pay him. Satin Doll sends him away, and years later in Los Angeles, Jo Jo finds success and a steady love in his future wife, Dawn (Barbara Williams), a white woman who loves him but who shares his weakness for alcohol, drugs, and the party life. At one wild party with unlimited cocaine, Jo Jo awakes from a stupor to find Dawn in a ménage à trois. After a time, Jo Jo is at a dance club where he spots Michelle (Debbie Allen), a beautiful black woman who becomes yet another wife. But even as Jo Jo begins to make movies, he abuses alcohol and drugs, and the relationship between him and Michelle disintegrates.

But when Jo Jo's grandmother dies, he loses the one person to whom he felt truly connected, and while freebasing cocaine, he attempts suicide by pouring rum over his body and torching himself. In the hospital, the Alter Ego pleads with Jo Jo not to give in to self-destruction, and in a closing segment on a concert stage, Jo Jo performs a stand-up routine using his troubled life and the burning incident as fodder for jokes.

Surprisingly, Pryor does an adequate job as a director. In a way, the techniques he uses in *Jo Jo Dancer* seem more in tune with the postmodern fragmentation and nontraditional structure found in a number of '90s independent films. In the script credited to Pryor, Paul Mooney, and Rocco Urbisci, the decision to personify the Alter Ego as a pivotal character adds a balance to Jo Jo's confused character. The Alter Ego becomes a character of reason that delivers the details of the story without relying solely on Jo Jo's viewpoints in all of their weaknesses. The Alter Ego permits a welcome cushion from the chaos of a talented but confused man spiraling toward a tragic demise.

Pryor does spend a lengthy amount of movie time on Jo Jo's early Cleveland days, but the point is to demonstrate the integrity and self-respect that Jo Jo possessed as his career was beginning—something obviously missing from his later years of success. But Pryor's directing achievement really emerges when showing the experiences of Little Jo Jo. In one sequence, after coming home with a good report card, and seeking the approval of his mother, Little Jo Jo ventures upstairs, only to find his mother with a strange man. The sadness of the moment is played out on Little Jo Jo's face, and the locked door that separates him from his mother symbolizes the barrier to the parental love he craves.

Another memorable moment of the film results from Pryor's effective use of quick cuts. In the opening and closing sequences that show Jo Jo's paranoia, the frenetic editing and diverse positioning of the camera punctuate the drug-induced state in which Jo Jo hallucinates. The jumping from shot to shot captures the bizarre nature of Jo Jo's distorted descent into depression.

Although Pryor did not direct another feature after *Jo Jo Dancer*, there are qualities in the movie that hint of his potential behind the camera. However, by his own admission, Pryor's inclination to direct this movie emanated from a need to be involved in telling his own story, not a consuming drive to be a filmmaker. But the courage to assume the responsibility as a director matches the courage it took to place his private life before the eyes of both fans and detractors.

Despite the fact that Pryor will not be remembered with adulation as a film director, his inescapable presence on film and television modified the manner in which comedy evoked responses across racial lines. Black author and scholar John A. Williams remarks: "Pryor spoke directly to us [black people], in our native language—there was no mistaking that—but he did it in a way that was slyly accessible to any white who dared eavesdrop. He was telling 'them' off and taking them to school even as he taught and entertained us [blacks]. And he didn't give a damn what anybody thought."[16]

Prince

I don't regret anything about Under the Cherry Moon. I learned that I can't direct what I didn't write. . . . I can't please everybody. I didn't want to make Die Hard 4. But I'm also not looking to be Francis Ford Coppola. I see this [Graffiti Bridge] more like those 1950s rock and roll movies.[17]   Prince

Prince was born in 1958 as Prince Roger Nelson and was raised in Minneapolis, Minnesota. His father was a musician and his mother a singer. Prince learned to play the piano by age seven, and five years later he had developed skills to play more than twenty instruments. He formed a band at the age of thirteen, and with a demo tape in hand, he took off for New York at seventeen to land a recording contract. After a year, he was able to negotiate a deal with Warner Bros., one that gave him the production control he sought. By age nineteen, Prince released his first album, *For You*, on which he played every instrument and wrote every song; the album went platinum, bringing Prince to mainstream recognition.[18] Of the twelve albums he released between 1978 and 1992, the most popular, selling 13 million copies, was *Purple Rain*, connected to the movie of the same title that launched Prince's Hollywood career. Following the film *Purple Rain* (1984), Prince appeared in and directed three additional projects—the fictional films *Under the Cherry Moon* (1986) and *Graffiti Bridge* (1990) and the concert film *Sign o' the Times* (1987).

The two fictional films that Prince directed failed to match the popularity of *Purple Rain*, and he moved from behind the camera and back to the creativity of the music studio. In 1992 Prince made music industry headlines with his staggering $100 million, six-album deal with Warner Brothers., but during the next four years, he sought publicity to criticize what he felt was "slave" treatment by the company. In 1996, when he was free of his ties to

Con artists Tricky (Jerome Benton, left) and
Christopher (Prince) prepare to crash the party
of their next wealthy victim in *Under the
Cherry Moon.*

Warner Brothers, he released a three-CD set, titled *Emancipation*.[19] By 1999, at age forty, with the release of the CD *Rave Un2 the Joy Fantastic*, Prince was still keeping himself a visible and musically innovative talent during a decade that ended with the domination of younger, less prolific hip-hop stylists.

As a film director, Prince must have felt the need to take his movie *Under the Cherry Moon* on a totally different route than the successful *Purple Rain.* With a script credited to Becky Johnston, the story is set in France, in the seaside city of Nice. Shot in black and white, the story opens with a woman's voiceover that tells viewers: "Once upon a time in France there lived a bad boy named Christopher Tracy. Only one thing mattered to Christopher— money." As the central character, Christopher Tracy (Prince), appears on the screen, the voiceover goes on to inform that Christopher eventually found a woman that he would die for because he learned the true meaning of love.

Christopher works the Riviera as a gigolo, along with his friend and business partner, Tricky (Jerome Benton); Christopher handles the romance while Tricky handles the money. Their techniques and strategy apparently work well, as illustrated by the successful connection that Christopher makes in the opening scene with the wealthy Mrs. Wellington (Francesca Annis). But when the partners find a newspaper announcement of the twenty-first birthday party for Mary Sharon (Kristin Scott Thomas), the daughter of shipping tycoon Isaac Sharon (Steven Berkoff) and his wife, Muriel (Alexandra Stewart), they determine that Mary's $50 million trust will be the next target.

Crashing the birthday party, Christopher eventually meets and shares an immediate attraction with Mary, but when Mary's friends inform her that Christopher and Tricky are known gigolos, she confronts Christopher with her resentment, particularly after discovering his liaison with the family's friend Mrs. Wellington. But Christopher woos Mary, helping her to have fun when away from her stuffy surroundings. However, Isaac Sharon has different plans for his daughter, and he offers Christopher a $100,000 check to disappear. Christopher rejects the money, and intercepting Mary before she flies off to New York, he drives her away and confesses his love. But Sharon and the police catch up with Christopher as he attempts to flee with Mary, and refusing to run and leave Mary behind, Christopher is shot and killed.

Having spent a great deal of time in front of a camera for music videos and in *Purple Rain*, Prince no doubt has a comprehension of the possibilities of the camera and editing. And in *Under the Cherry Moon* a number of interesting visual techniques surface, such as the high-angle aerial shots of the coastline; quick cuts between characters to convey inner longings; superimposition of images; and circular camera movements to capture the mise-en-scène. The problem with these various techniques in this movie is that they do not enhance or strengthen either the emotional content of the scene or the theme of the story. Rather, they appear without any particular purpose, though they might be pleasing aesthetically. In the same manner, the use of black-and-white film becomes questionable, as neither the fantasy nor the romantic tone of the story benefit from the lighting and shadows. Instead, as in the sequence for Mary's birthday party, the black-and-white sequence—with numerous bizarre characters, animals, fire-eaters, and fireworks—possesses a Fellini-esque feel. Consequently, in that same sequence, Christopher, who is supposed to come off as a cool, attractive, virile lover to Mary, emerges more as a sideshow with a traveling circus. Christopher's assumed sexuality and intensity gets lost within the black-and-white imagery, which merely highlights the soft facial qualities and heavy eye makeup worn by Prince.

Another problem develops from the conflicting tones created by the acting and the ongoing funk-rock music score provided by Prince and the Revolution. The funk-rock music—such as the celebrated song "Kiss"—doesn't blend with or reinforce the feelings and textures of given scenes. What results are songs whose style clashes with the look, style, and content of the movie. Additionally, when Kristin Scott Thomas and Steven Berkoff have their scenes together, their acting is strong and dramatic, contrasting severely with those scenes where Prince and Jerome Benton play out their cute and sometimes silly moments. At times, due to the disparity in music, acting, and moods, it is as if two different movies are being made.

With his next fictional feature, *Graffiti Bridge,* Prince attempts to go back and recapture the more satisfying aspects of *Purple Rain.* Returning to the same major characters from the original, Prince was surely hoping to achieve more success with *Graffiti Bridge,* but his preference for stylized eccentricity condemns a number of scenes to failure, undermining the overall impact of the movie.

Written and directed by Prince, the story concentrates on the rivalry between the Kid (Prince) and Morris (Morris Day), two creative megalomaniacs, each with his own musical style. As the movie opens, Morris informs his thug-band called the Time that in his efforts to control his area of the city, he needs to take over the club Glam Slam, which is run by the Kid. Using his club Pandemonium as a headquarters, Morris—with the support of his sidekick Jerome (Jerome Benton) and his sexy but jealous lover, Robin (Robin Power)—derides the Kid's music, serving up his own frantic dance tunes that make club patrons gyrate wildly. The Kid, distracted by the troubled past of his family, becomes depressed by his inability to create music that can challenge and defeat Morris. But a mysterious, sexy woman named Aura (Ingrid Chavez) appears on the scene, and her voiceovers and heavenly glances suggest that she is a muse-angel on a mission to help the Kid. Seeing how gorgeous she is, Morris determines he must possess Aura for his stable, which intensifies his rivalry with the Kid. Several songs and dance numbers later—many coming after the Kid's long poetic dialogues with Aura near an old stone bridge—the Kid challenges Morris that whoever performs the best song wins ownership of his club, Glam Slam. Bolstered by Aura's encouragement to never give up, the Kid takes on Morris. But Morris wins out, and soon after, Aura is struck by a speeding SUV and dies. Her death seals the Kid's determination, and he comes back and performs a slow ballad inspired by a poem given to him by Aura. The Kid's song moves everyone emotionally, including Morris, as the Kid and Morris hug one another in reconciliation.

Similar to *Under the Cherry Moon,* the most appealing aspect of *Graffiti Bridge* stems from the music. Prince's band, "The Revolution," that backed him in the musical score for *Under the Cherry Moon,* has been replaced in this movie with his new band, "The New Power Generation." Despite the different bands, the music still contains that recognizable Prince sound that blends funk, rock, and R&B, particularly displayed in the highly marketed song "Thieves in the Temple." But in *Graffiti Bridge,* Prince's character, when offstage, seems to have no connection whatsoever to the raving-syncopated-dancer-singer—the Kid—who performs onstage; in that schizophrenic characterization, Prince often seems to be doing a parody of his own stage image. Consequently, the musical performances that capture the viewer's attention the most are those presented by Morris Day and the Time, Tevin Campbell (singing the pop hit "Round 'n' Round"), and Mavis Staples.

As for the movie's story and directing, the former is elliptical and the latter more appropriate for a music video than a feature-length film. The direction cannot save the writing from blistering defects, and vice versa. Attempting a clashing mixture of symbolism, fantasy, humor, poetry, and spiritualism, Prince never quite integrates the various tones and plot points. The result is often confusion—as to where the setting is, from whose viewpoint the story is being told, or why the characters are motivated as they are. Scenes are linked back to back, like non sequiturs, without respect for logic and emotional development. And the effort to take the viewer into some complex, inner spiritual search of the Kid just doesn't ring true against the movie's backdrop. In this misfire of a script, Prince attempts to go deep with a host of shallow characters.

In both *Under the Cherry Moon* and *Graffiti Bridge,* Prince has a sexual energy that explodes dynamically across the screen, but it's an energy and persona that works better for a music video, which does not require a sustained, three-dimensional character. As a director, he has the creative talent to shape the look of a scene, but with the added duty of writing and/or appearing in that scene, his creativity becomes stifled and clumsy. With that stated, perhaps the biggest contribution of Prince has been himself—a "crossover" icon of '80s sex-rock and a harbinger of the '90s bad boy attitude. Prince, no doubt, prompted Hollywood power brokers to consider "different" and "alternative" as viable measurements for giving the nod to the projects of African American directors.

Robert Townsend

I always wanted to learn how to direct, and making the movie [*Hollywood Shuffle*] was like film school. I always watched the director I worked with. I'd ask Norman Jewison, "What size lens is that?," and I watched Walter Hill work with the camera and light certain scenes. I never went back to my trailer to count my per diem. I started doing my homework subconsciously.[20]

Robert Townsend

Usually, the designation of auteur is saved for American directors of drama, with perhaps the exception of Woody Allen. However, Robert Townsend deserves to be assessed seriously in regard to his body of feature films, which present recurring themes and characters, displaying the filmmaker's particular ethos. Although the comedy genre influences much of what is done in Townsend's films, the theme of redemption pervades his movies, leaving a stamp of the director's optimism concerning issues and situations often deemed hopeless by many. In addition, Townsend promotes a strong belief that the black community can be unified and proactive.

Townsend was born in Chicago in 1957, where he grew up in a poor background in the city's rough West Side. One of four children, he became involved in entertainment when he was sixteen, joining the Experimental Black Actors Guild and the Second City Comedy Group.[21]

Townsend then took off for New York to attend Hunter College in Manhattan while studying acting at the Stella Adler Acting School. Following college, he began doing stand-up routines in comedy clubs, acting in Off-Broadway plays, and appearing in commercials. The numerous commercial jobs enabled him to purchase video equipment to experiment with the visual medium.[22] In 1982 Townsend moved to Los Angeles, and he eventually won roles in the movies *Streets of Fire* (1984) and *A Soldier's Story* (1984); in addition, he did television appearances, while continuing to do commercials and other films, including *American Flyers* (1985), *Ratboy* (1986), and *The Mighty Quinn* (1989).

Between 1987 and 1997 Townsend directed five films for the big screen, but he was just as active in acting in and directing for television. His *HBO Partners in Crime* specials aired in the early '90s, and then his situation comedy, *The Parent 'Hood* ran on the WB network from 1995 to 1998.

It was with Townsend's directorial debut, *Hollywood Shuffle* (1987), that he became a contemporary legend of independent filmmaking. The content of the film was noteworthy, but the process through which Townsend completed the film brought both admiration and inspiration from other independent filmmakers. Using a script that he cowrote with Keenen Ivory Wayans, Townsend finished the film by using $100,000 of his own money raised through savings and acting jobs, as well as charging $40,000 to credit cards and department store cards.[23] At a screening of the film, Samuel Goldwyn Jr. took an interest, providing Townsend with money to cover the credit card debts[24] and signing the movie to his company, which put up $1 million to advertise it.[25]

Hollywood Shuffle follows Bobby Taylor (Robert Townsend), an aspiring black actor who struggles to break into films. Supported by his mother (Starletta Dupois), grandmother (Helen Martin), younger brother Stevie (Craigus R. Johnson), and girlfriend Lydia (Anne-Marie Johnson), Bobby goes to an audition for the title role in a movie called "Jivetime Jimmy's Revenge." Pleasing the writer, casting director, and director—who are all white—Bobby gets a callback for the role. But Bobby's perseverance and hard work just further alienate the black men with whom he works on his day job at "Winky Dinky Hot Dogs," including Donald (Keenen Ivory Wayans), Tiny (Ludie Washington); and his boss, Mr. Jones (John Witherspoon). Even more importantly, Bobby begins to have second thoughts about taking such a role, knowing that it is indeed a caricature, so he often slips into fantasy, seeing the tragic irony in the negative roles historically played by blacks. At the same time, in his fantasies, he envisions the kind of roles he would like to see—blacks as clever detectives or superheroes.

Bobby eventually wins the lead role in the movie, but he overhears his grandmother dismissing the role as another harmful stereotype. Later, on the set, Bobby begins a scene, but—with his younger brother, grandmother, and girlfriend watching—he can't lower himself to act out the part of Jivetime Jimmy.

The story not only satirizes the Hollywood treatment of minorities; it also criticizes those minority members who continue to take such negative roles. With vignettes of fantasies interspersed throughout the narrative, the film's linear structure is often interrupted. Early in the movie, while Bobby waits for his first audition, the camera pans across the long row of black actors and actresses waiting their turn to try out for the stereotyped roles. As Bobby watches, he slips into a fantasy, where black slaves, speaking in their broken drawls, run for their freedom. Then, a uniformed butler appears, and in a Stepin Fetchit parody, the butler questions why and where the blacks are running. Then, suddenly, Jasper the butler (Robert Townsend) breaks out of his "coon" persona and, joining the actors just seen as slaves, he speaks directly to the camera in a British accent, inviting viewers to consider signing up at his acting academy where they can learn how to "act black." Ironically, the instructors at the acting academy are white, and they demonstrate how they teach the black actors to talk jive and walk with a shuffle. Then, asking for a confessional from one of the successful graduates of the academy, the black actor proudly lists his litany of roles, including parts as a pimp and rapist. This fantasy sequence and others criticize directly the traditional approach of Hollywood toward minority characterizations and the dearth of substantive roles for black performers. As it draws humor, it also indicts the limitations for black actors and actresses whose skills are wasted and misused.

In a crucial part of the film, Townsend underscores a thematic point, as Bobby arrives for the first day of shooting at the studio. Bobby's reactions and his subjective point of view are intercut, as he observes on one set a white couple rehearsing a romantic scene and on another stage a white action hero holding an automatic weapon and demanding that he kill more people in his film. Then Bobby reaches his movie's set filled with black and Latino actors wearing their stereotypical wardrobes to portray their stereotypical characters. The sequence, and others before it, reveals that though whites might also be pigeonholed in certain films, a variety of images of whites has always been available—from the silly to the serious, from working-class to professional. That variety has remained elusive to blacks due both to the limited roles offered and to the lack of black involvement behind the camera in key decision-making positions.

When Townsend and Wayans wrote together again for their next fictional film—*The Five Heartbeats* (1991)—they kept humor as an important element of the film, but ventured to explore complex characters in a more dramatic way. The story, using the R&B music world as a backdrop, looks at the rise, fall, and redemption of five friends who find and lose success as the celebrated titular singing group.

Beginning in the 1980s, Donald "Duck" Matthews (Townsend), a graying man in middle age, sits on the back deck of his home facing the ocean as he reads the mail. Lifting and reading the cover of *Rolling Stone* magazine, Duck studies the photo of five black men beneath the caption "Where Are They Now?" Duck's thoughts focus on the past, as the scene flashes back to 1965 in New York City, where five childhood friends take their turn onstage at a music competition: Duck, the songwriter and piano player; J.T. (Leon), Duck's brother and a self-proclaimed ladies' man; Eddie (Michael Wright), the lead singer; Dresser (Harry J. Lennix), the bass singer; and Choirboy (Tico Wells), the tenor and son of a minister. Though the group loses the competition, they catch the eye of Jimmy Potter (Chuck Patterson), a manager with integrity and whose wife, Eleanor (Diahann Carroll), is weary of the heartbreak in the music business.

By 1967 the Five Heartbeats have found success, as their pictures appear on national magazine covers and as they rake in money, cars, and awards. Unfortunately, with that success, Eddie also begins using and abusing cocaine and alcohol. His addiction almost destroys the group, as it plays a part in Jimmy's murder. Into the early 1970s, the group takes on a new lead singer, as well as new tragedy when Duck discovers his fiancée and brother J. T. are having an affair. Consequently, the group falls apart. But by the film's end, the brothers forgive and reclaim one another, and the once-addicted Eddie follows a religious road to recovery. In a final sequence the Five Heartbeats, older and wiser, entertain family members with one of the old songs at a backyard cookout.

The overall story line of *The Five Heartbeats* might encourage one to dismiss it as just another soap opera put to music, but that would be a hasty assumption. The merit in this film emerges from Townsend's quest to reveal the hopes and failures of a group of black men in a manner that shows their maturation, and importantly for Townsend, their redemption. Five friends, all from the same background, are given distinctive qualities and talents, and their major struggle in this story is with their own demons. Racism and business corruption surface as ongoing enemies, but it's the internal enemies that the five friends must deal with, as well as the value of their love for one another. True, they don't question the nature of the fame they seek and the importance they give to materialism, and unabashedly Townsend proclaims the church as the ideal avenue toward hope and fulfillment. But these particular points don't matter to the objective the filmmaker has in mind—to show that humans can survive flaws and mistakes through love and find forgiveness.

To his credit, Townsend allows the musical aspect of the film to be handled through lip sync, as the marvelous R&B sounds of the Dells function as the vocals for the Heartbeats, while music from the Temptations is used as background score. In the concert scenes, Townsend does an impressive job of capturing the energy and style of the period and musical genre. The flamboyancy and showmanship of the various groups reflect the emphasis of the times, when melodic romantic lyrics were sung by lead vocalists who improvised and stretched their voices to their audiences. The audiences, for their part, consisted of men who would admire the synchronized choreography and women who would swoon at the balladeer's notions of love. Townsend creates this '60s music world effectively, as well as that of the later '70s, where funk rhythms, attitude, sexy choreography, and stage effects overwhelm the music's melodies and romantic appeal.

But Townsend also puts teeth into his smaller, intimate scenes, where characters' emotions and fragility become apparent. The scene, for example, where Dresser exposes Eddie's secret deal is played out in an alleyway, among the shadows of the darkened street where litter and an empty vacant lot symbolize the breakdown in the group's unity. In a later scene from the

Heroic teacher Jefferson Reed (Robert Townsend, third from left) has the support of his neighborhood, including buddy Michael (Eddie Griffin, far left), parents Mrs. Reed (Marla Gibbs, fifth from left) and Mr. Reed (Robert Guillaume), and friend Mrs. Walker (Marilyn Coleman) in the fantasy *The Meteor Man*.

'70s, when the new Heartbeats leave a performance, Eddie appears, wearing a costume from the old days, begging his way back into the group. He looks and sounds pathetic, as the four original members try to deal with their pity and shame for him.

The pageantry, drama, and intimacy of *The Five Heartbeats* are set aside for the elements of fantasy found in Townsend's *Meteor Man* (1993). In some ways, this movie seems an extension of the fantasy sequence in *Hollywood Shuffle* where the protagonist envisions a black superhero, à la Superman, who possesses extraordinary powers.

In Washington, D.C., substitute teacher Jefferson Reed (Townsend) lives in an urban neighborhood where he stays close to his parents—Mr. Reed (Robert Guillaume) and Mrs. Reed (Marla Gibbs)—and where he's known by his neighbors: Mr. Moses (James Earl Jones), Mrs. Walker (Marilyn Coleman), and the aloof junkman named Marvin (Bill Cosby). A bachelor himself,

Jefferson socializes with his fellow bachelor teacher, Michael (Eddie Griffin), a talkative science instructor. But Jefferson's neighborhood has one big problem—the Golden Lords, a black gang whose members wear black clothing and dye their hair blond. Led by Simon (Roy Fegan) and his henchmen, Goldilocks (Don Cheadle) and Uzi (Bobby McGee), the Golden Lords recruit elementary-age and older youngsters to vandalize, mug, steal, and extort the community.

One night Jefferson becomes a victim of the Golden Lords, and when he escapes their wrath, he finds himself isolated in an alleyway as a falling meteorite pins him against the wall, giving him third-degree burns and rendering him unconscious. The meteorite actually permeates Jefferson's body as it breaks into pieces, and as the ambulance carries him away, no one notices that Marvin has claimed an errant piece of the glowing meteorite for his junk collection.

Miraculously, Jefferson's burns heal, and he has been endowed with extraordinary powers: excessive physical strength, X-ray vision, speed, and flight. Unlike other superheroes, Jefferson reveals his powers to friend Michael, his parents, and his neighbors, all of whom urge him to fight the crime wave of the Golden Lords.

The efforts of Townsend in this movie are obvious—to entertain and to emphasize community unity. As an entertainment vehicle, Townsend provides an energetic comedy with slapstick and sight gags, but he simultaneously makes a point about the lack of black superheroes for ethnic children. Townsend provides a hero who, in addition to his powers, is educated, respectful to his parents, close to his friends, and loyal to his neighborhood. This last aspect about the neighborhood is significant, as Townsend stresses the connection of the superhero to the community. Unlike other such fantasy crime fighters (e.g., Batman, Spiderman), Meteor Man's identity is not a secret. There's an open link between the hero and the Community Watch Association via a telephone hot line. And at the end, though it appears the neighborhood will desert the hero, they eventually come through, fighting side by side to help him and to save their homes.

With equal and effective doses of silliness, verbal humor, gags, and poignancy, The Meteor Man offers up a satisfying movie that's family oriented. Once the fantasy tone of the story is established, Townsend keeps the pace moving quickly toward a predictable but happy Hollywood ending.

Townsend perhaps hoped to replicate the comedic level of The Meteor Man in his next film, B*A*P*S (1997), which is an acronym for Black American Princesses. However, the result is a movie that sadly suffers from being so over-the-top at the beginning that it never really recovers.

The story focuses on two working-class girlfriends—Deniece, aka Nisi (Halle Berry), and Tamika, aka Mickey (Natalie Desselle). Nisi, with her outlandish blond hairstyles, dreams of owning her own salon, and Mickey, heavy-set and short, just dreams of a better life than what they have in their inner-city neighborhood in Decatur, Georgia. Traveling to Los Angeles to audition as dancers for a music video, Nisi and Mickey are the proverbial fish-out-of-water, as they take in the city surroundings with their loud, crass behavior and their ornate outfits. Although they lose out at the audition, Nisi and Mickey are recruited by Antonio (Luigi Amodeo) to work for his wealthy Beverly Hills boss, Isaac (Jonathan Fried). Isaac makes a $10,000 proposition that Nisi pretend to be the granddaughter of the lost love of his dying uncle, Don Blakemore (Martin Landau). Accepting the job, the girls are assisted in their masquerade by the family butler, Manley (Ian Richardson), who is a proper British gentleman. With Nisi and Mickey around, Blakemore's health improves, as he spends all of his free time with them—dining, shopping, and dancing. Isaac, whose true intent was to hasten his uncle's death to inherit his wealth, tries to set up a robbery to implicate Nisi and Mickey, but when it fails, he attempts to get the family lawyer, Tracy Shaw (Troy Beyer), to declare Blakemore incompetent.

When Blakemore is rushed to the hospital, Nisi and Mickey feel guilty that they never told the ailing man of their arrangement with Isaac. Tracy tells them that Blakemore always knew they were frauds because his lost love never had any children at all. Blakemore dies, plunging everyone into sadness—except for Isaac. But at the reading of the will, they learn that Blakemore left nothing to Isaac, but all to Nisi, Mickey, and Manley.

With its broad humor and cartoonish characters, *B*A*P*S* is reminiscent of Michael Schultz's *Disorderlies*, which showcased the stooging of the Fat Boys. Although the screenplay is written by black actress-director Troy Beyer, the script doesn't appear to be too kind to its women protagonists. Nisi and Mickey are a-little-bit-country and a-little-bit-hip-hop, as their southern, uneducated background serves as the humorous side to both characters. Oddly enough, at the conclusion of the film, as the protagonists have developed affection for Blakemore and Manley, they become more mature. They lose their loudness, crassness, and country mannerisms. Is the writer suggesting that by living among wealthy whites in Beverly Hills these two black women have improved their personalities? Definitely, one of the weaknesses of the script and movie is that the tone changes abruptly toward the end in such a way that Nisi and Mickey seem like characters from another film. The movie takes them from exaggerated "Sapphire" and "Aunt Jemima" types to a semblance of a Meg Ryan/Goldie Hawn romantic-comedy cuteness. Unlike *The Meteor Man*, where the fantasy is intrinsic to the story's theme, and unlike *The Five Heartbeats*, where humor and drama find a balance, *B*A*P*S* misses as a vehicle of satisfying entertainment or thoughtful reflection. Instead, it becomes a painful experience of forced humor among characters and situations that fail to evoke any sympathy or concern. Townsend can't quite pull the pieces together in this movie, and its incoherence and flatness make it the least successful of his directorial efforts.

However, when weighing the total assemblage of his films, Robert Townsend must be appreciated for his attempts to use comedy to render significant themes of forgiveness, redemption, and community. He shows his abilities to excite and sometimes to incite an audience, whether looking at racial issues or personal issues of integrity and commitment.

Eddie Murphy

[*Harlem Nights*] was a question of wearing too many hats, and as a result, everything was half-assed. All my peers were directing: Keenen [Ivory Wayans], and Robert [Townsend] and Spike [Lee]. I was like "Shit," I'm the big cat on the block; let me see what it's like to direct. So I just did it. I didn't dig it.[26]   Eddie Murphy

During the latter half of the 1980s, Eddie Murphy ruled as the most popular comic star in America. Commanding a following across racial lines, he always held on to an attitude associated with black masculinity. Murphy was born in the Bushwick section of Brooklyn in 1961, and he endured an early childhood of separated parents, foster homes, and his father's death when Murphy was eight. After his mother remarried, the new family moved to Long Island, where Murphy became popular in high school. While still in secondary school, at age fifteen, he began doing stand-up comedy in the community, which ultimately led to appearances in Manhattan's comedy clubs. When appearing as a comedian in Fort Lauderdale, Florida, Murphy was observed by a producer for NBC's *Saturday Night Live*, and he was under contract and appearing on the show as a featured cast member in the fall of 1980. He remained with the show for four years, but with the national exposure it brought, he was able to get the part as Reggie Hammond in the 1982 feature *48 Hrs.*[27] Murphy's popular appeal in that film was replicated in a string of box-office hits in the '80s, including *Trading Places* (1983), *Beverly Hills Cop* (1984), *The Golden Child* (1986), *Beverly Hills Cop II* (1987), *Eddie Murphy Raw* (1987), a live comedy concert film, and *Coming to America* (1988). By mid-decade, Murphy's films had brought in more than $685 million for Paramount Pictures,[28] and for 1989–90, *Forbes* listed his income as $48 million.[29]

In *Harlem Nights,* despite their mutual irritation, Quick (Eddie Murphy), Sugar Ray (Richard Pryor), Vera (Della Reese), and Bennie (Redd Foxx) work together to outwit rival white mobsters.

With his 1989 feature, *Harlem Nights,* Murphy decided to take the bold step: in addition to acting, he served as the film's executive producer, writer, and director. Unfortunately, the film earned neither popular support nor critical praise, and Murphy's meteoric rise peaked.

The movie begins in 1918 Harlem, in an underground black speakeasy, where Sugar Ray (Richard Pryor) conducts a craps game and is confronted by an angry patron who dislikes the fact that there's a kid nearby. When the patron loses, he pulls a knife on Ray, but the kid shoots the patron dead. Twenty years later, Ray has raised the kid, called Quick (Eddie Murphy), as his son, and together they run an after-hours club, with the help of Benny (Redd Foxx) and Vera (Della Reese), who is in charge of the house prostitutes. But Bugsy Calhoune (Michael Lerner), a white mob boss, tries to force a takeover of the club, instructing his mistress, Dominique La Rue (Jasmine Guy), to seduce Quick, and using his hired police detective, Cantone (Danny Aiello), to apply pressure. But Ray and Quick devise a plan to outsmart the mob boss by stealing his gambling house money and getting out of

New York. They successfully destroy Bugsy's club, seize the gambling money from a heavyweight boxing match, capture Cantone, and set off a fatal explosion for Bugsy and his thugs.

With all the plot shifts and action in the story line, as well as music by Herbie Hancock and impressive set designs and costumes, *Harlem Nights* should have been something wonderful. But the film misfires at the beginning, in the scene where the kid kills the knife-wielding patron. After shooting a man in the head, the kid shows no emotions, and Ray's response is to take him out for ice cream. The whole scene plays out a joke in which the patron claims that kids bring him bad luck—a fact confirmed sarcastically by Ray as he looks down at the dead man. Taking away all the innocence from a seven-year-old kid might affirm the tough life he leads as an orphan, but the scene lacks humor and respect for the characters. The scene appears to be out of sync with the light and comic tone the film tries to offer.

Other scenes carry a similar cruelty to them as well. As an example, in one sequence, Vera feels insulted when Quick implies that she and her whores are skimming money from the evening's receipts. Forcing Quick into an alley for a fistfight, Vera beats him handily until Quick smashes her with a trash barrel. Upset that he would hit her with trash, Vera pulls a razor and then Quick pulls out his gun and shoots off her toe. The sequence plays much too long, the sight gags wear thin, and for all of its attempted verbal and physical humor, the impact of the scene works in an opposite way. Having the protagonist smash a woman over the head with a trash barrel and then shoot her in the foot does not endear that protagonist to the audience. Then, of course, the running joke for the remainder of the film is that Vera walks with a limp due to her missing toe.

Eddie Murphy's efforts in *Harlem Nights* show ambition, but his attempt to wear several significant hats obviously affected the end product. His instincts as a comedian, whether in stand-up or through a character, usually pay off on-screen. However, here, as he steps behind the camera, he is unable to achieve effective comic performances, to create engaging entertainment, or to salvage his weakly written script.

Keenen Ivory Wayans

Where I see myself in the '90s is becoming a full-fledged filmmaker, going to bigger budgets, and in doing that, hopefully opening the door for other black filmmakers to go above and beyond low-budget filmmaking. I think the '90s will be about studios making more movies that don't have big budgets, but carry big messages.[30]   Keenen Ivory Wayans

Born in 1957, Keenen Ivory Wayans was the second of ten children, and he grew up in the Fulton housing projects in Manhattan's Chelsea District. He aspired to be an engineer, attending Tuskegee University in Alabama. However, before completing the college program, he returned to New York and began pursuing jobs as a stand-up comedian. Traveling to Los Angeles in 1980, he appeared in a number of comedy clubs and managed to get an acting part in the 1983 movie *Star 80*.[31]

Wayans went on to appear on a number of television shows, including *Benson, Cheers, CHiPs*, and *A Different World*, and he made a personal mark on television by coproducing Robert Townsend's *HBO's Partners in Crime* (1987); by creating and producing Fox Television's Emmy Award-winning comedy series, *In Living Color* (1990–94); and by hosting and producing the late-night talk show *The Keenen Ivory Wayans Show* (1997). On the big screen, he cowrote and appeared in *Hollywood Shuffle* (1987), coproduced the feature concert film, *Eddie Murphy Raw* (1987), cowrote *The Five Heartbeats* (1991), coproduced *Don't Be a Menace to South Central While Drinking Your Juice in the Hood* (1996), and acted in the action movies, *The Glimmer Man* (1996) and *Most Wanted* (1997). Behind the camera as a director, Wayans has completed two films: *I'm Gonna Git You Sucka* (1988) and *A Low Down Dirty Shame* (1994).[32]

I'm Gonna Git You Sucka is one long parody of black urban action films —the so-called blaxploitation films of the early 1970s—and the celebrity images of a number of stars within those movies. Written and directed by Wayans, this comedy displays some of the episodic structure that later comprised the comedy skits of Wayans' television series, *In Living Color* (1990–1994). Some of the scenes seem to exist autonomously, disjointed from the other scenes, which, of course, results in a notable flatness when the comic level lags in parts of the movie.

The movie opens at night on an inner-city landscape, where a caption reads: "Any Ghetto, U.S.A." Police squad cars with screaming sirens race across the streets to arrive at a vacant lot where the body of June Bug Spade lays lifeless: the cause of death—he "OG'd." Specifically, he died of a "gold overdose" from wearing far too much trendy gold jewelry. Mourning the death are the mother, Ma Bell (Ja'net DuBois), and the young widow, Cheryl (Dawnn Lewis), but their grief turns to anger when two thugs, Willie (Kadeem Hardison) and Leonard (Damon Wayans), inform the women that June Bug owed money to their underworld boss, Mr. Big (John Vernon). Seeing that the women can't pay the money, the thugs opt to take Cheryl as a prize for Mr. Big. But the ineffective thugs are beaten up by the irrepressible Ma and thrown down the stairs as the oldest son, Jack (Keenen Ivory Wayans), arrives home in military uniform. Jack learns of his brother's death and the threats made by Mr. Big.

Jack goes out and seeks the help of John Slade (Bernie Casey), a former crime fighter who now works with youth gangs. The experienced Slade knows they'll need help, so he goes out to obtain guns and to get help from other retired crime fighters—Hammer (Isaac Hayes), Slammer (Jim Brown), and Kung Fu Joe (Steve James). Needing someone who knows the streets and Mr. Big's operations, Slade also recruits Flyguy (Antonio Fargas), a former pimp who was sent to jail by Mr. Big. Jack and the crime fighters hit Mr. Big's nightclub, and consequently Cheryl is kidnapped. But the heroes find Mr. Big's warehouse and make their assault, killing Mr. Big and his thugs and saving the girl.

From its title alone, it becomes apparent that *I'm Gonna Git You Sucka* seeks to hit the audience in the funny bone, or perhaps the silly bone. Yet, there are indeed some places where the humor comes close to being clever and satirical. For example, after agreeing to help Jack, Slade exits his apartment building wearing a black leather outfit. As Slade walks down the street, a band of musicians follow him playing the theme song to *Shaft*. When Jack asks Slade who the musicians are, Slade responds: "My theme music . . . every good hero should have some." In another scene in a bar, when Jack, like all good male heroes, picks up a sexy woman named Cherry (Anne-Marie Johnson), the two hurry to her place to indulge in a hot sexual encounter. As they begin to undress Jack confesses that he lied about the size of his penis. Cherry, though disappointed, takes the moment to confess a few secrets of her own as she removes a number of items: her colored contact lenses, her wig hiding her bald head, her false breasts, her false buttocks, and her false leg. Jack stares in shock and swiftly exits with Cherry hopping after him on one leg. This type of humor peppers the movie, with some scenes working more successfully than others. The unevenness of the humor is not as annoying as in other movies of similar, less-than-sophisticated comedic style, and the movie should be seen as a first-time feature of a director who honed his craft on television.

In his next film, Wayans presents a more linear narrative structure and better-developed characters than in his first. *A Low Down Dirty Shame* is constructed as an action-comedy, and on that level it works as effectively as any other Hollywood fare. In this movie Wayans proves that he has the screen appeal to be a viable draw in the genre, as validated in his later buddy action movie with Steven Seagal, *The Glimmer Man*, and his lead role in the action vehicle *Most Wanted*.

Working as both lead character and director in *A Low Down Dirty*

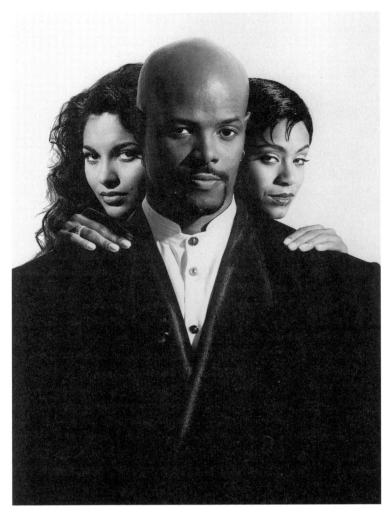

In *A Low Down Dirty Shame,* director Keenen Ivory Wayans portrays
private detective Shame, who is caught between his romantic
loyalties to former girlfriend Angela (Salli Richardson, left) and
Peaches (Jada Pinkett).

Shame, Wayans—in the same manner that his friend Robert Townsend negotiates the traditional superhero icon—shapes a traditional Hollywood icon
of the hard-boiled loner detective within an African American framework.
Shame (Wayans) is a near-bankrupt detective who lives in his inner-city
loft, which is large enough for him to park his car in its interior. When
Sonny Rothmiller (Charles Dutton), an old associate, brings him a job to

locate the girlfriend of a well-known drug dealer named Mendoza (Andrew Divoff), Shame is eager to take the work. He hesitates, however, when he discovers that the drug lord's girlfriend, Angela (Salli Richardson), is actually his old flame. By irritating a few criminal types and with the help and unpaid support of his secretary, Peaches (Jada Pinkett), Shame succeeds in finding Angela, only to discover that their meeting opens up old emotional wounds. Then, to his anger, Shame learns that Rothmiller lied, and is actually trying to locate Angela for Mendoza, for whom he works. Angela has Mendoza's money—some $20 million of it—and he and Rothmiller want it back. After Peaches is kidnapped by Mendoza and Rothmiller, Shame has to choose between saving her or going away with Angela with the stolen money to rekindle their old romance. Shame, finally confessing that he cares for Peaches, rejects Angela's offer, as he goes to save the woman for whom he really cares. As expected, Shame kills Mendoza, as Angela is taken off to jail. In the aftermath, Shame and Peaches realize that their business partnership has a foundation in their shared affection.

In this movie, Wayans does not offer anything experimental or unconventional in his direction, which appears to be his objective. The movie is presented as a genre piece that emphasizes black lead characters while covering the familiar ground of the "cool" hero confronting and winning over adversity. Keeping the movie on a strong comic edge, however, Wayans mixes verbal humor and physicality. The verbal humor picks up momentum with the frequent, snappy sparring that occurs between Shame and Peaches—humor linked to a hip-hop attitude and ebonics. The physical humor—often over-the-top, as in the sequences with Wayman (Corwin Hawkins), the gay roommate living with Peaches—is played for belly laughs, even at the expense of "typing" blacks, Latinos, and gays.

But Wayans knows his audience—the same group who flocked to his successful television series, *In Living Color*. And with both *I'm Gonna Git You Sucka* and *A Low Down Dirty Shame*, he aims to please that audience. And though he hasn't attempted to break with the conventional approach to directing, he has certainly given a recognizable ethnic flair to comedy and action movies. Without apology, he brings an African American comic perspective to a culturally diverse, mainstream audience, inviting that audience to laugh at itself without feeling uncomfortable or sensitive to the less-than-refined characterizations presented on the screen.

Wendell B. Harris Jr.

"Chameleon Street" is unique enough to be without precedent and Hollywood has always been suspicious of anything new. Everyone knows the existence of and can rally around the black ghetto. But just as there are a rainbow variety of black complexions in the world, there should be that same diversity in film.[33]   Wendell B. Harris Jr.

Wendell Harris is a filmmaker who, even by his own admission, expected a great deal to happen for him in commercial filmmaking. After his debut feature, *Chameleon Street,* won the Grand Jury Prize at the Sundance Film Festival in 1990, he was a hot black director who had numerous offers for his talents. However, the brilliant Hollywood career has not developed yet.

Born in Flint, Michigan, in 1954, Harris is the son of a doctor, who became a helpful consultant in fashioning his son's feature film script. Harris studied at Juilliard, where he was a classmate to Robin Williams,[34] and he nurtured his film interests on foreign directors such as Jean Cocteau, Jean-Luc Godard, Ingmar Bergman, and Ousmane Sembene.[35] He went to Los Angeles in 1976, hoping to make it into the industry as an actor and writer, but admits that he "spent two extremely frustrating years" as he "literally could not get in the door of casting directors or commercial auditions." So, with little success in Hollywood, Harris returned to Flint and with his family established the audio-video company that produced *Chameleon Street.*[36]

Harris and his family—his mother and brother served as executive producers—worked on developing *Chameleon Street* for seven years, eventually raising about $1.5 million.[37] With its success at the Sundance Film Festival, Harris found himself taking meetings to discuss the film as well as other possible projects for him to write and direct. But beyond the film festival, Harris endured disappointment. Distributors claimed that they didn't know how to market the film. Warner Bros. then made the most peculiar offer. Believing the film would "die on the art house circuit," the company wanted the rights to remake the story two years later "as a big-budget vehicle for Arsenio Hall."[38] However, Harris stood his ground, seeking the widest distribution possible, but he eventually settled for a deal with the Northern Arts Entertainment, which managed a screening for *Chameleon Street* in only two dozen theaters.[39]

Inspired by a true story and presented in black and white, the movie follows the amazing, but humorous, journey of William Street (Wendell B. Harris Jr.), a black man living in Detroit with his wife, Gabrielle (Angela Leslie). With financial pressures bearing down on him and nothing but a menial job to make ends meet, Street takes on the role of a con artist, trying various schemes. One scam involves him using fictional credentials to assume a job as a reporter for *Time* magazine. After a racially motivated attack, Street is taken to the hospital, and there he hatches the scheme to pass himself off as an intern, which he does successfully until a security check lands him in prison. In prison he undergoes psychiatric counseling, confessing that he takes on roles that people want to see in him.

Street escapes from the prison and goes east to New Haven, Connecticut, where he masquerades as a student and educates himself. Then, returning to Detroit after accidentally crossing paths with his wife at a party, he works for the city's Human Rights Commission, passing himself off as a lawyer. Eventually, however, his wife turns him in to the authorities, and Street faces prison once again.

As the award at the Sundance Festival confirms, Harris is celebrated by many who admire the independent tenacity that he displayed in getting *Chameleon Street* completed. Likewise, others have admired the symbols and political notions within the film that speak directly to the racial issues in America. Critic Ed Guerrero notes of the movie's protagonist: "Street's fantasy life . . . his frustrated ambition and intelligence, his dissembling in the face of a white professional class so eager to disavow its reflex feelings of racial superiority that it uncritically accepts him, all culminate in a dialectically shocking metaphor for the double consciousness, masked anger, and constant pretending that all blacks, to some degree, must deploy to live in a persistently racist society."[40]

If this film contains insights into social and psychological behavior on the one hand, and then on the other, if it presents what critic Harriet Robbins calls a "witty, perceptive study" that "provides excellent entertainment with solid production values,"[41] then why was it not released widely to a mainstream audience? It appears that the film's virtues of character insight and sociopolitical criticisms were the same aspects that frightened Hollywood away from it. This barrier continually faces independent filmmakers whenever they move beyond formula and the profitable genre movie. Following his unfulfilled hopes for *Chameleon Street*, Harris openly expressed his bitterness in *Variety*, the industry trade publication: "I would like to caution all those winners who pass through the pristine gates of Sundance—especially female filmmakers and filmmakers of color—not to be lulled into thinking that the rarefied hothouse atmosphere of Sundance extends into the whorehouse atmosphere of Hollywood."[42]

Reginald Hudlin

Whenever blacks succeed by crossing over, say, like Eddie [Murphy] or Bill Cosby or Arsenio Hall, they are made "honorary whites." There is still the perception in the movie business that blackness, real blackness, can only be negative, that black faces on a screen scare whites away, and that depictions of certain subjects, like black sexuality, are even scarier. We're out to prove that just isn't true."[43]   Reginald Hudlin

Given his academic background, one might not expect Reginald Hudlin to be listed in a hip-hop category of entertainment. But Hudlin, born in Centerville, Illinois, in 1961, has etched out a filmmaking career as an influential producer and director. Perhaps it was the experimental high school that Hudlin attended—with teachers that included the black writers Eugene Redmond, Shelby Steele, and Henry Dumas[44]—or perhaps it was having two parents who were teachers that played a large part in Hudlin attending Harvard, where he received his B.A. in 1983.[45]

While at Harvard he completed a short film version of *House Party*, and he directed two additional shorts, *Reggie's World of Soul* (1985) and *The Kold Waves* (1986). Then, with his brother, Warrington, who had attended Yale University, Reginald formed a company and produced music videos for R&B and hip-hop performers such as Heavy D, Guy, Blue Magic, and the Jamaica Boys.[46]

The significance of the Hudlin brothers' working together went beyond music videos. In 1978, aware of the dismal opportunities for black filmmakers, Warrington Hudlin helped establish and served as president of the Black Filmmaker Foundation, "an incorporated, nonprofit organization headquartered in New York" set up "to distribute films made by African Americans to libraries, museums, and colleges," and to serve as a "fiscal agent . . . to administer funds awarded to black filmmakers by other nonprofit organizations."[47] In addition, by the '90s, the foundation became a co-producer of the Acapulco Black Film Festival, creating an annual event that promotes and connects black actors, writers, producers, and directors.[48]

Attracted to the independent efforts of the Hudlin brothers, New Line Cinema offered financial support and distribution for the Hudlins to complete the feature-length *House Party* in 1990,[49] and the film went on to win the Filmmakers Trophy at the Sundance Film Festival.[50] The film's financial success was quickly evident, as its $2.5 million production budget grossed more than $30 million in the initial six months after its release.[51]

Reginald Hudlin has worked with his brother to produce *Bebe's Kids* (1992), the first black animated feature, and *Ride* (1998), directed by black director Millicent Shelton. As a director, he has helmed two of the most successful and popular black-oriented features of the '90s: *House Party* and *Boomerang* (1992).

House Party, discussed in the next chapter, opened the way for Hudlin to reach a youthful audience that followed hip-hop music and attitudes. With

Boomerang, Hudlin completed a black-oriented film that even popular critic Roger Ebert praises for its humor and casting.[52] Warrington produced with Brian Grazer, while Reginald directed this mainstream comedy that focuses on black yuppies, who are upwardly mobile but still rooted within their African American culture.

Boomerang follows Marcus Graham (Eddie Murphy), a marketing executive for a cosmetics company, who enjoys his lifestyle and reputation as a romantic player. His techniques of seduction are smooth, creative, and charming, as he moves from one lover to the next. When his company merges with another firm, the new head of marketing, Jacqueline (Robin Givens), is a gorgeous woman whom Marcus must possess. But soon Marcus finds his usual techniques fail to get the desired response. Instead, Jacqueline, a confident and liberated woman, assumes control, turning Marcus into a lovesick admirer; slowly, the cocky, self-assured Marcus becomes the target of intra-office laughter and disbelief. One clerk, named Bony T (Chris Rock), sadly remarks to Marcus: "I can't believe the way you let her [Jacqueline] dog you out like that! Where's your pride? . . . [F]irst the Fat Boys break up and now this. There's nothing to believe in!"

Marcus' other male friends are just as astounded by his defeat—Tyler (Martin Lawrence), a wannabe player, and Gerard (David Alan Grier), a sensitive conservative, have always looked at Marcus as the quintessential ladies' man. Angela (Halle Berry), an illustrator with the company, tries to console Marcus during his heartbreak, and though she and Gerard have been dating, Angela develops an attraction for Marcus. When Marcus and Angela become involved, Marcus' friendship with Gerard is threatened, but the bigger threat comes from Jacqueline, who decides she wants Marcus back in her life. In the end, Marcus realizes that being in love with Angela means being committed to her—the kind of relationship he's ready for. And with a bit of apologizing and begging, he wins her affections.

Reginald Hudlin, working with a script credited to Barry W. Blaustein and David Sheffield, makes a winning movie with a cast of characters—both leading and supporting—that have both comic and personable aspects. When the supporting characters come into the story, they add to another layer of entertainment rather than taking away from the major plot: characters such as the nasty and salacious commercial director, Nelson (Geoffrey Holder); the wild and forceful model, Strangé (Grace Jones); Marcus' crusading ex-lover, Yvonne (Tisha Campbell); and the sexily aggressive company matriarch, Lady Eloise (Eartha Kitt).

One of the numerous sequences that works well in merging the major and supporting characters occurs when Gerard's parents—Mr. and Mrs. Jackson—come to Marcus' house for dinner. With Angela and Tyler included, Mr. Jackson (John Witherspoon) and Mrs. Jackson (Bebe Drake-Massey) enter in all of their old-fashioned, crass, down-home glory. Mrs. Jackson brings a tub of uncooked chitlins and shows Angela how they should be prepared, while Mr. Jackson, displaying his mushroom-patterned wardrobe, instructs Marcus on how a man should "coordinate" his clothes. Then, already embarrassing Gerard with their behavior, Mr. and Mrs. Jackson disappear into the bathroom for an hour to enjoy a sexual tryst, and as they emerge with their clothes inside-out, even Marcus is speechless, as he hugs Gerard in an understanding of his shame.

Reginald Hudlin is to be commended for fashioning an entertaining movie that moves from the sublime to the overt, keeping elements of verbal humor, sight gags, and vulgarity all in balance. He elicits from Eddie Murphy one of his better comic performances, as his character moves from the confident to the pathetic and back again. And, finally, Hudlin is to be praised for bringing a black romance to the screen that highlights black characters who are intelligent and professionally successful, though just a bit confused by Cupid's mishandling of human affection.

Martin Lawrence

"Thin Line" was very personal. It was like my past before I got famous and before I got married. That was part of my old life. . . . I was always impressed with the Martin Scorseses and the action directors and the emotional directors who could put together a story and really make you feel. I wanted to give that a try. I wanted to get out and direct so people could have some understanding of the kind of person that Martin was like before.[53]

Martin Lawrence

Though in the media's eye during the late 1990s for his personal tragedies rather than his professional achievements, Martin Lawrence seems poised for comedic greatness or failure. Born in 1965 in Frankfurt, Germany, his father was in the U.S. Air Force and his mother was a salesclerk.[54] By eight, he was living in Landover, Maryland, when his parents separated, leaving his mother to take care of six children in a housing project.[55]

He began in entertainment by doing stand-up comedy in the Washington, D.C., area and later in New York. His big break occurred when he won the first round on television's *Star Search Showcase*, though he lost the final competition, but the exposure helped him land a regular part on the 1985–88 syndicated show *What's Happening Now!*[56] From that television work, he was able to get a role in Spike Lee's *Do the Right Thing* (1989). His other big-

Brandi (Lynn Whitfield) has a fatal attraction to womanizer Darnell (Martin Lawrence) in the comedy *A Thin Line Between Love and Hate.*

screen roles were in *House Party; House Party 2* (1991); *Talkin' Dirty After Dark* (1991); *Boomerang* (1992); *You So Crazy* (1994), his comedy concert film; *Bad Boys* (1995); *A Thin Line Between Love and Hate* (1996); *Nothing to Lose* (1997); *Life* (1999); and *Blue Streak* (1999). Other television appearances include his stint hosting *HBO's Russell Simmons Def Comedy Jam* (1994) and *Saturday Night Live;* then, from 1992 to 1996, he was the star and executive producer of the sitcom *Martin.*[57]

With the arrival of his popularity and success, his personal life faltered. In 1996, he was picked up for wandering and brandishing a gun while at a car wash in Sherman Oaks, California; he was detained and given two years' probation for trying to board a plane carrying a handgun; he was filing for divorce from his wife; and he was facing sexual harassment charges by his *Martin* costar Tisha Campbell.[58] In 1997 he was convicted of punching a man in a nightclub, and in 1999 he collapsed while jogging and lapsed into a three-day coma.[59] The high profile of his private life has made Lawrence topical, but by all box-office indications, with his most recent films, the audience that watches his humor has not dwindled.

With the movie *A Thin Line Between Love and Hate*, Martin Lawrence writes, acts, produces, and directs a story that has some striking similarities to Eddie Murphy's *Boomerang*. Although Martin stated in an interview that he wanted to use this film to present some aspects of his life and attitudes before marriage, the characters of Darnell in *Thin Line* and Marcus in *Boomerang* cover comparable ground: the player who toys with many women before committing to the one woman overlooked before.

The movie opens at the end of the story, showing three bodies falling from a second-floor window into a swimming pool below. One of the bodies and the voiceover belong to the protagonist, Darnell (Lawrence). From there, the scene cuts back in time, as Darnell and his friend Tee (Bobby Brown) work in a Los Angeles club called Chocolate City, owned by an older man named Smitty (Roger E. Mosley). Convincing Smitty to allow him and Tee to become partners in the club, Darnell now has another point of boasting as he meets numerous women. But Darnell is smitten by Brandi (Lynn Whitfield), a beautiful woman who, it turns out, is a rich real estate agent living in an ocean-front house. Darnell, still living at home in the inner city with his mother (Della Reese), maps out his strategy to conquer Brandi, even though his interest for an old girlfriend, Mia (Regina King), is rekindled when she comes homes on leave from the air force. Brandi finally comes to the Chocolate City club to see Darnell, and later together at her house, she shares details of her painful former marriage. But seeing her vulnerable state, Darnell maneuvers a sexual intimacy with Brandi by professing that he loves her. Following their night together and with his confessions of love, Brandi assumes that they have a committed relationship, but Darnell sees it as a one-night stand and begins pursuing Mia. However, Brandi refuses to be tossed aside, and she stalks Darnell at home, at the club, and around the city. Darnell fears for his life, and rightly so, as Brandi becomes psychotic, even to the point of bruising and hospitalizing herself in order to charge Darnell with assault. When Darnell plans to have a final showdown with Brandi at her house, she's prepared and ready to kill him. Fortunately, Tee and Mia arrive to prevent Darnell's death, but in a violent fight, Darnell, Brandi, and Tee all fly out of the second story window into the swimming pool below.

In some ways Lawrence has attempted to blend some traditional romantic comedy touches with a hip-hop feel, particularly in regard to language and music. That blending, however, is not always convincing, raising questions about Lawrence's targeted audience. Furthermore, the juxtaposition of inner-city and Malibu settings underscores the obvious class distinctions that exists between Darnell and Brandi, which contrasts as much as the personalities of the two characters. This points up one of the weaknesses in the story—namely, why would Brandi, given her past and background, find herself involved with Darnell?

This question highlights another weakness, which is the casting of Lawrence as the main character, Darnell. In *Boomerang*, the central playboy, Marcus, possesses an urbane smoothness, a natty confidence, and a romantic air—all of which are missing from Darnell. For Darnell, being romantic is buying a bouquet of flowers and busting into Brandi's office to deliver them with a smile. And with all respect to Lawrence, his Darnell is a narcissistic, crude hood rat who still lives at home with his mother. Why would Brandi and numerous other women be attracted to him?

But despite these criticisms, the movie accomplishes what Lawrence appears to be shooting for—a contemporary story about relationships with lessons to be learned. Darnell comes to understand that his exploitation of Brandi and other women does not enhance his manhood, but denies the humanity in himself and the women he hurts. He also learns that expressions of love, whether verbal or otherwise, have meaning and value, and should be approached carefully with respect.

Theodore Witcher

I didn't want to write a bourgeois fantasy, like "Boomerang." . . . Nor did I want to write something in the 'hood genre. All of my friends exist in between those worlds. We're not bourgeois, nor are we 'hood rats. We are a combination, and I was interested in making a movie about that group of people who never get to see movies about themselves.[60]   Theodore Witcher

When he was eleven, Theodore Witcher saw a screening of the movie *Raiders of the Lost Ark*, and he knew he wanted to be a filmmaker. His parents helped him get a Super-8 camera and editing equipment through a Sears catalog, which gave him his start in visual storytelling. Born in 1970, Witcher was raised in Chicago suburbs, and he attended the University of Iowa, though he returned to his home city to study at the Columbia College Film School. He landed a job as a production assistant on *The Jerry Springer Show* while also working as a waiter. He began sending out his scripts, and one made it to the Hughes brothers.[61]

He got the call to come to Los Angeles in 1994, to work with the Hughes brothers' company on a sequel to their successful film *Menace II Society*.[62] However, the sequel was never made, but Witcher obtained an entre to an executive at New Line Cinema, where he pitched several ideas, including the story for *Love Jones*.[63] Finding the story fresh in comparison to the inner-city gansgta stories that had grown jaded by 1995, *Love Jones* was accepted as a $7 million production with Witcher attached as the director.[64]

Love Jones goes a long way in exploring a serious romance between a contemporary, urban black couple who are, at the same time, attempting to define themselves individually as professionals. Witcher adheres to the basic boy meets girl–boy loses girl–boy finds girl at the end plot structure of the romance genre. However, within this genre-shaped plot, Witcher, as both writer and director, takes the audience along some fresh and revealing pathways. Unlike some of its contemporaries, such as *Booty Call* (1997) and *How to Be a Player* (1997), *Love Jones* refuses to reduce its characters to mere exploited types who are simply trendy and without depth. Instead, the film presents articulate, intelligent characters while examining African American cultural expressions, friendships, black masculinity, love, and marriage.

In Chicago, Nina (Nia Long), a photographer, is just coming out of a relationship that has left her doubtful about entering a union again. Those doubts are soon tested when she joins her friend, Josie (Lisa Nicole Carson), on an evening out at the Sanctuary, a lounge/coffeehouse where poetry readings and jazz performances serve as entertainment. Darius (Larenz Tate) is a regular at the Sanctuary, along with his close friends, Savon (Isaiah Washington), Sheila (Barnadette L. Clark), Eddie (Leonard Roberts), and Hollywood (Bill Bellamy). After a chance meeting at the bar, Darius dedicates his performance poem to Nina, and from there, the joys and convolutions of love and romance take off.

During the segments where Darius and Nina are dating, flirting, and lusting after one another, Witcher's blend of sharp dialogue and unobtrusive camera work makes the movie sparkle. Both Darius and Nina maneuver through urbane exchanges about literature and music for emotional protection; still, the close shots of their faces and body language reveal the inevitable. When Nina and Darius share a motorcycle ride and go out dancing, the two dominate the center of the frame, moving closer and closer, until they culminate the evening and their courting in sexual intimacy. The following morning Darius gets up and makes breakfast for a surprised Nina, as they both express that the previous night's intimacy does not bind them. But they know, and so does the audience, that they shared something special.

Darius and Nina have managed to step outside of the expected game-playing among singles, and certainly outside of the cinematic stereotypes of black singles in other films. It is only when they feel compelled to follow traditional gender games that they begin to crumble: Nina wants to test Darius' commitment by going off to New York, and Darius wants to affirm his "cool" masculinity by seeming indifferent to Nina's plan to move away.

Darius and Nina part ways, other lovers come into their lives, but they can't forget one another. And when they finally come together again, the director gives one of his more splendid visual scenes in the film. After an evening of dancing—dancing works consistently in this film as a sexual metaphor—Darius and Nina make their way in the late evening to a water fountain. The tones and textures of the frame are soft, smooth, and unblemished by the harshness of the city environment; the misty air and muted colors in the background interplay with the nondiegetic jazz strains that suggest a sophistication and maturity the couple in the foreground have finally reached in their relationship. The two lovers reaffirm their feelings for one another, and the world is balanced again for the two.

Most "romance" movies would end with the upbeat feelings in front of the water fountain, but Witcher forces his couple, and the audience, to travel into the mundane aspects of a relationship—the day-to-day interaction when a committed couple actually tries to live together. Dealing with jealousies about previous lovers and friends, and suffering from the neglect and inattention that can accompany a daily routine, Darius and Nina begin to annoy one another, as their arguments escalate. They break up again, and filled with pride and uncertainty, the couple go their separate ways, with Nina taking a job in New York. In the wake of the breakup, Darius discusses "true love" with his friend Eddie; the latter explains knowingly that "love . . . passion doesn't make sense. It is what it is." The filmmaker forces the audience to deal with that truth about relationships: love and passion are fundamental, but can not guarantee that a relationship will last. All love relationships— premarital and marital—are at risk; the excitement of the early dating and the passion of the early lovemaking must be continually fostered in an ongoing manner.

After a year, Darius has published his book of poetry, and Nina, a successful photographer, returns to Chicago. She visits the Sanctuary, and still in love with Darius, she reads a poem of her own that confesses the depth of her affection for him. She prefaces the reading by stating, "It's funny what you can do in front of a room full of people that you can't do in front of one person." Darius hears her poem, and outside as a downpour drenches the streets, Darius and Nina meet face-to-face. Reminiscent of the earlier scene before the fountain, the two now stand in the rain, a rain that's not as romantic as a fountain, but a rain that baptizes the two in the reality of their love.

Just as the passion is still there, so too are the challenges. With Nina working in New York, and Darius still living in Chicago, a relationship will not be easy. But as Darius tells Nina, the first thing is to get out of the rain; in other words, they need to take each difficulty as it comes and to keep their relationship centered in the passion they share.

Love Jones is an impressive accomplishment for a first film for writer-director Witcher. His movie tackles legitimate fears and complexities of the contemporary efforts of men and women to connect and share meaningful lives in relationships. The director is not afraid to examine the painful and the erotic aspects of his lovers' union. Witcher fashions a memorable and engaging film, and hopefully, he'll get the opportunity to do so many times again in the future.

George Tillman Jr.

Everyone has a script, but if you really go out and make a film, you'd be surprised what you can make a film for. There's no better way to learn your craft. To wait on Hollywood to give you a break is hard, but if you have a completed film, they will recognize that initiative and will take a meeting with you.[65]

George Tillman Jr.

Before going to study filmmaking at Columbia College in Chicago, George Tillman began working with videos as a teenager in Milwaukee. While there he also put together a public access show for cable television that he called *Splice of Life.* But it was his short film at Columbia, entitled *Paula,* which won him the Midwestern Student Academy Award and the Black Filmmakers Hall of Fame Award, as well as screenings at seven film festivals.[66]

The short film gave him the experience to move toward a feature, and along with his partner, Robert Teitel, Tillman put a group of investors together for a production budget of $140,000. Once completed, Tillman and Teitel took their feature, *Scenes for the Soul,* to Los Angeles, where they eventually obtained a $1 million distribution deal with Savoy Pictures. The feature was never released, but Tillman had the means to begin his next script, which was *Soul Food* (1997).[67]

With the help of agents, Tillman began to package the script, seeking help with a sound track at Yabyum Entertainment, which was run by Tracey Edmonds. Edmonds was impressed with the script and, along with her husband, Kenneth "Babyface" Edmonds, decided to take on the project as the first movie for the newly established Edmonds Entertainment.[68]

Soul Food has a number of captivating aspects to pull in an audience: a talented ensemble cast, an impressive music track, and a compelling story.

Director George Tillman Jr. (second from left) takes a break on the set of *Soul Food* with Mekhi Phifer, far right, who portrays Lem, and producer Robert Teitel, left. Courtesy of The Museum of Modern Art/Film Stills Archive.

Written and directed by Tillman, the story focuses on an African American family in Chicago that spends Sunday afternoons over dinners containing generous dishes from the cultural tradition—fried chicken, smoked ham, collard greens, cornbread, peach cobbler. Through the preparation and sharing of the food, the family members maintain their love and, too often, their conflicts. As seen through the perspective of preteen Ahmad (Brandon Hammond), the family is led by Mother Joe (Irma P. Hall), whose love and wisdom keep all situations in balance. Mother Joe's three daughters include Brandon's mother, Maxine (Vivica A. Fox), Teri (Vanessa L. Williams), and Bird (Nia Long). The three sisters have strikingly different personalities, as well as different lifestyles shared with their husbands. Kenny (Jeffrey D. Sams), the stable family man, is married to Maxine. Miles (Michael Beach), a lawyer who has a passion to be a musician, is married to Teri. Lem (Mekhi Phifer), an ex-con trying to get established, is married to Bird.

When Mother Joe dies, the bickering between the three sisters escalates to the point of a split and the ending of the Sunday tradition of making and sharing dinner as a family. Fueling the flames of sibling conflict is the arrival of Faith (Gina Ravera), a cousin whose failing dancing career in Los Angeles brings her home to Chicago. A sexual encounter between Faith and Miles results in a rift in his marriage to Teri that can never be repaired.

Young Ahmad sees the family drifting apart, and he attempts to bring them back together with the lure that he has discovered the long-rumored hidden money in the house. Although Ahmad's plan falls apart, the legendary money is found to actually exist, and as the movie ends, Ahmad sits on the back steps of Mother Joe's house watching Maxine, Teri, and Bird picking vegetables in the garden to prepare the Sunday feast.

Soul Food emerges as a satisfying movie in a number of respects. First and foremost, it confirms the positive family ties that can weather the stormy dilemmas that often trouble close relationships. The urban backdrop, the weight of economics, busy schedules, and personal ambitions all ring true in reflecting the extremities of interactions and conflicts facing a family.

Secondly, Tillman manages to pull strong performances from his cast, as both the major and smaller roles shine brilliantly. His work with Brandon Hammond is particularly successful, as the character Ahmad captures the wonder, admiration, confusion, and love of the youngster toward the adults around him who shape his world and his modes of behavior within that world.

Thirdly, Witcher directs large, complicated scenes, such as Bird and Lem's marriage reception, where the energy, excitement, and enjoyment of the occasion run headlong into the threatening appearance of one of Lem's old girlfriends. Then, in opposition to the broader comedy of the reception sequence, Tillman shapes smaller, sensitive scenes, such as when Maxine and Ahmad walk the city streets discussing the family's future as well as his own.

Soul Food stands out as one of the most memorable films to present contemporary black family life, displaying the flaws and spirit of people struggling and surviving together. In seeking to present three-dimensional characters, the filmmaker shows respect for his subjects, while acknowledging their faults. Furthermore, the film proves that a compelling story with fresh characters, regardless of ethnicity, can be appealing artistically and rewarding financially. For its $6.5 million budget, the film earned more than $43 million at the box office,[69] which is indeed a success in Hollywood's lexicon. But beyond the box office, *Soul Food* demonstrates again that a movie oriented in African American experiences and helmed by an African American director can possess elements that entertain and embrace members of a diverse audience.

Kevin Rodney Sullivan

When I go to the movies, I want a filmmaker to make me feel something. . . .
If you give me some information, or show me something I've never seen, or
expand my point of reference on a particular issue, that's cool, but make me
feel something—that's the job.[70]   Kevin Rodney Sullivan

A San Francisco native who took a job at age ten as a movie extra, Kevin
Rodney Sullivan, who was born in 1959, went on to be an actor on television's
Happy Days during its last years.[71] His formal acting training began when
he was fourteen, as he entered San Francisco's American Conservatory Theater. By nineteen, Sullivan was in Los Angeles, getting parts in the movies
More American Graffiti (1979), *Night Shift* (1982), and *Star Trek: The Wrath
of Khan* (1982). He was twenty-two when he sold a television script—an episode of *Fame*—to the ABC network; this good fortune opened the door for
a working relationship that resulted in his creating, writing, and directing
the drama series *Knightwatch*.[72] With that background, Sullivan was able to
springboard into directing movies for HBO: the short film *Long Black Song*,
which was one of three in the *America's Dream* anthology movie, and *Soul
of the Game*.[73]

The movie *How Stella Got Her Groove Back* (1998) afforded Sullivan a
chance to blend drama and comedy in a story from the novel that had already found a wide audience. Following the literary and cinematic success
of *Waiting to Exhale* (1995), which also centered on black women, *Stella* was
a highly anticipated film. With the novel's author, Terry McMillan, serving
as coscreenwriter and executive producer, the movie brought a closer look
at African American women to mainstream audiences that had previously
been encouraged to recognize only stereotypes about black women.

Living in San Francisco, the protagonist, Stella (Angela Bassett), works as
a stockbroker, as she survives her stressful job, a recent divorce, and being
a single parent to her son, Quincy (Michael J. Pagan). With further irritation
coming from her meddling sisters, Angela (Suzanne Douglass) and Vanessa
(Regina King), Stella finds solace in talking over the phone with her close
friend Delilah (Whoopi Goldberg), who lives in Manhattan. Delilah convinces Stella to vacation in Jamaica, and the friends meet at a resort in the
Caribbean. Resisting Delilah's efforts to fix her up with some vacationing
"players," Stella meets Winston Shakespeare (Taye Diggs), a local man who
is half her age. But their mutual attraction and later passion for one another
are obvious.

Trying to settle back into her routine in San Francisco, Stella gets fired
from her job, but is encouraged when Winston phones. Returning to Jamaica

---

While shooting *How Stella Got Her Groove Back,* director Kevin Rodney Sullivan is flanked by his stars, Angela Bassett, right, playing the title character, and Whoopi Goldberg.

with her son and niece Chantel (Sicily), Stella and Winston enjoy an affectionate reunion. But when Winston introduces Stella to his affluent parents, his mother (Phyllis Yvonne Stickney) confronts Stella about the age difference. The ensuing discussion brings on the first of many arguments between Stella and Winston about the subject. When Delilah dies, Winston travels to the funeral to support Stella, then decides to live with her while considering his options about employment or attending medical school. When Winston learns of Stella's passion for furniture making, he encourages her to follow her dream, and just as sincerely, he proposes marriage. Concerned with the twenty years that separate them—and what turns out to be emphatic "taste" differences in food, movies, and video games—Stella hesitates to marry. When she finally does accept, Winston has grown weary of waiting, and has decided to leave for Jamaica to attend medical school. But catching him at the airport, Stella convinces Winston that they should be together.

In some ways, the movie runs the risk of putting off its perceived audience of women; in many ways, Stella is not a "typical" American woman with whom female viewers would identify. It might be difficult for the average woman to earn Stella's salary, to own her spacious house, and to fly off to

Jamaica twice within a few months. However, Sullivan, Bassett, and Diggs erase those alienating elements of the script by providing the main characters with warmth, intelligence, and integrity. Sullivan, for his part, makes the best of the scenes shared by the two main characters. Whether serious or humorous, the scenes play authentically without the cutesy, lost-in-the-clouds aspects found in the romantic comedies of Julia Roberts or Sandra Bullock.

Early in the film when Stella and Winston first meet at a patio restaurant, Winston joins her at her table over breakfast. As they talk, Sullivan shows the encounter from Stella's point of view, intercutting subjective shots of Winston's eyes, mouth, and biceps with Stella's voiceover providing sensual sighs of approval at what she sees. Later when the two are living together, they argue at dinner about who will pay the check. Paying the tab becomes linked to questions of manhood for the jobless Winston, but to Stella, the fact that she has a steady income dictates that she pays. Both of these scenes, which play out over meals, contain the realistic qualities to which audiences connect—one carrying the excitement of a first encounter, the other the realities of maintaining a relationship. In the many scenes that work well in presenting the evolution of their relationship, Sullivan keeps the pace intact, allowing the emotional rhythms to shape the segments.

With a comedic talent like Whoopi Goldberg in the cast, Sullivan certainly allows her moments in the spotlight—often through verbal humor, but also through physical humor. In one scene, Delilah attempts a morning workout with Stella, whose athletic fitness has been established during her strenuous jogging under the opening credits. Stella's toned body and precise stretching is juxtaposed with Delilah's halfhearted calisthenics and need for an easy chair. Delilah would prefer to be running to the bar, rather than running on the beach.

How Stella Got Her Groove Back carries many of the expected aspects of a romantic comedy, including the happy ending. However, this should not necessarily be viewed as a fault, given that black couples have had few such happy cinematic endings. Importantly, along the way, the story moves through particular challenges that plague a number of contemporary relationships. For those reasons, the movie targets and reaches a wide audience. Still, at the same time, Sullivan—like Theodore Witcher in *Love Jones*—provides a movie that speaks in a recognizable way to a black audience, particularly black women who have found themselves omitted from serious screen depiction over the decades. This achievement is not an easy one, but Sullivan meets the challenge, contributing in a positive way to the possibility of future projects in the same vein.

Christopher Scott Cherot

I wanted to show a black male character who wasn't a player, who wasn't try-ing to hit on all the women around him. I was also very careful not to specify what class he was from. And there's no 'hood talk [from him]. Most of the dirty language comes from Hav and her friends—the upper-class people.[74]

Christopher Scott Cherot

In some ways, Christopher Scott Cherot followed a pathway to his debut fea-ture that seems penned by a Hollywood writer. As actor, writer, editor, and director of his first film, Cherot took large risks, but he accomplished his goal and completed a piece that possesses enough quirkiness to make it note-worthy. Born in 1968 in the Bronx, Cherot studied filmmaking for three years at Manhattan's Tisch School of the Arts.[75] But he decided to leave school to put together a feature film, so he worked as a cabdriver and borrowed money from friends and family. Most of the money for the feature came from his mother, a physical therapist who applied for a fifth mortgage on her home.[76] So with about $65,000, Cherot began shooting his film, taking the lead role when his cast actor left the project to work on a larger movie.[77] Eventually, Cherot finished *Hav Plenty*, getting it to Miramax Films, which paid $1 mil-lion for the movie.[78]

There's something wickedly biting about *Hav Plenty*—from the names of its characters, to the underlying tone, to the glib protagonist who serves as the focus of the story. Following a caption of a New Testament verse about "being content in any and every situation,"[79] as well as the legend that "what follows is a true story," the movie opens on a home video where an attrac-tive black woman, Havilland "Hav" Savage (Chenoa Maxwell), poses for her fiancé, Michael Simmons (Hill Harper), who is running the camera.

From a wider angle, sitting on the couch, Lee Plenty (Cherot) watches Hav's image on the monitor, his obvious fascination with her telegraphing his romantic feelings. When the phone rings, Hav is on the other line, invit-ing Lee down to Washington, D.C., for New Year's Eve.

With nothing to do, he accepts and hurries down to what turns out to be an emotionally draining weekend. In addition to dealing with Hav's caustic and icy personality, Lee meets her black women friends: Caroline (Tammi Katherine Jones), a woman obsessed with her own importance; Bobby Mont-gomery (Kim Harris), a snooty, arrogant woman; and Alexandria Beaumont (Margie St. Juste), a sharp-tongued, insensitive woman. Added to this group is Hav's sister, Leigh Darling (Robinne Lee), a photographer who has a bumpy marriage with the moody Felix (Reginald James).

After Lee rejects Caroline's sexual proposition and, later, a flirtatious

In *Hav Plenty,* director Christopher Scott Cherot, second from left, portrays Lee Plenty, an aspiring filmmaker who spends an uneasy weekend with his love interest, Havilland "Hav" Savage (Chenoa Maxwell, third from left); her friend, Caroline (Tammi Katherine Jones, left); her brother-in-law, Felix (Reginald James); and her sister, Leigh (Robinne Lee).

kiss from Leigh, hurt feelings and misunderstandings abound, but every time Lee attempts to leave to return to New York, Hav finds a reason for him to stay. Finally, Hav and Lee find themselves in bed, and after kissing passionately, Hav informs him that she won't have sex. Lee understands, which, in turn, infuriates Hav, who wants to enjoy the power of denying Lee what he wants—namely her. Lee realizes Hav's desire to always be in control, manipulating those around her, and he returns to New York.

Later, when Lee breaks down to write a letter to Hav, proclaiming his love, Hav is forced to make a decision about confessing her affections in turn. Instead, she chooses to attend a party with a friend and avoid the commitment. One year later, Lee's feature film, based on that New Year's weekend, premieres at a film festival. All the characters attend, and at a reception following the film, Hav finally tells Lee that she loves him. Lee, receiving an offer for a movie distribution deal for his film, acknowledges that he got the deal and the girl—but does he want them both?

Cherot makes a watchable film that has numerous moments of humor and observations about class differences among blacks. When it works well, the script delivers clever and insightful dialogue that prompts reflection, even as one laughs. But the element that doesn't quite work here is the main characters—most of whom come off as being shallow, self-absorbed whiners. Although this may in fact be one of the points of the story, the problem is that the viewer never quite finds a character to connect with or to care about. Even the protagonist, Lee Plenty, with all his wisecracking quips, eventually becomes as irritating as the snooty characters that surround him. Consequently, the romantic attraction that Lee and Hav avoid until the end of the film doesn't seem like a final fulfillment of delayed love; instead, one wonders what aspects, beyond good looks, either finds worth loving in the other. And certainly, when they finally reach that point of expressing their true feelings, the likelihood of the relationship working out seems a miracle at best. In the movies *Love Jones* and *How Stella Got Her Groove Back*, one hopes that the main couples can make a commitment because they're decent, likable people who deserve an opportunity at happiness. However, with Lee and Hav, their final outcome never proves to be of much importance.

With such a small budget, Cherot must be commended for telling a story that is coherent and developed with detail. Since this is a character study, through a generous use of close-ups and tight framing, he doesn't lose focus, as he keeps Lee and Hav linked to each situation and event in the story. With the help of hip-hop and R&B music, as well as a score by Wendy Melvoin and Lisa Coleman, the director paces the film well, keeping most of his scenes moving with crisp dialogue and through smooth editing.

There are two elements, however, that don't work to the film's advantage: breaking the fourth wall and sound effects. At various places in the story, Lee looks into the camera and speaks directly to the audience, informing viewers of what he thinks, plans, and feels. Although the technique has worked in many other romantic comedies, such as Woody Allen's *Annie Hall* (1977), the use of it in this movie appears to be just another way of displaying Lee's flippant response to the characters and situations. However, this point about his nature has been firmly established, and conversing with the audience fails to be revelatory about his situation or life in general. Likewise, there are three occasions when the sound of a loud heartbeat reverberates over a scene—specifically, when Lee is tempted sexually by Caroline, Leigh, and Hav. The sound effect is supposed to reflect Lee's increasing temptation and indecision about either giving in or turning away from the proffered affection. But the dialogue and the acting serve that purpose without the aural element added, which comes off as a distraction in both its loudness and its abrupt insertion.

Another odd element included in the story is the overuse of profanity. Here with a group of young, upper-class blacks, Cherot must believe that scatological language will somehow emphasize "ethnicity" and connect his characters to a hip-hop audience. But in this movie the language seems out of place—not because upper-class people do not use profanity, but because with these characters, it sounds forced and inconsistent with other aspects of their dialogue and personalities.

Hav Plenty seeks to take us into a similar territory as the aforementioned films—*Boomerang, Love Jones,* and *How Stella Got Her Groove Back.* For its efforts the movie can be praised as an example of the personal and private choices that differ among African Americans. The film helps destroy the myth that African Americans are a monolithic group. Unfortunately, the movie is not as successful in making its characters rounded and three-dimensional, and thus more interesting. But Cherot's skills as a writer and director are apparent, and the movie signals his emerging, and impressive, talents.

In American cinema, comedy has taken on many shapes, and romance has assumed many designs to suit the diverse tastes of mainstream viewers. Each genre poses its own particular challenges, and directors attempt to craft a level of humor that entertains or to develop screen relationships that exhilarate. But those black directors who have felt compelled to respond to the racial stereotypes of the past have sought to balance aspects of race, culture, and age in comic and romantic stories that can connect to the largest audience. Regardless of their motivations, black directors of comedy or romance have provided a collection of films that often excel and sometimes stumble in these two essential genres of the Hollywood system.

CHAPTER TEN

Off the Hook: Comedy and Romance with a Hip-Hop Flavor

Among those who study American popular music, arguments are made that "rap music" is an evolutionary outcome of numerous factors: the African oral tradition; African American work songs; the call-and-response tradition; the doo-wop of the '50s; soul and funk music of the late '60s–early '70s; and the union of music and poetry by artists such as Gil Scott-Heron, the Last Poets, and Don L. Lee (aka Haki Madhubuti). In explaining the origins of contemporary rap forms, in his book *Black Popular Music in America*, author Arnold Shaw asserts that as early as 1974 in the Bronx, rhyming words spoken above dual turntable mixing began at house parties, but it was promoted by a group that came to be known as Grandmaster Flash and the Furious Five. Over the next five years, the "rap" and mixing became commonplace in New York neighborhoods, until a New Jersey record company, called Sugar Hill records, released the 1979 tune "Rapper's Delight," by the Sugar Hill Gang. By 1982, Grandmaster Flash and the Furious Five were signed to the same record label, releasing their tune "The Message," which reached music critics and a larger mainstream audience.[1] Black cultural critic Michael Eric Dyson underscores the impact of "The Message" in this manner: "The picture this song painted of inner-city life for black Americans . . . screeched across the canvas of most suburban sensibilities."[2] Specifically, through the reflective refrain, the lyrics commented on the oppressive limitations of the environment posed to any who tried to escape: "It's like a jungle sometimes/It makes me wonder how I keep from goin' under."[3]

Early-'80s street dancing in New York called "breaking" and in Los Angeles called "pop-locking" was showcased in the movie *Beat Street* (1984), which also integrated "rap" music into its story.[4] *Beat Street* validated the marriage of rap music and street dance, as the umbrella term "hip-hop" was used to label the creative expressions of this street culture, which also included language, attitude, and clothing.

Hip-hop music spread to mainstream America, assuming different shapes and tones, and by the time Public Enemy's "Fight the Power" served as a thematic spine to Rosie Perez's opening choreography for Spike Lee's film *Do the Right Thing* (1989), hip-hop was in vogue. In the '90s, hip-hop music splintered further, as gangsta rap emerged on the West Coast and as hip-hop moved away from its more melodic origins. However, as the decade closed, extensive "sampling"—that is, integrating segments from other songs—began bringing back into fashion a fusion of hip-hop with R&B, reggae beats, Latin rhythms, and jazz riffs.

The hip-hop influence on a bevy of movies is displayed in a number of ways—the story lines, characters, tone and attitude, language, music sound track, and presence of hip-hop performers both in front of and behind the camera. All of these elements do not necessarily apply to all of the films in this chapter, but enough elements are present to warrant categorizing numerous '90s movies as hip-hop flavored, such as *CB4* (1993), *House Party 3* (1994), *Phat Beach* (1996), *Booty Call* (1997), *Fakin' Da Funk* (1997), and *Woo* (1998).

The hip-hop flavored movies that have been helmed by black directors have been as varied as the directors themselves. Certainly, one of the more interesting black personalities on both sides of the camera has been Master P, born Percy Miller. After moving from the slums of New Orleans to the inner city of Richmond, California, Master P began his No Limit Records in 1992. He used the company as a springboard to become a powerful force in rap music, music videos, and movies.[5] Acting, writing, producing, and directing his first film, *I'm Bout It,* which went straight to video, he sold over 200,000 copies on his $1 million investment, together with enough sound track copies to go platinum.[6] As he did with his successful records, which made millions over a six-year period, Master P marketed his movies directly to African American communities. He continued to mine the black audience for his second movie, *I Got the Hook Up,* in which he served as writer, actor, and executive producer.[7] In 1998, *Forbes* magazine put him in tenth place on its list of highest-paid entertainers, estimating his earnings at $57 million for that year alone.[8] In addition to his music and movie works, Master P also owns a clothing line and a sports management company,[9] and in 1999 he had a development deal with MTV to star in and produce a thirty-minute "dramedy" about a boot camp for juvenile delinquents.[10]

Other rappers, if not so entrepreneurial as Master P, have had considerable success in both hip-hop music and Hollywood movies: Queen Latifah, Ice Cube, Mark Wahlberg, Ice-T, Tupac Shakur, Busta Rhymes, and Tone-Loc, to name a few of the better known. These rappers turned actors and, for some, directors, brought a measurable audience with them from the music world to the movie theaters. Their "crossover" appeal to black and nonblack youth has been a crucial factor in studios making decisions about movie projects.

Nine black Hollywood directors have celebrated hip-hop sensibilities in their comedy and romance movies in the '90s. These directors have made movies that are "off the hook"—that is, extraordinary or outstanding, in terms of their vital recognition of hip-hop culture. At the same time, in addition to the various configurations of hip-hop, these filmmakers, while targeting specific youthful audiences—both black and nonblack—have promoted the absorption of hip-hop into the center of American culture.

Reginald Hudlin

As indicated in his biographical sketch in Chapter 9, Reginald Hudlin gained success in directing his first feature, *House Party* (1990). In the film, Hudlin visually captures a younger generation of African American teens often absent from the contemporary films that focus on the angst and confusion of white teens. Like *Cooley High* (1975) did years earlier, *House Party* examines the concerns close to teens—peer acceptance, image, sexuality, clothing, music, and dance—while it manages to slip in some serious social and cultural messages to the same audience that it celebrates.

Using the popularity of the rap duo called "Kid 'n' Play," the story centers on Kid (Christopher Reid), who despite restrictions imposed by his father, Pop (Robin Harris), sneaks off to attend a party thrown at the home of his friend Play (Christopher Martin). At the party, another close friend, Bilal (Martin Lawrence), serves as the deejay, while two girls in particular capture Kid's attention—Sharane (A. J. Johnson) and Sidney (Tisha Campbell). Sharane, a girl from the projects, is sexy and stylish, and her best friend, Sidney, who lives in a middle-class neighborhood, is smart and sensitive.

As the night evolves, Pop angrily arrives at the party looking for Kid, but Sidney covers for him. Later, walking the girls home, Kid is lustful after Sharane, but winds up at Sidney's house, where their intimacy is cut short when her parents come home. On his way to and from the party, Kid has to dodge several muscular bullies (the group Full Force), who are led by the school tough guy, Stab (Paul Anthony). The after-party confrontation lands Kid and the bullies in jail, but Kid's friends bail him out. Making his way home, Kid attempts to slip quietly into bed, but Pop waits with his leather belt. Over the closing credits, the sounds of Pop's disciplinary action mix with Kid's pleadings for forgiveness.

House Party has an engaging innocence about it. As writer and director, Reginald Hudlin avoids the gross-out and vulgar elements often included in teen-oriented movies. He was not merely attempting to do an imitation of *Fast Times at Ridgemont High* (1982) in blackface. Rather, Hudlin has a genu-

Director Reginald Hudlin envisions a shot on the set of his influential comedy *House Party.* Courtesy of The Museum of Modern Art/Film Stills Archive.

ine affection for his characters, and even as he makes them entertaining, he tries to provide them with attributes that show their vulnerabilities.

The relationship between Kid and Pop touches upon the reality of a single-parent household with the twist of the father as the solo parent. Having lost the mother, Pop is determined to keep Kid in line and to prevent him from becoming a teenage father. One sequence explores that issue when Kid and Sidney are alone at her house. As the petting and kissing lead toward possible intercourse, the parents appear, becoming a deciding factor. But later, when riding in the car with Play and Bilal, Kid confesses that he didn't have sex because he lacked a condom. Although his friends berate him and argue that a pregnancy becomes the girl's problem, Kid stands firm on his commitment not to make that kind of mistake.

Another conspicuous message revolves around the avoidance of alcohol. At the party the teens dance, laugh, joke, and flirt, but they don't drink alcohol. The one teen who does drink eventually passes out on the floor and suffers the criticism of the other kids. Drinking and drug abuse is not a part of being "cool" among these young people.

Hudlin provides a pace and energy level to match the exuberance of his characters. The dialogue is quick and sprinkled with humor, particularly the lines delivered by Robin Harris as Pop. And with the accompanying hip-hop music, Hudlin creates scenes that suggest authenticity without seeming to be forced and squeezed over the top. From the opening dream sequence where the camera moves through the smoky interior of a party where the roof is literally blown off, Hudlin keeps the movie at a light level of storytelling that doesn't descend into an unnecessary stringing together of tasteless jokes and routines.

House Party opened the way for other films intent upon using the hip-hop aspect as a way of tapping into an existing audience of black and white rap fans. It also demonstrated that rap performers could translate their video appearances into effective screen presences. *House Party* began a decade where hip-hop would shape the sounds and images of profitable Hollywood films.

James Bond III

I've rewritten a lot of my own stuff over the years, and I basically watched and learned from director Stan Lathan [*Beat Street*], who was a real role model for me. . . . I like horror because it's so intertwined with spirituality—I believe very strongly in God, so it's a natural arena.[11]

James Bond III

James Bond III, who was born in Harlem in 1966, was a busy child star, beginning at age eight he when appeared in an elementary school play. In fact, it was as a result of that play that his parents found an agent. James eventually won a role on the NBC children's series *The Red Hand Gang*.[12] During his career, Bond appeared on a number of television shows, such as *B.J. and the Bear, The Waltons, Vegas, Wonder Woman*, and *The Love Boat*,[13] while working in more than seventy commercials.[14]

Bond also used his talents in the feature *The Fish That Saved Pittsburgh* (1979), and he delivered a strong performance in the short film *The Sky Is Gray* (1980), based on the short story of the same title by black author Ernest J. Gaines. Additionally, Bond portrayed a young James Baldwin in the made-for-television movie *Go Tell It on the Mountain* (1984). In the late 1980s, Bond began writing scripts, hoping to make a transition into more adult roles,[15] and he scored Hollywood support with the comedy-horror film

Portraying the naive protagonist Joel, director James Bond III, left, shares a scene with actor Kadeem Hardison in *Def by Temptation*.

Def by Temptation (1990), where he functioned as actor, writer, producer, and director. Film reviewer Maitland McDonagh summarizes the movie's plot as a focus on a beautiful but evil Temptress (Cynthia Bond), who dispatches several victims in her vampire lust. She then targets Joel (James Bond III), a religion student, as her next challenge. When a psychic (Melba Moore) discloses the otherworldly powers of the Temptress, Joel inevitably defeats the demon through the religious strength he shares with his Grandma (Minnie Gentry).[16]

The critical response to the movie is mixed, though most give praise to the skillful cinematography by Ernest Dickerson. In a less than exciting assessment, one critic states the movie "blends music video aesthetics and horror-genre ethics to just about the effect you'd expect: foolishness."[17] In contrast, a more favorable observation highlights Bond's direction, indicating that "Mr. Bond is best at letting . . . actors . . . exude a breezy, unselfconscious charm, and in eliciting the jokey, improvised-sounding small talk that breaks up the horror sequences."[18] Another critic concludes: " 'Def By

Temptation' is vital and funny, but is reflective in ways not typical of genre fare. . . . Underneath the humor and gore, however, we're able to perceive, indeed feel, a genuine struggle between good and evil."[19]

Since *Def by Temptation* Bond's work as a director has been as scarce as his work as an actor. The factors that contribute to the silencing of a career are a frequent conundrum of Hollywood filmmaking. Though several of the people that Bond worked with—such as Ernest Dickerson, Kadeem Hardison, and Bill Nunn—have gone on to build reputable work in films, James Bond III is open to evaluation for only one movie that, unfortunately, is out of circulation, even for a video audience.

George Jackson

The point of the movie [*House Party 2*] is not necessarily to go to college, but to make a commitment and do the best you can. Community and commitment is something you don't see in movies a lot. . . . We have to use the opportunity to not just make people laugh, but also to make people think. This movie . . . stresses responsibility, friendship, the value of education. . . .[20]

George Jackson

Similar to his partner, Doug McHenry, whose profile appears in Chapter 7, George Jackson ventured into the academic arena, but he found himself easing into filmmaking after getting his college degree. The younger of the two, Jackson was born in Harlem in 1960. He graduated from Fordham Preparatory in 1976. He went on to attend Harvard University, obtaining a degree in sociology and economics in 1980. Aiming at a career in the business world, he spent two years working in marketing and sales at Proctor & Gamble.[21]

Making his way to Los Angeles, he began working in the film business with Garry Marshall when he was at Paramount Studios. Later Jackson worked as a production assistant at Universal Studios before connecting with Richard Pryor's company. When Jackson teamed up with Doug McHenry in 1985, they decided to take advantage of the new craze in rap music, and they produced the $3 million movie *Krush Groove* (1985). From that beginning, the two have gone on to produce nine films together,[22] with both receiving credits for coproducing and codirecting *House Party 2* (1991).

In 1996, along with white agent Rob Lee, Jackson and McHenry formed Elephant Walk Entertainment, a company containing a film production division, a television department, a recording area, and an artist management section.[23] Then, in January 1999, Jackson and two friends shaped the idea for an Internet company that would be aimed at urban minorities, and one year later the Urban Box Office Network was established with planned websites for hip-hop music and young Latinos. Unfortunately, shortly thereafter, Jackson died of a stroke in February 2000.[24]

Although using the featured characters from the original *House Party*, this predictable sequel unfortunately possesses uneven humor. Even though it attempts to present more black cultural messages than the first movie, the overall achievement with story and characters falters.

Following the death of his Pop, Kid (Christopher Reid) keeps his promise to attend college, as his girlfriend, Sidney (Tisha Campbell), joins him on campus and his homeboy, Play (Christopher Martin), begs him to choose a music career instead of academics. Play's argument is strengthened when record producers, Sheila (Iman) and Rick (Louie Louie), offer a record deal. However, Kid maintains his commitment to his education, bolstered by the $10,000 donated to him by his church.

On campus Kid meets a number of influential people: his hip-hop roommate, Jamal (Kamron), a white rapper who considers himself black; Professor Sinclair (Georg Stanford Brown), a scholar of black studies; and Mr. Lee (Tony Burton), the rigid Supervisor who runs the kitchen in the faculty cafeteria. But as classes begin, Kid deals with two challenging problems: losing his scholarship money when Play gives it to the record producers and losing Sidney to the political spell of her feminist roommate, Zora (Queen Latifah). Without money and his girl, Kid faces expulsion from college, but Play, realizing that the record producers have scammed him for the money, looks for a way to raise money and keep Kid in school. With the help of their deejay friend, Bilal (Martin Lawrence), Kid and Play finally plan to have a Pajama Jam, where the men will be charged to attend but the women will be allowed in free if they dress in lingerie or sleeping attire.

With most of the action occurring on the college campus, the directors weave a number of topics into the story line: the value of higher education, the rich legacy of black history, the positive nature of protest, and the need for self-esteem and self-reliance. Using the characters of Professor Sinclair and Zora to impart most of these messages, these two characters present perspectives that offset the film's broad antics. There's an obvious respect that emerges for issues connected to black struggle and women's rights, and the filmmakers are careful to protect those areas within the more serious moments of the movie.

The sequence that works best, in regard to the energy level established by the first movie, is the Pajama Jam. Well-known hip-hop performers Ralph Tresvant and "Tony!Toni!Tone!" deliver upbeat songs as the students get into their grooves, but the rapping and dancing of Kid 'n' Play steal the segment. Though obviously choreographed, the dance numbers have a spontaneous, exuberant feel, and the actors seem genuinely to be enjoying themselves.

House Party 2 offers an interesting combination of entertainment and message that, targeted toward its young audience, makes it a movie worth recommending. The campus life projected in the film contains a refreshing optimism, though a rather romantic, unrealistic vision of classes, studying, and learning. Devoid of the cynicism, drug and alcohol abuse, and sexual obsessions found in a number of high school– and/or college-based films that came after it, the movie encourages the audience to believe in the possibilities of higher education in opening doors and shaping progressive attitudes.

Rusty Cundieff

Some black directors enjoy doing that whole violent gang thing. And there's nothing wrong with that. It's the equivalent of Scorsese doing *Mean Streets, Goodfellas,* and *Casino.* I like telling stories from the black experience, but the last thing you want is to become known as a black director who does only one kind of movie.[25]   Rusty Cundieff

In an interview, Rusty Cundieff commented further upon the pigeonholing that occurs in Hollywood. He observed: "The business finds it very easy to corner creative people into specific tasks. . . . [W]riters and directors and even actors, to some extent, can get short-changed when it comes to the type-casting process that happens. . . . "[26] Cundieff goes on to indicate that he has consciously and deliberately changed genres to demonstrate his versatility to the Hollywood power brokers.

Cundieff grew up in Pittsburgh, where he was born in 1965. He studied journalism at Loyola in New Orleans, but he later attended the University of Southern California, majoring in philosophy of religion.[27] Following college, he began doing stand-up comedy in Los Angeles, while writing and looking for acting parts. He landed a small part in the comedy series *Benson,* but made an impact when he received a year-long job on the daytime soap opera *Days of Our Lives.*[28] While participating in a small role in Spike Lee's *School Daze,* Cundieff decided to pursue feature writing and directing,[29] so he partnered with writer-producer Darin Scott.[30] The two collaborated on the project *Fear of a Black Hat* (1995), which opened up the doors for their next two collaborations—*Tales from the Hood* (1995) and *Sprung* (1997).

Inspired by the mock-documentary *This Is Spinal Tap* (1984) and the obscenity trial of the rap group 2 Live Crew, *Fear of a Black Hat* offers a fresh and humorous take on hip-hop performers. The movie opens with black professor Nina Blackburn (Kasi Lemmons) speaking directly to the audience, informing it that this documentary is part of her doctorate work in sociology. The remainder of the documentary follows a year in the rise of the rap group N.W.H., or Niggaz With Hats, which is composed of rappers Ice Cold (Rusty Cundieff) and Tasty Taste (Larry B. Scott) and deejay Tone Def (Mark Christopher Lawrence). In various interviews—within the group's tough inner-city neighborhood, in recording studios, behind stage, on the road, and at their individual homes—Dr. Blackburn collects the data and intercuts music videos by the group that profile their talents both collectively and as solo artists. With songs such as "Grab Your Shit," "Guerillas in the Midst," "Kill Whitey," and "Booty Juice," the hard-core rapping style takes the group to a number one status. Along the way the group suffers adversity, such as the accidental shooting deaths of seven managers, police censorship, competition from other rappers, public criticism from conservatives, and a groupie named Cheryl C (Rosemarie Jackson), who becomes the catalyst for the group's breaking up. The rappers all achieve success as solo artists, but in the aftermath of Tone Def's victimization by a New York City taxi driver, the three hip-hoppers join together again and go back out on tour.

The script by Cundieff parodies the language and attitudes of real-life rappers, exposing the ignorance, machismo, and shallow creativity that often exist. Although genuine educational and economic challenges confront numerous rappers in real life, the rap world, as the movie points out, sometimes becomes a self-serving outlet for rappers' emotions and cloudy philosophies.

This latter aspect surfaces in the movie when the group explains their name—Niggaz With Hats. According to the group members, the name connects back to slavery when blacks were compelled to work in the hot sun all day—hatless. Consequently, the sun-soaked blacks were too tired to rebel; but now as black men in the '90s, they wear hats of all shapes and colors to show their intentions to rebel. And later when questioned about the political implications of their song "Booty Juice," the trio respond: "the butt is like society, which we want to see as being opened and expanded, but the white man wants to keep it clogged, and we're trying to get a foot up in there . . . and when the butt is at its juiciest, we gonna get that ass." Again the cloudy philosophy delivered in hip-hop cadence shows the rappers' unusual political perspectives.

As the movie unfolds, Cundieff does an eye-catching job as director, incorporating handheld cameras, shaky camera movements, oblique angles, low angles, natural lighting, and ambient sounds in duplicating the authentic aspect of a documentary film. In addition, he uses the character of Dr. Blackburn effectively, cutting away to show her nodding and reacting to all she sees and hears. As the movie progresses, she moves further away from the prissy, glass-rimmed intellectual look at the beginning with her affected speech and straightened hair that assert her professional status. Eventually, with every hairstyle change and diction change, she moves deeper into the hip-hop world.

Cundieff's next project left behind the strong satirical edge of *Fear of a Black Hat*, though humor was still evident in the movie's journey into the macabre. *Tales from the Hood* (1995) is an anthology movie that surprises in both its visual aspects and its content. The movie spins off from the popular HBO series *Tales from the Crypt*, which presented disturbing tales in often graphic and grisly detail. Like its predecessor *The Twilight Zone*, *Tales from the Crypt* inserted the supernatural into stories that usually carried ironic twists or ethical lessons. Written by Cundieff and Darin Scott, the episodes in the movie *Tales from the Hood* center on African American characters who find that immoral deeds receive appropriate punishment with a little help from the supernatural.

As the movie opens, three inner-city gangstas—Bulldog (Samuel Monroe Jr.), Ball (De'Aundre Bonds), and Stack (Joe Torry)—pay a visit to a funeral home where they're greeted by a mysterious and peculiar Mortician, Mr. Simms (Clarence Williams III). The gangstas are there to make a drug buy, but Mr. Simms delays the business deal as he leads them from one room to another, from one casket to another, telling them four stories that he insists are true. As he tells the stories, the viewers see each one played out, with the action coming back to the Mortician and the gangstas between each story.

"Rogue Cop Revelation" follows the story of three white policemen, played by Wings Hauser, Michael Massee, and Duane Whither—who detain, brutally beat, and kill a black activist, Martin Moorehouse (Tom Wright). Witnessing this attack is a black rookie cop, Clarence (Anthony Griffith), who never reports the tragedy, and one year later, he's summoned by the voice of the dead black activist to bring the cops to his graveside. Once there, the dubious white cops are violently killed by the zombie manifestation of Moorehouse.

The second story, "Boys Do Get Bruised," examines a grade school black child named Walter (Brandon Hammond) who blames his physical bruises on nightly visits from a big green monster, which he illustrates with a crayon drawing. His teacher, Richard (Cundieff), of course disbelieves the story, so he visits the mother, Sissy (Paula Jai Parker), and her live-in boyfriend, Carl (David Alan Grier). Afterward, the audience sees that Carl physically abuses Walter, and from the young boy's viewpoint, Carl is indeed a monster who

Director Rusty Cundieff, wearing the cap, plays Richard, a concerned schoolteacher, in one of the episodes in *Tales from the Hood*. Behind him is producer Darin Scott, who directed the action movie *Caught Up* (see Chapter 7). Courtesy of The Museum of Modern Art/Film Stills Archive.

growls orders and punishes. But with Richard's help and some assistance from the supernatural, Walter tortures and destroys Carl the monster.

"KKK Comeuppance" focuses on a former Ku Klux Klan member, Duke Metger (Corbin Bernsen), who is running for governor. A pronounced racist, Metger takes up residence in an old plantation that harbors a myth that at slavery's end, the white master killed all of his slaves rather than allow them to go free. Buried in a mass grave, the souls of the slaves were transferred into small dolls by an old voodoo woman. Metger laughs at the myth until the images come to life from a wall painting, attack, and kill him.

The final vignette is "Hard Core Convert," and it looks at an inner-city gangsta, Crazy K (Lamont Bentley), who guns down a rival gang member. Before Crazy K can escape, three other gang members riddle his body with bullets, leaving him on the brink of death. Crazy K then finds himself in limbo, confronted by a Dr. Cushing (Rosalind Cash) who offers the young man a chance at redemption—specifically to undergo a behavior modification program of looking at violent images and visions of victims from his past. Crazy K rejects the program and suddenly finds himself back on the street riddled with bullets and dying.

After hearing the four stories, the three gangstas tell the Mortician he has been wasting their time, but in one last room, they see their own dead bodies. The Mortician explains that they were the three gangstas who killed Crazy K, and he reveals his true identity—the devil—as the walls of the funeral home dissolve amid a lake of hellfire.

Each one of the vignettes possesses entertaining elements, as well as dashes of the surreal. With the aid of special visual effects and sound effects, Cundieff manages to put together an intriguing mixture of humor and terror. And though some of the images are purposely graphic, the intent doesn't seem to be to sensationalize but to enhance the horror element. Cundieff understands the youthful age of his targeted audience and knows that it has become accustomed to visuals that leave little to the imagination.

Of the four vignettes, the final story holds the strongest message and most physically violent images. In one instance, Crazy K is placed in a small cell next to a neo-Nazi with tattoos proclaiming racist slogans of death to blacks. Crazy K quickly lashes out at him for killing black people; then the neo-Nazi asks what color are the people that Crazy K kills. The indictment of Crazy K's murdering of other black people is confirmed when the neo-Nazi adds: "I like you a lot." Crazy K, like the neo-Nazi, has been systematically destroying the black neighborhood. And later, as Dr. Cushing initiates the treatment, Crazy K is bombarded with a montage of visuals—live action, still photographs, and news footage—that intercut between three topics: black gang members killing each other, black victims of lynching, and hooded KKK members parading and burning crosses. The vignette is powerful in capturing the collective result of both random and deliberate political violence that steals the lives and dreams of black victims.

When Cundieff went to his next project, he jumped back into the comedy arena to present a softer, romantic story. In its efforts to develop a contemporary love story between young professional African Americans, *Sprung* might arguably be placed in the category of romantic comedies with other films such as *Boomerang, A Thin Line Between Love and Hate,* and *Love Jones.* But without subtlety in both the comedy and the romantic moods, and lacking a more sophisticated story line, *Sprung* floats in a netherworld between a hip-hop comedy and a Hollywood fantasy.

Before the opening credits are completed, Montel (Rusty Cundieff) speeds up to a church and into a room where his close friend, Clyde (Joe Torry), chastises him for being late. The wedding ring having been left in the car, both Montel and Clyde run outside, when a freeze-frame stops the action. Over the frozen image, Montel's voiceover reflects his surprise that a wedding day ever arrived. From there, the action goes back to a year earlier, as Montel and Clyde dress trendily for a party that evening. On the other side of town two friends—Brandy (Tisha Campbell) and Adina (Paula Jai Parker)—also dress for the same party. Both sets of friends, in crosscutting scenes, display the concerns and expectations of the dating lives of singles.

At the party, Clyde, with sex as his priority, has borrowed a friend's Porsche and has taken a discarded receipt left behind at an ATM machine in order to suggest his wealth. Adina, searching for the easy life, is intent upon catching someone rich. Both Clyde and Adina think they've found in each other the kind of person each desires, but after their one-night stand of wild sex, both soon learn the truth.

In contrast, Montel, a photographer, and Brandy, a law clerk, seek someone who possesses a personality and dreams. Soon, Montel and Brandy become an item and, eventually, move in together. When their friends' relationship reaches this level of commitment, Clyde and Adina reluctantly work together to tear them apart.

Cutting back to the opening freeze-frame, it turns out that Clyde and Adina are actually the ones getting married at the church. But as Adina throws her bridal bouquet, Brandy completes an acrobatic leap to catch the prize, sealing her impending marriage to Montel.

There are particular places in *Sprung* when the movie appears to be on the verge of providing something heartfelt and provocative about affection, commitment, and integrity in relationships. Yet, Cundieff retreats time and again to a level of inconsistency in the writing. On the one hand, he goes for broad, over-the-top humor with Clyde and Adina, while aiming for a more realistic style with Montel and Brandy. Although the technique works to distinguish the attitudes and personalities of the characters early on, eventually the shifting modes become disconcerting. One abrupt shift occurs toward the movie's finale, when Montel and Brandy return to a dance pavilion in the park. No one is there except the two as they begin to dance to music that only they and the audience hear. Visually, the couple is silhouetted in sparkles, as they suddenly wear formal gown and tails, dancing à la Astaire and Rogers to "Write a Song of Love" by Earth, Wind, and Fire.

One sequence that works more effectively in balancing the broad and the subtle occurs when the four characters meet at the opening party segment. As Montel strikes out with his weak "rap" to the ladies, Clyde studies the bodies in motion on the dance floor. Showing Clyde's point of view as if he possessed X-ray vision, he, and the audience, sees all the women on the floor in thongs and lacy lingerie. Cutting to the women, Brandy, from her subjective viewpoint, sees all the men actually transforming into dogs wearing human clothing. For her part, Adina, whose point of view becomes a digital scanner, evaluates each man in regard to the price and authenticity of his clothing and jewelry. Adina's quick ranking of each man appears as a single-word caption on the screen, such as "Dog," "Fake," "Crackhead," "Buckwheat," "Wimp," and "Pimp." Although cutting to-and-from the subjective points of view is gimmicky, at this early point in the story, it works successfully in showing the personalities of the main characters.

With the three movies he has directed, Cundieff has accomplished one of his articulated goals—not to be limited to one type of film. His works so far demonstrate his ease at handling differing visual textures and characterizations. At this point in his career, Cundieff needs to engage his talents in more rigorous material that will not sacrifice quality for the sake of trendy entertainment.

F. Gary Gray

As his biographical sketch in Chapter 11 points out, F. Gary Gray made his way to a director's spot through his years of work in hip-hop music videos. With *Friday* (1995) as his first feature, he connected to the music and audience with which he had become familiar, and since its theatrical release, *Friday* has developed an even larger audience, who enjoy the movie's rather simple plot and juvenile, sometimes crude, humor.

The story covers the events that occur on a Friday in a particular inner-city neighborhood. As the camera pans through the interior of a house where the Jones family sleeps, the voiceover of the son, Craig (Ice Cube), tells the audience that "after this Friday, the neighborhood would never be the same." Craig, having lost his job at a factory, exchanges morning quips with his family—Mr. Jones (John Witherspoon), Mrs. Jones (Anna Maria Horsford), and sister Dana (Regina King)—as each heads off to work. The remainder of his day is filled with "chillin'" on the porch with his friend Smokey (Chris Tucker); talking on the phone with his girlfriend, Joi (Paula Jai Parker); flirting with his beautiful neighbor, Debbie (Nia Long); avoiding the neighborhood bully, Deebo (Tiny Lister Jr.); tolerating the neighborhood crackhead Ezal (Anthony Johnson); talking with a neighborhood friend Red (DJ Pooh); and observing the antics of married neighbors, Mrs. Parker (Kathleen Bradley) and Mr. Parker (Tony Cox).

For Craig, the major stress in the day comes from two areas. First, having smoked a joint with Smokey, Craig feels obliged to help Smokey get $200 still owed to the drug dealer, Big Worm (Faizon Love). Second is an encounter with Deebo, the physically huge aggressor who shakes down anyone for money and jewelry. When Deebo punches Debbie for insulting him, Craig hurries to defend her. In the ensuing fistfight, Craig takes a beating, but he manages to fight back and defeat Deebo in front of a cheering neighborhood.

If one is looking for depth of characters and fascinating dialogue, this movie is not the first choice. With a script by Ice Cube and DJ Pooh, the movie unfolds as one long situation where characters move in and out of dialogue with Craig. At times it attempts to pass along a message: for example, Mr. Jones catches Craig with a handgun and challenges him to be a man without a gun. However, this scene is short and not typical of this cartoonish comedy.

In a peculiar way, F. Gary Gray doesn't appear to place much of a stamp on this film; instead, the movie focuses on Ice Cube's stoic persona in collision with Chris Tucker's fast-talking, over-the-top screen image. In fact, the energy that emerges in the movie flows from Tucker's frenetic character. Unpredictable, explosive, and ethnic, Tucker steals his scenes, as he couples vulgarity and spontaneous reactions. His character actually becomes more interesting than Craig, and it's Tucker's Smokey who in the last scene breaks the fourth wall and speaks directly to the audience in one final joke and freeze-frame.

The cultlike popularity of *Friday* rests perhaps in the throwback to a well-worn situation: specifically, the smaller underdog defeats a bigger enemy to become a hero. The David-versus-Goliath theme must still appeal to a younger audience, especially when wrapped in a hip-hop sound track.

Paris Barclay

I think that Black filmmaking in Hollywood is on an upswing in a big way. That's because Hollywood has finally discovered that there is a box office for more serious and diverse Black movies. They have acknowledged that there are more than enough competent Black directors around who can do them. They see that Black people are hungry for more diverse movies and will pay for them.[31]   Paris Barclay

Paris Barclay was born into a working-class family in 1956 in Chicago Heights, Illinois. One of seven children, he left home at fourteen to attend an all-white prep school called La Lumiere in La Porte, Indiana. A scholarship student and football player, he earned the grades to gain acceptance into Harvard University.[32] He went on to earn a B.A. in English and American literature,[33] but he spent more time in the creative area, writing sixteen musicals while at the university.[34]

Moving to New York City after graduation, Barclay found employment as an advertising copywriter, before landing a job at the Theater Workshop for the American Society of Composers, Authors and Publishers (ASCAP). From there, Barclay began directing commercials and music videos, working with performers such as Harry Connick Jr., Barry White, Bob Dylan, New Kids on the Block, and Luther Vandross.[35] Transferring his writing and directing experience over to television, he worked on episodic shows such as *ER* and *NYPD Blue*.[36] In 1998, Barclay won an Emmy Award for his direction of an *NYPD Blue* episode,[37] and he also received the Marianne Williamson Founders Award for his volunteer work with the Project Angel Food Agency, which prepares and delivers daily meals to more than nine hundred people living with AIDS.[38] An outspoken advocate for gay rights, as well as the need for opportunities for African American directors, Barclay earned the position of coexecutive producer on the black-oriented hospital drama *City of Angels* in 1999, but by July 2000 he resigned from the position following creative differences with the show's creator and producer, Steven Bochco.[39] In addition to directing the parody *Don't Be a Menace to South Central While Drinking Your Juice in the Hood* (1996), Barclay also helmed the HBO movie *The Cherokee Kid* (1996), with black comedian Sinbad in the title role.[40]

The title of Barclay's first feature suggests the tone that's appropriate to the level of comedy within this movie. *Don't Be a Menace to South Central While Drinking Your Juice in the Hood* is a blatant send-up of the collection of movies from the late 1980s and 1990s—specifically *Boyz N the Hood, Menace II Society, Poetic Justice, Juice, Higher Learning, Jason's Lyric, Def by Temptation*, and *Dead Presidents*—that dictated the screen images of young black males surviving their hostile urban environments. Additionally, the movie makes references to Hollywood films such as *Apocalypse Now* (1979) and *Nine 1/2 Weeks* (1986), while making light of rapper M.C. Hammer.

In a spoof of '90s "hood films," Loc Dog (Marlon Wayans, left), Dashiki (Tracey Cherelle Jones), and Ashtray (Shawn Wayans) are troubled youth in *Don't Be a Menace to South Central While Drinking Your Juice in the Hood.*

As the movie parodies the "hood" movie trend, it incorporates elements that are familiar to the category: a violent urban setting, black youth abusing alcohol and drugs, black characters with low self-esteem, overt sexist behavior, and a barrage of scatological language. There is less of a plot here than a stringing together of sequences that interface the satiric re-creation of scenes from the aforementioned movies. It's possible to actually rearrange the order of a number of sequences without harming the effect on the whole movie. With a script by Shawn Wayans, Marlon Wayans, and Phil Beauman—along with the production team of Keenen Ivory Wayans and Eric Gold—*Don't Be a Menace* certainly contains the pacing and level of humor found in the successful *In Living Color* television show.

When Ashtray (Shawn Wayans) moves in with his father (Lahmard J. Tate) to learn how to be a man, Ashtray spends most of his time with the neighborhood gangsta, Loc Dog (Marlon Wayans). Along with their homies, the two friends journey in and out of misadventures, with Ashtray finally deciding to move out of the hood with a popular girl named Dashiki (Tracey Cherelle Jones), who is unfortunately the mother of seven children with absentee fathers. From an environment of hopelessness to confrontations with other gang members and the police, Ashtray and Loc Dog deal with odds that are never in their favor.

Barclay maintains the ridicule and humor through the tidal wave of sight gags and verbal jokes. Along the way, he does, however, take a couple of strong blows at the manner in which race and oppression form an inextricable bond. In one sequence, actor Omar Epps makes a cameo appearance as Malik, a character from John Singleton's *Higher Learning.* As Malik walks with Astray and Loc Dog up the stairway of a university campus, the latter congratulates Malik for being the first from the neighborhood to attend college. After they wish him well, Malik is gunned down by a white sniper, and the camera cuts to show the sniper crossing Malik's name off a list of black celebrities he has assassinated.

With *Don't Be a Menace,* Barclay reminds the viewer of the pervasive way in which Hollywood can seize a significant concept and wring it dry of any freshness until the resulting formula has lost all depth and importance. The "hood" movies serve a purpose in exploring some legitimate issues and situations challenging certain African American communities; however, the redundancy within some of the movies suggests a perspective that African American youth are a monolithic group. Barclay allows his movie to be a visual commentary on the legacy and problematic nature of those collective films as their treatment of various issues becomes an exploitation for the sake of box-office receipts.

Lionel C. Martin

I think the issues in the film [*How to Be a Player*] are represented in a very balanced way. There are different types of characters in the story, men and women, black and white. I think it's just going to come across as a funny, universal type of film.[41]   Lionel C. Martin

Lionel C. Martin began his career on public television, first serving as a production assistant and later the production manager for the children's

BLACK DIRECTORS IN HOLLYWOOD

series *3-2-1 Contact*. He went on to gain his master's degree in film and television from the New York Institute of Technology, before making his way into directing music videos. In his extensive directing experience in that area, Martin worked with a diverse collection of performers, including Public Enemy, Bobby Brown, Boyz II Men, Whitney Houston, Toni Braxton, R. Kelly, Stevie Wonder, Jodeci, and TLC.[42]

Martin's feature, *Def Jam's How to Be a Player* (1997), works as long as a viewer suspends logic and ethics; consequently, it is a fantasy—one that journeys through the regions of adolescent male sexual desires. On one level, it has the same escapist approach toward sexual intimacy that's found in most James Bond films, where the hero's number of sexual conquests confirms his manhood, power, and status among men. Specifically, *How to Be a Player* presumes to illustrate how the game of conquests can be played out within the black community, as the reality of the four-to-one ratio of black women to available black men serves the patriarchal system quite well.

Drayton "Dray" Jackson (Bill Bellamy) is a bona fide "player"—a male who is intimate with numerous women lovers at the same time without commitment—and without being caught. But Dray finds himself being challenged by his sister, Jenny (Natalie Desselle), who is herself a onetime statistic of a player, and who wants to teach her brother a lesson. With the help of her friend, Katrina (Mari Morrow), Jenny sets a strategy to reform his behavior. However, Dray's romantic ways are exemplary to his homies—David (Pierre), Spootie (A. J. Johnson), and Kilo (Jermaine "Big Hugg" Hopkins)—who try to learn his techniques. Most of the movie focuses on Dray and his four friends making the holiday rounds at a cookout and a party, stopping off at various locales for Dray to have sex with his lovers—including a married woman, a dominatrix, an aerobics instructor, a spiritualist, and a white actress.

In order to put their plan in place, Jenny and Katrina initiate their tactics by inviting all of Dray's main women to an evening party, hoping to trap him. But at the party, Dray discovers their scheme and manages to juggle the women from one room to another until he can escape. Back at his apartment, where he's scheduled to meet Lisa (Lark Voorhies) for a late-night rendezvous, Katrina appears unexpectedly and seduces Dray. When Lisa enters the apartment, she finds Katrina's underclothes tied to the refrigerator door with the words written in red lipstick: "Busted! Adapt!" Lisa realizes that another woman has indeed been with Dray, and as she yells angrily for Dray to explain, Dray looks into the camera in defeat.

The ending of the movie suggests that Dray must pay for his deceitful actions, yet the events that precede detail and in some ways validate Dray's

Director Lionel C. Martin, left, goes over notes
with actor-comedian Bill Bellamy, who portrays
a slick womanizer in *How to Be a Player.*

actions as a player. In other words, most of the movie dwells on the exploitive
nature of Dray's behavior and suggests that the worst consequence is getting
caught.

As director, Martin exposes a great deal of naked flesh in the movie, but
doesn't address some of the contemporary issues of safe sex, pregnancy, and
AIDS—but after all, it is a fantasy. And though Bill Bellamy has a natural
comic flair, the reasons why his character attracts so many different women
are never quite divulged. At one point, Dray refers to his job at Def Jam
Records, but exactly what he does there remains unclear. Since he is neither
rich nor handsome, it often appears that it is his reputation alone that becomes the magnet for women. And the movie would imply that this reputation is founded on Dray's being an accomplished lover who sexually satisfies
each and every woman he meets—perhaps the biggest fantasy of all?

One sequence that Martin presents does work effectively for its visual
content. In the foreground of the frame, Dray and David talk about the upcoming party, while in the background a large clock sits on the wall, showing
that it's seven o'clock. The camera moves forward to an extreme close-up of
the clock, and as the second hand sweeps in a circle, the faces of Dray's vari-

ous women appear, each woman preparing for the party. Over these images that move in a circle and dissolve into one another, Jenny's voiceover sarcastically repeats Dray's rules for being a player, while Dray's voiceover repeats his confident line about succeeding as a player. The sequence shows the simultaneity of actions as everyone prepares to attend the same function, and it helps to heighten the impending showdown when Dray's abilities will be put to the test.

One the one hand, *How to Be a Player* does a positive service in presenting a number of attractive, talented black actresses to an audience. The movie reminds viewers that there are so few roles in Hollywood for the many black actresses available. On the other hand, the movie reinforces the tradition that the roles that do come to black actresses are often shallow and exploitive. And what happens to older talented black actresses? Where are their roles in the contemporary hip-hop movies that appeal to a younger, adolescent audience?

On a final cultural note, the movie also questions the manner in which the messages about power are delivered to a male audience. In his 1992 feature film, entitled *The Player*, white director Robert Altman presents a character who is a "player" in the film business. Altman's player is a white male who also exploits women as sexual objects, but the ultimate prize is the political and economic power that comes from running a major Hollywood studio. For Lionel C. Martin's player, the major impetus is sexual gratification and a power that comes from controlling women. In a game of patriarchal power, the black player seeks a rather limited objective, while the white player reaches for a greater sense of control in society. The movies in a salient manner provide a disturbing juxtaposition of the ambitions and definitions of manhood that are prescribed to the two protagonists of different racial groups. Certainly, such disparaging perceptions about manhood were not the intentions of the filmmakers, but these pejorative messages of black masculinity remain present nonetheless.

Ice Cube

I think what [my directing] does is it inspires new directors, creators, writers —people who never went to drama school, never been on set. I never went to any director's school or film school. No one taught me to write a script. I just looked at scripts I was getting and followed the formula.[43]   Ice Cube

Born in Los Angeles in 1969, Ice Cube was named O'Shea Jackson by his father, a machinist/groundskeeper, and his mother, a hospital clerk. From 1986 to 1989, he was a member of the rap group calling itself N.W.A., which stood for Niggaz With Attitudes.[44] The material created by the group ushered in the "West Coast gansta rap" that carried strong homicidal and misogynistic messages. The debate over the commercial shaping of gangsta rap versus the political messages of the form still continues today, but the bottom line is that gangsta rap has sold extensively in the crossover marketplace and has catapulted performers, such as Ice Cube, Dr. Dre, Tupac Shakur, and Snoop Doggy Dogg, into hip-hop stardom.

In his individual endeavors, by 1990 Ice Cube had formed his Street Knowledge record label and production company and was beginning to receive laudations as a solo performer, completing nine albums between 1990 and 1998. In 1990, he was chosen the Best Male Rapper by *Rolling Stone* magazine; in 1993 he earned two gold records, and in 1996 he received an NAACP Image Award nomination for his supporting role in the movie *Higher Learning.*[45]

It was in 1991 that he entered a new arena of performance—acting. Over the next decade, he appeared in numerous movies, including *Boyz N the Hood* (1991), *Trespass* (1992), *CB4* (1993), *The Glass Shield* (1994), *Friday* (1995), *Dangerous Ground* (1997), *Anaconda* (1997), *The Players Club* (1998), *I Got the Hook Up* (1998), and *Three Kings* (1999).

Reflecting on the inspiration for his first directorial feature, *The Players Club,* Ice Cube recounts visiting a strip club in Atlanta. He remarks: "I went to a [strip] club and it just blew my mind. . . . But when I started writing and tried to figure out the story . . . the only thing I could think of was telling the story from the point of view of one of the girls."[46]

Although it contains an interesting beginning, *The Players Club* gets off track by the end of the first act. As the burned-out skeleton of a building, bearing the singed logo—"The Players Club"—fills the screen, a stunning black woman, Diana Armstrong, aka Diamond (LisaRaye), walks through the remnants. With her voiceover, the story flashes back to a montage that takes the viewer through Diana's angry confrontation with her father, her pregnancy and rejection by her boyfriend, and her job working as a salesclerk in a shoe store. There at the store, two black women patrons—Ronnie (Chrystale Wilson) and Tricks (Adele Givens)—invite Diana to use her good looks to hustle money as they do at the Players Club. Diana, in need of money, goes to the club, where she's immediately hired by the sleazy owner, Dollar Bill (Bernie Mac).

Attending college classes during the day while working nights at the club, Diana's plans go successfully until her senior year, when her cousin, Ebony (Monica Calhoun), moves in with her and her boyfriend, Lance (Monte

Director Ice Cube, right, sets up a scene for his protagonist Diana, aka Diamond (LisaRaye, center), in *The Players Club.*

Russell). Ebony gets a job at the club as well, but is soon caught up in the fast money, party life, drugs, and an affair with Lance.

Diana severs her connection with Ebony, but later, when Ebony is sexually assaulted at a private party arranged by Ronnie, Diana physically battles Ronnie and emotionally saves Ebony. As Diana plans to graduate from college, Ebony realizes that Diana's earlier advice rings true: "make the money, but don't let the money make you."

The beginning of this film promises to examine a rather interesting premise—a college-educated black woman achieves financial independence by exploiting the male-dominated system that seeks to exploit her. If the writer and director, Ice Cube, had kept this particular theme in mind, *The Players Club* would have been a revealing movie in its exposure of gender and economic issues. Unfortunately, the filmmaker appears more interested in exposing the naked bodies of black women characters, whose motivations are oversimplified and often unclear.

For example, though committed to college and her child, Diana permits herself to stumble into emotional and violent confrontations with people from the club. However, she appears to be too smart to allow dead-end people to ruin what she has built for herself. Likewise, Ebony is even more enigmatic, as she descends into the sleaziness of the club life. The story suggests that among her reasons for following such a hellish path was her discovery that years earlier Diana became an unknowing participant in one of Ronnie's sexual exhibitions at a party. But Diana's past is too far removed from Ebony to be such a controlling force in her decision making, so Ebony's motivation remains a mystery. In an interesting way, of the three significant women characters, Ronnie is the most consistent. However, as a black lesbian woman with long, bleach-blond hair, Ronnie is presented as an anomaly, and the script inappropriately suggests that Ronnie's lesbianism is inextricably tied to her sinister nature.

Not too far along in the movie, it becomes evident that this is not a story about women's perceptions, but a story about a man's perceptions about women who work at strip clubs. And with the inclusion of action sequences —with shootouts, mobsters, crooked black cops, and explosions—Ice Cube directs the film best when it functions as an action-comedy for males.

Without a doubt, Ice Cube does better as a director than as a writer. At one part, when Diana leaves the dressing room and enters the club to dance for the first time, the camera does a full 360-degree pan to provide the subjective viewpoint of the smoky, dimly lit, male-populated room. The room, like the strip club world, is small, oppressive, and stifling. In another segment, Ice Cube successfully employs parallel cutting to contrast the lives of Diana and Ebony. As the former is having a pleasant dinner with Blue (Jamie Foxx) in a well-lit café, the latter is cornered in the darkened bedroom at a bachelor's party desperately phoning for help. The juxtaposition of the settings underscores the quality of life attained by each character, as the sequence ends with Ebony being beaten and raped.

The Players Club misses the chance to set a standard about black women characters with a younger generation of viewers who, no doubt, responded to Ice Cube's image as a hip-hop icon, more so than to the movie itself. Rather than setting itself apart, however, the movie offers more of the same misogynistic and homophobic vibes that have been found in much of the more controversial gangsta rap lyrics of the '90s.

Without question, the decade of the 1990s witnessed a significant rise in the number of black directors in Hollywood. From one perspective, the hip-hop-flavored movies merely serve as the most recent example of white-owned studios seizing the opportunity to reap profits from cultural elements rooted within African American communities. Yet, from another viewpoint, the proliferation of hip-hop flavored comedies and romances edifies and legitimizes that aspect of African American culture to the larger society. The latter viewpoint recognizes that the co-opting of black culture has been an ongoing reality in America, but it also recognizes that in this case—as opposed to the black urban action films of the late '60s and '70s—many of the actors, writers, producers, and directors have been African American, creating a formidable presence in front of and behind the camera.

CHAPTER ELEVEN

Redefining Crossover Films

The concept of "crossover" has been an operative idea in the marketing of Hollywood films for decades. It took on a particular relevance to African American representation in movies as the early-1970s formula of black urban action movies began to wane in popularity. In his study *American Film Now*, critic James Monaco places the term "crossover" into the context of black-white audience appeal and story lines. By the early '70s, films such as *The Godfather* (1972) and *The Exorcist* (1973) pulled in not just white audiences, but also audiences that were composed of over one-third black viewers despite the absence of on-screen black characters in those films. Likewise, successful films with serious black themes such as *Sounder* (1972) and *Lady Sings the Blues* (1972) were actually written and directed by whites.[1] For Monaco, these films translated into box-office receipts that pleased the Hollywood studios, so the "crossover" perspective shaped the decision making to green-light future projects.

During the latter part of the decade, the notion of "crossover" expanded in meaning as it identified a black actor who could attract audiences beyond black viewers. At the time, comedian Richard Pryor was the primary crossover black performer, and then in the 1980s, it was comedian Eddie Murphy who ruled as the premier crossover personality. Additionally, in the '80s the black-white buddy films, such as *Lethal Weapon* (1987), served as crossover movies as the interracial protagonists affirmed racial harmony while offering heroes who represented both black and white viewers. In the 1990s, the crossover appeal of black performers, such as Denzel Washington, Whoopi Goldberg, and Will Smith, was still a prominent aspect in the deal-making process, as were the buddy films with black-white pairings, such as *The Glimmer Man* (1996) with Steven Seagal and Keenen Ivory Wayans and *Nothing to Lose* (1997) with Tim Robbins and Martin Lawrence.

However, in the '90s the crossover idea attained yet another configuration. During the decade a small number of black directors helmed commercial movies with white characters who lived and interacted in predominantly white-oriented environments. This type of film should not be seen as a cause célèbre for the erasure of racial barriers for black filmmakers, nor should it be seen as an anomaly for a black director to tell a nonblack story. After all, black people, in general, have a familiarity with the environments and experiences of whites more often than the reverse. However, in Hollywood, it did become an unusual occurrence for a black filmmaker to be chosen to direct the stories of whites, given the history and limitations of blacks in the film industry.

In noting the origins of this black directing of white experiences, one would certainly have to consider the role that Michael Schultz assumed when completing the movies such as *Scavenger Hunt* and *Sgt. Pepper's Lonely Hearts Club Band*. Although largely forgettable movies for reasons explained in Chapter 5, the responsibility given to Schultz demonstrated a confidence in his ability to render movies that would satisfy a popular audience across racial lines. One of the notable aspects of the '90s crossover movies was that black directors were not restricted to the comedy genre. Kevin Hooks, F. Gary Gray, and Antoine Fuqua developed action films, while Bill Duke, Carl Franklin, Thomas Carter, and Forest Whitaker completed films that highlighted drama and/or romance. These black crossover directors became examples of the skills and talent that existed within the community of black filmmakers—the capabilities to take on diverse characters, stories, and historical settings beyond their own ethnic and cultural backgrounds. Their collective success offered strong evidence that filmmaking, in some instances, enables creative people to transcend sociopolitical boundaries, even as they validate or deconstruct those boundaries.

Kevin Hooks

I think one of the most difficult things for a director, when doing television or whatever, is to be consistent. . . . As a director you're telling a story and the audience is going to react to that story based on the way you present it. And when I'm finished telling this story, that's the *only* way it's going to be told; this is the first impression this audience is going to have. That became extremely important to me and I think it made me a more sensitive, knowledgeable filmmaker.[2]   Kevin Hooks

Raised in Philadelphia, the city of his birth in 1959, Kevin Hooks grew up with entertainment as a part of his environment. His talented father, actor Robert Hooks, was a series regular on the television show *N.Y.P.D.*, when at the age of nine Kevin Hooks won a role as a delivery boy.[3] Hooks continued to work as a child and teen actor, appearing in several notable films, such as *Sounder, Aaron Loves Angela* (1975), and *A Hero Ain't Nothin' But a Sandwich* (1978).

After graduating from high school, Hooks moved to the West Coast, attending Los Angeles City College for a year to study in the Theater Arts Program. After acting in the television film *Just an Old Sweet Song* (1976)—with his father and Cicely Tyson in the lead roles—Hooks received a regular role on the television series *The White Shadow*, which aired from 1978 to 1981, giving him national recognition and a promise to direct from executive producer Bruce Paltrow. That opportunity came when Paltrow's new dramatic series *St. Elsewhere* provided Hooks with his chance to get behind the camera.[4] From there, other assignments came his way, and Hooks directed numerous series episodes on *China Beach, Doogie Howser, M.D., Equal Justice, Homicide: Life on the Street, I'll Fly Away, Midnight Caller, Tales from the Crypt, 21 Jump Street,* and *The Young Riders.* Additionally, he completed television pilots and made-for-television movies, including *To My Daughter with Love* for NBC, *Roots: The Gift* for ABC, and *Best Intentions* and *Boys and Girls* for CBS.[5]

In 1989, Hooks was a Directors Guild of America nominee for his direction of the CBS Schoolbreak Special *Home Sweet Homeless,*[6] and nine years later, he garnered considerable praise for his direction of Turner Network Television's original film *Glory and Honor.*[7] In between those two television films, he completed four feature films that demonstrated his seasoned skills in handling both comedy and action for a mainstream audience: *Strictly Business* (1991), *Passenger 57* (1992), *Fled* (1996), and *Black Dog* (1998).

Hooks' first feature, *Strictly Business,* begs to be compared with two similar comedies of the '90s—*Boomerang* (1992) and *A Thin Line Between Love and Hate* (1996). Similar to *Boomerang,* the story focuses on characters who were buppies, and similar to *A Thin Line,* the story minimizes the class differences that exist among blacks. But in *Strictly Business* the attitudes of black urban professionals and aspects of class distinctions become more significant to the plot, and the film should be credited for the effort to acknowledge the different shadings—in regard to complexion, economics, and tastes—that are found within the black community.

Strictly Business follows the cultural journey of Waymon Tinsdale III (Joseph C. Phillips), a black executive at a Manhattan real estate firm who is on the verge of gaining a partnership if he can close a pending deal. His streetwise friend, Bobby Johnson (Tommy Davidson), seeks Waymon's help in moving up in the company from his mailroom job, and Waymon's lawyer girlfriend, Diedre (Anne-Marie Johnson), pressures him to be successful and to commit to marriage. Waymon seems to be on track until he meets Natalie (Halle Berry), a beautiful black woman who works as a nightclub personality and who knows Bobby.

When Waymon and Natalie meet, the two develop a relationship, but it's one that takes Waymon's time from his business and from Deidre. Added to that pressure is the sneaky sabotage of Waymon's real estate project conducted by David (David Marshall Grant), a white colleague competing for Waymon's position of partner. Blaming his failing project on excessive time spent with Natalie and on Bobby's incompetence, Waymon loses his woman and his friend all at once. But in the end, Bobby comes through and hooks Waymon up with the Halloran brothers (Paul Butler and James McDaniel), who are wealthy black bankers. With their financial investment, Waymon is able to complete his real estate deal, get the partnership, fund a nightclub for Natalie to own, and give Bobby a promotion.

In his first feature, Hooks puts together a very likable movie that takes a few punches at issues of cultural expression, as well as at the racial politics pervading the business world. At the heart of the story, cowritten by Nelson George and Pam Gibson, perceptions of "blackness" are tested. For Bobby, being in and of the black neighborhood, regardless of a corporate job, is a necessity; for Waymon and Deidre, being too "ethnic" is viewed as a deplorable condition. These two extremes tug away at Waymon, as he realizes that Natalie lives within the black world that he avoids. By the movie's end, Waymon has moved more toward his ethnic identity via his language, clothing, walk, style of dancing, and attitude, while Bobby's promotion has certainly pushed him into the requirements of corporate culture. In the end, Hooks suggests that Waymon, Bobby, Natalie, and the Halloran brothers have managed to reach and find a middle ground that allows for a celebration of "blackness" and a successful negotiation of the white corporate world.

Rather than going for over-the-top humor, Hooks keeps the verbal and physical comedy in an effective balance in the movie. Joseph C. Phillips has just the right degree of stiffness, allowing his clumsy efforts at being "ethnic" to be funny and nonderogatory. At the same time, Tommy Davidson's one-liners and rapid-fire wit provide sufficient venom to take on both the black bourgeoisie and the white establishment.

In *Strictly Business* Hooks engages a wide audience, with subject matter and genre that invite a younger audience, across ethnic lines, to feel comfortably entertained. Both Davidson and Phillips had made connections with mainstream audiences through television—the former on *In Living Color* and the latter on *The Cosby Show*. Hooks doesn't require either actor to go too far beyond the personas they exuded on their respective television shows, and he shapes the distinction between the personalities toward his goal of validating the diversity that exists among young urban blacks—a diversity that doesn't necessarily mean a separation.

Unfortunately, the focus on the two male characters means that the black women characters suffer from a lack of depth. Halle Berry is both gorgeous and captivating as Natalie, the beautiful fantasy; Hooks' slow-motion introduction of her to Waymon and the audience is sexy and tasteful. But despite Natalie's drive to own her own nightclub, the audience never gets to know more about her or her perspectives on corporate America and ethnicity. By contrast, Deidre's politics are as visible as her haughty disdain for Waymon's socializing with Bobby; Deidre remains more of a "buppie type," yet without connections to anything other than her buppie girlfriends.

Strictly Business, however, has more going for it than against it, and it certainly shows Hooks' facility with taking black characters to a mainstream audience without compromising their ethnic qualities. He manages to accomplish a similar objective with his next feature, *Passenger 57*, an action film that offers an example of Hooks' skill at excelling in that genre. The movie delivers a black action hero who, unlike the heroes of the black urban action movies of the early '70s, functions outside of the black neighborhood and interacts within mainstream America's codes of heroics.

At the center of the movie is John Cutter (Wesley Snipes), a security strategist who works with airline employees in preparing for hostile in-flight situations. As the title character, Cutter is flying aboard a plane that's taken over by international terrorist figure Charles Rane (Bruce Payne) and his followers. With the aid of a black flight attendant, Marti Slayton (Alex Datcher), Cutter manages to dump fuel, forcing the plane to land in a small southern town. Once it does, Cutter gets off the plane and is arrested by local law enforcement agents, but the bigoted cops are set straight by federal agent Dwight Henderson (Robert Hooks) and airline supervisor Sly Delvecchio (Tom Sizemore). The authorities work with Cutter as he reenters the refueled plane to continue his rescue. Eventually, Cutter whittles away at Rane's group, until the two fight one-on-one, with Cutter sending a beaten Rane tumbling through the opened door of the speeding jet.

With his martial arts skills, cool-under-pressure resourcefulness, and glib attitude, John Cutter is an action hero in the Stallone, Schwarzenegger, Willis tradition. Snipes—who would continue to show his physical prowess alongside Sean Connery in the black-white buddy action movie *Rising Sun* (1993)—assumes the Cutter persona with an appropriate physical display and cool demeanor. With the flashback of the character's haunting memory of losing his wife in a hostage standoff with a killer, Cutter has become a driven, no-nonsense good guy. Hooks and Snipes present a tough, take-charge hero with a sexy edge who confidently moves between black and white worlds.

Director Kevin Hooks, right, explains his goals for a scene with his buddy characters Charles Piper (Laurence Fishburne, center) and Luke Dodge (Stephen Baldwin, left) in the movie *Fled.* Courtesy of The Museum of Modern Art/Film Stills Archive.

Cutter's world, like that of most heroes, is more accurately populated with "good" and "bad" people, more so than "ethnic" people.

Keeping within the action vein, Hooks then directed *Fled,* a formula film that borrows from other movies, most notably *The Defiant Ones* (1958) and *The Fugitive* (1993). The movie opens with a bang, as a witness held in safekeeping by the Feds is killed in an explosion planned by a hit man named Santiago (Victor Rivers). Learning that the key witness has been killed, federal attorney Chris Paine (David Dukes) gives Federal Marshall Schiller (Robert John Burke) one weekend to come up with evidence needed to put away the mob boss who was believed to have ordered the hit, Manta-jano (Michael Nader).

The scene shifts to a prison gang working a rural Georgia road. White convict Luke Dodge (Stephen Baldwin) and black convict Charles Piper (Laurence Fishburne) are chained together, and when an inmate seizes a gun and begins shooting, everyone scatters. Piper and Dodge escape, battling one another as they elude the authorities. Eventually, Dodge, a computer hacker who stole $5 million from a corporation, agrees to give Piper half of the hidden money if they work together to reach Atlanta. Once there, Piper and Dodge hijack a car and its driver, Cora (Salma Hayek), forcing her to take them to her house. When Dodge goes out to locate his girlfriend, Faith (Brittney Powell), and his former partner, Puffy (K. Addison Young), he's tracked down by Santiago, who has been hired by Mantajano. Faith is killed, and Dodge is tortured to divulge the location of a computer disc that contains data about Mantajano's money laundering and financing schemes. Piper rescues Dodge, as the former confesses that he is actually an ex-cop, who can get back onto the force by helping authorities locate Dodge's disc. Making a deal for exoneration with the Attorney General's Office, Piper and Dodge defeat Santiago to safely deliver the computer disc.

In a script written by black writer and later director Preston A. Whitmore II (*The Walking Dead*), *Fled* contains less of the freshness of *Passenger 57* and all of the staples of the action genre—violence, car chases, beautiful and accessible women, and victorious heroes. The success of the movie, then, rests on its ability to fulfill the requirements of the genre, and at the same time that becomes its weakness.

There's not much to surprise the viewer in the film, either with characters, plot points, or themes. Hooks takes his audience on a roller-coaster journey through fights, shootouts, explosions, and chases at an exhilarating speed. One of the most effective chase scenes occurs toward the end of the film as Piper and Dodge flee on Suzuki motorbikes with Santiago and his thugs speeding behind them in a dark sedan. Edgy and visually stimulating with its quick cuts, the sequence culminates when Piper separates from Dodge and spins his bike to a stop in the center of the road. On foot, he confronts Santiago's speeding sedan, and shooting with precision Piper hits Santiago behind the steering wheel, and the black sedan flips over numerous times toward Piper before exploding.

Another aspect of most Hollywood action films revolves around the tongue-in-cheek wisecracking of the protagonist. That element emerges within the dialogue between Piper and Dodge, but in this movie, an interesting variation of that humor is found in the continual allusions and references to popular Hollywood movies, such as *The Fugitive, Deliverance, The Godfather,* and *Shaft.* Whenever Dodge faces a particular situation, he references one of the movies to illustrate a point or to validate a course of behavior; Piper, for his part, impatiently dismisses the movie connections.

The ongoing name-dropping of movies works an additional joke in the last scene. When Dodge punches Piper, the former asks the latter if he ever saw *What's Love Got To Do with It*—a film that starred Laurence Fishburne as an abusive husband.

Still another staple popping up in recent action movies is the obligatory visit to a strip club, where several bottomless and topless women— usually blond—gyrate and sashay in front of wildly enthusiastic male customers. In *Fled*, Hooks creates the appropriate ambience of such a club, merging music, smoke, colored lights, curvaceous young women, and voyeuristic men. Dodge goes to such a club to find his blond girlfriend, Faith (aka Cindy), who in a later scene confirms that she's paying her way through college by working as a stripper. On the other end of the love-interest pattern, Piper and Cora develop a relationship that promises to become an intimate one after the movie ends. Although Cora—dark-haired, beautiful, and sexy—keeps her clothes on, she is still cooperative with Piper and Dodge, later confessing that she was once married to a cop and suspected that Piper was one all along. Cora, who obviously had no life and friends before Piper and Dodge kidnapped her, becomes pivotal to the plot, and her pronounced Chicana ethnicity complements Piper's African American ethnicity. Hooks doesn't fashion the traditional nude love scene between the two, but he treats the interracial romance respectfully, not exploiting the sexual aspect. Piper and Cora share a long passionate kiss and a promise that they will connect after Piper's business is complete.

With Hooks' next feature, *Black Dog*, all the elements of an escapist action movie burst across the screen in the appropriate places and times. The problem, however, is that writers William Mickelberry and Dan Vining neglected to provide a worthwhile story with intriguing characters. Hooks once again demonstrates his ease with handling the action genre, but the visual style cannot make up for the forgettable content.

Opening with an action sequence in which FBI and ATF agents give chase to a truck filled with crates of illegal guns, the rhythm established at the outset promises an exciting movie to follow. But shifting to a truck warehouse, Jack Crews (Patrick Swayze), an ex-con with a suspended trucker's license, is offered $10,000 by his boss, Mr. Cutler (Graham Beckel), to drive a truckload of bathroom fixtures from Atlanta to New Jersey. With a foreclosure notice on his house and an obligation to his wife, Melanie (Brenda Strong), and daughter, Avery (Lorraine Toussaint), Crews accepts the job.

In Atlanta, Crews faces a suspicious truck yard supervisor named Red (Meat Loaf), and he's forced to accept the company of extra drivers: Earl

(Randy Travis), an aspiring country-and-western singer, and Sonny (Gabriel Casseus), an easygoing black man, who later turns out to be an undercover FBI agent. On the road, Crews and company confront violent efforts to steal the cargo, while Mr. Cutler threatens Crews' family if the latter fails to deliver the cargo. When Crews discovers the cargo is actually crates of automatic weapons, he understands the willingness of Red and Cutler to kill for the load. Setting a rendezvous at a warehouse and informing the FBI, Crews fights and defeats Cutler and his thugs, while the FBI arrives in time to take the bodies away.

For viewers who care, by the third act of the movie, the "Black Dog" of the title is given meaning. With no link to race or ethnicity, the title identifies a trucker legend that suggests that when a trucker greedily pushes too hard and too long to make money on a run, a Black Dog appears on the highway, causing an accident. This legend directly related to Jack Crews who, guilty of such greed, fell asleep at the wheel and rammed his truck into a stranded car with a family inside. Although this legend explains Crews' two-year prison sentence for vehicular manslaughter, its philosophical injection into the story seems forced and inconsequential.

The material here is far beneath Hooks' abilities, as well as those of a slightly plump Patrick Swayze. The most dynamic action sequences occur on the road, as Crews handles his trailer along winding roads and down steep hills despite the forces that attempt to stop him. In one specific segment, two motorcycles chase the speeding truck, and amid gunshots and dangerous road hazards, Crews maneuvers from the truck cab and onto the hitch as he fights a cyclist who has climbed aboard his truck. The stunt work is impressive, as is the editing that captures the battle between the hero and the thug. With high aerial shots followed by various angles of the speeding vehicles from within the cab, alongside the cab, and beneath the truck, all shots culminate to create a thrilling ride. But the predictability and familiarity of the plot render a disappointing piece, which—given its trucker theme and country-and-western music—appears to be targeted at a particular male audience.

With *Strictly Business* and *Passenger 57*, Hooks made a strong argument for his ascendancy into the ranks of the outstanding action directors. Even *Fled*, with all of its flaws, possesses a notable charm and self-conscious homage to other Hollywood movies. However, *Black Dog* misfires and fails to distinguish itself in any memorable way. But this one venture into mediocrity cannot erase Hooks' previous work, and it may serve more as a litmus test for his ability to rise again to his proven level of impressive filmmaking.

Bill Duke

There are a lot of films I want to make about America, films that have to do with issues that *affect* black people, but don't involve them. They happen in corporate offices and in halls of justice, in congressional halls—the politics of this country. Black people have no access to this reality. Those are things I want to talk about, the films I want to make. . . . I want to be able to make a film . . . because I'm the best director for the film.[8]   Bill Duke

In his career as a director, actor, writer, and educator, Bill Duke has demonstrated a commitment to creative professionalism and to helping others reach their artistic goals. Born in 1943 in Poughkeepsie, New York, Duke received a B.A. from Boston University's School of Fine Arts before gaining an MFA at New York University's Tisch School of the Arts.[9]

Influenced by black director Lloyd Richards, Duke studied acting, writing, and directing, obtaining work with the Negro Ensemble Company and Joseph Papp's Public Theater. By the mid-1970s, Duke was in Los Angeles, working on KCET's *Visions* series and finding an agent to represent him as actor. While developing an acting career, he decided to attend the American Film Institute as a Directing Fellow. In 1979 his student film, *The Hero*, won the institute's Best Young Director award, which he was able to negotiate into a directing job on the series *Knots Landing*.[10]

Extending his television directing credits, Duke also worked on series such as *Cagney & Lacey, Dallas, Hill Street Blues, Miami Vice,* and *Fame*.[11] He directed the PBS specials *The Meeting* and *A Raisin in the Sun,* and in 1996 he won the Cable ACE Award for directing HBO's *America's Dream: The Boy Who Painted Christ Black*. At the same time, he became a notable actor on television shows, such as *Palmerstown, U.S.A.* (1980–81), and in a number of films, most notably *Car Wash* (1976), *American Gigolo* (1980), *Commando* (1985), *Predator* (1987), *Action Jackson* (1988), *Bird on a Wire* (1990), *Menace II Society* (1993), *Payback* (1999), and *The Limey* (1999).[12]

In 1998, Duke took on a different role; he became the mentor to a number of Hollywood hopefuls during a ten-week seminar "to study acting and industry survival techniques."[13] Working with a group of thirty-five black performers, Duke participated in the seminar to inspire and educate the young talent about the realities of making it in Hollywood. In that same year, he took the educational aspect of his profession a step further, accepting the position as the chair of the Department of Radio, Television, and Film at Howard University in Washington, D.C. Duke saw the university post as an opportunity to combine "classroom instruction at one of black

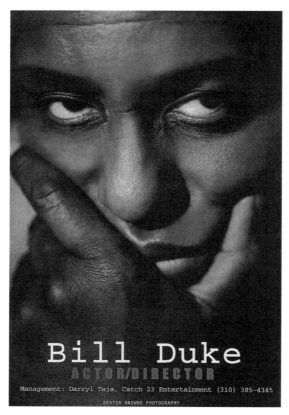

Director Bill Duke in a pensive mood.
Courtesy of Bill Duke Media.

America's premier institutions of higher learning with Hollywood movie production."[14]

Serving as Duke's first feature film, *A Rage in Harlem* (1991) is a movie that entertains, though jarringly so due to its uneven tones. With a mixture of broad comedy and subtle humor, the movie often bolts into graphic violence that undermines its possible charm. With a strong cast in both the lead and supporting roles, Duke might have leaned more on their talents, rather than reaching for the harder-edged aspects of the action genre.

Opening in Natchez, Mississippi, in 1956, a gold-for-money exchange goes sour between a group of black hoodlums, led by Slim (Badja Djola), and local white thugs. Before a bloody shootout, Slim learns that a mobster in

Harlem is already primed to buy the gold, but when the chaos erupts, Slim's woman, Imabelle (Robin Givens), escapes in a truck with the crate full of gold, leaving everyone else for dead.

In Harlem, the curvaceous Imabelle seeks out the black mobster known as Easy Money (Danny Glover), and their mutual flirtation leads to closing a deal, but unfortunately, two local black detectives—Coffin Ed Johnson (Stack Pierce) and Gravedigger Jones (George Wallace)—break in and arrest Easy Money for his role in a numbers racket. Left on her own, Imabelle decides to attend the Undertakers' Ball, hoping to find a flunky she can take advantage of.

As if made-to-order, she finds Jackson (Forest Whitaker), a naive, hard-working bachelor who lives in a small apartment with paintings of his mother and Jesus hanging over his bed. Jackson loses his virginity and heart to Imabelle and proposes marriage. Imabelle's tough exterior melts as she moves in with Jackson, his naïveté and honest emotions evoking her tender side.

But the rumors of gold in Harlem quickly spread through the neighborhood, sparking the interest of a local hustler, Goldy (Gregory Hines), who happens to be Jackson's estranged half-brother. But to Imabelle's surprise, Slim arrives in Harlem, still alive and hungry to reclaim his crate full of gold, and Imabelle. Jackson is forced to go to Goldy for help to find Imabelle, promising him the gold. Inevitably, Jackson fights Slim man-to-man, with Imabelle shooting Slim to save Jackson. In the end, forfeiting his share of the money to his brother, Jackson runs to catch the train that's taking Imabelle back to Mississippi.

Based on the novel written by black author Chester Himes, the allure of this movie revolves around its energy and its variety of characters. In an interesting twist, the femme fatale is a woman from the country, while the inexperienced man is an urban dweller. Jackson's devotion to his mother and his religion, coupled with his job as an undertaker, are played for laughs, but not at the expense of the character's human dimensions. His idealism becomes infectious to other characters in the story as well as to the audience. When Jackson's character is thrown in with fast women, deadly hoodlums, deadlier detectives, obsessive undertakers, and courageous transvestites, the combination of motley personalities proves to be a workable mix. Duke's direction doesn't falter when revealing these characters to the audience, as he manages to give each a peculiar appeal. The brisk movement in the exterior scenes that capture the rhythms of the urban streets matches the witty dialogue in the interiors where the physical action slows down. But Duke is at ease with the comedy sequences as well as the action and dramatic sequences, with the former igniting visceral response while the latter evokes more emotional intensity.

Again, the major criticism rests with the integration of graphic violence, which seems a bit too harsh for the otherwise comic levels in the film. Unlike a predecessor, *Cotton Comes to Harlem* (1970), also based on a Chester Himes novel, *A Rage in Harlem* accents the action with blood and profanity. In the opening sequence when Slim's gang confronts the white thugs, Slim has one of his men torture a white leader with a knife before the gunfight ensues, detailed with shotgun blasts spraying blood throughout the setting—a bit more than necessary for a comedy. Later, the shootout between Slim and Easy Money's gang brings about a similar result, and when Slim has the transvestite Big Cathy killed, a close shot of his throat being cut is included.

Duke could have saved these violent touches for his next film, as violence relates directly to the themes and situations of its story. *Deep Cover* (1992) is perhaps one of those films that missed a great deal of attention in the shadows of the burgeoning "hood" films, but it stands as a very accomplished work in its style and content. The film develops as a character study, but at the same time, it serves as a study of the politics of drug enforcement.

The story begins in Cleveland in 1972 under a voiceover of John Hull (Laurence Fishburne) who "unwraps his pedigree" by narrating the visuals of his drug-using father being shot dead while robbing a liquor store. Twenty years later, Hull, in police uniform, is recruited by Carver (Charles Martin Smith) a manipulative white man heading operations for the federal Drug Enforcement Agency (DEA). Carver's one question while interviewing Hull and other black men seems inflammatory: "What's the difference between a black man and a nigger?" Hull response shows his intelligence, pride, and perceptiveness: "The nigger is the one who would even answer that question."

Two weeks later, Hull is relocated to Los Angeles, where he plans his mission: to bring down a high-level official named Hector Guzman (René Assa) by going through the ranks of his drug distribution family. As Hull settles into a cheap hotel room, across from a junkie and her son, he makes the rounds on the street, attracting the attention of a vice cop, Taft (Clarence Williams III).

Hull makes the right moves and soon finds himself introduced to a local supplier, David Jason (Jeff Goldblum), a Jewish lawyer whose intelligence is compromised by his sexual appetites, drug use, and greed. But as Hull gets closer to David, the two develop a friendship, as David introduces Hull to Betty (Victoria Dillard), a black art dealer who launders drug money outside of the country. While Hull kills and sells drugs to people of color, he questions his direct participation in destroying the black community.

But Hull presses on, bringing down Barboza and Gallegos (Gregory Sierra and Arthur Mendoza) and moving in on the top boss, Guzman. However, abruptly, Carver thwarts the efforts, explaining that the State Department has just negotiated an alliance with Guzman to gain political access into his foreign country. Hull erupts at the insanity of the whole situation, realizing that he permitted the government's game to turn him into a murderer and drug dealer. Hull regrettably kills David, and holding on to millions taken from Guzman's drug family, Hull arranges for Betty's freedom from prosecution and takes custody of the young son of the aforementioned junkie.

With strong performances by Fishburne, Goldblum, and Sierra, Duke takes the viewer into the extremes and ultimate destructiveness of the drug scene. Giving due respect to the action genre, Duke nonetheless devotes ample time to examining the characters who commit themselves to a lifestyle that speeds them toward a void. When David's wife begs him to quit the drug business—reminding him that besides the "things" he has a wife and daughter who love him—David explains that he wants it all. His greed has become an addiction.

But the pivotal character in the film, from first scene to last, remains Hull, and the movie shows his cautious idealism when he first takes the undercover assignment, through to his disillusionment with what he's doing. If there is a weakness in this character, it might be seen in the closing sequence where he shoots David for killing Taft. David reminds Hull that they have $11 million and a clear escape. David says, "Wake up, my brother," as he dismisses Hull's sobbing about morality and legal codes. Hull's personality has been altered so drastically at this juncture that his choice to reclaim his old identity is questionable.

In a smaller part, the character of Betty adds some interesting dynamics to the movie. Victoria Dillard—still another black actress with far too few roles for her talents—constructs an intelligent woman whose independence and business savvy, not a plunging neckline or tight-fitting wardrobe, become the attributes that attract Hull. Betty and Hull share a relationship, as opposed to one exploiting the other, and when Hull finally negotiates with the Feds, he demands Betty's freedom as a part of his deal, confirming his commitment to her. Duke presents their relationship as one that develops slowly, but one that has both passion and respect.

With this second film, Bill Duke confirms his skillful directing in bringing black characters to a mainstream audience without losing expectations for entertainment or compromising black cultural perspectives. In his third film, *The Cemetery Club* (1993), he goes a step further and proves that he can also complete a story with dominant white characters in the most difficult of genres—the comic drama.

With this mainstream project, *The Cemetery Club*, Duke tells the story of three Jewish women in their senior years who weather the difficult situation of living as single women following the deaths of their spouses. Basing the screenplay on his play of the same title, writer Ivan Menchell provides Duke with a story that examines friendship, romance, love, and insecurity. The focus of the piece is the link between three friends: Esther Moskowitz (Ellen Burstyn), a level-headed, congenial woman; Doris Silverman (Olympia Dukakis), a conservative, feisty woman; and Lucille Rubin (Diane Ladd), an assertive, fun-loving woman. When all three lose their husbands, they remain loyal by regularly journeying together to visit the grave sites. Lucille, who knew her husband had cheated on her, wants to stop grieving and to enjoy her life again, but Doris insists that it's their duty as wives to maintain their vigilance. Esther, after a year of mourning, meets Ben Katz (Danny Aiello), a former cop turned taxi driver, who has been dating a number of women since his wife's death.

When Doris dies of heart failure, Ben makes an effort to see Esther again, confessing that he was afraid of getting married again. Esther tells him she doesn't want marriage, and that she's not afraid of living alone or being independent. In concluding, Lucille sits at Doris' graveside, telling her dead friend that Esther and Ben will probably wind up together, and that she, Lucille, will remember Doris, not by visiting the cemetery, but by living and treasuring the good times they had together.

Having a trio of experienced actresses such as Burstyn, Dukakis, and Ladd certainly makes Duke's job easier, as each actress provides a distinctive personality and roundness to her character through dialogue and nuances. At those places where the dialogue carries the humor, Duke doesn't have his actresses push the lines, but rather communicate them in an understated manner. For example, when the trio is at the cemetery, Lucille and Doris argue about remaining faithful in attending the graves. The former announces that she's ready to live and not ready to join a cemetery club, stating: "I refuse to be in a club where half the members are dead."

But much of the strength of the film comes from such interactions, as casual conversations evolve into humorous moments or, just as quickly, into heated arguments. Duke allows these many friendly discourses to develop naturally without overplaying either the comic touches or the heavier dramatic moments. Duke seems to understand the restraints needed to transfer a stage piece, with its emphasis on dialogue, into a film work, where the visuals and tones require a more subtle shaping.

As the film develops, Esther's character takes the spotlight, much of it dealing with her growing relationship with Ben. After being married to her deceased husband for thirty years, Esther is tentative about dating, being alone with a man, and allowing herself to show affection to someone new.

But when Esther and Ben decide to spend the night together, one of the movie's funniest sequences develops. Nervously undressing one another, Esther asks for the lights to be lowered; in the dimness, she confesses her physical wounds that befit her age—a scar from a hysterectomy and a mark from gall bladder surgery. Not to be outdone, Ben confesses a bullet wound and a scar from his removed kidney stones. Having undressed each other via their confessed scars, Esther asks Ben if he has "one of those things"—her reluctance to say "condom" another sign of her generation. Ben confirms, and like a nervous teen, goes off to the bathroom, but waiting in the dark room, Esther, and the audience, hear the snapping of rubber and Ben's crying out in pain. Ben hobbles back into the bedroom and Esther has to assist him in getting aroused and putting on the condom. In the sequence Duke keeps his characters true to who they are at that point in the story. He allows the anxiety, awkwardness, and tenderness of their time together to play out without raw language, graphic visuals, or intruding music.

There is a sweetness and honesty about *The Cemetery Club* that makes it a very endearing film. Similar to what director Ron Howard did with *Cocoon* (1985), Duke doesn't exploit the senior characters as fodder for laughter; rather, the film reveals that people in their early sixties can be as cautious, thoughtful, witty, and sexual as younger folks. Moving to the other end of the age scale, Duke completed *Sister Act 2: Back in the Habit* (1993) as his next film. Following the box-office success of *Sister Act* (1992), Duke took on the task of making a sequel, with the major cast reprising their roles. The audience's familiarity with characters is both a plus and minus when making a sequel, because of expectations, so this sequel places familiar characters into a familiar teachers-saving-at-risk-ethnically-diverse-teens-in-a-crumbling-school plot.

While headlining her Las Vegas show, Deloris Van Cartier (Whoopi Goldberg) receives a visit from her old friends, Sister Mary Patrick (Kathy Najimy), Sister Mary Lazarus (Mary Wickes), and Sister Mary Robert (Wendy Makkena). They implore Deloris to return to San Francisco with them because they need her help at the troubled St. Francis High School. Unable to let her good friends down, Deloris goes, meeting up again with the calm and steadfast Mother Superior (Maggie Smith). Mother Superior explains that Deloris has a gift of inspiration that's needed to reach the kids at the school, and donning the nun's habit, Deloris proceeds to help out, keeping her true identity a secret from the principal, Father Maurice (Barnard Hughes), and the administrator, Mr. Crisp (James Coburn).

Deloris' first challenge comes from her music class, a group of annoying, disrespectful, and unruly teens, including characters played by two newcomers who would later emerge as stars in music and movies, respectively—Lauryn Hill and Jennifer Love Hewitt. Deloris' next challenge comes from the news that Mr. Crisp is leading the campaign to close St. Francis for good and to put up a more profitable parking lot in its place. Determined to prevent the school's demise, Deloris, with the help of the nuns, shapes the music class into a chorus and enters them into a state competition in Los Angeles. Despite nerves, the chorus goes on to perform a rendition of "Joyful, Joyful" with a mixture of gospel, R&B, and hip-hop stylings. The chorus wins the competition, the school is saved, and Deloris triumphs again.

Sister Act 2 completes its main objective—to entertain while noting the importance of following one's dreams and working together for a common goal. Duke wisely allows the film to speed along without adding on the messages too heavily. He presents a fine balance between the comic and the emotional, as characters reach out for one another across shared insecurities and pain.

At the center, of course, is the comic performance of Whoopi Goldberg, who at this point knows the character of Deloris quite well—irreverent, gutsy, sardonic, but caring. It's a character Goldberg has played before, and one that suits her comic timing. Likewise, a young Lauryn Hill delivers a notable performance, balancing her acting with scene-stealing vocals. Her proficiency and confidence as a singer shine throughout the film, and she makes otherwise predictable scenes interesting to watch.

One of the predictable sequences is the Hollywood ending obligatory in most studio films. Here, despite only singing together for a few weeks, the St. Francis School chorus manages to beat other choirs that appear to have been more experienced. But even though the audience knows what will transpire, Duke still delivers a payoff with a production number of "Joyful, Joyful" that has been set up in small pieces earlier in the film. When first teaching the unruly music class, Deloris tells the students that she has an eclectic approach to music, loving all forms equally. This homage to fusion is realized in the final performance, as the multiethnic chorus sings, dances, raps, and improvises their way to the championship.

Perhaps in an effort to return to the intense drama and character study he had explored in *Deep Cover*, Duke went on to helm *Hoodlum* (1997) as his next project. Serving also as one of the executive producers, and teaming again with Laurence Fishburne, Duke constructed a film that is his strongest work to date and an obvious celebration of African American culture and the gangster genre.

The focus of the film is the protagonist Ellworth "Bumpy" Johnson, a character Fishburne first played in a much smaller role in *The Cotton Club* (1984). In *Hoodlum*, there seems to be a continual battle within Bumpy, where good and evil are jockeying for the right to dominate. Bumpy sees himself as a businessman providing jobs for the people in Harlem. Yet, Bumpy is volatile and selfishly vengeful, willing to endanger those same Harlem people in a mob crossfire in order to maintain his power over the Harlem numbers racket. From the earliest scene where the audience sees Bumpy alone in his Sing Sing jail cell to the later scene when Bumpy, all-powerful, sits alone in a gloomy office, Duke emphasizes the complexity of the character and the many shadings of his personality. Bumpy seems a realist and a nihilist all at once, charging forward toward a vision of economic independence for black people, but not noticing the black people he steps on along the way.

First and foremost, this is a gangster film, filled with the testosterone-driven dialogue, action, and violence inherent in the genre. Along the way, Bumpy crosses paths and gunfire with two white mobsters attempting to muscle their way into the 1930s Harlem numbers business—Dutch Schultz (Tim Roth) and Lucky Luciano (Andy Garcia). To his credit, Duke succeeds in putting together an excellent gangster film while also managing to provide a visual landscape of an ethnic community. *Hoodlum* is as slick, polished, and accomplished as Francis Ford Coppola's *Godfather* (1972), where underworld figures are tainted by personal neurosis and eccentricities, but yet compelling and electrifying. Duke plays with tones—amber at places to emphasize the historical setting, as well as dark and shadowy in those interior scenes of confrontation, isolation, and violence.

Duke gives the audience a moral tale using just enough symbols to make his point. One of the initial symbols is a black undertaker (Ellis Foster) who literally blocks Bumpy's path as the latter returns to Harlem from jail. Ominous and recurring throughout the film, the mortician tells Bumpy that everyone has to one day face death. Duke uses this character to foreshadow the impending bloodbath in their streets and the death of Illinois Gordon (Chi McBride), who is Bumpy's cousin and business partner.

Early within the film, when Bumpy meets Francine (Vanessa L. Williams), he warns her that he doesn't go to church. God stays out of Bumpy's busi-

Bill Duke discusses an upcoming scene for his lead character Bumpy Johnson (Laurence Fishburne) in *Hoodlum* as producer Frank Mancuso Jr. looks on.

ness, and Bumpy stays out of God's house. He refuses to attend the church funeral of his cousin's mistress, and unlike *The Godfather* gangsters, Bumpy never consoles himself with prayers or religious rituals. But conceding at the end of the film, Bumpy steps into a church, attending his cousin's funeral, carrying the guilt of the relative's death and all the related violence. Then, as he leaves the church, he stands alone, again seeing the same mortician waiting to carry the body away. At this juncture, the film ends in a freeze-frame, a close-up on Bumpy's face. Bumpy has reached his isolated and lonely end. Similar to Michael Corleone in *The Godfather II* (1974), Bumpy has gathered complete power and complete loneliness at the same time.

The tragedy in the film is explored on a grand scale, the implications going far beyond the mere bloody deaths of characters. Duke goes for something more complex—for example, the sequence where Bumpy joins Madame (Cicely Tyson) on a trip to the opera. Madame, running the numbers racket that Bumpy eventually takes over, tells Bumpy that the opera is all about passion, life, and death. En route, Bumpy, Madame, and her body-

guards are ambushed on the street, their car caught within a carefully designed crossfire. As the jolting, bloody sequence draws to a close, a soothing,
comforting operatic voice comes over the visuals, a woman's voice singing
a requiem for the black and white gangsters lying dead in the streets. The
film cuts to an interior as the vocals continue, and sitting together in their
bloody formal clothes, Bumpy and Madame quietly listen to the phonograph
of the operatic voice that sounds so beautiful against the ugly violence of the
preceding scene.

Despite such an artistic sequence within the film, Duke savors the exces-
siveness allowed within the gangster genre: tough, sexual language; smooth
dissolves juxtaposed with quick cuts; frenetic action sequences sandwiched
between scenes with lengthy dialogues; graphic and bloody violence; and
fiery explosions. At one point, Duke pays homage to earlier gangster films
of the '30s and '40s with a familiar use of montage to show the passage of
time and the gaining of fame and power: newspaper headlines are superim-
posed over gun battles that dissolve into money floating downward within
the frame, which dissolves to Bumpy and Francine's frolicking, which dissolves into a long shot of Bumpy walking into the camera along a Harlem
street followed by his car and his thugs.

Whether one admires or rejects Bumpy Johnson and his Harlem, Duke
is stating that there were African Americans active in the underworld, not
just the passive victims often presented in other gangster films. In addition,
Duke highlights the historical setting for a black urban community during
the early years of the Depression. There were certainly the entertainment
icons shown in other films, such as the Cotton Club and Duke Ellington, but
there were also followers of black minister Father Divine and black nation-
alist leader Marcus Garvey. There were food drives, rent parties, and black
businesspeople. At one point when Bumpy and Francine are discussing options for blacks in the community, Bumpy rejects shoe shining and luggage
handling as suitable careers for a black man. But Francine counters that there
are also colored doctors, lawyers, writers, and musicians. Duke's cultural objective in the film appears to be the celebration of what did exist in the black
community, and all the possibilities of what could happen if the community
had the same economic base as white-owned downtown Manhattan.

From *A Rage in Harlem* to *Hoodlum*, Bill Duke has demonstrated a measurable growth as a mainstream director. Since 1991 he has ventured into
established genres and crossed ethnic and racial lines to pursue films that
tell stories that provoke and entertain. In some ways, he has done it without
the self-indulgence of many other contemporary directors. Given the scope
of his directorial skills and his seeming commitment to variety, Duke will

be a director who will one day receive the attention he deserves for his impressive filmmaking.

Carl Franklin

America is a very conservative, puritanical country and I think Hollywood has always reflected that. It's only natural that you tell stories that feature your dreams, but for most people in Hollywood, those are white male dreams. That's why it's important to let other artists in, so they can bring their dreams with them.[15]   Carl Franklin

Raised in a rough neighborhood in Richmond, California, where he was born in 1949, Franklin saw his future as an actor. He studied in UC-Berkeley's Dramatic Arts Program in 1967.[16] Franklin then moved to New York to pursue stage performance, gaining roles in the Joseph Papp Public Theater productions of *Cymbeline, Timons of Athens,* and *Twelfth Night* for the New York Shakespeare Festival.[17]

Franklin moved into movie acting with a part in *Five on the Black Hand Side* (1973), then had a number of appearances in television shows, including *Caribe, The Fantastic Journey, Cannon, Streets of San Francisco,* and *McClain's Law.*[18] His television career hit a new level of popularity in the 1980s when he received a recurring role as Captain Crane on the hit series *The A-Team,*[19] but Franklin's disappointment with the cartoonish nature of the show led him to attempt to make a film. He even mortgaged his house to fund it.[20] However, the film was never completed, and he decided to study filmmaking at the American Film Institute in 1986.[21] While at the institute, he directed his student film, titled *Punk,* which was "a story of ignorance and fear" that examines a nine-year-old boy from inner-city Los Angeles who becomes a killer.[22]

Franklin's accomplishments at the American Film Institute brought him to the attention of famed B-movie producer Roger Corman, who hired him to direct three features.[23] But it wasn't until the critical response to *One False Move* (1992) surfaced that Franklin was taken seriously as a director, an assessment sustained with the praise he received for his direction of the HBO miniseries *Laurel Avenue.*[24]

Perhaps his days of shooting films with economy and leanness for Roger Corman prepared Carl Franklin for his feature thriller *One False Move.* Based on a script written by Billy Bob Thornton and Tom Epperson, the story considers how the smallest decisions and moves in life can have irrevocable consequences. The story begins under the darkness of a Los Angeles evening, as a large sedan pulls up before a house, and a beautiful black woman, Fantasia

(Cynda Williams), steps out and gains access into the house. Bursting in behind her is Ray (Thornton), her white boyfriend, and Pluto (Michael Beach), their partner in crime. While a videotape still rolls, Ray and Pluto round up the few party-goers in the house, beating two of them to find the location of an associate. The man is found, along with $15,000 and numerous bags of cocaine. With the desired treasure in hand, Pluto brutally kills several of the revelers, while Ray murders the rest. Fantasia hides the one survivor—a young boy—undetected in a back room closet.

Fantasia, Ray, and Pluto take off for Houston, Texas, to sell the drugs to a buyer Pluto has set up, with a promise to travel on to Arkansas so that Fantasia can visit her family. But getting clues from the videotape, two Los Angeles detectives, Dud Cole (Jim Metzler) and John McFeely (Earl Billings), travel to Star City, Arkansas, to await the arrival of the trio. Greeting them is a young, overeager police chief, named Dale Dixon (Bill Paxton), who has ambition to one day work in big-city law enforcement.

As the trio make their way through Texas, they leave a number of dead bodies. Meanwhile Dale has recognized photos of Fantasia. He knew her six years earlier as Lila Walker, when he arrested her for shoplifting and then allowed her to go. Arriving at the outskirts of Star City to secretly meet her five-year-old son, Byron, Fantasia is confronted by Dale, and they both face their common past. They were lovers, and Byron is their son. In an explosive encounter, Dale, though seriously wounded, manages to shoot and kill Ray and Pluto. Fantasia, caught within the crossfire, is fatally shot also. As Dale awaits an ambulance, he calls for Byron, and the two talk to one another as the scene fades out.

Layering with themes of race relations and unfulfilled dreams, Franklin shapes a movie that emerges as a suspense-thriller, but ultimately succeeds because it goes beyond a simple genre piece. With a sturdy script, Franklin slowly peels back layers of his characters to reveal what simmers beneath. Fantasia and Dale, each missing out on their big-city dreams, must inevitably deal with their shared past. The movie moves them steadily toward that conflict, as it shows the viewers the frustrations that make up their lives. Fantasia hides from her past in sex and drugs, while Dale hides within his job and his small-town reputation. Likewise, Ray and Pluto try to run away from their lives as petty thieves and killers, both hoping that one big drug deal will give them entre into the easy life. Franklin allows these characters to display what they want the world to see, but manages to provide reaction shots and close-ups that tell the audience much more than the dialogue reveals. In this way, Franklin appears to trust his actors and their skills to actualize the subtleties of their characters.

Even as Franklin weaves this psychological drama, he stays attuned to the aspects of a suspense-thriller. One successful sequence finds Fantasia and Ray in a convenience store, when a state trooper comes in for coffee. Pluto, sitting in the car, looks in anxiously through the store window, knowing Ray's volatility. Intercutting from Ray and Fantasia, to the Trooper eyeing them, to Pluto—all adds to an escalating tension. And immediately in the next sequence, the Trooper follows the trio along a dark, deserted stretch of highway, pulling them over. Ironically, cautious of the two men as he forces them out of their car, the Trooper turns his back on Fantasia, who surprises the Trooper and the audience when she shoots him in the head.

One of the elements that helps these two sequences is the omission of nondiegetic music. Franklin seems a minimalist when it comes to using a music score to enhance the intensity of a scene. Without flourishing strings or thumping chords, the sequences have an eeriness about them. The absence of sounds, other than those intrinsic to the scene, suggests a realist rather than a theatricalist approach. Franklin takes this cautionary approach to music not only in this film, but in his next two as well.

Franklin's second feature, *Devil in a Blue Dress* (1995), is the film version of the popular detective novel written by black author Walter Mosley. Franklin adapted the novel to the screen, and with Denzel Washington in the lead role, the hopes for the movie were high. Unfortunately, the resulting film, though well made, didn't find a wide popular audience.

In Los Angeles in the late 1940s, Ezekiel Rawlins (Washington), an army vet, searches for a job. Ezekiel, or Easy as he's known, is introduced by his friend, Joppy (Mel Winkler), to DeWitt Albright (Tom Sizemore), a white man who's looking for a white woman, Daphne Monet (Jennifer Beals), who socializes in the black community. After dead bodies bring on police suspicions of Easy as the killer, he realizes he has to call in an old friend, Mouse (Don Cheadle), for a bit of muscle support.

Easy eventually puts all the pieces into place in the immoral puzzle where two wealthy mayoral candidates compete for power. Daphne, the secret girlfriend of one candidate, Todd Carter (Terry Kinney), attempts to secure incriminating photos of Carter's opponent. But at the bottom of all the violence and politics is the fact that Daphne is biracial and is passing for white, a fact that Carter can't quite accept. Daphne's black background alienates her from Carter and his socialite family, a lesson she learns painfully at the end when Carter refuses to acknowledge her publicly despite her success at delivering him the damning photos.

Using the detective-suspense genre as a background, Franklin pulls splendid performances from Denzel Washington and Don Cheadle as he weaves an intricate story line with understatement. Franklin begins his movie with a slow pace, but allows it to pick up energy with every scene, particularly at the juncture when the character Mouse appears. Laying Easy's voiceover atop the visuals connects the movie in another way to traditional detective movies of the past, while providing a black male's perspective of the racial, economic, and emotional dynamics of the characters and their Los Angeles urban environment.

Rather than pepper the movie throughout with gratuitous sex and violence—which may have lessened its popular appeal—Franklin controls those areas, integrating them only to provide a direct link to the story's development. Franklin chooses to approach his audience as a sophisticated one that looks for a balance between entertainment and thought-provoking elements. He wants the audience to indulge in the suspense, but to recognize the gravity of the characters' situations. For example, in the section when Easy is interrogated and beaten by the cops, he realizes his situation as a black man charged with a crime. Rather than responding like the popular wisecracking hero, Easy fears for his life and plays the game of "cops-and-niggers," knowing his very survival is at stake. And later when Easy and Mouse hurry to a rural cabin to save Daphne from Albright and his thugs, the violent shootout shows Easy's careful maneuvering, as opposed to breaking through the door with guns blazing.

Franklin also makes an effort to maintain some of the '40s ethnic and cultural aspects that author Mosley integrated into the book: the presentation of a peaceful neighborhood of black homeowners, the black businesses and nightlife of L.A.'s historical Central Avenue, the racial segregation of the city, the corruption of the city's law enforcement officers, and the exploitive aspects of the municipal political structure. Franklin even adds a symbolic character not in the novel to underscore the issues of ethnicity and culture— namely, a black man in overalls who walks the neighborhood, cutting down trees with his gardening tools. More than just a comic element, this man seems to represent forces—historical and contemporary—that try to uproot and create disorder within the black neighborhood. Easy constantly chases the man away from his house, as well as his neighbors' yards.

With *Devil in a Blue Dress*, Franklin presents engaging characters and creates a palpable emotional level without lapsing into sentimentality. This ability no doubt contributed to his selection to direct the mainstream family drama *One True Thing* (1998). This movie becomes Franklin's crossover film, as he examines a white, suburban family living in Connecticut. With a marquee cast that includes Meryl Streep, William Hurt, and Reneé Zellweger, Franklin tackles a familiar story of the impending death of a family member that transforms the relationships within the remaining family.

Ellen Gulden (Zellweger) speaks to an investigator about the death of her mother, Kate (Streep), who had been suffering from cancer. Flashing back, viewers learn about the truths that Ellen comes to know about her parents. Ellen, living in Manhattan as an ambitious journalist for *New Yorker* magazine, doesn't want to become trapped domestically like her mother, but when her father, George (Hurt), reveals that Kate's biopsy has turned up positive, he insists that Ellen come back home and take care of her mother. George, a university professor, will not change his established campus schedule, and Ellen's brother, Brian (Tom Everett Scott), has moved a distance away. As Kate's health declines and as Ellen gives more time to her mother's world, Ellen comes to understand the sacrifices her mother has made for the family, as well as for her marriage. George has engaged in affairs with students and has made his career a priority—qualities and truths that slowly anger Ellen.

Witnessing the extreme pain endured by her mother, Ellen is grateful when she dies. In a final sequence at Kate's graveside, Ellen and George have a revealing discussion. Each mistakenly believes that the other helped Kate to die, but it becomes apparent that Kate herself saved her medication until she had a sufficient amount of drugs to commit suicide. George, despite his weaknesses, admits that he deeply loved Kate: "She was my muse. My lovely wife. My one true thing."

Although *One True Thing* has a sense of déjà vu about it, Franklin pulls an Academy Award–nominated performance from Meryl Streep, and he presents a film that triumphs in its subtleties. Franklin manages to put together a number of effective scenes that have an evenness of tone, though the characters' eyes and expressions hint at numerous emotions lying dormant beneath. Early in the movie, following the party sequence where neighbors and friends dressed in corny disguises, Ellen and her brother watch their parents embrace, kiss, and slow dance to Bette Midler's cover of "Do You Wanna Dance." Franklin juxtaposes shots of the parents locked in their enjoyment of one another and the adult children watching and marveling at the two people who, flaws and all, have shaped their lives. The scene plays on for minutes over the length of the song, and the combined visuals and music result in a simplicity and honesty of emotions that captivate the viewer. If the scene had been shorter, the audience would have been nothing more than a voyeur, catching a quick glimpse of closeness, but as

Despite infidelities, Kate Gulden (Meryl Streep) remains a dutiful wife to husband George (William Hurt) in the drama *One True Thing*.

directed, the audience is invited inside to savor those fulfilling moments for the characters.

Later in the film, when Kate and Ellen picnic in the park, they engage in a discussion of fiction written by Jane Austen. Kate criticizes the author's depiction of domestic women characters as weak and unfulfilled, while Ellen attempts to explain the reasons for the author's attack on domesticity. In their opposing points of view, it becomes clear that mother and daughter have both generational and political differences. Both endeavor to protect the preferred version of womanhood, and both expose their vulnerability. It is a short scene that soon fades into the next, but the attitudinal differences will obviously not fade away as quickly.

In this film where there are no black characters or suggestions of racial strife, Franklin ably presents a character study through which the characters Ellen, Kate, and George are fully realized, showing their flaws as well as their fervent efforts to reach across their differences to connect with one another. More specifically, Franklin constructs a mother-daughter study that doesn't force either character to undergo a forced Hollywoodish transformation. Franklin proves once again that he can effectively tell a story—anyone's story—through unobtrusive, subtle camera work that permits authentic characters to remain the focus of the narrative.

Thomas Carter

[M]y job as a director was to take what was written and try to say it in a way that went beyond the words. To enhance the words by figuring out how I can say the same thing with where I put the camera or with the colors I choose or how we use sound or music. Once you start playing the game that way, filmmaking becomes so much fun.[25]   Thomas Carter

Thomas Carter has enjoyed an enviable career as a television director. Beginning in 1982, he has been fortunate enough to direct seven television pilots that all became regular series.[26] Born in Naples, Italy, in 1954—though some sources state Smithville, Texas, as his birthplace—Carter graduated from high school in Smithville before attending Southwest Texas State University, where he studied drama. With acting as his goal, Carter went to Los Angeles in 1975, and after only a few months he lucked into his first professional acting role as a bit player in a television pilot film. The role got him into the Screen Actors Guild but not much more, as he took on various jobs to support himself.[27]

But his commitment to breaking into the business paid off, as he eventually earned acting roles in several television series, including *The Blue*

In *Swing Kids,* lovers of swing music Peter (Robert Sean Leonard, left) and Thomas (Christian Bale, right) run to evade the restrictions of Nazi Germany.

Knight, Medical Story, and *Poppi.*[28] In 1978, he became a series regular on the show *The White Shadow*—along with his peer and future director Kevin Hooks. It was on that show that Carter was given a chance to direct an episode, and from there, he went on to complete ten episodes of *Hill Street Blues.*[29] His reputation increasing, Carter helmed notable television pilots, including *St. Elsewhere, Miami Vice, Call to Glory, A Year in the Life,* and *Midnight Caller.*[30] In 1990, he was a cocreator and executive producer of the ABC legal series *Equal Justice,* on which he also directed,[31] earning an Emmy Award for Outstanding Director of a Drama Series in 1991.[32]

In 1993, the years of work behind television cameras finally led Carter to his first feature film, *Swing Kids.* With this film, Carter offers an unusual perspective on the familiar story of Nazi Germany. Set in 1939, the movie opens with what appears to be an incongruous situation: Two young white "hep cats" enter a dance club where other young white people are wildly dancing the jitterbug to black big band music; the caption on the screen reads "Hamburg, Germany, 1939." The two swingers of focus are Peter (Robert Sean Leonard) and Thomas (Christian Bale), two close friends who share a passion for American music, especially by Duke Ellington, Count Basie, and Benny Goodman. Along with their friends Arvid (Frank Whaley) and Otto (Jayce Bartok), Peter and Thomas submerge themselves into the "swing" culture, as they share music, language, long hair, and distinctive fashions.

Peter, however, reenters his German life whenever at home. There, living with his mother, Frau Muller (Barbara Hershey), and his younger brother, Willi (David Tom), he's haunted by the vacancy of his father, who was arrested and tortured by the Gestapo of the popular Nazi Party. At his home, Thomas reluctantly bears the tyranny of his father, Dr. Berger (David Robb), an opportunist who voted for Hitler as a way of securing his social position.

Although all young men are required to join the Nazi Party's "Hitler Jugend," known as the H.J., Peter and Thomas, as well as Arvid and Otto, refuse to volunteer for the ranks of the stoic, aggressive, and hateful H.J. members. But, when a prank goes sour, Peter is forced to join the H.J., and Thomas does so just to be close to his friend. As they are exposed to the Nazi's military training, newsreels, and lectures, Thomas softens and embraces the Nazi position. At one point, Thomas even reports on his father and has him taken away for interrogation.

Finally, one day Peter discovers that, following the orders of the H.J., a small box he delivers contains human ashes. In his rage he goes to a club that night and dances to the music he loves, but the H.J. break into the club and force the patrons into waiting trucks. Among the H.J. troopers is Thomas, and he and Peter fight one another in the same club where they once enjoyed both music and friendship. Peter is placed on a truck to be taken to a work camp, and as the truck pulls away, Thomas connects with an old part of himself and yells out their old swing salute to Peter: "swing heil!"

In addition to the heartfelt story surrounding Peter and Thomas, the film triumphs with a production design by Allen Cameron and choreography by Otis Sallid. Carter takes both elements and utilizes them effectively throughout the film. In particular, the dance sequences in the clubs carry an infectious exuberance, representing not only the function in the plot, but signifying the freedom and enjoyment inherent within the "swing" lifestyle that enamors Peter and his friends. Carter lets his camera follow the action as dancers move athletically and dynamically, with arms flailing and women's bodies tossed over shoulders and through the opened legs of their partners. Using swish pans, high angles, and tracking shots, the camera reveals the unleashed ecstasy of young people obsessed by rhythm. Carter carefully supplies long shots, allowing viewers to see the entire bodies of the dancers as they cut their jitterbug designs around the floor. The dancing of the swing kids displays a wild abandon, a spirit, and an individualism that blatantly contradicts the stiff, uniformed, militaristic group identity posed by the H.J., and as the movie goes along, Carter juxtaposes both worlds in a convincing manner.

Carter's movie undulates between musical-dance moments of pure energy and powerful, dramatic moments that underscore the hatred and fears of living with the Nazi regime. One of several such moments occurs when Peter and Thomas argue as to whether or not Arvid is a traitor for criticizing the Nazi Party. Thomas insists that Arvid is wrong in defending Jews, and Peter reminds him that "Benny is Jewish"—meaning Benny Goodman, one of their swing heroes. Thomas adds that Peter's father was a "Jew lover," and the two friends fight each other physically for the first time. When pulled apart, they stare at one another in shock, seeing a stranger instead of a close friend.

Carter accomplishes much in *Swing Kids,* as the movie personalizes the emotional and psychological struggle that results when a society turns to scapegoating and persecution. For his first feature film, Carter chooses a challenging historical canvas to fill in, but he meets the test with proficiency and skill, pulling exceptional performances from his actors, particularly Robert Sean Leonard and Barbara Hershey.

For his second feature, Carter embarks on a drastically different cinematic experience, as he ventures into the action-comedy genre with Eddie Murphy in the lead role. The movie *Metro* (1997) took Carter back toward some of the urban police material he had worked with earlier on television, and unlike *Swing Kids,* the messages in *Metro* require viewers to use little of their intellectual or emotional faculties.

In *Metro* Murphy appears to be playing a character that is a combination of the Reggie Hammond–Jack Cates duo from his earlier blockbuster, *48 Hrs.* (1982). Murphy portrays a cop named Scott Roper, a hostage negotiator who is funny, clever, and tough all at the same time.

With the story set in contemporary San Francisco, Roper demonstrates his success on his job by defusing a drug-crazed bank robber holding hostages after bungling a holdup. Afterward, he sees his ex-girlfriend journalist, Ronnie (Carmen Ejogo), whom he tries to woo back, but with little success. She has had far too much of Roper's gambling and emotional distance. Settling for a night at the ball game with his friend Lt. Sam Baffert (Art Evans), Roper is jolted into despair when Sam is killed by a sinister jewel thief named Michael Korda (Michael Wincott).

As Roper tries to return to his regular duties, he undertakes the task of training a new partner, Kevin McCall (Michael Rapaport). McCall, a SWAT sharpshooter, possesses perceptive skills that impress Roper, particularly when the two have to respond to a hostage situation at a jewelry store. Roper recognizes the thief is Michael Korda, and Roper and McCall give chase along the San Francisco streets, finally cornering Korda in a parking structure. In a concluding battle, an escaped Korda takes Ronnie hostage, but Roper, with McCall's help, outsmarts the thief and saves his woman.

Metro contains all the bells and whistles needed to be the entertainment vehicle that it is. Following the success of a milder Eddie Murphy in *The Nutty Professor* (1996), *Metro* reaches out to those fans who enjoy Murphy's patented wisecracking, fast-talking, quick-cussing black hero. Carter makes certain that Murphy satisfies those viewers by providing sequences that offer mixtures of humor and tension, humor and action, and humor and romance.

The tension works well in the segments that highlight hostage standoffs. Carter wrenches as much life-and-death drama as possible in those scenes via the helpless, frightened people held at gunpoint. Likewise, Carter's best action sequence occurs during the second act of the film, when Korda's jewelry store heist goes wrong. As Korda makes his escape in an SUV with a woman hostage, Roper and McCall are speeding after him in an old Cadillac. Using the streets and hills of San Francisco, Carter provides the necessary staccato rhythms to thrill viewers as innocent pedestrians are threatened and unsuspecting cars are smashed and destroyed. But unsatisfied with the usual street chase, Carter adds a cable car fight between Roper and Korda. Once Korda jumps off the racing cable car, Roper discovers that he can't get the brakes to work, and so jumping back into the speeding Cadillac, he has McCall angle the big sedan across the tracks in front of the trolley, using the car's weight to brake the cable car and prevent it from plowing through the pedestrians and buildings waiting at the end of the line.

Carter's sharp ability to move from the serious drama of *Swing Kids* and into the genre trappings of *Metro* wins him praise for versatility. He proves that the demands of each type of film, though different, can be achieved effectively. Having demonstrated his success at reaching a mainstream audience through television projects, Carter possesses the experience and skills to continue his crossover success in feature films. The hope now is that he can find the kind of material that displays the compelling content of a *Swing Kids*, while offering the entertainment of a *Metro*.

Forest Whitaker

You get to tell the whole story when directing—the picture, the color, the words—in a way that shapes the whole story. As an actor, you can try to tell the story of who you think you are. . . . [Y]ou don't know what the filmmaker will choose to do. . . . As an actor, I have no control over that. But as a director, I do.[33]   Forest Whitaker

Born in Longview, Texas, in 1961, Forest Whitaker had a mother who was a teacher and a father who was an insurance salesman. The family moved to Carson, California, where Whitaker distinguished himself as a high school football player. Becoming a standout defensive lineman helped him get an athletic scholarship to California State University at Pomona, where he majored in music.[34] When he later transferred to USC to study drama and opera, he drifted into acting and began to appear in local Los Angeles productions. His talent earned him the Sir John Gielgud Scholarship to attend the Berkeley, California, branch of the Drama School of London.[35]

As an actor he was able to find roles in both small- and big-screen productions. His television appearances included parts on *Hill Street Blues, Amazing Stories,* and the miniseries *North and South;* similarly, he received parts in made-for-television movies, including Showtime's *Last Light,* HBO's *Criminal Justice,* and the cable film *Lush Life.* In theatrical films, he became a visible performer in numerous movies of the 1980s and 1990s, including *The Color of Money* (1986), *Platoon* (1986), *Good Morning, Vietnam* (1987), *A Rage in Harlem* (1991), *The Crying Game* (1992), *Jason's Lyric* (1994), *Species* (1995), *Phenomenon* (1996), and *Light It Up* (1999). In addition, for his lead role as the title character in Clint Eastwood's direction of *Bird,* Whitaker won a Best Actor award at the 1988 Cannes Film Festival.[36]

As a director, he had an auspicious debut with the HBO drama *Strapped* (1993), which earned him the recognition as the Best New Director at the Toronto Film Festival.[37] From there, he was able to make the move to the big screen with his first feature, *Waiting to Exhale* (1995).

With several black women directors to choose from, surprisingly Whitaker received the nod to helm *Waiting to Exhale* as his first film. Since the movie was based on Terry McMillan's popular novel of the same title, the audience for the film already existed, particularly among African American women who seldom saw themselves represented on the big screen.

With author McMillan joining screenwriter Ron Bass to complete the script, the story follows the personal lives and friendship among four African American women. Savannah (Whitney Houston), a television news producer, endures empty, uncommitted relationships and a mother who pressures her to have a man in her life, even if he's married. Bernadine (Angela Bassett) endures infidelity and betrayal by her husband, John (Michael Beach), who leaves her for a white coworker. Robin (Lela Rochon) endures several un-

---

healthy, dead-end relationships, with one leading to her pregnancy. And Gloria (Loretta Devine) endures rejection from an estranged husband who admits that he's gay. With all of this *enduring* going on, the emotional pain suffered by these four friends mounts up emotionally over the year that the film's story takes place. The friends support, criticize, and love one another, which appears to be the medication needed for each to individually arrive at a position where she can achieve the victory of self-pride and self-love. Of the four friends, Bernadine and Gloria both fulfill the responsibilities of motherhood, and these two appear to have the promise of positive relationships with men at the story's end. Bernadine develops a friendship with a stranger (Wesley Snipes), a businessman in town who's losing his wife to cancer, and Gloria becomes close with Marvin (Gregory Hines), the new next-door neighbor who's a widower.

Whitaker makes a point of giving each of the four women equal screen time, as he uses generous subjective shots and voiceovers by each to tell the audience their inner feelings during various segments. Each woman's story is indeed worthy of attention, though Savannah and Robin seem to create situations that they later whine about. But before allowing these two to be too annoying and self-engrossed, Whitaker moves to either Bernadine or Gloria, who indeed emerge as the two most engaging characters.

One of the more popular scenes with women viewers, and one of the better-directed sequences, occurs when Bernadine takes out her wrath on John's belongings. Having personally sacrificed to help John build his business, Bernadine's anger is legitimate. As she gathers John's clothes and sets them ablaze in his sports car, Whitaker uses zoom shots, quick cuts, subjective shots, and close-ups to create a dynamic emotional sequence. The visceral ride, coupled with Bassett's sharp acting, turns the segment into a memorable delight where vengeance on material things works effectively on both a literal and a symbolic level.

In a more humorous tone, Whitaker takes the audience into a sexual liaison between Robin and her coworker, Michael (Wendell Pierce). As Robin waits in her sexy lingerie for her lover to come out of the bathroom, her voiceover narrates the scene. Michael, physically chubby and unintentionally funny, attempts to be sexy, as he maneuvers into bed and prematurely ends their lovemaking. Confident that he has thoroughly satisfied Robin, Michael begins to boast about the material things he can provide. The sequence is funny, but provides the audience a clear view of Robin's emotional weaknesses and needs.

From one perspective, it's surprising that *Waiting to Exhale* was so successful with audiences because at its foundation, it's really little more than a slick daytime drama centering on issues of "love and romance." Indeed, the refreshing element here revolves around a presentation of African American women, all of whom are professional and educated, and who serve as the movie's focus—a rare cinematic sight. Along with an equally popular music score by Kenneth "Babyface" Edmonds, in which most of the vocals were also performed by black women, the movie becomes a celebration of African American womanhood. At the same time, with the gender concerns shaping the story, the movie, as well as the book, crosses over racial lines and touches black and nonblack women alike. Women are famished for women protagonists—as opposed to adolescent sex kittens—who are dealing with situations relevant to contemporary life, balancing areas of professional success, family, love, and marriage.

Having completed a movie that examines the intimate and professional lives of four contemporary women, Whitaker seemed a likely choice for directing a movie that focuses on one contemporary woman suddenly overwhelmed by deceit and infidelity. Unlike the emphasis on African American women in *Waiting to Exhale*, the movie *Hope Floats* (1998) follows one white woman's struggle toward independence.

Birdee Pruitt (Sandra Bullock) appears on a television talk show thinking her best friend is treating her to a makeup session. Instead, Birdee discovers, on national television, that the friend has been having an affair with her husband, Bill (Michael Pare). Following her humiliation, Birdee packs up her belongings and her daughter, Bernice (Mae Whitman), and drives from Chicago back to her hometown of Smithville, Texas. Birdee and Bernice move in with Birdee's eccentric but caring mother, Ramona (Gena Rowlands), who is raising Travis (Cameron Finley), the son of Birdee's peripatetic sister. Having been a former high school cheerleader and beauty queen, Birdee is remembered by everyone and pitied for her embarrassment on "ambush" television. But Birdee is pursued by Justin Matisse (Harry Connick Jr.), a former high school friend who has recently returned to Smithville following a stay in California.

Birdee and Bernice hope for Bill to return to them, and as Birdee waits, she wallows in self-pity. When Justin finally convinces Birdee to have dinner with him, he reminds her that in their youth, Birdee was audacious and full of life. But Birdee's depression makes her reject Justin's romantic proclamations, and even causes a rift with Bernice. When Ramona dies of a stroke, Bill shows up for the funeral to ask for a divorce. Birdee realizes Bill's selfishness and shallowness, confessing that she tried to make herself over into the wife he wanted and lost herself in the process. Getting an agreement to the divorce, Bill hurries away, leaving his daughter Bernice devastated. And

Director Forest Whitaker reviews a scene with his star and executive producer Sandra Bullock, who portrays the protagonist Birdee in *Hope Floats*.

as Birdee decides to stay in the small town, the final images show Birdee, Justin, Bernice, and Travis attending a street fair together.

Hope Floats has the feel and pacing of an independent film—a character study that aims to take the audience deep beneath the surface of the protagonist and her various relationships. With Sandra Bullock serving as both the executive producer and the star, the movie is obviously a vehicle to showcase her talents in a serious, dramatic turn. But, surprisingly, the movie tries too hard to be emotional in some places, and then it doesn't quite do enough with character development in other places. For example, Birdee's character, despite what all of the other characters say about her bold and assertive qualities, never seems to fulfill her pronounced vigor. The rumors of her dynamic personality seem to be greatly exaggerated. Since Birdee spends most of the movie suffering from feelings of inadequacy, it's difficult to picture her ever having been a lightning bolt of a personality. At the same time, Justin's character remains a bit too mysterious. His time in California appears to have been disappointing for him, but without details, his return to Smithville seems more convenient for the plot than revealing of his personality.

The rhythmic construction of Whitaker's direction in *Hope Floats* is inconsistent. Some scenes develop through pauses that are supposed to suggest deep meanings, but instead only slow the movie's pace. And, then, Whitaker uses a rather odd transitional device on several occasions: instead of a traditional dissolve, he uses a rippling frame as the final image in one scene becomes the new image of the next scene. Perhaps the technique is meant to connect to the job that Birdee gets as a film developer and cutter at a one-hour photo lab; however, the effect merely brings attention to itself.

Whitaker actually creates more effective sequences when he makes the characters move to the edges of their fears. In one segment, Birdee enters an employment agency being run by Dot (Dee Hennigan), an old high school classmate who used to be teased by Birdee because of her weight. Dot, having the power to assist Birdee in finding a job, relishes the revenge she can now take, as she keeps Birdee waiting for forty-five minutes and then declines to send her out on any job. Then, in her desperation, Birdee apologizes for the past and pleads for a job in the present. It is a painful, but honest moment when the protagonist has to reach out to seek help while trying to hold on to as much pride as possible.

Although *Waiting to Exhale* and *Hope Floats* achieve certain levels of success, both films point out the confidence of Forest Whitaker to tackle issues of gender across racial lines. Similar to Bill Duke with *The Cemetery Club*, Whitaker demonstrates a proficiency in rendering a story that takes him out of the familiar. Whatever projects Whitaker chooses in the future, he has proven himself as a director who has few limitations in regard to material and themes.

F. Gary Gray

Directing is a love it or leave it job. There's no in between. You have to give up a big chunk of your freedom to do it, so you'd better love it. . . . You have to deal with attitudes and egos, you have to convince people to do things they wouldn't normally do, you have to convince performers to be people that they're not—and be convincing. . . . [S]ometimes you think, am I out of my mind for doing this? But then you sit back . . . take a really deep breath and you say, "It was *all* worth it."[38]   F. Gary Gray

Similar to Hype Williams and Antoine Fuqua, F. Gary Gray worked his way as a director through the demanding area of music videos. Born in 1969 and

Director F. Gary Gray sits reflectively on the set of *The Negotiator.* Photo by Sam Emerson; courtesy of F. Gary Gray.

named "Felix,"[39] Gray grew up in inner-city Los Angeles and studied film and television at Los Angeles City College. But he dropped out of school at the age of twenty to pursue jobs as a cameraman, working for Fox Television, CNN, and E! His experiences with those positions helped him find work as a director on music videos, as he completed projects with performers such as Ice Cube, TLC, Coolio, and Whitney Houston.[40]

By 1998, Gray had received sixteen awards and twenty-three nominations for his direction of music videos. Two of the more noted awards display his versatility and creativity: the 1995 Billboard Music Video Award for Best Rap Video for Coolio's *Fantastic Voyage* and the 1995 MTV Music Video Award for Video of the Year for TLC's *Waterfalls.* He also received an NAACP Image Award for *Waterfalls,* and in 1998 he was nominated for a Grammy Award for directing Stevie Wonder and Babyface's video, *How Come, How Long*.[41]

With his celebrated background as a music video director, Gray was able to direct his first feature—New Line Cinema's urban comedy *Friday* (1995), starring Ice Cube and comedian Chris Tucker. The film achieved remarkable popularity and financial success, allowing Gray to direct the more dramatic story of *Set It Off* (1996), also for New Line Cinema.

Gray's first feature, *Friday*, which certainly reached a crossover audience, works better as an example of the hip-hop-flavored comedies of the 1990s. However, Gray made certain that he struck a more powerful note with his next film, *Set It Off*, a movie containing all the necessary elements of the contemporary black urban films: an inner-city setting; the street language, clothing, and ethos; African American cultural expressions, especially music; violence; and sex. Notably, Gray shifts the focus from the world of black masculinity and forces the viewer into a world of working-class African American women struggling to survive a tense Los Angeles environment.

Lita "Stony" Newsome (Jada Pinkett) possesses an independent spirit and a strong set of shoulders, as she takes on the responsibility for her younger brother, Stevie (Chaz Lamar Shepard), following the death of their parents. Hungry for a life beyond daily desperation, Stony sacrifices to make college a real option for Stevie. Cleo (Queen Latifah), by her own admission, is a "hood rat," excited by fancy cars, the thrill of auto theft, and the companionship of her lover, Ursula (Samantha MacLachlan). Frankie (Vivica A. Fox), a sassy, energetic woman, longs to be treated fairly in the world. Tisean (Kimberly Elise), a single mother, tries to break through her insecurities to establish an independent life.

Early in the movie, Frankie loses her bank teller position when she neglects to follow the bank's standard procedures during a robbery at gunpoint. At the same time, Stony, Cleo, and Tisean work for a janitorial service under the watchful eye of their demanding supervisor, Luther (Thomas Byrd). Complications occur when Tisean faces the possibility of losing her daughter to the authorities, and Stony learns that Stevie never applied to college. Then, when Stevie is mistakenly shot and killed by the police, Stony's anger and hatred of the system erupt.

With the economic pressures bearing down, the four decide to rob a bank, and with Frankie's knowledge of bank procedures, they stake out their target. In the process, Stony meets Keith (Blair Underwood), an upper-class bank vice president, who is immediately attracted to her. Stony and Keith begin a romance, even as Stony and her friends continue to rob banks. When a bank job goes awry, Tisean is shot, and soon afterwards, so too are Cleo and Frankie. Escaping with the money, Stony heads south to Mexico, from where she phones Keith one more time before going off to start a new life.

F. Gary Gray assembles a rather stimulating movie with *Set It Off* as he blends action, romance, and class issues together. Seldom does one find women protagonists—particularly, black women protagonists—as the focus of an urban action movie. But, despite some places in the script by Takashi Bufford and Kate Lanier where situations are a bit too convenient, the combination works here, offering an appeal to a wide audience. Certainly, the women live in a black neighborhood, but their enemy in the story is a common one to all—a power system that constantly places barriers across life's pathways. An audience member doesn't have to be from the "hood" to recognize that particular enemy.

In a distinctive manner, Gray doesn't allow the romance to overshadow the primary story. Stony's loyalty to her friends and her affection for Keith each tug at a different side of her personality and dreams. In doing so, her character becomes much more complex and her decisions more crucial. Connected to the romantic side is the issue of class, as Stony's working-class environment appears to clash at first with Keith's upper-class background. Although the differences are obvious, what the characters and the viewers come to understand is that Stony and Keith have much in common—primarily, both believe in dreaming and working hard for those dreams. In Keith's case, his hard work has paid off—helped by the fact that he's a male in the banking world. For Stony, her hard work didn't result in a similar material success—connected to the fact that as a female, additional barriers still exist. Stony and Keith are both intelligent enough to understand their similarities and their differences, even as they relish their growing affection. In a sequence that might suggest *My Fair Lady* (1964), when Stony arrives in her best evening outfit, Keith takes her to purchase a more appropriate, expensive evening gown on their way to his bank's social function. But Keith doesn't patronize Stony in the Dr. Higgins–Eliza Doolittle fashion, nor does he try to make her different from who she is. Once they reach the party, she is dressed appropriately because of Keith, but it's Stony's own articulation and personality that makes her fit into the social event.

Gray also presents another romantic couple in the film, though in a minor way compared to Stony and Keith. Cleo and Ursula don't hide their affection for one another, whether in the presence of friends or in public. Gray integrates the lesbian couple into the story, showing the impatience on the faces of Stony and Frankie, but not shying away from presenting the strength and sexiness that both Cleo and Ursula possess. Although their affection is shown only through touching, embracing, and an on-screen kiss, the director's message is clear that these two lovers are as passionate, affectionate, and committed as Stony and Keith.

In addition to developing these uncommon, romantic story lines, which do include a very sensual love scene between Stony and Keith, Gray's achievement in directing the action sequences is noteworthy. In these sequences the genre, and not gender, remains the significant factor, as Gray shapes bank robberies, chase scenes, and escape segments that rank on a par with other comparable action films. In one memorable part of the movie, Stony, Cleo, and Frankie elude the cops following the botched bank robbery. Trapped in a tunnel by squad cars and a helicopter overhead, Cleo makes her friends get out and escape on foot while she continues to drive through the roadblock. Gray maintains his focus on Cleo's suicidal decision, and as she's cornered with no way out, the poignant melody from the song "Up against the Wind" comes over the visuals. Gray decreases the ambient sounds, as the song, with vocal by Lori Perry, ushers Cleo through the shootout where dozens of cops return fire and she dies. In that juxtaposition of music and visuals, Cleo is raised to heroic status, forcing the viewers to connect to Cleo's final sacrifice.

Gray takes his skillful handling of action sequences into his third feature, *The Negotiator* (1998), which achieves its crossover status by returning to the black-white buddy genre of the 1980s. With the strong acting of Samuel L. Jackson and Kevin Spacey, this movie opens with a fresh story of intrigue, though by midway, the script begins to lose its edginess, and the film ends with a rather jumbled conclusion.

In Chicago, Danny Roman (Jackson), a hostage negotiator for the police department, ends another critical standoff, to the praise of his peers and the media. But when his partner is killed, evidence points to Roman as being the killer and the thief who stole money from the department's disability fund. Since his wife, Karen (Regina Taylor), is the only person who believes him, Roman executes a kidnapping as a way of forcing the department and the media to look into the fabrication of evidence. Among his hostages are Grant Frost (Ron Rifkin), Roman's commander and friend, and Terence Niebaum (J. T. Walsh), an internal affairs inspector whom Roman suspects is part of a conspiracy to frame him. Additionally, Roman demands that Chris Sabian (Spacey) be called in to negotiate the siege, because Sabian is a well-respected negotiator outside of Roman's division.

Despite the aggressive actions urged by police leaders Al Travis (John Spencer) and Adam Beck (David Morse), Roman shares information that he gathers from Niebaum with Sabian. Eventually, Niebaum confesses that he was indeed involved in a ring of cops who embezzled money from the disability funds, but he's killed in a surprise assault by a SWAT team. By the time the FBI takes over the hostage situation, Sabian decides to help Roman, which means going to Niebaum's house to find files that contain evidence necessary to show Roman's innocence. As the cops follow, Sabian manipulates a confession from Commander Frost. Frost is killed, and Roman survives the ordeal.

The Negotiator doesn't attempt to challenge the genre, but marches alongside the many explosive, loud, and masculine-centered action films with military-esque music à la the Jerry Bruckheimer productions The Rock (1996) and Con Air (1997). With two splendid performers such as Jackson and Spacey, the movie commands attention and provides a happy-ending payoff that validates its heroes. But the significant aspects of the movie revolve around Gray's handling of characters, story, themes, and visuals. Having shown in Set it Off that he's up to the task, Gray doesn't fail here. The script for The Negotiator, while not as complex as that for Set It Off, does show Gray's ability to make African American characters accessible to a mainstream viewer. As with Set It Off, Gray's characters confront an enemy common to everyone—a corrupt system that forces the protagonist to cross a moral line. By the setup of Roman as a hero in the opening sequence via his successful freeing of hostages, the viewer is drawn emotionally to Roman; his character is then strengthened further by the relationships with his wife and colleagues.

There are numerous areas where Gray choreographs segments that exude suspense and physical titillation. One such scene develops when the Hostage Assault Team mounts a secret night assault through air ducts, through office windows, and with helicopters. Trying to force Roman into surrender, the cacophony of automatic weapons, shattering glass, helicopter blades, and yelling voices erupts into a tumult of confusion and chaos as Roman and the hostages scramble to survive. With quick cutting among the attackers, the street crowd, and the command post, along with extreme close-ups, askew angles, and ominous lighting, the action makes for an irresistible emotional ride. As the assault fails, Roman discovers that Niebaum has been shot, confirming his earlier confession that members of the force were involved in the embezzlement. Roman emerges from this segment as a valiant fighter for justice, just as he did in an earlier scene when he stood in an open window before the lights of media helicopters, indicating that to kill him was to kill the truth. Forcefully, both scenes are true to the genre and raise the stature of Roman's character, a protagonist who is willing to die for innocence and the truth—a crossover hero.

Antoine Fuqua

Hip-hop videos tend to have a lot of action and are story based. Also, MTV audiences are familiar with video directors because they put our names on the screen at the end of the video. So we have an audience and fans, which probably makes [studio execs] feel like they can market our names with the film. After I did *Gangsta's Paradise,* the studios were really on to me.[42]

Antoine Fuqua

Fuqua's journey into feature films resembles the professional track followed by his contemporaries Hype Williams and F. Gary Gray. Like them, he distinguished himself in the music video world and parlayed that experience into his position behind the Hollywood camera. Born in 1966 in Pittsburgh, Pennsylvania, Fuqua matriculated at West Virginia University, where he was an athlete while studying electrical engineering. But by 1987 he had decided upon a film career, moving to New York City and finding work as a production assistant.[43]

Fuqua's next step was to gain positions as associate producer and first assistant director for a music video firm. From there he formed his own company, called Reel Power, directing a short film titled *Exit.* The short film got him signed on with Propaganda Films as one of their commercial and music video directors.[44] His "eye-catching spots" for Giorgio Armani and Big Star Jeans brought him attention,[45] as well as his ads for Miller Lite, Reebok, Seiko, Honda, and Toyota. In addition, he directed music videos for Arrested Development, Prince, Zhané, Al B. Sure, Chante Moore, and Toni Braxton, and in 1994 he was nominated for an MTV Music Video Award. In 1996 Fuqua went on to win the MTV Music Video Award for Best Video for directing *Gangsta's Paradise.*[46]

Many action directors would envy Fuqua's unique position for his first feature—to have legendary action director John Woo as an executive producer, and international action star Chow Yun-Fat as the leading actor. This was Fuqua's situation with *The Replacement Killers* (1998), an action thriller that combines the visual stylization of music videos with John Woo-isms. In addition, the movie serves as an interethnic buddy film with a man-woman duo at the center.

The movie opens with John Lee (Chow Yun-Fat) completing an assassination of several men in a nightclub. The story cuts to the docks where Detective Zedkov (Michael Rooker) leads his team of officers on a drug bust that ends with Peter Wei (Yau-Gene Chan) being killed. As it turns out, Peter is the son of notorious underworld boss Terence Wei (Kenneth Tsang), who vows vengeance on Zedkov. Wei gives Lee the job, but Lee cannot complete the hit—which later in the film is revealed to be a hit on Zedkov's seven-year-old son. Wei wants a son for a son.

By disobeying Wei's command, Lee knows he has placed his family in danger back in China, so he goes to obtain a forged passport from the black market expert Meg Coburn (Mira Sorvino). From their initial business meeting, Lee and Coburn suddenly find themselves targets for Wei's thugs, led by the ruthless Michael Kogan (Jürgen Prochnow). Through several shootouts, Lee and Coburn survive, along the way saving Zedkov and his son from being killed. Lee finally decides the only way to stop Wei is to confront him directly, and with Coburn's help, the two invade Wei's business site and defeat his forces. When Zedkov and the cops arrive, Zedkov repays the two by allowing them to go free.

The Replacement Killers delivers all that audiences have come to expect from the action team of Chow Yun-Fat and John Woo: a story sparse on dialogue and long on stylized, lyrical violence and noble courage. Fuqua adds his own particular directorial nuances, and the result is a fast-paced movie driven by plot and two interesting, if underdeveloped, characters.

The opening sequence is indicative of Fuqua's style integrated into the action genre. A high-angle shot reveals the city at night, as the camera passes over and looks down at the maze of lights. A cut to an interior of a busy nightclub shows, from a low angle, the back of a man walking in slow motion. His body takes most of the frame as dancers, frolicking under the colored lights, fill the spaces around him. The bodies move to uptempo, techno-pop music as a reverse cut shows the man, his face shadowed, walking toward the camera. There's a cut to the man's footsteps hitting the dance floor in reverberation, until a shift to a high-angle shot captures the crowded dance floor as the man reaches a corner table. As the man places a bullet at the table's center, the film moves from slow motion into real time, and the man—John Lee—stares at the thugs who comprehend his presence. Chaos erupts above the techno-pop and screaming people as the thugs dispatch their guns, and in swift cuts, Lee moves even quicker, his body fluid, graceful, and dangerous as he takes out five thugs with his deft shooting. As Lee surveys the carnage, he thoughtfully observes his face in a triptych-designed wall mirror.

This sequence shows the influence of Fuqua's music-video style on the film—tight framing, slow motion, and pounding music combined with muted lighting obscured by smoke and flailing bodies in motion. The con-

Professional hit man John Lee (Chow Yun-Fat) survives *The Replacement Killers* by teaming up with streetwise Meg Coburn (Mira Sorvino).

spicuous enjoyment of the nightclub patrons is contrasted sharply with the violence that erupts. Fuqua's introduction of John Lee confirms the character as a deadly individual of quiet power, yet, as Lee stares at his image in the broken mirror, his complexity is suggested.

The character who adds an intriguing dynamic to the movie is that of Coburn. Given an appealing mixture of ruthlessness and sexiness, the character seems a compilation of Sigourney Weaver's Ripley in *Alien* (1979) and Geena Davis' Charly Baltimore in *The Long Kiss Goodnight* (1996). Mira Sorvino provides the effective tough shell that permits Meg Coburn to propel herself into John Lee's world of killers. In the scene when Coburn is first interrogated by Zedkov at police headquarters, Fuqua gives just enough exposition to inform viewers of her troubled past, but it's Coburn's restraint and sarcasm that affirm her toughness. Later, as she finds herself entangled within lethal shootouts, Coburn releases her repressed emotions, screaming wildly like a banshee as she eradicates her foes.

The one element obviously missing from the movie is the obligatory romance and love scene. Most action films take a breath by allowing the male hero to become involved with the sexy female lead. Here, the sexy female is the hero's partner-in-survival, so the romance would have been more believable than in most action movies. However, the movie backs away from an interracial union, and similar to *The Long Kiss Goodnight*—which contained black man–white woman duo—the movie only flirts with the audience, strongly indicating the sexual attraction but avoiding an on-screen display of that attraction. Whether this decision was Fuqua's or his producers is unclear, but the "love scene" is all the more noticeable for its absence.

Given the other genre accomplishments in the movie, the lack of an interracial "love scene" is indicative of the Hollywood traditions rather than some weakness in Fuqua's skills. As a director, he pulls together an entertaining action vehicle with the appropriate elements to satisfy the mainstream audience. In doing so, Fuqua delivers a feature film that crosses ethnic lines in its characterizations as well as its targeted audience. With his first feature, he asserts his ability to assemble a film that contains the market value worshiped by Hollywood studios.

The African American directors explored in this chapter have reached the noteworthy position of making movies that sometimes emphasize race and culture—and sometimes not. Some critics will see this status as testament to the acceptance that black directors have gained as a whole—chosen to direct because of skill and not because of color. Still other critics will chide the lament expressed by James Monaco: "Once again, the seemingly insoluble dilemma of the Black situation in America. . . . how to make a significant and fair contribution to the general culture while at the same time maintaining a separate and thriving Black identity."[47]

Intrinsic in Monaco's observation is the legitimate concern that if black directors fail to develop black-oriented material, those projects will not be made. With few exceptions, such as a Steven Spielberg (*The Color Purple, Amistad*) or a Norman Jewison (*A Soldier's Story, The Hurricane*), white directors don't display a passion to tell stories about African American experiences. Yet, to be successful by Hollywood's standards, black directors will need to pursue a variety of materials that speak to a diverse audience. As more and more black directors get the opportunity to make studio films, they will collectively continue to affirm African American culture and experiences in a manner accessible to a mainstream audience, and on some occasions, they will venture into unfamiliar areas that stretch their knowledge and skills as filmmakers. The key to this progressive phase remains the same as it was in earlier decades: black directors have earned and must receive the opportunity to work within the Hollywood system.

The following list contains the theatrical releases of the directors' feature films, but wherever possible, cable and network television movies (TV); documentaries (D); performance concert (C); and straight-to-video (V) films have been identified.

Maya Angelou
> Down in the Delta (1998)

Paris Barclay
> The Cherokee Kid (TV) (1996)
> Don't Be a Menace to South Central While Drinking Your Juice in the Hood (1996)

Troy Beyer
> Let's Talk About Sex (1998)

James Bond III
> Def by Temptation (1990)

Charles Burnett
> Killer of Sheep (1977)
> My Brother's Wedding (V) (1983)
> America Becoming (D) (1991)
> To Sleep with Anger (1990)
> The Glass Shield (1995)

Topper Carew
> Talkin' Dirty After Dark (1991)

Thomas Carter
> Swing Kids (1993)
> Metro (1997)
> Save the Last Dance (2001)

Christopher Scott Cherot
> Hav Plenty (1998)

Rusty Cundieff
> Fear of a Black Hat (1994)
> Tales from the Hood (1995)
> Sprung (1997)

Julie Dash
> Daughters of the Dust (1991)
> Subway Stories (TV) (1996)
> Funny Valentines (TV) (1998)
> Incognito (TV) (1999)
> Love Song (TV) (2001)
> The Rosa Parks Story (TV) (2002)

Ossie Davis
> Cotton Comes to Harlem (1970)
> Kongi's Harvest (1971)
> Black Girl (1972)
> Gordon's War (1973)
> Countdown at Kusini (1976)

Ernest Dickerson
> Juice (1992)
> Surviving the Game (V) (1994)
> Tales from the Crypt Presents Demon Knight (V) (1995)
> Bulletproof (1996)
> Ambushed (TV) (1998)
> Blind Faith (TV) (1998)
> Future Sport (TV) (1998)
> Strange Justice (TV) (1999)
> Bones (2001)
> Big Shot: Diary of a Campus Bookie (TV) (2002)

Ivan Dixon
> Trouble Man (1972)
> The Spook Who Sat by the Door (1973)

Bill Duke
> The Killing Floor (TV) (1984)
> Johnnie Mae Gibson: FBI (TV) (1986)
> A Rage in Harlem (1991)
> Deep Cover (1992)
> The Cemetery Club (1993)
> Sister Act 2: Back in the Habit (1993)
> America's Dream: Long Black Song (TV) (1996)
> Hoodlum (1997)
> The Golden Spiders: A Nero Wolfe Mystery (TV) (2000)

Cheryl Dunye
   The Watermelon Woman (1997)
   Stranger Inside (TV) (2001)
Jamaa Fanaka
   Penitentiary (1979)
   Penitentiary II (1982)
   Penitentiary III (1987)
Carl Franklin
   Eye of the Eagle 2 (V) (1988)
   Nowhere to Run (V) (1989)
   Full Fathom Five (V) (1990)
   One False Move (1992)
   Laurel Avenue (TV) (1993)
   Devil in a Blue Dress (1995)
   One True Thing (1998)
   High Crimes (2002)
Antoine Fuqua
   The Replacement Killers (1998)
   Training Day (2001)
Berry Gordy Jr.
   Mahogany (1975)
F. Gary Gray
   Friday (1995)
   Set It Off (1996)
   The Negotiator (1998)
Leslie Harris
   Just Another Girl on the I.R.T. (1993)
Wendell B. Harris Jr.
   Chameleon Street (1989)
Kevin Hooks
   Heat Wave (TV) (1990)
   Strictly Business (1991)
   Passenger 57 (1992)
   *Murder without Motive: The
   Edmund Perry Story* (V) (1992)
   Fled (1996)
   Black Dog (1998)
   Mutiny (TV) (1999)
Reginald Hudlin
   House Party (1990)
   Boomerang (1992)
Albert and Allen Hughes
   Menace II Society (1993)
   Dead Presidents (1995)
   American Pimp (D) (1999)
   From Hell (2001)

Ice Cube
   The Players Club (1998)
George Jackson
   House Party 2 (codirected with
   Doug McHenry) (1991)
David Clark Johnson
   Drop Squad (1994)
Stan Lathan
   Amazing Grace (1974)
   Beat Street (1984)
Martin Lawrence
   A Thin Line Between Love and Hate
   (1996)
Spike Lee
   She's Gotta Have It (1986)
   School Daze (1988)
   Do the Right Thing (1989)
   Mo' Better Blues (1990)
   Jungle Fever (1991)
   Malcolm X (1992)
   Crooklyn (1994)
   Clockers (1995)
   Girl 6 (1996)
   Get on the Bus (1996)
   4 Little Girls (D) (1997)
   He Got Game (1998)
   Summer of Sam (1999)
   Bamboozled (2000)
   The Original Kings of Comedy (C)
   (2000)
   The 25th Hour (2002)
Kasi Lemmons
   Eve's Bayou (1997)
   The Caveman's Valentine (2001)
Darnell Martin
   I Like It Like That (1994)
Lionel C. Martin
   Def Jam's How to Be a Player (1997)
Doug McHenry
   House Party 2 (codirected with
   George Jackson) (1991)
   Jason's Lyric (1994)
Gilbert Moses
   Willie Dynamite (1973)
   The Fish That Saved Pittsburgh
   (1979)

Eddie Murphy
Harlem Nights (1989)
Ron O'Neal
Super Fly T.N.T. (1973)
Euzhan Palcy
Sugar Cane Alley (1984)
A Dry White Season (1989)
Ruby Bridges (TV) (1998)
The Killing Yard (TV) (2001)
Gordon Parks
The Learning Tree (1969)
Shaft (1971)
Shaft's Big Score! (1972)
The Super Cops (1974)
Leadbelly (1976)
Solomon Northup's Odyssey (TV) (1984)
Gordon Parks Jr.
Super Fly (1972)
Thomasine and Bushrod (1974)
Three the Hard Way (1974)
Aaron Loves Angela (1975)
Robert Patton-Spruill
Squeeze (1997)
Sidney Poitier
Buck and the Preacher (1972)
A Warm December (1973)
Uptown Saturday Night (1974)
Let's Do It Again (1975)
A Piece of the Action (1977)
Stir Crazy (1980)
Hanky Panky (1982)
Fast Forward (1985)
Ghost Dad (1990)
Prince
Under the Cherry Moon (1986)
Sign o' the Times (C) (1987)
Graffiti Bridge (1990)
Richard Pryor
Jo Jo Dancer, Your Life Is Calling (1986)
Tim Reid
Once Upon a Time . . . When We Were Colored (1996)
Matty Rich
Straight Out of Brooklyn (1991)
The Inkwell (1994)

Hugh A. Robertson
Melinda (1972)
Michael Schultz
Cooley High (1975)
Car Wash (1976)
Greased Lightning (1977)
Which Way Is Up? (1977)
Sgt. Pepper's Lonely Hearts Club Band (1978)
Scavenger Hunt (1979)
Carbon Copy (1981)
The Last Dragon (1985)
Krush Groove (1985)
Disorderlies (1987)
Livin' Large! (1991)
Darin Scott
Caught Up (1998)
Oz Scott
Bustin' Loose (1981)
Millicent Shelton
Ride (1998)
John Singleton
Boyz N the Hood (1991)
Poetic Justice (1993)
Higher Learning (1995)
Rosewood (1997)
Shaft (2000)
Baby Boy (2001)
Raymond St. Jacques
Book of Numbers (1973)
Kevin Rodney Sullivan
America's Dream: Long Black Song (TV) (1996)
Soul of the Game (TV) (1996)
How Stella Got Her Groove Back (1998)
George Tillman Jr.
Soul Food (1997)
Men of Honor (2000)
Robert Townsend
Hollywood Shuffle (1987)
Eddie Murphy Raw (C) (1987)
The Five Heartbeats (1991)
The Meteor Man (1993)
B*A*P*S (1997)
Love Songs (TV) (1999)

Livin' for Love: The Natalie Cole Story (TV) (2000)
Holiday Heart (TV) (2000)
Carmen: A Hip Hopera (TV) (2001)
Ten Thousand Black Men Named George (TV) (2002)
Mario Van Peebles
New Jack City (1991)
Posse (1993)
Panther (1995)
Melvin Van Peebles
The Story of a Three-Day Pass (1967)
Watermelon Man (1970)
Sweet Sweetback's Baadasssss Song (1971)
Identity Crisis (1990)
Keenen Ivory Wayans
I'm Gonna Git You Sucka (1988)
A Low Down Dirty Shame (1994)
Scary Movie (2000)
Scary Movie 2 (2001)
Forest Whitaker
Strapped (TV) (1993)

Waiting to Exhale (1995)
Hope Floats (1998)
Hype Williams
Belly (1998)
Fred Williamson
Adiós Amigo (1976)
Mean Johnny Barrows (1976)
Mr. Mean (V) (1977)
One Down, Two to Go (1982)
The Last Fight (1983)
Foxtrap (V) (1986)
The Messenger (V) (1987)
The Kill Reflex (V) (1989)
Steele's Law (V) (1991)
South Beach (V) (1992)
3 Days to a Kill (V) (1992)
Silent Hunter (V) (1995)
Preston A. Whitmore II
The Walking Dead (1995)
Theodore Witcher
Love Jones (1997)

The abbreviation MHL/MPA indicates materials researched in the Archival Files, Margaret Herrick Library, The Motion Picture Academy, Beverly Hills, CA.

Introduction

1. David Finnigan, "DGA Committee for Blacks Taps Helmer Barclay," *Hollywood Reporter*, 24 March 2000, 114.
2. Mario Falsetto, *Personal Visions: Conversations with Contemporary Film Directors* (Los Angeles: Silman-James Press, 2000), xiv.

Chapter 1

1. Gordon Parks, *Voices in the Mirror* (New York: Anchor, 1990), 319.
2. Martin Bush, *The Photographs of Gordon Parks* (Wichita, KS: Edwin A. Ulrich Museum of Arts at Wichita State University, 1983), 15–16.
3. Parks, *Voices in the Mirror*, 281.
4. Charles Michener, "Black Movies," in *Black Films and Film-makers*, ed. Lindsay Patterson (New York: Dodd, Mead, and Co., 1975), 239.
5. Parks, *Voices in the Mirror*, 308.
6. James Murray, "Now a Boom in Black Directors," in *New York Times Encyclopedia of Film*, vol. 10, ed. Gene Brown (New York: Times Books, 1984).
7. Parks, *Voices in the Mirror*, 308.
8. Ibid.
9. Jay Cocks, "Batman and Robin," *Time*, 22 April 1974, 70.
10. Parks, *Voices in the Mirror*, 319.
11. Ibid., 342.
12. Karen Jaehne, "Melvin Van Peebles: The Baadasssss Gent," *Cineaste* 18, no. 1 (1960): 6–7.
13. "Melvin Van Peebles," *African American Almanac*, 7th ed., ed. L. Mpho Mabunda (Detroit: Gale, 1997), 853.
14. Philip T. Hartung, "Guess Who's Coming to Lunch," *Commonweal* 88 (August 1968): 571.
15. Jaehne, "Melvin Van Peebles," 7.
16. Ibid.
17. "Black Workshop Charges Racial Sabotage in 'Sweet'," *Los Angeles Times*, Calendar Section, 21 November 1971, 22.
18. "Black Workshop Charges Racial Sabotage," 22.
19. Jesse Algernon Rhines, *Black Film/White Money* (Brunswick, NJ: Rutgers University Press, 1996), 43–44.

Chapter 2

1. Ossie Davis and Ruby Dee, *With Ossie and Ruby* (New York: Morrow, 1998), 341.
2. Jesse Algernon Rhines, *Black Film/White Money* (New Brunswick, NJ: Rutgers University Press, 1996), 46–47.

3. Ibid., 46.

4. Ibid.

5. Howard Thompson, "Gordon's War," *New York Times*, 10 August 1973, 26.

6. Vincent Canby, "Countdown at Kusini," *New York Times*, 11 April 1976, Sec. 2, 15.

7. Lawrence Van Gelder, "Countdown at Kusini," *New York Times*, 17 April 1976, 10.

8. Renee Ward, "The Crossover Goes Beyond Blaxploitation," *Los Angeles Times*, Calendar Section, 28 December 1975, 28–29.

9. "Sidney Poitier," *African American Biography*, vol. 1 (Detroit: Gale Research, 1994), 582.

10. Sidney Poitier, *This Life* (New York: Knopf, 1980), 333.

11. Ibid., 322.

12. Ibid., 346–348.

13. Ibid., 348–349.

14. Donald Bogle, *Toms, Coons, Mulattoes, Mammies, and Bucks* (New York: Continuum, 1996), 277.

Chapter 3

1. Paul Gardner, "Hollywood Is Crossing the Last Racial Barrier," *New York Times*, 6 October 1974, in *New York Times Encyclopedia of Film*, vol. 10, ed. Gene Brown (New York: Times Books, 1984).

2. Elizaeth V. Foley, "Gordon Parks, Jr," in *Encyclopedia of African-American Culture and History*, ed. Jack Salzman, David Lionel Smith, and Cornel West, vol. 4 (Simon and Schuster, 1996), 2100–2101.

3. Jay Cocks, "Quick Cuts," *Time*, 6 May 1974, 91.

4. Donald Bogle, *Blacks in American Film and Television: An Encyclopedia* (New York: Garland Publishing, 1988), 215.

5. Nelson George, *Blackface: Reflections on African Americans and the Movies* (New York: Harper Perennial, 1995), 62.

6. Jesse Algernon Rhines, *Black Film/White Money* (New Brunswick, NJ: Rutgers University Press, 1995), 44.

7. Walter Burrell, "Interview: Ivan Dixon," *Soul Illustrated*, April 1969, 48.

8. "The Sergeant's Hard Climb from the Ranks," *TV Guide*, 16 September 1967, 36.

9. Don Page, "Ivan Dixon's Curious Career," *Los Angeles Times*, 22 June 1967, 14.

10. "Ivan Dixon," *Hollywood Reporter*, 28 April 1966, MHL/MPA.

11. Ibid.

12. James Robert Parish and George H. Hill, *Black Action Films* (Jefferson, NC: McFarland and Co., 1989), 282.

13. Ibid., 283.

14. Gerald Martinez, Diana Martinez, and Andres Chavez, *What It Is . . . What It Was* (New York: Hyperion, 1998), 124.

15. Ibid., 91.

16. Andy Webster, "Filmographies: Fred Williamson," *Premiere*, May 1996, 104.

17. Ibid.

18. Melvin Durslag, "Fred Willamson May Have a Big Head, but It Isn't Empty," *TV Guide*, 26 December 1970, 16.

19. Ibid.

20. Jim Murray, " 'Hammer' Can't Stop Making Hits," *Los Angeles Times*, 10 December 1995, C14.

21. Wayne Warga, " 'Shaft' Editor Directs First Film," *Los Angeles Times*, 4 June 1972, 20.

22. Roxie Frances-Nuriddin and Myrna Traylor-Herndon, series eds., *Voices of Triumph: Creative Fire, African Americans*, vol. 3 (New York: Time-Life Books, 1994), 65.

23. "Hugh Robertson," *New York Times*, 14 January 1988, MHL/MPA.

24. "Hugh Robertson," *Hollywood Reporter*, 22 January 1988, MHL/MPA.

25. Warga, " 'Shaft' Editor Directs First Film," 20.

26. James P. Murray, "The Subject Is Money," *Black Films and Film-makers*, ed. Lindsay Patterson (New York: Dodd, Mead, and Co., 1975), 257.

27. Charles Michener, "Black Movies," in *Black Films and Film-makers*, ed. Lindsay Patterson (New York: Dodd, Mead, and Co., 1975), 243.

28. Frances-Nuriddin and Traylor-Herndon, *Voices of Triumph*, 65.

29. Maurice Peterson, "Ron Was Too Light for 'Shaft', but . . . ," *New York Times*, 17 September 1972, 29.

30. Susan King, " 'Red Dawn' Marks a New Day for Actor Ron O'Neal," *Los Angeles Herald Examiner*, 24 August 1984, MHL/MPA.

31. Lois Baumoel, "Producer and Star of 'Super Fly' Are Interviewed in Cleveland," *Box Office*, 9 October 1972, MHL/MPA.

32. King, " 'Red Dawn' Marks a New Day."

33. Samir Hachem, "Director Gilbert Moses Works to Humanize Roles for Blacks," *Hollywood Dramalogue*, 22 November 1979, 1.

34. "Gilbert Moses," *Hollywood Reporter*, 17 October 1979, MHL/MPA.

35. "Gilbert Moses," *Los Angeles Times*, 1 May 1995, MHL/MPA.

36. Parish and Hill, *Black Action Films*, 335.

37. James, *That's Blaxploitation!* 81.

38. "Two's Company," *Los Angeles Magazine*, November 1978, 72.

39. Hachem, "Director Gilbert Moses," 1.

40. Maurice Peterson, "He's Making a Big 'Numbers' Racket," *New York Times*, n.d., MHL/MPA.

41. Ibid.

42. Joseph McBride, "St. Jacques, 60, Dies of Cancer," *Variety*, 29 August 1990, 14.

43. Ibid.

44. Peterson, "A Big 'Numbers' Racket."

45. Parish and Hill, *Black Action Films*, 64.

Chapter 4

1. David Sheff, "Playboy Interview: Berry Gordy," *Playboy*, August 1995, 130.

2. Margo Jefferson, "My Town, Our Town, Motown," *New York Times*, 5 March 1995, 1.

3. Robert Hilburn, "Motown's Berry Gordy Looks Back on 25 Years," *Los Angeles Times*, Calendar Section, 22 March 1983, 3.

4. Jefferson, "My Town, Our Town, Motown," 26.

5. Sheff, "Playboy Interview: Berry Gordy," 52.

6. Jefferson, "My Town, Our Town, Motown," 26.

7. Diane Haithman, "Talk! In the Name of Love!" *Los Angeles Times*, Calendar Section, 11 December 1994, 76.

8. Hilburn, "Motown's Berry Gordy," 3.

9. Bill Barol and David Friendly, "Motown's 25 Years of Soul," *Newsweek*, 23 May 1983, 75.

10. Haithman, "Talk!" 76.

11. Hilburn, "Motown's Berry Gordy," 3.

12. Jefferson, "My Town, Our Town, Motown," 26.

13. Darrell L. Hope, "AACS Hosts 'Directing in the '70s'," *Directors Guild of America Magazine*, May 1999, 50.

14. Kris Gilpin, "Breaking the Uncle Tom Myth: 'Cabin' Director Stan Lathan," *Drama-Logue*, 11–17 June 1987, 7.

15. Tammy Sims, "Struggles of Black Film Maker Jamaa Fanaka," *Los Angeles Times*, 28 July 1988, 6.

16. Ibid.

17. David Robb, "DGA Suspends Fanaka 2 Years," *Hollywood Reporter*, 14 October 1998, 3

18. James Robert Parish and George H. Hill, *Black Action Films* (Jefferson, NC: McFarland and Co., 1989), 130.

19. Ibid., 131.

20. Ibid., 232.

21. Sims, "Black Film Maker Jamaa Fanaka," 6.

22. Parish and Hill, *Black Action Films*, 233.

Chapter 5

1. Bob Mazza, "Aiming to Make the Mark," *Hollywood Reporter*, 9 July 1975, 5.

2. *Disorderlies*, Production Notes, MHL/MPA.

3. Julio Martinez, "'Spirit' Director Michael Schultz," *Drama-Logue*, 28 August–3 September 1986, 4.

4. Emory Holmes, "Introduction" to "Michael Schultz: The People's Director," by Walter Rico Burrell, *Players*, February 1983, 9.

5. Ibid.

6. Martinez, "'Spirit' Director Michael Schultz," 4.

7. Louie Robinson, "Michael Schultz: A Rising Star behind the Camera," *Ebony*, September 1978, 95.

8. *Variety*, 24 July 1986, 9.

9. Walter Rico Burrell, "Michael Schultz: The People's Director," *Players*, February 1983, 22.

10. Phil DiMauro, "'Groove' Hews to Tight Sked, Lean Budget," *Daily Variety*, 6 November 1965, MHL/MPA.

11. Cary Darling, "The Last Hip-Hop Movie?" *BAM*, 15 November 1985, 24.

12. DiMauro, "'Groove' Hews to Tight Sked."

Chapter 6

1. Marlaine Glicksman, "Spike Lee's Bed-Stuy BBQ," *Film Comment*, July–August 1989, 18.

2. Jim Haskins, *Spike Lee: By Any Means Necessary* (New York: Walker and Co., 1997), 2.

3. Ibid., 4–5.

4. Ibid., 18.

5. "Spike Lee," *African American Biography*, vol. 3 (Detroit: Gale Research, 1994), 468.

6. Haskins, *Spike Lee*, 24.

7. Ibid., 25–28.

8. "Spike Lee," 469; Haskins, *Spike Lee*, 30.

9. bell hooks, "'Whose Pussy Is This': A Feminist Comment," *Talking Back: Thinking Feminist, Thinking Black* (Boston: South End Press, 1989), 138.

10. "Spike Lee," 469.

11. Nelson George, "Do the Right Thing: Film and Fury," *Five for Five: The Films of Spike Lee* (New York: Stewart, Tabori, & Chang, 1991), 80.

12. Glicksman, "Spike Lee's Bed-Stuy BBQ," 12.

13. "The Edge of Hollywood," *America Cinema Journal*, Video Series, The Annenberg/CPB Collection, 1994.

14. James Robert Parish. *Today's Black Hollywood* (New York: Pinnacle Books, 1995), 360.

15. Haskins, 103.

Chapter 7

1. Bernard Weintraub, "Winners Circle," *Hollywood Reporter*, 8 August 1994, MHL/MPA.

2. Phyllis Klotman, ed., *Screenplays of the African American Experience* (Bloomington: Indiana University Press, 1991), 95–96.

3. "The Films of Charles Burnett: Witnessing for Everyday Heroes," Program Notes, The Film Society of the Lincoln Center, Human Rights Watch International Film Festival, 31 January–13 February 1997.

4. Klotman, *Screenplays*, 95.

5. "Films of Charles Burnett."

6. Weintraub, "Winners Circle."

7. "Films of Charles Burnett."

8. Nathan Grant, "Innocence and Ambiguity in the Films of Charles Burnett," in *Representing Blackness: Issues in Film and Video*, ed. Valerie Smith (New Brunswick, NJ: Rutgers University Press, 1997), 149.

9. Sandy Kreiswirth, "Single-Minded Director," *Daily Breeze*, 21 February 1997, K11.

10. James Ryan, "John Singleton," *Premiere*, August 1991, MHL/MPA.

11. James Robert Parish, *Today's Black Hollywood* (New York: Pinnacle Books, 1995), 247–252.

12. Elias Stimac, "Matty Rich," *Drama-Logue*, 28 April–4 May 1994, MHL/MPA.

13. Ibid.

14. Bruce Feld, "Mario Van Peebles," *Hollywood Drama-Logue*, 7–13 March 1991, 5.

15. Ibid.

16. Tim Cogshell, "Going Solo," *Entertainment Today*, 30 August 1996, MHL/MPA.

17. *Solo*, Production Notes, MHL/MPA.

18. Cogshell, "Going Solo," 5.

19. *Solo*, Production Notes.

20. *Highlander: The Final Dimension*, Production Notes, MHL/MPA.

21. Kari Granville, "Finally, He Gets His Shot," *Los Angeles Times*, Calendar Section, 28 July 1991, 28.

22. Nick Ravo, "Ernest Dickerson Would Rather Be Called Director," *New York Times*, 18 April 1993, 19.

23. Ibid.

24. Granville, "Finally, He Gets His Shot," 3, 28.

25. Sean Mitchell, "The Hughes," *Los Angeles Times*, Calendar Section, 1 October 1995, 5.

26. *Dead Presidents*, Production Notes, MHL/MPA.

27. Mitchell, "The Hughes," 86.

28. Henry Louis Gates Jr., "Niggaz with Latitude," *New Yorker*, 21 March 1994, 143.

29. Bob Thomas, "Producers Cross Line with Movie Success," *UCLA Daily Bruin*, 15 April 1996, MHL/MPA.

30. *Jason's Lyric*, Production Notes, MHL/MPA.

31. Thomas, "Producers Cross Line."

32. *Jason's Lyric*, Production Notes.

33. Thomas, "Producers Cross Line."

34. *Drop Squad*, Production Notes, MHL/MPA.

35. Ibid.

36. *The Walking Dead*, Production Notes, Press Kit, Savoy Pictures, 1995.

37. *Fled*, Production Notes, MHL/MPA.

38. Claudia Puig, "Caught in a Time Warp," *Los Angeles Times*, 24 January 1996, F8.

39. *Once Upon a Time . . . When We Were Colored*, Production Notes, MHL/MPA.

40. Ibid.

41. Ibid.

42. Ibid.

43. David Cobb Craig and Macon Morehouse, "Who's the Boss?" *People*, 7 September 1998, 103–104.

44. "Short Takes," *Variety*, 15 March 1999, MHL/MPA.

45. Jonathan Soroff, "The Next Big Thing," *Improper Bostonian*, 9–22 October 1996, 24.

46. Ibid.

47. "Breaking Out," *Hollywood Reporter*, Special Issue, 5 August 1998, MHL/MPA.

48. Soroff, "The Next Big Thing," 24.

49. "Winners Circle: Darin Scott," *Hollywood Reporter*, 8 August 1994, MHL/MPA.

50. Ibid.

51. Anna Sui, "Hype Williams," *Interview*, October 1999, MHL/MPA.

52. *Belly*, Production Notes, MHL/MPA.

Chapter 8

1. Christine Spines, "Behind Bars," *Premiere*, Special Issue (2000): 45.

2. Ibid., 45–48.

3. Tara Roberts, "Independents' Day," *Essence*, September 1998, 105.

4. Ibid., 105–106, 174–175.

5. Eileen Orr, "Interview: 'Sugar Cane's' Euzhan Percy [*sic*]," *UCLA Daily Bruin*, 22 May 1984, MHL/MPA.

6. Ephraim Katz, *The Film Encyclopedia*, 3d ed. (New York: Harper Perennial, 1998), 1058.

7. Gwendolyn Audrey Foster, *Women Film Directors: An International Bio-Critical Dictionary* (Westport, CT: Greenwood Press, 1995), 297.

8. Julie Dash, *Daughters of the Dust* (New York: New Press, 1992), 40.

9. Foster, *Women Film Directors*, 99.

10. Phyllis Rauch Klotman, ed., *Screenplays of the African American Experience* (Bloomington: Indiana University Press, 1991), 193–195.

11. Steve Garland, "Straight Outta Cleveland, *L. A. Village View*, 9–15 April 1993, 13.

12. Foster, *Women Film Directors*, 173.

13. Ibid.

14. Ibid.

15. Kenneth Turan, "Loves Movies, Hates the Biz," *Los Angeles Times*, 19 May 1994, F1.

16. Foster, *Women Film Directors*, 244.

17. Ibid.

18. Emory Holmes, "A New Song of the South," *Los Angeles Times*, 6 November 1997, 12.

19. Ibid., 14.

20. *Eve's Bayou*, Production Notes, MHL/MPA.

21. Holmes, "A New Song," 14.

22. Steve Hochman, "Whatever: Millicent Shelton/Writer-Director," *Los Angeles Times*, 15 March 1998, MHL/MPA.

23. *Ride*, Production Notes, MHL/MPA.

24. Hochman, "Whatever."

25. Karen Moore, "Troy Beyer Talks about Sex," *Venice*, September 1998, 10.

26. Minna Towbin, "Belle Troy," *Elle*, May 1988, 40.

27. Susan King, "Her Dynasty Is Just Beginning," *Los Angeles Herald Examiner*, 3 October 1987, MHL/MPA.

28. Towbin, "Belle Troy," 40.

29. Ibid.

30. King, "Her Dynasty Is Just Beginning."

31. *Eddie*, Production Notes, MHL/MPA.

32. Tom Provenzano, "Keeping It Real," *Backstage West Drama-Logue*, 17 September 1998, MHL/MPA.

33. Ernest Hardy, "A Woman of Independent Mien," *Los Angeles Weekly*, 28 March–3 April 1997, 37.

34. Amy Stockwell, "Cheryl Dunye," *Advocate*, 17 September 1996, 70.

35. Ibid.

36. Hardy, "A Woman of Independent Mien," 37.

37. Stockwell, "Cheryl Dunye," 70.

38. Ibid., 69.

39. Michelle Wallace, "Sexin' the Watermelon," *Village Voice*, 4 March 1997, MHL/MPA.

40. Ibid.

41. Dana Kennedy, "A Poet, at 70, Ventures into the Unknown," *New York Times*, 15 November 1998, 13.

42. Melvin Donalson, *Cornerstones: An Anthology of African American Literature* (New York: St. Martin's Press, 1996), 674.

43. Ibid., 674–675.

Chapter 9

1. *Bustin' Loose*, Studio Biography, MHL/MPA.

2. Ibid.

3. "Oz Scott's Standing Broad Jump from Off-B'way 'To Film for U'," *Variety*, 31 May 1981, 12.

4. Lee Margulies, "Comedies Take a Dramatic Turn," *Los Angeles Times*, 6 November 1981, Part 4, 14.

5. *D.C. Cab*, Studio Biography, MHL/MPA.

6. Ibid.

7. Margulies, "Comedies Take a Dramatic Turn," 14.

8. Terrie M. Rooney, ed., *Contemporary Theatre, Film, and Television*, vol. 13 (Detroit: Gale Research, 1995), 81.

9. Richard Pryor and Todd Gold, *Pryor Convictions and Other Life Sentences* (New York: Pantheon Books, 1995), 211.

10. Ibid., 28–30.

11. Richard Goldstein, "The Funniest Man in America Is Richard Pryor, Yes!" *Evening Outlook*, 24 July 1983, Family Weekly Section, 5–6.

12. Donald Bogle, *Toms, Coons, Mulattoes, Mammies, and Bucks* (New York: Continuum, 1990), 259.

13. John Baxter and David E. Salamie, "Richard Pryor," in *International Dictionary of Films and Filmmakers: Actors and Actresses*, 3d ed., ed. Amy L. Unterberger (Detroit: St. James Press, 1997), 981.

14. Pryor and Gold, *Pryor Convictions*, 220–224.

15. Ibid., 210.

16. John A. Williams and Dennis Williams, *If I Stop, I'll Die: The Comedy and Tragedy of Richard Pryor* (New York: Thunder's Mouth Press, 1991), 216.

17. Neal Karlan, "Prince Talks," *Rolling Stone*, 18 October 1990, 59.

18. *Purple Rain*, Studio Biography, MHL/MPA.

19. Anthony DeCurtis, "He's Back—but Don't Call It a Comeback," *New York Times*, 12 September 1999, 92.

20. "Comic-Cum-Director Townsend on a Roll Following 'Hollywood'," *Variety*, 10 December 1986, 23.

21. Steve Pond, "Robert Townsend," *Vogue*, March 1991, 248.

22. *The Five Heartbeats*, Studio Biography, MHL/MPA.

23. Todd McCarthy, "Comedian Townsend on Roll with Directorial Projects," *Variety*, 30 October 1996, 6, 13.

24. Esther B. Fein, "Robert Townsend Has Fun at Hollywood's Expense," *New York Times*, 19 April 1987, 35.

25. Greg Tate, "Hollywood Shuffle's Fancy Dancer," *Village Voice*, 31 March 1987, MHL/MPA.

26. James Robert Parish, *Today's Black Hollywood* (New York: Pinnacle Books, 1995), 233.
27. Ibid., 215–222.
28. Ed Guerrero, *Framing Blackness: The African American Image in Film* (Philadelphia: Temple University Press, 1993), 132.
29. Parish, *Today's Black Hollywood*, 231.
30. *Hollywood Reporter*, 59th Anniversary Ed., 1989, MHL/MPA.
31. *A Low Down Dirty Shame*, Production Notes, MHL/MPA.
32. McMurray, Emily J., ed. *Contemporary Theatre, Film, and Television*, vol. 10 (Detroit: Gale Research, 1993), 432–433.
33. Steve Weinstein, "Maybe He Should Have Impersonated a White Studio Boss," *Los Angeles Times*, Calendar Section, 14 July 1991, 26.
34. Ibid.
35. Jean Oppenheimer, "Man on the Street," *Village View*, 19–25 July 1991, MHL/MPA.
36. Ibid.
37. Rex Weiner, "One-Way Street," *Variety*, 22 January 1996, MHL/MPA.
38. Michael Fleming, "Youthful Black Helmers Fear a Hollywood Whitewash," *Variety*, 21 February 1990, 1.
39. Weiner, "One-Way Street."
40. Guerrero, *Framing Blackness*, 174.
41. Harriet Robbins, "Chameleon Street," *The Motion Picture Guide: 1992 Annual* (New York: Baseline, 1992), 50.
42. Weiner, "One-Way Street."
43. Patrick Pacheco, "The Hudlin Brothers Set Out to Prove Black Is Bountiful," *New York Times*, 26 July 1992, 9.
44. Ibid., 12.
45. McMurray, *Contemporary Theatre, Film, and Television*, vol. 1, 238.
46. *Boomerang*, Production Notes, MHL/MPA.
47. Jesse Algeron Rhines, *Black Film/White Money* (New Brunswick, NJ: Rutgers University Press, 1996), 60–61.
48. *Ride*, Production Notes, MHL/MPA.
49. Rhines, *Black Film/White Money*, 63.
50. McMurray, *Contemporary Theatre, Film, and Television*, vol. 1, 239.
51. Rhines, *Black Film/White Money*, 64.
52. Roger Ebert, *Roger Ebert's Video Companion, 1997 Edition* (Kansas City, MO: Andrews and McMeel, 1997), 94.
53. Rick Sherwood, "Martin Lawrence," *Hollywood Reporter*, 22 February 1996, S16–S18.
54. Joshua Kondek, ed., *Contemporary Theatre, Film, and Television*, vol. 21 (Detroit: Gale Research, 2000), 231.
55. Allison Samuels, "A Comic's Erratic Ride," *Newsweek*, 21 July 1997, 73.
56. Sherwood, "Martin Lawrence," S8.
57. Kondek, *Contemporary Theatre, Film, and Television*, vol. 21, 231–232.
58. Samuels, "A Comic's Erratic Ride," 73.
59. Dan Jewel, Lorenzo Benet, and Ron Arias, "A Bad Run," *People*, 13 September 1999, 79–80.

60. Jamie Diamond, "From Gangsta Scripts to Poetry's Romance," *New York Times*, 9 March 1997, H16.

61. Cheo Hodari Coker, "Can a Real 'Love' Conquer?" *Los Angeles Times*, 20 March 1997, 8, 10.

62. Ibid., 10.

63. Diamond, Gangsta Scripts to Poetry's Romance," 16.

64. Coker, "Can a Real 'Love' Conquer?" 12.

65. Chris Petrikin, "'Food' for Thought," *Variety: Vibe Biz*, August 1998, 4.

66. *Soul Food*, Production Notes, Press Kit, Twentieth Century Fox, 1997.

67. Ibid.

68. Ibid.

69. Richard Natale, "Looking for Clout in Hollywood? It Takes Some to Get Some," *Los Angeles Times*, Calendar Section, 14 June 1998, 9.

70. Juan Morales, "Sullivan's Travels," *Detour*, September 1998, MHL/MPA.

71. Ibid.

72. *How Stella Got Her Groove Back*, Production Notes, MHL/MPA.

73. Ibid.

74. Amy Wallace, "Cherot Bets the House—and Wins," *Los Angeles Times*, 18 June 1998, MHL/MPA.

75. Ibid.

76. Ibid.

77. Juan Morales, "Christopher Cherot," *Detour*, August 1998, 105.

78. Wallace, "Cherot Bets the House."

79. Philippians 4:12, New International Version.

Chapter 10

1. Arnold Shaw, *Black Popular Music in America* (New York: Schirmer Books, 1986), 292–293.

2. Michael Eric Dyson, *Reflecting Black: African-American Cultural Criticism* (Minneapolis: University of Minnesota Press, 1993), 4.

3. Ibid.

4. Shaw, *Black Popular Music in America*, 292–293.

5. Mike Allen, "Hit Rapper Dreams of Becoming Hip Hoop Artist," *New York Times*, Sunday Metro Section, 15 November 1998, 40.

6. Cheo Hodari Coker, "Master P's Theater," *Los Angeles Times*, Calendar Section, 14 September 1997, 6.

7. *I Got the Hook Up*, Production Notes, MHL/MPA.

8. Allen, "Hit Rapper Dreams," 40.

9. *Foolish*, Production Notes, MHL/MPA.

10. Marc Weingarten, "Master P's Hollywood Takeover," *Rolling Stone*, 29 April 1999, 35.

11. Karen Moline, "Bond—James Bond (III)," MHL/MPA.

12. "James Bond III," *Ebony*, March 1982, MHL/MPA.

13. Ibid.

14. Moline, "Bond—James Bond (III)."

15. Ibid.

16. Maitland McDonagh, "Def by Temptation," *The Motion Picture Guide: 1991 Annual* (New York: Baseline, 1991), 39.

17. Joe Wood, "She-Devil," *Village Voice,* 11 September 1990, 68.

18. Janet Maslin, "The Lady Has Fangs (and Uses Satin Sheets)," *New York Times,* 7 September 1990, MHL/MPA.

19. Kevin Thomas, "A 'Def' Reworking of Vampire Genre," *Los Angeles Times,* 7 September 1990, F16.

20. Claudia Puig, "Taking the Inside Track," *Los Angeles Times,* 23 October 1991, F12.

21. Melody Peterson, "George Jackson, Movie Producer, Dies at 42," *New York Times,* 15 February 2000, MHL/MPA.

22. Bob Thomas, "Producers Cross Line with Movie's Success," *UCLA Daily Bruin,* 15 April 1996, MHL/MPA.

23. Kirk Honeycutt, "WMA Agent Lee Going for Elephant Walk," *Hollywood Reporter,* 23 October 1996, 1.

24. Peterson, "George Jackson."

25. Sean O'Neill, " 'Sprung' Fever," *Boxoffice,* April 1997, 48.

26. Erich Leon Harris, *African-American Screenwriters Now: Conversations with Hollywood's Black Pack* (Los Angeles: Silman-James Press, 1996), 61.

27. Ibid., 41.

28. O'Neill, " 'Sprung' Fever," 48.

29. Robert Levine, "Meet the Ice Cold King of Gansta Rap," *Los Angeles Times,* 2 June 1994, F7.

30. *Tales from the Hood,* Production Notes, MHL/MPA.

31. David Barr, "Prominent Black Film Director," *Ebony Man,* March 1997, 45.

32. Paul Brownfield, "Laying Down His Own Law," *Los Angeles Times,* Calendar Section, 31 January 1999, 66–67.

33. *Don't Be a Menace . . . ,* Production Notes, MHL/MPA.

34. Brownfield, "Laying Down His Own Law," 67.

35. Ibid., 66–67.

36. Barr, "Prominent Black Film Director," 44–45.

37. Brownfield, "Laying Down His Own Law," 66.

38. "Paris Barclay," *Advocate,* 15 September 1998, MHL/MPA.

39. Greg Braxton, "Call It 'City of Arch Angels'," *Los Angeles Times,* 1 July 2000, F1.

40. Barr, "Prominent Black Film Director," 44.

41. *Def Jam's How to Be a Player,* Production Notes, Press Kit. Island Pictures/ Polygram Filmed Entertainment, 1997, MHL/MPA.

42. Ibid.

43. Steve Hochman, "Whatever," *Los Angeles Times,* 5 April 1998, MHL/MPA.

44. Joshua Kondek, ed., *Contemporary Theatre, Film, and Television,* vol. 22 (Detroit: The Gale Research, 1999), 206.

45. Ibid.

46. B. Love, "Ice Cube—Renaissance Man?" *Insite,* May 1999, 23.

Chapter 11

1. James Monaco, *American Film Now* (New York: New American Library, 1979), 193.

2. Kris Gilpin, "Kevin Hooks: Going for the 'Heart' of the Matter," *Drama-Logue,* 27 November–3 December 1986, MHL/MPA.

3. *Strictly Business*, Production Notes, MHL/MPA.

4. Gilpin, "Kevin Hooks."

5. *Black Dog*, Production Notes, MHL/MPA.

6. *Strictly Business*, Production Notes.

7. Ibid.

8. Alex Demyanenko, "Straight Up: An Interview with Filmmaker Bill Duke—without the Chaser," *Village Voice*, 10–16 May 1991, 22.

9. Eric Harrison, "Boot Camp, Hollywood Style," *Los Angeles Times*, Calendar Section, 1 November 1998, 31.

10. Yardena Arar, "Hollywood Is Doing Double Take on Duke," *Los Angeles Daily News*, Life Section, 6 May 1991, 11.

11. *Hoodlum*, Production Notes, MHL/MPA.

12. Ibid.

13. Harrison, "Boot Camp, Hollywood Style," 31.

14. Ibid., 32.

15. Patrick Goldstein, "Easing into Old L.A.," *Los Angeles Times*, Calendar Section, 24 September 1995, 79.

16. Sheila Benson, "Director: Carl Franklin," *Premiere*, July 1992, 46.

17. *Devil in a Blue Dress*, Production Notes, MHL/MPA.

18. Ibid.

19. Ibid.

20. Philip French, "Black and White and Real All Over," *London Observer*, Arts Section, 4 April 1993, 54.

21. Benson, "Director: Carl Franklin," 46.

22. French, "Black and White," 54.

23. Benson, "Director: Carl Franklin," 46.

24. Goldstein, "Easing into Old L.A.," 79.

25. Steve Weinstein, "From Hired Gun to Top Gun," *Los Angeles Times*, Calendar Section, 11 February 1990, 94.

26. Ibid., 102.

27. *Almost Summer*, Studio Biography, Universal Studios, MHL/MPA.

28. Ibid.

29. Elias Stimac, "*Swing Kids* Director Thomas Carter Makes All the Right Choices," *Drama-Logue*, 25 February–3 March 1993, 6.

30. *Metro*, Production Notes, MHL/MPA.

31. Stimac, "*Swing Kids* Director Thomas Carter." 6.

32. *Metro*, Production Notes.

33. Tom Provenzano, "Forest Whitaker: Career Phenomenon," *Drama-Logue*, 11–17 July 1996, 6.

34. *Hope Floats*, Production Notes, MHL/MPA.

35. Alex Lawrence, "Forest Whitaker," *Premiere*, November 1988, MHL/MPA.

36. *Hope Floats*, Production Notes.

37. Ibid.

38. David McKenna, "How to Make an American Movie," *Detour*, November 1996, 70.

39. George Christy, "The Great Life," *Hollywood Reporter*, 31 July 1998, MHL/MPA.

40. Ernest Hardy, "Black Like Who? Notes on Black Films and the Career of F. Gary Gray," *Los Angeles Weekly*, 31 July–6 August 1998, 38.

41. *The Negotiator*, Production Notes, MHL/MPA.

42. Marc Graser and Daniel Lorber, "Hip-Hop Breeds New Storytellers," *Variety*, August 1998, 8.

43. *The Replacement Killers*, Production Notes, MHL/MPA.

44. Ibid.

45. Chris Petrikin, "Antoine Fuqua, Director," *Variety*, 25 August 1997, MHL/MPA.

46. *The Replacement Killers*, Production Notes.

47. Monaco, *American Film Now*, 193.

aspect ratio The measurement between the height and width of the images on the movie or television screen.

auteur theory The analytic approach to film that identifies the film's director as the author or dominating presence in giving shape and vision to the final film (see the introduction).

Bernard Hermann–esque Music that replicates the arrangements of movie music composer Bernard Hermann—particularly the orchestral strings to produce tension and terror.

blocking The arranged physical movements of characters within a setting.

close-up A camera shot of a character or object that magnifies the image until it appears to fill the frame.

cinema verité A technique of "true film" in which the filmmaker shoots the subjects and action as they develop and occur in order to present the authentic and unrehearsed nature of that segment.

crosscutting Moving between shots of different locations to establish simultaneous or parallel actions.

cutaway Within a scene, a quick view of some specific object within the scene to give emphasis and explanation before returning back to the original scene.

diegetic A term that identifies events, actions, sounds, music, etc., that occur within the fictional world of the movie and, therefore, experienced by the movie's characters.

Dutch angle A shot in which the normal lines of an image are askew and titled to suggest an ominous tone, imbalanced reality, or distorted perception.

fabula The mental or verbal process in which a viewer completes the chronological organization of a movie's narrative, when that narrative is presented in a disjointed or impressionistic manner.

Fellini-esque In reference to legendary Italian film director Federico Fellini, a style of filmmaking that resembles the unusual, bizarre, dreamlike, and/or circuslike aspects of a sequence.

fisheye lens A lens that creates a visual effect by elongating and curving the images within the frame.

fourth wall The transparent "wall" that separates the audience from the movie's characters and world, allowing the audience to voyeuristically observe actions. When "breaking the fourth wall," a character will speak directly to the audience.

framing Maintaining the desired images within the borders captured by the camera's eye.

freeze-frame A visual effect where the image is locked on the screen like a still photograph to punctuate and heighten the intensity of a dramatic moment.

genre film A motion picture that contains certain story, thematic, and visual attributes that qualifies its inclusion within a body of similar films. Genre films, such as gangster, horror, comedy, etc., seek the fulfillment of expected elements that influence the resulting success of the movie.

high-angle shot A visual perspective obtained by placing the camera above the subjects and objects to film from that position.

independent film A film that is produced outside of a major studio and therefore is devoid of funding and creative control by a studio. By the late 1990s, however, some Hollywood studios created their own "independent" branches that sought to support low-budget film projects that would be targeted to a specialized audience with little marketing costs (see Introduction).

John Woo–ism Any visual technique that resembles the noted style of famed action director John Woo. These techniques might include slow-motion ballets of violence, abrupt subjective shots, expressionistic stunts, and lengthy, fast-paced chase scenes.

jump cut An abrupt and quick edit, changing from one image to another to create a jolting or disturbing effect on the viewer.

key lighting The primary or major lighting that is focused and concentrated on a given object or subject in a scene.

lap dissolve The slow, manipulated blending of one image over another, often used as a transitional device or a method of suggesting the passage of time.

long shot A shot in which the camera is placed in a manner to allow a perspective of the full character from head to feet.

malapropism When humor is created by misusing words that are confusing or contradictory because of their similar sound.

mise-en-scène A term that refers to all of the collective staging, setting, and composition that appears before the camera in a given scene.

montage An essential concept in the recognition of the power of images to affect a viewer's imagination and emotional response. In European films in the early twentieth century, the concept identified the simple but dynamic results when placing one image after or next to another. In American films, the concept labels a use of successive images to suggest the passing of time or the developing nature of a character or situation.

nondiegetic This term denotes the events, action, sound, music, etc. that occur outside and beyond the world of the film. In this case, the objective is to affect and enhance the audience's response to the film being viewed.

pacing The rhythm and movement of the movie's action perceived by the viewer, as a result of staging within a scene and the editing among scenes.

panning shot A shot in which the camera moves horizontally across a setting, usually from left to right.

production design The resulting look and dimensions of a set's environment in regard to its detail, authenticity, and creativity.

real time The semblance of normal action and behavior of characters before and following any special effect or story shift, such as slow motion or flashbacks.

sequence A unit of meaning in a story comprising of several related scenes.

slow motion An effect that exaggerates the actions and behavior of characters and events by making them appear to occur more slowly than they actually do.

stop action Movement before the camera that is not shot continuously, but in a process of repeatedly stopping and then restarting the filming, creating a visual effect of interrupted action.

strobe effect Movement before the camera in which continuous action is filmed while a blinking light source rapidly alternates brightness and darkness, creating a visually distorting effect of staccato-like flashing images.

subjective viewpoint A sequence that displays the action as seen through the perspective of a particular character.

swish pan A rapid and swift panning shot that obscures the images in a frame until the movement stops on a sharply defined image.

three-shot A shot that shows three characters within the frame.

tight framing A shot that shows a frame filled with subjects and objects to create feelings of immediacy, claustrophobia, and/or tension in the viewer.

title card Used to display credits and captions, the framed card that contains the given text to be shown to the viewer.

tracking shot The shot that results from the camera moving along with the action in a scene while the camera is fastened to a mobile unit on wheels.

two-shot A shot that shows two characters within the frame.

visual style The various ways, methods, techniques, and patterns employed by the filmmaker to tell a story in images and sound.

wide-angle shot A camera shot that presents the most expansive inclusion of subjects and objects, in terms of both the horizontal perspective and depth perception.

wipe An optical effect when one scene is replaced with another following a vertical line that moves across the frame from left to right, or vice versa.

BIBLIOGRAPHY

The abbreviation MHL/MPA indicates materials researched in the Archival Files, Margaret Herrick Library, The Motion Picture Academy, Beverly Hills, CA.

African American Biography. Vols. 1 and 3. Detroit: Gale Research, 1994.

Allen, Mike. "Hit Rapper Dreams of Becoming Hip Hoop Artist." *New York Times,* 15 November 1998, Sunday Metro Section, 40.

Almost Summer. Studio Biography. Universal Studios. 15 March 1978. MHL/MPA.

Anderson, Lisa M. *Mammies No More: The Changing Image of Black Women on Stage and Screen.* Lanham, MD: Rowan & Littlefield Publishers, 1997.

Arar, Yardena. "Hollywood Is Doing Double Take on Duke." *Los Angeles Daily News,* 6 May 1991, Life Section, 11.

Banks, William M. *Black Intellectuals.* New York: W. W. Norton, 1996.

Baraka, Amiri. "Malcolm as Ideology." In *Cornerstones: An Anthology of African American Literature.* Edited by Melvin Donalson, 742–755. New York: St. Martin's Press, 1996.

Barol, Bill, and David Friendly. "Motown's 25 Years of Soul." *Newsweek,* 23 May 1983, 75–76.

Barr, David. "Prominent Black Film Directors." *Ebony Man,* March 1997, 44–53.

Baumoel, Lois. "Producer and Star of 'Super Fly' Are Interviewed in Cleveland." *Box Office,* 9 October 1972. MHL/MPA.

Baxter, John, and David E. Salamie. "Richard Pryor." In *International Dictionary of Films and Filmmakers: Actors and Actresses.* 3rd ed. Edited by Amy L. Unterburger, 979–981. Detroit: St. James Press, 1997.

Beaver, Frank. *Dictionary of Film Terms: The Aesthetic Companion to Film Analysis.* New York: Twayne Publishers, 1994.

Belly. Production Notes. MHL/MPA.

Benson, Sheila. "Director: Carl Franklin." *Premiere,* July 1992, 46.

Bernstein, Abbie. "Director Kevin Hooks Reveals 'Honor' of Unsung." *Drama-Logue,* 26 February–4 March 1998, 7.

Black Dog. Production Notes. MHL/MPA.

"Black vs. Shaft." *Newsweek,* 28 August 1972, 88.

"Black Workshop Charges Racial Sabotage in 'Sweet.'" *Los Angeles Times,* 21 November 1971, Calendar Section, 22.

Bogle, Donald. *Blacks in American Films and Television: An Encyclopedia.* New York: Garland Publishing, 1988.

———. *Toms, Coons, Mulattoes, Mammies, and Bucks.* 3rd ed. New York: Continuum, 1996.

Borie, Marcia. "Williamson Not on 'Social' Trip, Means to Do Business in Cannes." *Hollywood Reporter,* 10 May 1977, C45, C48.

Braxton, Greg. "As Robert Townsend Sees It." *Los Angeles Times*, 3 August 1993, F1, F6–F7.

"Breaking Out." *Hollywood Reporter*, Special Issue, 5 August 1998. MHL/MPA.

Brownfield, Paul. "Laying Down His Own Law." *Los Angeles Times*, 31 January 1999, Calendar Section, 4–5; 66–67.

Burrell, Walter. "Interview: Ivan Dixon." *Soul Illustrated*, April 1969, 21–23, 40, 48.

Burrell, Walter Rico. "Michael Schultz: The People's Director." *Players*, February 1983, 9, 22, 26, 67.

Bush, Martin. *The Photographs of Gordon Parks*. Wichita, KS: Edwin A. Ulrich Museum of Art at Wichita State University, 1983.

Bustin' Loose. Studio Biography. MHL/MPA.

Canby, Vincent. "Countdown at Kusini." *New York Times*, 11 April 1976, Sec. 2, 15.

———. "Review: Willie Dynamite." *New York Times*, 24 January 1974, 45.

Christy, George. "The Great Life." *Hollywood Reporter*, 31 July 1998. MHL/MPA.

Cocks, Jay. "Batman and Robin." *Time*, 22 April 1974, 70.

———. "Quick Cuts." *Time*, 6 May 1974, 91.

Cogshell, Tim. "Going Solo." *Entertainment Today*, 30 August 1996. MHL/MPA.

Coker, Cheo Hodari. "Can a Real 'Love' Conquer?" *Los Angeles Times*, 20 March 1997, 8, 10, 12.

———. "Master P's Theater." *Los Angeles Times*, 14 September 1997, Calendar Section, 6, 62.

Coleman, John. "Outlaws Incorporated." *New Statesman* 86 (14 December 1973): 918.

"Comic-Cum-Director Townsend on a Roll Following 'Hollywood.'" *Variety*, 10 December 1986, 23.

Cook, David A. *A History of Narrative Film*. 3rd ed. New York: W. W. Norton, 1996.

Craig, David Cobb, and Macon Morehouse. "Who's the Boss?" *People*, 7 September 1998, 103–105.

Cripps, Thomas. *Black Film as Genre*. Bloomington: Indiana University Press, 1978.

———. *Making Movies Black: The Hollywood Message Movie from World War II to the Civil Rights Era*. New York: Oxford University Press, 1993.

———. *Slow Fade to Black: The Negro in American Films, 1900–1942*. New York: Oxford University Press, 1977.

Cullum, Paul. "Matty Rich." *Hollywood Reporter, Independent Producers and Distributors Special Edition*, August 1998, 28–29.

Darling, Cary. "The Last Hip-Hop Movie?" *BAM*, 15 November 1985.

Dash, Julie. *Daughters of the Dust*. New York: New Press, 1992.

Davis, Ossie, and Ruby Dee. *With Ossie and Ruby: In This Life Together*. New York: Morrow, 1998.

D.C. Cab. Studio Biography. 4 November 1983. MHL/MPA.

Dead Presidents. Production Notes. MHL/MPA.

DeCurtis, Anthony. "He's Back—but Don't Call It a Comeback." *New York Times*, 12 September 1999, 89, 92.

Demyanenko, Alex. "Straight Up: An Interview with Filmmaker Bill Duke—without the Chaser." *Village View*, 10–16 May 1991, 22.

Derry, Charles. "Spike Lee." In *International Dictionary of Films and Filmmakers: Directors*. 2nd ed. Edited by Nicholas Thomas, 496–497. Chicago: St. James Press, 1991.

Devil in a Blue Dress. Production Notes. MHL/MPA.

Diamond, Jamie. "From Gangsta Scripts to Poetry's Romance." *New York Times,* 9 March 1997, H15–16.

Diawara, Manthia, ed. *Black American Cinema.* New York: Routledge, 1993.

Dick, Bernard. *Anatomy of Film.* New York: St. Martin's Press, 1990.

DiMauro, Phil. "'Groove' Hews to Tight Sked, Lean Budget." *Daily Variety,* 6 November 1965.

Disorderlies. Production Notes. MHL/MPA.

Donalson, Melvin. *Cornerstones: An Anthology of African American Literature.* New York: St. Martin's Press, 1996.

Don't Be a Menace. Production Notes. MHL/MPA.

Drop Squad. Production Notes. Press Kit. Gramercy Pictures, 1994.

Durslag, Melvin. "Fred Williamson May Have a Big Head, but It Isn't Empty." *TV Guide,* 26 December 1970, 15–17.

Dyson, Michael Eric. "Malcolm X: The Man, the Myth, the Movie." *Christian Century* 109, no. 38 (23–30 December 1992): 1186–1189.

———. *Reflecting Black: African-American Cultural Criticism.* Minneapolis: University of Minnesota Press, 1993.

Ebert, Roger. *Roger Ebert's Video Companion.* 1997 Edition. Kansas City, MO: Andrews and McMeel, 1997.

Elle, Claudia. "Anger on the Airwaves." *Los Angeles Times,* 18 August 1994, F1, F5.

Eve's Bayou. Production Notes. Press Kit. Trimark Pictures, 1997.

Falsetto, Mario. *Personal Visions: Conversations with Contemporary Film Directors.* Los Angeles: Silman-James Press, 2000.

Fein, Esther B. "Robert Townsend Has Fun at Hollywood's Expense." *New York Times,* 19 April 1987, 18, 35.

Feld, Bruce. "Mario Van Peebles." *Hollywood Dramalogue,* 7–13 March 1991, 5.

Fessier, Michael. "A War Ivan Dixon Is Winning." *New York Times,* 29 January 1967, D19.

"The Films of Charles Burnett: Witnessing for Everyday Heroes." Program Notes. The Film Society of Lincoln Center. Human Rights Watch International Film Festival. 31 January–13 February 1997.

Finnigan, David. "DGA Committee for Blacks Taps Helmer Barclay." *Hollywood Reporter,* 24 March 2000, 7, 14

The Five Heartbeats. Studio Biography. MHL/MPA.

Fled. Production Notes. MHL/MPA.

Fleming, Michael. "Youthful Black Helmers Fear a Hollywood Whitewash." *Variety,* 21 February 1990, 1, 6.

Foley, Elizabeth V. "Gordon Parks, Jr." In *Encyclopedia of African-American Culture and History.* Edited by Jack Salzman, David Lionel Smith, and Cornel West. 4:2100–2101. New York: Simon and Schuster, 1996.

Foolish. Production Notes. MHL/MPA.

Ford, Timothy. "The Culture of Paris." *Code: The Style Magazine for Men of Color,* July 1999, 100–105.

Foster, Gwendolyn Audrey. *Women Film Directors: An International Bio-Critical Dictionary.* Westport, CT: Greenwood Press, 1995.

France-Nuriddin, Roxie, and Myrna Traylor-Herndon, Series Directors. *African Americans: Voices of Triumph — Creative Fire.* Vol. 3. New York: Time-Life Books, 1994.

French, Philip. "Black and White and Real All Over." *London Observer,* 4 April 1993, Arts Section, 54–55.

Gates, Henry Louis, Jr. "Niggaz with Latitude." *New Yorker,* 21 March 1994, 143, 146–147.

George, Nelson. *Blackface: Reflections on African Americans and the Movies.* New York: HarperCollins, 1994.

———. "Do the Right Thing: Film and Fury." In *Five for Five: The Films of Spike Lee.* Edited by Spike Lee and David Lee, 77–81. New York: Stewart, Tabori & Chang, 1991.

———. "Menace to Society." *Voice Film Special,* 25 May 1993, 21, 23.

Gilpin, Kris. "Breaking the 'Uncle Tom Myth': 'Cabin' Director Stan Lathan." *Drama-Logue,* 11 June 1987, 7.

———. "Kevin Hooks: Going for the 'Heart' of the Matter." *Drama-Logue,* 27 November–3 December 1986. MHL/MPA.

Goldstein, Patrick. "Easing into Old L. A." *Los Angeles Times.* 24 September 1995, Calendar Section, 3, 79.

Goldstein, Richard. "The Funniest Man in America Is Richard Pryor: Yes!" *Evening Outlook,* 24 July 1983, Family Weekly Section, 4–6.

Grant, Nathan. "Innocence and Ambiguity in the Films of Charles Burnett." *Representing Blackness: Issues in Film and Video,* edited by Valerie Smith, 135–155. New Brunswick, NJ: Rutgers University Press, 1997.

Granville, Kari. "Finally, He Gets His Shot." *Los Angeles Times,* 28 July 1991, Calendar Section, 3, 27–28.

Graser, Marc, and Daniel Lorber. "Hip-Hop Breeds New Storytellers." *Variety,* August 1998, 8.

Guerrero, Ed. *Framing Blackness: The African American Image in Film.* Philadelphia: Temple University Press, 1993.

Hachem, Samir. "Director Gilbert Moses Works to Humanize Roles for Blacks." *Hollywood Dramalogue,* 22 November 1979, 1, 14.

Haithman, Diane. "Talk! In the Name of Love!" *Los Angeles Times,* 11 December 1994, Calendar Section, 5, 75–76.

Halliwell's Film and Video Guide. New York: Harper Perennial, 1998.

Hardy, Ernest. "Black Like Who? Notes on Black Films and the Career of F. Gary Gray." *Los Angeles Weekly,* 31 July–6 August 1998, 38.

———. "A Woman of Independent Mien." *Los Angeles Weekly,* 28 March–3 April 1997, 37.

Harpole, Charles, general ed. *History of the American Cinema Series.* 10 vols. New York: Charles Scribner's Sons, 2000.

Harris, Erich Leon. *African-American Screenwriters Now: Conversations with Hollywood's Black Pack.* Los Angeles: Silman-James Press, 1996.

Harrison, Eric. "Boot Camp, Hollywood Style." *Los Angeles Times,* 1 November 1998, Calendar Section, 6, 31–32, 36, 38.

Hartung, Philip T. "Guess Who's Coming to Lunch." *Commonweal* 88 (23 August 1968): 571.

Haskell, Molly. "Are Women Directors Different?" In *Women and the Cinema.* Edited by Karyn Kay and Gerald Peary. New York: Dutton, 1977.

Haskins, Jim. *Spike Lee: By Any Means Necessary.* New York: Walker and Company, 1997.

Highlander: The Final Dimension. Production Notes. MHL/MPA.

Hilburn, Robert. "Motown's Berry Gordy Looks Back on 25 Years." *Los Angeles Times,* 22 March 1983, Calendar Section, 1, 3.

———. "'Superfly' Is Case of More Being Too Much." *Los Angeles Times,* 16 January 1998, Calendar Section, F26.

Hindes, Andrew. "Indie 'Baby' Boyz." *Daily Variety,* 26 February 1999, 7.

Hochman, Steve. "Whatever" (Column). *Los Angeles Times,* 5 April 1998. MHL/MPA.

———. "Whatever: Master P/Rapper—Filmmaker." *Los Angeles Times,* 7 June 1998. MHL/MPA.

———. "Whatever: Millicent Shelton/Writer-Director." *Los Angeles Times,* 15 March 1998. MHL/MPA.

Hollywood Reporter. 22 January 1988. MHL/MPA.

———. 28 April 1966. MHL/MPA.

———. 17 October 1979. MHL/MPA.

———. 59th Anniversary Edition, 1989. MHL/MPA.

Holmes, Emory. "A New Song of the South." *Los Angeles Times,* 6 November 1997, 12, 14.

Hoodlum. Production Notes. MHL/MPA.

hooks, bell. *Black Looks: Race and Representation.* Boston: South End Press, 1992.

———. "'whose pussy is this?': a feminist comment." In *Talking Back: Thinking Feminist, Thinking Black,* 134–141. Boston: South End Press, 1989.

Hope, Darrell L. "AASC Hosts 'Directing in the 70s.'" *DGA Magazine,* May 1999, 48–51.

Hope Floats. Production Notes. MHL/MPA.

How Stella Got Her Groove Back. Studio Biography. MHL/MPA.

How to Be a Player. Production Notes. MHL/MPA.

Jaehne, Karen. "Melvin Van Peebles: The Baadasssss Gent." *Cineaste* 18, no. 1 (1960): 4–8.

James, Darius. *That's Blaxploitation!: Roots of the Baadasssss 'Tude.* New York: St. Martin's Griffin, 1995.

Jason's Lyric. Production Notes. MHL/MPA.

Jefferson, Margo. "My Town, Our Town, Motown." *New York Times,* 5 March 1995, 1, 26.

Jewel, Dan, Lorenzo Benet, and Ron Arias. "A Bad Run." *People,* 13 September 1999, 79–80.

Jones, G. William. *Black Cinema Treasures, Lost and Found.* Denton: University of North Texas Press, 1991.

Karlan, Neal. "Prince Talks." *Rolling Stone,* 18 October 1990, 58–60, 104.

Katz, Ephraim. *The Film Encyclopedia.* 3rd ed. New York: Harper Perennial, 1998.

Kauffmann, Stanley. "Hit and Myth." *New Republic,* 10 August 1968, 14, 23.

Kennedy, Dana. "A Poet, at 70, Ventures into the Unknown." *New York Times,* 15 November 1998, 13, 35.

King, Susan. "Her Dynasty Is Just Beginning." *Los Angeles Herald-Examiner*, 3 October 1987. MHL/MPA.

———. "'Red Dawn' Marks a New Day for Actor Ron O'Neal." *Los Angeles Herald-Examiner*, 24 August 1984. MHL/MPA.

Klotman, Phyllis Rauch, ed. *Screenplays of the African-American Experience*. Bloomington: Indiana University Press, 1991.

Klotman, Phyllis, and Gloria J. Gibson. *Frame by Frame: A Filmography of the African American Image, 1978-1994*. Bloomington: Indiana University Press, 1997.

Kondek, Joshua, ed. *Contemporary Theatre, Film, and Television*. Vol. 24. Detroit: Gale Research, 2000.

Lawrence, Alex. "Forest Whitaker." *Premiere*, November 1988. Archival Files. Margaret Herrick Library. The Motion Picture Academy. Beverly Hills, CA.

Leab, Daniel. *From Sambo to Superspade*. Boston: Houghton Mifflin, 1976.

Lee, Spike. *Uplift the Race: The Construction of School Daze*. New York: Simon and Schuster, 1988.

Levine, Robert. "Meet the Ice Cold King of Gangsta Rap." *Los Angeles Times*, 2 June 1994, F1, F7.

Love, B. "Ice Cube—Renaissance Man?" *Insite*, May 1999, 23.

A Low Down Dirty Shame. Studio Biography. MHL/MPA.

Magill's Cinema Annual. Detroit: Gale Research, 1999.

Margulies, Lee. "Comedy Takes a Dramatic Turn." *Los Angeles Times*, 6 November 1981. Part 4: 14.

Martinez, Gerald, Diana Martinez, and Andres Chavez. *What It Is . . . What It Was: The Black Film Explosion of the 70s in Words and Pictures*. New York: Hyperion, 1998.

Maslin, Janet. "The Lady Has Fangs (and Uses Satin Sheets)." *New York Times*, 7 September 1990. MHL/MPA.

Mazza, Bob. "Aiming to Make the Mark." *Hollywood Reporter*, 9 July 1975, 5–6.

McBride, Joseph. "St. Jacques, 60, Dies of Cancer." *Variety*, 29 August 1990, 14.

McCarthy, Todd. "Comedian Townsend on Roll with Directorial Projects." *Variety*, 30 October 1996, 6, 13.

McDonagh, Maitland. "Def by Temptation." In *The Motion Picture Guide: 1991 Annual*, 38–39. New York: Baseline, 1991.

McKenna, David. "How to Make an American Movie." *Detour*, November 1996, 67–70.

McMillan, Terry, "Thoughts on *She's Gotta Have It*." In *Five for Five: The Films of Spike Lee*. Edited by Spike Lee and David Lee, 19–29. New York: Stewart, Tabori & Chang, 1991.

McMurray, Emily J., ed. *Contemporary Theatre, Film, and Television*. Vols. 10–12. Detroit: Gale Research, 1993–94.

Metro. Production Notes. MHL/MPA.

Michener, Charles. "Black Movies." In *Black Films and Film-makers*, edited by Lindsay Patterson, 235–246. New York: Dodd, Mead, and Co., 1975.

Miller, Lynn Fieldman. *The Hand That Holds the Camera: Interviews with Women Film and Video Directors*. New York: Garland Publishing, Inc., 1988.

Mitchell, Sean. "The Hughes One-Two Punch." *Los Angeles Times*, 1 October 1995, Calendar Section, 5, 86–87.

Moline, Karen. "Bond—James Bond (III)." *Brief Lives*, 3 September 1990. MHL/MPA.

Moon, Spencer. *Reel Black Talk: A Sourcebook of 50 American Filmmakers*. Westport, CT: Greenwood Press, 1997.

Moore, Karen. "Troy Beyer Talks about Sex." *Venice*, September 1998, 10.

Morales, Juan. "Sullivan's Travels." *Detour*, September 1998. MHL/MPA.

The Motion Picture Annual Series. New York: CineBooks, 1988–1999.

Murray, James P. "Now a Boom in Black Directors." *New York Times*, 4 June 1972. In *New York Times Encyclopedia of Film*. Vol. 10. Edited by Gene Brown. New York: Times Books, 1984.

———. "The Subject Is Money." In *Black Films and Film-makers*, edited by Lindsay Patterson, 247–257. New York: Dodd, Mead, and Co., 1975.

———. *To Find an Image: Black Films from "Uncle Tom" to Super Fly*. Indianapolis: Bobbs-Merrill, 1973.

Murray, Jim. "'Hammer' Can't Stop Making Hits." *Los Angeles Times*, 10 December 1995, C1, C14.

Natale, Richard. "Looking for Clout in Hollywood? It Takes Some to Get Some." *Los Angeles Times*, 14 June 1998, Calendar Section, 8–9, 25–28.

The Negotiator. Production Notes. Archival Files. MHL/MPA.

Once Upon a Time . . . When We Were Colored. Production Notes. MHL/MPA.

O'Neill, Sean. "'Sprung' Fever." *Box Office*, April 1997, 48.

Oppenheimer, Jean. "Man on the Street." *Village View*, 19–25 July 1991. MHL/MPA.

"Oz Scott's Standing Broad Jump From Off-B'way 'To Film for U.'" *Variety*, 31 May 1981, 12, 38.

Pacheco, Patrick. "The Hudlin Brothers Set Out to Prove Black Is Bountiful." *New York Times*, 26 July 1992, 9, 12–13.

Page, Don. "Ivan Dixon's Curious Career." *Los Angeles Times*, 22 June 1967, 14.

"Paris Barclay." *Advocate*, 15 September 1998. MHL/MPA.

Parish, James Robert. *Today's Black Hollywood*. New York: Pinnacle Books, 1995.

Parish, James Robert, and George H. Hill. *Black Action Films*. Jefferson, NC: McFarland & Co., 1989.

Parks, Gordon. *Voices in the Mirror*. New York: Anchor, 1990.

Peterson, Maurice. "He's Making a Big 'Numbers' Racket." *New York Times*. MHL/MPA.

Petrikin, Chris. "'Food' for Thought." *Variety: VibeBiz*, August 1998, 4, 42.

Phillips, William H. *Film: An Introduction*. Boston: Bedford Books, 1999.

Poitier, Sidney. *The Measure of a Man*. San Francisco: HarperCollins, 2000.

———. *This Life*. New York: Knopf, 1980.

Pond, Steve. "Robert Townsend." *Vogue*, March 1991, 248, 252, 256.

Provenzano, Tom. "Forest Whitaker: Career Phenomenon." *Drama-Logue*, 11–17 July 1996, 6.

Pryor, Richard, and Todd Gold. *Pryor Convictions and Other Life Sentences*. New York: Pantheon Books, 1995.

Purple Rain. Studio Biography. 1984. MHL/MPA.

Pym, John. *Time Out: Film Guide*. 6th ed. London: Penguin Books, 1997.

Ravo, Nick. "Ernest Dickerson Would Rather Be Called Director." *New York Times*, 18 April 1993, 14, 19.

Reid, Mark A. *Redefining Black Film*. Berkeley: University of California Press, 1993.

The Replacement Killers. Production Notes. MHL/MPA.

Rhines, Jesse Algeron. *Black Film/White Money*. New Brunswick, NJ: Rutgers University Press, 1996.

Richards, Larry. *African American Films through 1959: A Comprehensive Illustrated Filmography*. Jefferson, NC: McFarland and Co., 1998.

Ride. Production Notes. MHL/MPA.

Robb, David. "DGA Suspends Fana 2 Years." *Hollywood Reporter*, 14 October 1998, 3, 37.

Robbins, Harriet. "Chameleon Street." In *Motion Picture Guide: 1992 Annual*, 50. New York: Baseline, 1992.

Roberts, Tara. "Independents' Day." *Essence*, September 1998, 105–106, 173–175.

Robinson, Louie. "Michael Schultz: A Rising Star behind the Camera." *Ebony*, September 1978, 94–102.

Rooney, Terrie M., ed. *Contemporary Theatre, Film, and Television*. Vol. 13. Detroit: Gale Research, 1995, 80–81.

Rossini, Lauren, ed. *Hollywood Creative Directory: Film Directors*. 15th ed. Hollywood, CA: ifilm publishing, 2001.

Ryan, James. "John Singleton." *Premiere*, August 1991. MHL/MPA.

Sampson, Henry T. *Blacks in Black and White: A Source Book on Black Films*. 2nd ed. Metuchen, NJ: Scarecrow Press, 1995.

Samuels, Allison. "A Comic's Erratic Ride." *Newsweek*, 21 July 1997, 73.

"The Sergeant's Hard Climb from the Ranks." *TV Guide*, 16 September 1967, 35–36.

Shaw, Arnold. *Black Popular Music in America*. New York: Schirmer Books, 1986.

Sheff, David. "Playboy Interview: Berry Gordy." *Playboy*, August 1995, 47–52, 124–132.

Sherwood, Rick. "Martin Lawrence." *Hollywood Reporter*, 22 February 1996, S8, S16–S20.

"Short Takes." *Variety*, 15 March 1999. MHL/MPA.

Sims, Tammy. "Struggles of Black Film Maker Jamaa Fanaka." *Los Angeles Times*, 28 July 1988, 6–7.

Sklar, Robert. *Movie-Made America: A Cultural History of the Movies*. New York: Vintage Books, 1975.

Snead, James. *White Screens, Black Images*. New York: Routledge, 1994.

Solo. Production Notes. 1996. MHL/MPA.

Soroff, Jonathan. "The Next Big Thing." *Improper Bostonian*, 9–22 October 1996, 24.

Soul Food. Production Notes. Press Kit. Twentieth Century Fox, 1997.

"Spike Lee." *African American Biography*. Vol. 3. Detroit: Gale Research, 1994, 467–470.

Spines, Christine. "Behind Bars." *Premiere*. Special Issue: *Women in Hollywood*, 2000.

Spotnitz, Frank. "Dialogue on Film: Sidney Poitier." *American Film*, September/October 1991, 18–21, 49.

Stimac, Elias. "Matty Rich Takes Smooth Trip from 'Brooklyn' to Hollywood." *Drama-Logue*, 28 April–4 May 1994, 23.

———. "*Swing Kids* Director Thomas Carter Makes All the Right Choices." *Drama-Logue*, 25 February–3 March 1993, 6.

Stockwell, Amy. "Cheryl Dunye." *Advocate*, 17 September 1996, 69–71.

Strictly Business. Production Notes. MHL/MPA.

Sui, Anna. "Hype Williams." *Interview*, October 1999. MHL/MPA.

Tales from the Hood. Production Notes. MHL/MPA.

Tate, Greg. "Hollywood Shuffle's Fancy Dancer." *Village Voice*, 31 March 1987. MHL/MPA.

Thomas, Bob. "Producers Cross Line with Movie's Success." *UCLA Daily Bruin*, 15 April 1996. MHL/MPA.

Thomas, Kevin. "A 'Def' Reworking of Vampire Genre." *Los Angeles Times*, 7 September 1990, F16.

Thompson, Howard. "Gordon's War." *New York Times*, 10 August 1973, 26.

Towbin, Minna. "Belle Troy." *Elle*, May 1988, 38–40.

Trenz, Brandon. "Belly." In *The Motion Picture Guide: 1999 Annual*, edited by Edmond Grant, 25–26. New York: Cinebooks, 1999.

"Two's Company." *Los Angeles Magazine*, November 1978, 72.

Van Gelder, Lawrence. "Countdown at Kusini." *New York Times*, 17 April 1976, 10.

Van Peebles, Melvin, director. *Sweet Sweetback's Baadasssss Song*. Special Collection Video. Xenon Entertainment Group, 1996.

Variety. 26 July 1999. MHL/MPA.

The Walking Dead. Production Notes. Press Kit. Savoy Pictures, 1995.

Wallace, Michelle. "Sexin' the Watermelon." *Village Voice*, 4 March 1997. MHL/MPA.

Ward, Renee. "The Crossover Goes Beyond Blaxploitation." *Los Angeles Times*, 28 December 1975, Calendar Section, 26, 28–29.

Warga, Wayne. "'Shaft' Editor Directs First Film." *Los Angeles Times*, 4 June 1972, 1, 20.

Webster, Andy. "Filmographies: Fred Williamson." *Premiere*, May 1996, 104.

Weiner, Rex. "One-Way Street." *Variety*, 22 January 1996. MHL/MPA.

Weingarten, Marc. "Master P's Hollywood Takeover." *Rolling Stone*, 29 April 1999, 35.

Weinraub, Bernard. "Winners Circle." *Hollywood Reporter*, 8 August 1994. MHL/MPA.

Weinstein, Steve. "From Hired Gun to Top Gun." *Los Angeles Times*, 11 February 1990, Calendar Section, 5, 94, 102.

———. "Maybe He Should Have Impersonated a White Studio Boss." *Los Angeles Times*, 14 July 1991, Calendar Section, 22, 26.

Williams, John A., and Dennis Williams. *If I Stop I'll Die: The Comedy and Tragedy of Richard Pryor*. New York: Thunder's Mouth Press, 1991.

Wood, Joe. "She-Devil." *Village Voice*, 11 September 1990, 68.

Page numbers in italics indicate photographs.

BLACK DIRECTORS IN HOLLYWOOD